P9-DTV-248

WITHDRAWN
UTSA LIBRARIES

RENEWALS 458-4574

Culture and Psychiatric Diagnosis

A DSM-IV Perspective

Culture and Psychiatric Diagnosis
A DSM-IV Perspective

Edited by
Juan E. Mezzich, M.D., Ph.D., Arthur Kleinman, M.D.,
Horacio Fabrega, Jr., M.D., *and* Delores L. Parron, Ph.D.

Washington, DC
London, England

Note: The authors have worked to ensure that all information in this book concerning drug dosages, schedules, and routes of administration is accurate as of the time of publication and consistent with standards set by the U.S. Food and Drug Administration and the general medical community. As medical research and practice advance, however, therapeutic standards may change. For this reason and because human and mechanical errors sometimes occur, we recommend that readers follow the advice of a physician who is directly involved in their care or the care of a member of their family.

Books published by the American Psychiatric Press, Inc., represent the views and opinions of the individual authors and do not necessarily represent the policies and opinions of the Press or the American Psychiatric Association.

Copyright © 1996 American Psychiatric Press, Inc.
ALL RIGHTS RESERVED
Manufactured in the United States of America on acid-free paper
99 98 97 96   4 3 2 1
First Edition

American Psychiatric Press, Inc.
1400 K Street, N.W., Washington, DC 20005

Library of Congress Cataloging-in-Publication Data
Culture and psychiatric diagnosis / edited by Juan E. Mezzich ... [et al.] — 1st ed.
        p. cm.
    Includes bibliographical references and index.
    ISBN 0-88048-553-1 (alk. paper)
    1. Cultural psychiatry. 2. Mental illness—Diagnosis—Social aspects. I. Mezzich, Juan E.
    [DNLM: 1. Mental Disorders—diagnosis. 2. Cross-Cultural Comparison. WM 141 C968 1996]
RC455.4.E8C826 1996
616.89'075—dc20
DNLM/DLC
for Library of Congress   95-26288
                                                                    CIP

British Library Cataloguing in Publication Data
A CIP record is available from the British Library.

Library
University of Texas
at San Antonio

Contents

Contributors

Victor R. Adebimpe, M.D.
Attending Psychiatrist, Mercy Psychiatric Institute, Pittsburgh, Pennsylvania

Renato D. Alarcón, M.P.H., M.D.
Professor and Vice Chairman, Department of Psychiatry, Emory University, Atlanta, Georgia

Morton Beiser, M.D.
Professor of Psychiatry, Program Head, Culture, Community and Health Studies Program, University of Toronto, Toronto, Ontario, Canada

Magda Campbell, M.D.
Professor of Psychiatry, New York University, New York, New York

Glorisa Canino, Ph.D.
Professor of Pediatrics and Director, Behavioral Sciences Research Institute, University of Puerto Rico, San Juan, Puerto Rico

Etzel Cardeña, Ph.D.
Assistant Professor, Department of Psychology, Trinity College, Hartford, Connecticut

Dora Cárdenas, M.D.
Resident in Psychiatry, New York State Psychiatric Institute, Columbia University, New York, New York

Ellen Corin, Ph.D.
Assistant Professor of Psychiatry, Douglas Hospital Psychosocial Research Unit, McGill University, Montreal, Quebec, Canada

Sharon Davies, R.N.
Research Scientist, New York State Psychiatric Institute, New York, New York

Dona L. Davis, Ph.D.
Professor of Anthropology, University of South Dakota, Vermillion, South Dakota

Leon Eisenberg, M.D.
Presley Professor of Social Medicine and Professor of Psychiatry Emeritus, Harvard University, Boston, Massachusetts

Horacio Fabrega, Jr., M.D.
Professor of Psychiatry and Anthropology, University of Pittsburgh, Pittsburgh, Pennsylvania

Michael B. First, M.D.
Assistant Professor of Clinical Psychiatry, New York State Psychiatric Institute, Columbia University, New York, New York

Michael Flaum, M.D.
Assistant Professor of Psychiatry, University of Iowa, Iowa City, Iowa

Edward F. Foulks, M.D., Ph.D.
Sellars-Polchow Professor of Psychiatry and Neurology, Tulane University, New Orleans, Louisiana

Allen Frances, M.D.
Chair, DSM-IV Task Force, Professor and Chair, Department of Psychiatry, Duke University, Durham, North Carolina

Carlos A. González, M.D.
Assistant Professor of Psychiatry, Director of the Hispanic Clinic, Connecticut Mental Health Center, Yale University, New Haven, Connecticut

Byron J. Good, Ph.D.
Professor of Anthropology and Social Medicine, Harvard University, Boston, Massachusetts

Ezra E. H. Griffith, M.D.
Professor of Psychiatry, Director, Connecticut Mental Health Center, Yale University, New Haven, Connecticut

Peter J. Guarnaccia, Ph.D.
Associate Professor of Anthropology, Institute for Health, Health Care Policy and Aging Research, Rutgers University, New Brunswick, New Jersey

Charles C. Hughes, Ph.D.
Professor of Anthropology and of Family and Preventive Medicine, University of Utah, Salt Lake City, Utah

Janis H. Jenkins, Ph.D.
Associate Professor of Anthropology and Psychiatry, Case Western Reserve University, Cleveland, Ohio

Gloria Johnson-Powell, M.D.
Professor of Psychiatry, Harvard Medical School, Director, Partnerships in Prevention, Judge Baker Children's Center, Boston, Massachusetts

Carlos Jusino, M.D.
Research Psychiatrist, New York State Psychiatric Institute, New York, New York

Marvin Karno, M.D.
Professor of Psychiatry and Biobehavioral Sciences, Director, Division of Social Psychiatry, University of California at Los Angeles, Los Angeles, California

Marianne C. Kastrup, M.D., Ph.D.
Expert Consultant, World Health Organization, Associate Professor of Psychiatry, University of Copenhagen, Copenhagen, Denmark

J. David Kinzie, M.D.
Professor of Psychiatry, Oregon Health Sciences University, Portland, Oregon

Laurence J. Kirmayer, M.D.
Professor of Psychiatry and Director, Division of Social and Transcultural
Psychiatry, Institute of Community and Family Psychiatry, McGill University,
Montreal, Quebec, Canada

Arthur Kleinman, M.D.
Professor of Anthropology and Psychiatry, Chair, Department of Social
Medicine, Harvard University, Boston, Massachusetts

Robert F. Kraus, M.D.
Professor of Psychiatry, University of Kentucky, Lexington, Kentucky

Tina K. Leonard-Green, M.S., R.D.
Lecturer, Department of Family and Community Medicine, University of
Arizona, Tucson, Arizona

Michael Liebowitz, M.D.
Professor of Clinical Psychiatry, Director, Anxiety Disorders Clinic, New York
State Psychiatric Institute, Columbia University, New York, New York

Keh-Ming Lin, M.P.H., M.D.
Professor of Psychiatry, Director, National Institute of Mental Health Research
Center on the Psychobiology of Ethnicity, University of California at Los Angeles,
Los Angeles, California

Roland Littlewood, M.B., D.Phil.
Director, Center for Medical Anthropology, University College, London, England

Enrique Madrigal, M.D.
Regional Advisor on Alcohol and Drug Abuse, Pan American Health Organization, Washington, D.C.

Spero M. Manson, Ph.D.
Professor and Director, National Center for American Indian and Alaska Native
Mental Health Research, University of Colorado, Denver, Colorado

Juan E. Mezzich, M.D., Ph.D.
Chair, National Institute of Mental Health Group on Culture and Diagnosis,
Professor of Psychiatry and Head, Division of Psychiatric Epidemiology, Mount
Sinai School of Medicine of the City University of New York, New York, New
York

Delores L. Parron, Ph.D.
Associate Director for Special Populations, National Institute of Mental Health,
Rockville, Maryland

Bruce Pfohl, M.D.
Professor of Psychiatry, University of Iowa, Iowa City, Iowa

Harold A. Pincus, M.D.
Deputy Medical Director, Director, Office of Research, American Psychiatric
Association, Washington, D.C.

Raymond Prince, M.D.
Professor of Psychiatry, McGill University, Montreal, Quebec, Canada

Cheryl Ritenbaugh, M.P.H., Ph.D.
Professor, Arizona Prevention Center, University of Arizona, Tucson, Arizona

Lloyd H. Rogler, Ph.D.
Albert Schweitzer University Professor of the Humanities, Hispanic Research Center, Fordham University, Bronx, New York

William H. Sack, M.D.
Professor of Psychiatry, Oregon Health Sciences University, Portland, Oregon

Ester Salman, B.S.
Research Assistant, New York State Psychiatric Institute, New York, New York

Catherine Shisslak, Ph.D.
Associate Professor, Department of Family and Community Medicine, University of Arizona, Tucson, Arizona

David Spiegel, M.D.
Professor of Psychiatry and Behavior Sciences, Stanford University, Stanford, California

Nicolette Teufel, Ph.D.
Assistant Professor, Department of Family and Community Medicine, University of Arizona, Tucson, Arizona

James W. Thompson, M.P.H., M.D.
Professor of Psychiatry, University of Maryland, Baltimore, Maryland

Wen-Shing Tseng, M.D.
Professor of Psychiatry, University of Hawaii, Honolulu, Hawaii

Mitchell Weiss, M.D., Ph.D.
Lecturer, Department of Social Medicine, Harvard Medical School, Boston, Massachusetts

Joseph Westermeyer, M.D., Ph.D.
Professor of Psychiatry, University of Minnesota, Minneapolis, Minnesota

Janet B. W. Williams, D.S.W.
Professor of Clinical Psychiatry, New York State Psychiatric Institute, Columbia University, New York, New York

Ronald M. Wintrob, M.D.
Professor of Psychiatry, Brown University, Providence, Rhode Island

Foreword

The fact that a Conference on Culture and Psychiatric Diagnosis was convened by the National Institute of Mental Health and the American Psychiatric Association in preparation for DSM-IV (American Psychiatric Association 1994) is an indication of progress in this area. Much is at stake. The United States will no longer have a white majority in the second half of the 21st century. Thus, the domestic as well as the international utility of DSM-IV and its successors will depend on suitability for use with many different cultures.

There is another problem. Taking culture into account is not simply an issue of whether it is legitimate to apply mainstream schemata to people from other cultures. Diagnosis itself is a cultural issue in mainstream society. All medical diagnoses are socially constructed. This does not imply that diseases would not exist as phenomena in the world if people did not recognize them; it is precisely their existence that makes it necessary to try to make sense of them to diminish suffering. However, the concepts we invent to account for disease come to shape not only the observations we make and the remedies we prescribe but also the very manifestations of disease itself. Concepts of pathophysiology are "constrained fictions"— "constrained" in that they must at least approximately match events of the world, and "fictions" in that their ability to make sense of those events, or even to predict them, does not establish their correspondence to the fundamental principles of nature (Eisenberg 1988).

Beliefs about mental disorder have real consequences for the behavior of patients, physicians, and society. Recall the extraordinary clinical manifestations in the patients Charcot diagnosed as experiencing hysteria. Repeatedly put on display to international medical audiences assembled in the amphitheater of the Salpetriere Hospital, these patients would reliably enact a spectacular range of pathological phenomena from dysesthesias to pseudoepileptic fits to opisthotonos. The patient brought to see Charcot knew she was being examined by a formidable personage. Once Charcot had diagnosed her as hysteric, he would (unwittingly) choreograph her performance (Veith 1965). What he expected, she performed; what she performed confirmed his conviction that his diagnosis was correct. A century later, the diagnosis of hysteria is made much less often, the performance is much less flamboyant, and the term itself has been replaced. Perhaps Charcot's hysteria should be designated a *culture-bound syndrome—France, late 19th century*—and be included in Appendix I of DSM-IV!

Despite this, separating out a cluster of symptoms that can be differentiated from other clinical presentations—the first step in a long process—permits the clinician to study course and outcome well before cause has been discovered. Medical ability to predict course (i.e., to cast a prognosis) is of considerable value to patient and family in planning the future. Reliable specification of disease characteristics permits the organization of epidemiological studies to identify incidence, prevalence, and risk factors, all of which provide clues to cause. Case identification makes possible the comparative evaluation of therapeutic outcomes. The ultimate hope is to identify a specific cause for each disease, a cause we can treat and ultimately prevent. There are many intervening steps between the first halting attempts to define a new syndrome on clinical grounds and the discovery of a consistent pathological anatomy and a necessary and sufficient cause. In that sequence the provisional definition may be altogether abandoned, or the "disease" itself may no longer be regarded as an entity. Some disease categories are hotly contested in the community at large by groups with a financial or an emotional stake in the outcome. The fight over the criteria for defining coal miner's black lung as a compensable occupational disease was a long union-management struggle, with physician-partisans presenting scientific (or so they said) arguments on both sides. Currently, lay advocacy groups and their medical sponsors argue that chronic fatigue and immune dysfunction syndrome, chronic Lyme disease, and multiple chemical sensitivities are each organic (i.e., "real") rather than functional (i.e., "imaginary") disorders.

The ultimate criterion for the longevity of a classification is utility; the difficulty is that there is not one utility but many utilities, each serving different purposes. What suits one may not fit another. A research classification, which is relatively specific but not very sensitive, may be splendid for investigators but a disaster for clinicians, because it leaves too many clinical problems unclassified. A clinical classification that captures most outpatient attenders may be poorly suited for research uses because of the penumbra of uncertain cases in each category. Neither classification may suit health services researchers, who are concerned with the statistics of patient flow and health care costs. Furthermore, case inclusion criteria have major consequences for what is counted as a case and, therefore, for reimbursement. As Blacker and Tsuang (1992) have pointed out,

> One of the problems with DSM-III-R is that it tries to be all things to all people. It is meant to be used for treatment decisions, billings, courtrooms, epidemiologic research, clinical trials, genetic linkage studies, and so on . . . a classification system that suits everyone's needs and conforms to the same structure across a broad range of conditions [may be] a laudable goal [but] its pursuit entails compromises that might, in the long run, cause more problems than it solves. (p. 1481)

Acknowledging that diagnostic categories and classification schemes are acts of the imagination rather than real things in the world enhances rather than diminishes the magnitude of the accomplishment. It is, however, the very success of these schemes in "making sense" of things that makes it easy to mistake them for reality itself. For clinicians the problem is that the more these schemes are believed, the more their prophecies become self-fulfilling. Accounts of disease, through the expectations they arouse, influence the course of disease. There is no escaping the paradox except to recognize it as such. The clinician who understands that he or she is a participant in, as well as an observer of, the drama of health and sickness will be better able to fashion new remedies for old problems.

Leon Eisenberg, M.D.

References

American Psychiatric Association: Diagnostic and Statistical Manual of Mental Disorders, 4th Edition. Washington, DC, American Psychiatric Association, 1994

Blacker D, Tsuang MT: Contested boundaries of bipolar disorder and the limits of categorical diagnosis in psychiatry. Am J Psychiatry 149:1473–1483, 1992

Eisenberg L: The social construction of mental illness. Psychol Med 18:1–9, 1988

Veith I: Hysteria: The History of a Disease. Chicago, IL, University of Chicago Press, 1965

Introduction

Diagnosis is a central concept in psychiatry and medicine. It defines the core domain of the field, and as Feinstein (1967) has pointed out, it establishes the patterns according to which clinicians observe, think, remember, and act. Its specific meaning and scope, however, range from the identification of a disorder to the characterization of the patient's entire clinical condition. The latter corresponds etymologically to *diagnosis* as "knowing thoroughly" and fits a biopsychosocial model of psychiatry and general medicine as well as of health as propounded by the World Health Organization. This more comprehensive concept of diagnosis also implies a focus on the personhood of the patient. Strauss (1992) has reminded us that the historical, Hippocrates-inspired concern and responsibility of clinicians has been to care, not just for diseases, but for people who happen to be experiencing health problems. Understanding and engaging the patient and thoughtfully considering all essential informational perspectives is consistent with a commitment to clinical effectiveness and ethical responsibility and represents a valid framework for articulating the role of cultural factors in psychiatric diagnosis.

An early anthropological challenge to a universalistic and decontextualized concept of psychiatric diagnosis, particularly in its platonic "disease entity" version, was carried out under the banner of cultural relativism (Devereux 1956; Mead 1928). The misconceptions of this position were embodied in the excesses of sociological labeling theory and became associated with antipsychiatric writings (Scheff 1966; Szasz 1964). The outcome was a devaluation of the insights afforded by that early anthropological challenge.

Building in part on relatively recent epidemiologically oriented cross-cultural studies (Leighton et al. 1963; Sartorius et al. 1978), a new generation of anthropological psychiatric research has been emerging. This research is based on a concept of culture as a pervasive set of symbols that provide meaning to social interactions and that, reciprocally, can be built up out of everyday experiences of social life. Implied in a cultural approach is a sensitive understanding of patients and their worlds, an appreciation of social burdens stemming from ethnic marginalization, and sensitive dialogues aimed at furthering the richness of patients' lives (Fabrega 1974; Kleinman 1986). This body of work documents and clarifies how cultural factors influence 1) the experience of psychopathology; 2) the manifestations, assessment, and course of mental disorders; and 3) response to treatment, wherever these processes take place, not only in exotic locations (Fabrega 1987; Hooper 1991; Kleinman 1988; Mezzich and Berganza 1984; Rogler 1989).

Making the consideration of anthropological factors in psychiatric diagnosis and care even more compelling is the growing multiculturality of society in both Western and non-Western countries. In the United States the presence of diverse communities of African (or black) Americans, Asian Americans, Native Americans (or American Indians), and Latinos (or Hispanic Americans) is indeed increasing in both demographic magnitude and cultural differentiation. Also enriching and extending social and ethnic diversity is the ongoing flow of immigrants and refugees. Notably, evidence indicates that misdiagnosis occurs more frequently in minority populations (Good 1993; Lin 1990; Manson et al. 1985; Parron 1982). Finally, there is the challenging recognition of intracultural diversity with differences across the lines of gender, age, cohort, class, and locality (Sakauye et al. 1993; Ware and Kleinman 1992). Ignoring this diversity can lead to serious problems such as stereotyping and overlooking the perspectives of women and the poor.

The National Institute of Mental Health Culture and Diagnosis Group

The urgency argued previously for articulating cultural principles in the organization and content of a psychiatric diagnostic manual did not find much resonance in DSM-III or DSM-III-R (American Psychiatric Association 1980, 1987) beyond a brief reference in the introductory sections. This seemed to reflect the long-standing gap between, on one hand, universalistic biomedical nosologists and, on the other, anthropological scholars—reminiscent, mutatis mutandis, of C. P. Snow's 1995 *The Two Cultures and the Scientific Revolution.*

An opening emerged in 1990 as the process of preparing the fourth edition of DSM (American Psychiatric Association 1994) took form. The leadership of this serial endeavor decided then to explore the possibility of taking culture more seriously into consideration. Experts working at the interface of psychiatry and anthropology were approached. Perceiving an unusual opportunity to advance the field, they responded positively to the overture.

The Conference on Culture and Psychiatric Diagnosis, held in Pittsburgh in April 1991, offered a forum for a meeting of minds. Under the auspices of the National Institute of Mental Health (NIMH) and the American Psychiatric Association, 15 nosologists (members of the DSM-IV Task Force), chaired by Allen Frances, M.D., met with a multidisciplinary group of 45 experts in cultural psychiatry (anthropological and cross-cultural scholars and psychiatrists standing as representatives of prominent ethnic minorities), coordinated by Juan E. Mezzich, M.D., Ph.D. (alsoa member of the DSM-IV Task Force), Arthur Kleinman, M.D., Horacio Fabrega, Jr., M.D., and Delores L. Parron, Ph.D. Major conclusions of the conference included the identification of specific points for culturally enhancing DSM-IV (i.e., in the Introduction to the manual, with cultural considerations pertinent to the various diagnostic categories and the multiaxial schema, and with a glossary of culture-bound syndromes), the need to appraise the ethnic representativeness of the DSM-IV field trial samples, and plans to prepare pertinent research documentation and educational materials. A key strategic recommendation was the formation of a study group to carry out the agenda outlined previously (Mezzich et al. 1992).

The Office for Special Populations of the NIMH accorded crucial sponsorship and funding to establish the Culture and Diagnosis Group. This group has included 50 cultural experts, both clinicians and scholars, coordinated by a steering committee made up of J. E. Mezzich, A. Kleinman, H. Fabrega, D. L. Parron, B. Good, K.-M. Lin, and S. Manson; G. Johnson-Powell also participated during the initial phase of the project. To accomplish each identified task, the committee designated a writing workgroup and a primary reader, to which several advisors and consultants were added as needed. Literature reviews were conducted, and extensive communications among scholars were carried out, in writing and orally, including numerous conference calls.

Specific cultural proposals (initial and revised versions) were prepared and distributed to the DSM-IV Task Force by the NIMH Culture and Diagnosis Group from April 1992 to September 1993. The NIMH Group also produced booklets (January 1993, January 1994) in which were assembled concise papers in support of the proposals made. The final set of these short papers constituted the *DSM-IV Source Book* section on cultural issues (Mezzich et al., in press).

Cultural Contributions to DSM-IV

The major cultural contributions prepared for DSM-IV are outlined below. Not all aspects of these cultural proposals were incorporated into DSM-IV. A new NIMH conference will critically evaluate this process and its outcome. The individual authors and the NIMH Culture and Diagnosis Group offer in this book the thrust of these cultural proposals, regardless of their inclusion or lack thereof in DSM-IV, and the rationales articulated for their development, with the hope that this information will stimulate further advancement of psychiatric diagnostic systems and enrich the practice of clinical care.

1. *Cultural statement for the Introduction to the manual.* This statement alerts the clinician to the challenge of using DSM-IV thoughtfully in a multicultural society. It outlines the concepts of culture and ethnicity, refers to the substantial anthropological research findings underlying the specific recommendations offered, and encourages the clinician to be aware of his or her ethnocentric biases and to keep in mind the personal perspectives of the patient being assessed.

2. *Cultural considerations for various diagnostic categories.* Included in the text associated with specific psychiatric disorders are paragraphs summarizing information on cultural variations in distress idioms, symptom patterns, dysfunctions, correlates, and course of the disorder. The aim of these inclusions is to stimulate culturally sensitive use of the corresponding diagnostic criteria. To uphold cultural sensitivity implies an examiner is able to understand the criteria that define a disorder and take into account the cultural context of the person being examined in order to ascertain whether the criteria are applicable in the present cultural context of the patient.

As justified by available research findings, statements have been prepared for the following major classes of mental disorders:

a. Childhood-onset disorders
b. Cognitive impairment disorders
c. Substance-related disorders
d. Schizophrenia and other psychotic disorders
e. Mood disorders
f. Anxiety disorders
g. Somatoform disorders
h. Dissociative disorders
i. Sexual disorders
j. Eating disorders
k. Sleep disorders
l. Impulse control disorders
m. Adjustment disorders
n. Personality disorders
o. Other clinically significant conditions

In addition, comments were offered for factitious disorders, but given the scarcity of cultural research in this area, no specific cultural considerations were developed.

3. *Cultural annotations for the multiaxial schema.* Although the multiaxial system embodies most patently the biopsychosocial underpinnings of DSM-IV, proper use of its purportedly standardized typologies and scales requires attention to how cultural factors can influence the standing of the individual being assessed. This applies to all mental disorders included in Axis I and, especially, Axis II; general medical disorders (Axis III), which can be differentially distributed across ethnic groups and often display complex interactions with psychopathology; the psychosocial stressors (Axis IV) particularly frequent in minority and multidisadvantaged populations; and functioning levels (Axis V), the accurate rating of which can be enhanced by considering the collective experience of the individual's reference group.

4. *Cultural formulation guidelines.* This contribution, included in an appendix of DSM-IV, evolved relatively recently but has attracted considerable interest. It

supplements the nomothetic or standardized diagnostic ratings with an idiographic statement emphasizing the perspectives of the patient's personal experience and the corresponding cultural reference group. Its components include the cultural identity of the patient, cultural explanations of the individual's illness, cultural factors related to psychosocial environment and functioning, cultural elements of the relationship between the individual and the clinician, and overall cultural assessment for diagnosis and care. Field trials with various ethnic groups have yielded illustrative case formulations.

5. *Glossary of culture-bound syndromes and idioms of distress.* This collection, placed in a DSM-IV appendix, defines some of the popular, or "folk" psychiatric syndromes and the by-no-means-always-pathological idioms for describing distress that may present in clinical practice in multicultural U.S. society. It illustrates the importance of an anthropological framework for understanding any disorder. Culture-bound syndromes are often organized with regard to perceived cause as well as symptom clusters, representing both distinctive forms of illness experience and local approaches to explaining, classifying, and responding to them. The glossary focuses on items that are widely acknowledged both in non-Western societies and in North America, for example, among African Americans (e.g., *rootwork, falling out*), Native Americans (e.g., *ghost sickness, pibloktoq*), Asian Americans (e.g., *shenjing shuairuo, taijin kyofusho*), and Latinos (e.g., *susto, ataque de nervios*). Also recognized are Western culture-bound syndromes, found almost exclusively or in distinctive form in Western countries or highly Westernized segments of other societies (e.g., anorexia nervosa, multiple personality disorder). Western culture-bound syndromes also reflect the cultural assumptions of psychiatry.

Organization of Culture and Psychiatric Diagnosis

The present work reviews and discusses the relationship between culture and psychiatric diagnosis within the framework governing an effort to enhance the cultural sensitivity and validity of DSM-IV.

A key feature of this volume is that it constitutes a collaborative enterprise of cultural experts, members of the NIMH Culture and Diagnosis Group, nosologists, and members of the DSM-IV Task Force and Work Groups, as listed in the roster of contributors.

The volume is organized according to several principles. The most apparent one, as displayed in the Contents, corresponds to the components of DSM-IV to which cultural contributions have been made. Section I, "General Issues," is particularly pertinent to the cultural statement prepared for the DSM-IV Introduction. Sections II through IX discuss cultural factors required to understand the emergence, manifestations, and course of standard mental disorders, and thus underlie the cultural considerations paragraphs prepared for the text of the DSM-IV chapters on specific categories of mental disorder. Section X reviews the concept and various forms of culture-bound syndromes and idioms of distress, a theme included in Appendix I of DSM-IV. Section XI considers multiaxial diagnostic issues, including the pertinence of an idiographic cultural formulation, a development also presented in DSM-IV Appendix I. An epilogue (Chapter 47) completes the core text of the book.

Another organizing principle guiding the structure of each section of this volume is plurality of perspectives. In Section I, chapters on the historical and anthropological bases of psychiatric diagnosis are followed by presentations of African American, Native American, Asian American, and Hispanic perspectives, as well as nosological views from the chairperson of the DSM-IV Task Force. In Sections II through XI, an overview article is typically followed by cultural comments from members of the NIMH Cultural and Diagnosis Group and nosological comments from DSM-IV Task Force representatives, as well as, in certain sections, international comments from World Health Organization experts and consultants.

Colophon

Culture has a fundamental role in the articulation of diagnostic systems, which are children of their history and circumstances. Contributions have recently been made to upgrade the cultural suitability of DSM-IV for its use in a multicultural world where collective differences and cultural commitments of professionals themselves constrain the encounter between patient and practitioner. This book presents the theoretical and empirical bases of these efforts, with the hope that it will stimulate further work on enhancing the validity of psychiatric diagnosis and higher effectiveness and thoughtfulness in patient care.

Juan E. *Mezzich*, M.D., *Ph*.D.
Arthur Kleinman, M.D.
Horacio Fabrega, *Jr.*, M.D.
Delores L. *Parron*, *Ph*.D.

References

American Psychiatric Association: Diagnostic and Statistical Manual of Mental Disorders, 3rd Edition. Washington, DC, American Psychiatric Association, 1980

American Psychiatric Association: Diagnostic and Statistical Manual of Mental Disorders, 3rd Edition, Revised. Washington, DC, American Psychiatric Association, 1987

American Psychiatric Association: Diagnostic and Statistical Manual of Mental Disorders, 4th Edition. Washington, DC, American Psychiatric Association, 1994

Devereux G: Normal and abnormal, in Some Uses of Anthropology: Theoretical and Applied. Edited by Casagrande J, Gladwin T. Washington, DC, Anthropological Society of Washington, 1956

Fabrega H, Jr: Disease and Social Behavior: An Interdisciplinary Perspective. Cambridge, MA, MIT Press, 1974

Fabrega H, Jr: Psychiatric diagnosis: a cultural perspective. J Nerv Ment Dis 175:383–394, 1987

Feinstein AR: Clinical Judgment. Huntington, NY, Krieger, 1967

Good BJ: Culture, diagnosis and comorbidity. Cult Med Psychiatry 16:427–446, 1993

Hooper K: Some old questions for the new cross-cultural psychiatry. Med Anthropol 5:299–330, 1991

Kleinman A: Social Origins of Distress and Disease. New Haven, CT, Yale University Press, 1986

Kleinman A: Rethinking Psychiatry: From Cultural Category to Personal Experience. New York, Free Press, 1988

Leighton AH, Lambo TA, Hughes CC, et al: Psychiatric Disorder Among the Yoruba. Ithaca, NY, Cornell University Press, 1963

Lin KM: Assessment and diagnostic issues in the psychiatric care of refugee patients, in Mental Health of Immigrants and Refugees. Edited by Holzman WH. Austin, University of Texas Press, 1990

Manson S, Shore JH, Bloom JD: The depressive experience in American Indian communities: a challenge for psychiatric theory and diagnosis, in Culture and Depression. Edited by Kleinman A, Good B. Berkeley, University of California Press, 1985

Mead M: Coming of Age in Samoa: A Psychological Study of Primitive Youth for Western Civilization. New York, Dell, 1928

Mezzich JE, Berganza CE: Culture and Psychopathology. New York, Columbia University Press, 1984

Mezzich JE, Fabrega H, Kleinman A: Cultural validity and DSM-IV (editorial). J Nerv Ment Dis 180:4, 1992

Mezzich JE, Kleinman A, Fabrega H, et al (eds): Section on Cultural Issues, in DSM-IV Source Book. Edited by Widiger T, Frances A, Pincus HA, et al. Washington, DC, American Psychiatric Press (in press)

Parron DL: An overview of minority group mental needs and issues as presented to the President's Commission on Mental Health, in Perspectives in Minority Group Mental Health. Edited by the President's Commission on Mental Health. Washington, DC, University Press of America, 1982

Rogler LH: The meaning of culturally sensitive research in mental health. Am J Psychiatry 146:296–303, 1989

Sakauye KM, et al: Reflecting on the studies of Asian American elderly by Asian American researchers. Asian American Psychological Association Journal 8:22–33, 1983

Sartorius N, Jablensky A, Shapiro R: Cross-cultural differences in the short-term prognosis of schizophrenia. Schizophr Bull 4:102–113, 1978

Scheff TJ: Being Mentally Ill: A Sociological Theory. Chicago, IL, Aldine, 1966

Strauss JS: The person—key to understanding mental illness: towards a new dynamic psychiatry, III. Br J Psychiatry 161(suppl. 18):19–26, 1992

Szasz TW: The Myth of Mental Illness. New York, Harper & Row, 1964

Ware NC, Kleinman A: Culture and somatic experience: the social course of illness in neurasthenia and chronic fatigue syndrome. J Psychosom Med 54:546–560, 1992

Section I

General Issues

Chapter 1

Cultural and Historical Foundations of Psychiatric Diagnosis

Horacio Fabrega, Jr., M.D.

his book, compiled from conference proceedings, is an effort to improve the system of psychiatric diagnosis. Its specific purposes are to draw together and synthesize knowledge pertaining to the role of cultural factors in the diagnosis, epidemiology, course, and treatment of psychiatric disorders, in such a way that they enhance the suitability and sensitivity of diagnostic systems.

In this chapter, I examine the cultural and historical foundations of psychiatric diagnosis and classification.

A Cultural Approach to Psychiatric Classification

A study of society, history, and culture shows that illness problems are ubiquitous and recurring and that all cultures reflect knowledge about the nature, importance, and modes of control of illness (Fabrega 1974; Kleinman 1979). Important aspects of a society's culture are, in fact, incorporated in the way illness problems are explained and handled. Psychiatric illnesses are always represented in this knowledge and in the experiences that various peoples have had with illness.

From a general standpoint, psychiatric illnesses are human behavioral anomalies and breakdowns that are culturally shaped, explained, and dealt with in terms of established conventions and meanings. Societies differ greatly in terms of how they define and explain such breakdowns. In Western society, psychiatric illnesses have special meanings and, with difficulty and with the commission of logical errors, can be equated with other formulations of behavior problems. Workers in the field of comparative medicine have found analogues of Western psychiatric illnesses in the bodies of knowledge of Indian, Chinese, Islamic, Greek, and Roman medicine, as well as in the medical traditions of contemporary preindustrial societies (Dube 1978; Grmek 1989; Haldipur 1984; Jackson 1986; Lloyd 1979; Tseng

1973; Veith 1965). Pertinent studies of a cross-cultural or historical nature should be seen as offering alternative versions of psychiatric illness. Historical and cultural factors, in conjunction with biological and physical environmental factors, are integral to the production of social psychological behavior—the material of psychiatric illness. Such factors are also integral to the production, definition, classification, and mode of handling illnesses. It is in light of this generic dialectical interplay among history, culture, and biology as it affects psychiatric illnesses and their classification that the clinician must view the contemporary diagnostic statistical manual.

The Western Cultural Approach to Psychiatric Classification

General Introduction

A prominent characteristic of descriptions of psychiatric illnesses in antiquity was its integration with general medicine. Some of these illnesses involved delusions, and all included bodily manifestations that implicated prominent alterations in well-being and function. During the medieval period, Christian religious themes, including exorcistic elements, were added. Conditions one could view as madness and/or insanity were well represented as were conditions characterized by prominent somatic symptoms such as hysteria. Thus, from a very early period, psychiatric illness carried special intellectual, moral, and literary meanings (Fabrega 1990a). This included social stigma, conditions for which were well established in the classical period and which was accentuated during the medieval period. These special meanings appear to have been associated mainly with the part of Western psychiatric illness encompassed by madness (namely, acute and chronic behavioral dilapidations).

Intellectual Foundations of the Modern Approach to Psychiatric Illness

Three major theoretical characteristics of the history of Western medicine during the early modern period (roughly the 16th–18th centuries) may be viewed as laying the intellectual foundations for the development of contemporary diagnostic and classification systems in psychiatry. These are 1) the doctrine concerning the ontology of disease; 2) the rise of the mechanistic philosophy and its application to medicine; and 3) the use of the nervous system as a major concept in the system of nomenclature, classification, and explanation (Cohen 1961; Fabrega 1990b; Hudson 1983; Kraupl-Taylor 1980, 1982; Nutton 1983; Pagel 1972; Pagel and Winder 1968; Rather 1959; Temkin 1963).

Theories and explanations of illness in antiquity and up to the early modern period are described by historians of medicine as having a predominantly *functional* emphasis. Illnesses may have been conceived of as entities having distinctive identities insofar as these were named and described. However, the main concern of the medical tradition was that of explaining illness in light of special characteristics pertaining to the individual. Yet, historians of medicine are of the opinion that a requirement for a general, formal, and authoritative system of classification was the development of an *ontological* approach. This approach emphasized that illnesses were naturalistic entities having independent existence, each with its own distinct structure and course and each of which could be named, classified, explained, and made objects of concern in the society.

The second development leading to modern psychiatric diagnosis and classification was the rise of the mechanical philosophy, beginning in the 17th century, which involved the work of individuals such as Descartes, Boyle, and Newton. This philosophy led to the wide use of scientific explanations in terms of particles of varying shapes, sizes, and motions. Eventually, medical writings in the late 17th to early 18th centuries drew heavily on the mechanical philosophy and led to the *mechanistic* emphasis in medicine, which gave an almost modern cast to medical theorizing. This emphasis was initially reflected in general medical conditions, with the organs conceived mechanistically and positivistically to constitute part structures affecting each other and the whole.

The third development leading to modern psychiatry was an emphasis on the brain and nervous system as a basis for understanding and classifying diseases. This development has deep roots and encompasses contributions from celebrated individuals such as Syndenham, Willis, Hoffman, and Boerhaave. Medical figures of the Scottish Enlightenment during the 18th century continued this trend and gave central emphasis to human sensibility, to its effects on the economy of the individual, and to its correlates in nervous fluids, nervous energies, and nervous forces (Porter 1987). The writings of Enlightenment medical scientists influenced central figures in the early development of classifications of disease. Developments during the 19th century should be viewed as refinements of the emerging tradition of classifications of disease pertaining to the nervous system. These three intellectual developments, then, set the foundations for the modern Western academic approach to psychiatric classification.

Ingredients of the Western Medical Approach

In Western intellectual efforts pertaining to psychiatric diagnosis and classification, one sees two themes: 1) the progressive loss of lay conceptualizations and meanings about madness and related conditions and 2) the progressive elaboration of impersonal biomedical concepts. In effect, an exchange occurred as naturalistic semantic themes pertaining to socioculturally rooted persons gave way to scientific or objective/neutral themes descriptive of mechanical objects or human machines. To some extent, this secularization and materialization of illness is found in descriptions of psychiatric illness of all of the great traditions of medicine, but such descriptions typically handle illness functionally and cast it in a social and moral context. What distinguishes the Western tradition is, on the one hand, the progressive authority given to neuroanatomy, neurophysiology, and scientific psychology and, on the other, the absence of moral considerations. The result is the elaboration of a descriptive language of psychopathology—a "pure" phenomenological description of mental pathology allegedly devoid of material connected to situational and personal characteristics of the individual.

This new form of illness is said to have become neutral and impersonal and to be grounded in scientific objectivism. Yet, the ontology and epistemology that are found in contemporary psychiatry are different from those in general medicine, because indicators of psychiatric disorders are linked to symbolic behavior and hence to the self. The current mode of describing and defining psychiatric illness is viewed as but temporarily expedient until truly biological markers (which are disconnected from behavior) are uncovered and linked to discrete disorders—a molecular biological approach to psychiatric diagnosis and classification, if you will. The misconceptions as well as the problems—theoretical, practical, and ethical— implicit in this picture of psychiatric diagnoses and classification cannot be fully discussed here.

Special Meanings Linked to Psychiatric Illness in Western Societies

An interest and fascination with, as well as a social condemnation of, madness and insanity was a feature of classical and medieval societies (Fabrega 1990a). During the early modern period there appears to have taken place an accentuation of such special meanings (Porter 1987). In addition, heavily somatized "psychiatric" conditions (hysteria, mood disorders) became more closely associated with madness and its special social meanings. In the process, all of these psychiatric illnesses also became more naturalized, demystified, and secularized because they were very prevalent in many individuals who could not easily be classified as marginal, impaired, or socially dilapidated or, as previously defined, as mad or insane.

The Importance of an Institutional Foundation for Psychiatric Discourse

A document such as DSM-IV symbolizes the institutional basis of psychiatric practice in American-influenced societies. Like other national and international systems, it constitutes the official protocol for certifying official psychiatric practice by professionally accredited practitioners. DSM-IV operates as a guide for legitimate reimbursement for psychiatric services, provides a rationale or guideline for the domain of appropriate research in psychiatry, and validates expert testimony in courts of law. Wherever one points to psychiatric discourse in contemporary American psychiatry, DSM-IV will stamp it with the authority of the profession, the scientific establishment, and the state.

The central role played by the state and the psychiatric profession in the contemporary Western approach to psychiatric illness, as symbolized in protocols such as DSM-IV, is a result of the demographic, social, and political economic transformations that took place in the early modern and modern periods in western Europe (Butler 1985; Castel 1986; Fabrega 1989; Goldstein 1987; Scull 1979). An underlying accompaniment to these transformations was an increased number of poor, marginal, ill, and socially dependent persons who were unable to fit into the newly established occupational structures of modern society. One consequence was an increased prevalence of psychiatrically compromised persons who could no longer be controlled and cared for by traditional social institutions. The problems posed by the management and control of people forced the government to play a larger administrative role. An important generalization is that the movement toward state intervention in the handling of psychiatrically ill persons, and more generally, toward social welfare and collectivism (DeSwann 1988), promoted and hastened a bureaucratic, impersonal, and managerial approach to mentally ill individuals. Associated with this, professions such as asylum superintendents and related personnel proliferated. The establishment of an institutional basis for psychiatric discourse in modern societies is not complete until the professional sector becomes differentiated, specialized, and hierarchically organized within and dominant with respect to competing institutions dealing with mentally ill persons.

The development of an institutional framework for psychiatric practice was dependent on and influenced greatly by the purely conceptual changes discussed earlier. These two sets of developments did not take place coincidentally; each promoted the other. Segregation of mentally ill persons and subsidies to the medical profession provided a setting in which observations, description, analysis, and theoretical developments culminated in new knowledge about psychiatric illness. Conversely, refinement of the language of psychopathology and psychiatric diagnosis greatly aided the ease with which state-influenced personnel and state-managed institutions were able to efficiently identify, segregate, and process psychiatrically ill persons. It was on the shoulders of these developments that systems of classification of psychiatric illness became enlarged as to geographic domain—in many instances extending across national boundaries—and eventually, in the late 20th century, extended in scope and content so as to include multiaxial elements.

The institutional approach was based on and came to greatly affect the general social meanings associated with psychiatric illness. The negative view that these illnesses could produce behavioral dilapidations and contribute to deviance and marginalization helped promote the asylum movement, and this in turn, through institutionalization, added a special chapter to the increasing stigmatization of mentally ill persons.

The Psychiatric Enterprise as a Product of Conflicts With the Criminal Justice System

Criminal actions by psychiatric persons have always been a feature of organized social groups and, in Western societies, have long occasioned social dilemmas and debates (Rosen 1968). The insanity defense for criminal actions (usually for the gravest of these actions—namely, homicide) has been a consequence of this debate. In contemporary times, a new wrinkle or threat implicit in this defense has been manifest in the treatment of political dissidents in the Soviet Union. There, the exercise of basic civic rights in opposition to prevailing political and social conditions has culminated in actions that the state, in alliance with the psychiatric profession and mental health system, has deemed as illness. These developments are clear instances of state-sanctioned applications of the insanity defense.

An alliance similar to the one in the Soviet Union between state representatives pursuing social, political, and medical ends and physicians and public health officials has been manifest in the evolution of European medicine during the 19th century. Issues of political opposition to civil liberties, as these are currently understood, were not explicitly in evidence in the earlier period. The alliance nonetheless clearly had political overtones. Thus there is a precedent for the political needs of the state to be pursued through medical and public health channels; this is a dangerous border region for psychiatry (Butler 1985; Castel 1986; Foucault 1965, 1979; Goldstein 1987; Scull 1979).

Issues devolving from the opposition between the psychiatric profession and the criminal justice system with respect to the insanity defense are in certain respects cultural in nature and thus fall within the area of our concerns here. What is criminal is in many instances culturally conditioned; similarly, how psychiatric illness is construed is also culturally based. Because criminality and psychiatric illness definitions are both influenced by cultural conventions, it is necessary to ensure that these conventions are clearly specified and independent. In certain respects the universalistic language of psychopathology and psychiatric diagnosis described earlier was forged in the opposition between the psychiatric profession and the criminal justice system. This language evolved as a result of the need to incorporate psychiatrically ill persons who surfaced as wards of the criminal justice system without unduly compromising criminal justice formulations and thus creating institutional conflicts.

To allow cultural factors to affect psychiatric illness determinations is to risk politicizing the psychiatric enterprise. Having said this, one cannot but acknowledge that such kinds of conflicts are and have been implicated in the criteria for the definition of many Axis I and Axis II disorders. One has but to review quandaries involving definitions of psychosis, neurosis, homosexuality, the sexually assaultive male syndrome, adjustment disorders, and personality disorder to appreciate how often psychiatric concerns intrude into, contaminate, and in some instances logically implicate sociopolitical concerns. In most instances the potential problems of untangling medical-psychiatric and sociopolitical concerns are never allowed to materialize, or if they do materialize, are bypassed or ignored.

Is a Universalistic Language of Psychiatric Illness and Psychopathology Possible?

A basic assumption in psychiatry is the need for objectivity, rationality, and empiricism. In claiming the authority of science, psychiatry stipulates applicability to all peoples. However, from a cultural point of view, one can ask whether diagnosis is ever in fact truly culture free and universally applicable. The topic can be stated thus: Does not the language of DSM-IV reflect culturally particularistic assumptions about the nature of mind, behavior, and personhood drawn from Western European culture? Specifically, is not DSM-IV a product of the interplay of 1) special biosocial factors producing illness conditions; 2) Western academic conventions about rationalism, voluntarism, and autonomy; and 3) sociocultural standards about behavior?

Schizophrenia has a bona fide claim to status as a psychiatric disorder. So, also, does depression or melancholia. However, many of the earlier descriptions of such bona fide disorders contained elements that seem inappropriate, wrong, or misguided, given our current understanding of their nature. Differences between earlier and current versions of bona fide disorders are ascribed to error or to the tendency to confound disorders we currently regard differently. This is understandable and can in many instances be accepted. Yet, it could be that earlier bona fide disorders looked different partly because the social and cultural circumstances of individuals and the way these individuals responded to stress were different. Not surprisingly, and to complete the circle, these disorders were constructed by physicians in a different form and with a different content.

If the social constructionist view of psychopathology can be said to apply to so-called bona fide psychiatric disorders, can not a stronger and more compelling argument be made for such application to other sorts of disorders of DSM-IV? As an example, are narcissistic personality disorder and schizotypal personality disorder universal and culture free? On the one hand, one can suggest that narcissistic personality disorder is culture bound in a positive sense. The conventions of our society and culture directly create much of the narcissistic posture and the abnormalities in social relations associated with it. However, its features are unlikely to be found similarly depicted cross-culturally, because in other societies attitudes about the self, objects, the sexes, emotion, intimacy, and interpersonal power carry different conventions. It is excesses of Western conventions that color abnormalities of social relations. On the other hand, one can regard schizotypal disorder as culture bound in a negative sense: remnants of social psychological conventions long ago devalued, deemphasized, and superseded by rationalistic and scientific modes of thinking and feeling "create" this disorder and render it abnormal in our culture and society. However, in other societies, and in earlier ones in European history, in which magical thinking and magical beliefs were and still are normal and acceptable, this "disorder" as such does not and cannot exist, as it merges with the way ordinary citizens think about themselves and their behavioral world. The stipulation that these two styles of personality are disorders is a consequence of cultural and historical factors as much as biological ones. That psychiatric illnesses and classification systems are culturally shaped has been illustrated with respect to melancholia, anorexia nervosa, and *taijin kyofusho* (Kirmayer 1984).

Culturally Sensitizing Psychiatric Classification Systems

Culturally sensitizing a society's diagnostic classification system is a complex undertaking. One must ensure that all people of a society who are "psychiatrically" ill be adequately incorporated. The diagnosis of bona fide disorders should embody criteria that take into account relevant phenomena in all persons regardless of their cultural, social, or linguistic background. In addition, culturally unique illness, sickness, or suffering pictures that implicate "the psyche" need to be included in the protocol. The culturally oriented nosologist has the responsibility to decide whether ethnic-specific syndromes are sufficiently well understood to be judged as medical and, especially, "psychiatric." Next, it must be decided whether these are to be incorporated under more abstract categories or simply allowed as variants of a separate category especially created for atypical or culture-specific entities. Finally, it must also be decided to what extent a multiaxial formulation should incorporate cultural/ethnic factors pertaining to diagnosis in a broad frame of reference. This would include ensuring that stressors and social functioning are evaluated with an appreciation of their cultural rootedness.

The addition of a special axis that would incorporate cultural factors is one way of culturally sensitizing a diagnostic system. An axis as currently embodied in DSM-IV suggests a category of information that is widely applicable to patients and that, when properly codified and/or quantified, aids in the understanding of the patients' overall condition. As an example, Axis II reflects the impact of psychoanalytic theory in psychiatry and symbolizes the important role that personality can play in making sense of the patients' problems and symptoms and the formulation of an effective treatment plan. A cultural axis on this account would reflect the impact that sociocultural research has had in psychiatry and symbolize the potential contribution it can make to diagnosis. It might embody the extent to which local cultural factors influence patients' clinical condition and/or accessibility to treatment. Thus, the extent to which cultural and linguistic factors (local traditions of meaning) cloud the presentation of symptoms might be measured. Alternatively, one might consider codifying patients' linguistic skills and understanding and acceptance of the "disease model," level of acculturation in American society, and capacity to participate in and comply with a treatment regimen.

The conceptual issues involving classification can be viewed from a formal psychiatric standpoint. In this instance, one should ensure that criteria of a bona fide illness promote reliable and valid diagnosis. The criteria should isolate and point to essential elements of the disorder in question. According to this logic, disorders should be relevant and applicable across societies and cultures. There exists an obvious conflict between the cultural and psychiatric points of view. This conflict is that posed by cultural relativism and has constituted an incentive for research. Ideally, a culturally sensitive and scientific description of psychiatric illness, and the criteria for its diagnosis, should be formulated in such a way that they remain independent from descriptions and criteria pertaining to strictly criminal or political considerations. The special ontology and epistemology of psychiatric illness as currently stipulated render this goal difficult if not impossible to achieve.

Given that a dialectical interplay involving biology, society, and culture produces psychiatric disorders and leads to the development of psychiatric knowledge and systems of diagnosis and classification, it should be evident that neither DSM-IV nor any classification system in psychiatry will ever be complete. Our goal should be tempered by this awareness and be correspondingly modest: to achieve the best synthesis we can of the knowledge we have accumulated about the topic of culture and psychiatric illness and to incorporate this knowledge in the system of diagnosis.

Conclusion

In considering the cultural and historical foundations of psychiatric illness classification, the following 11 generalizations seem worthy of mention:

1. The raw material to which psychiatric systems of classification apply consists of behavioral phenomena that are formed by the interplay of genetic factors, neurobiological factors, social and ecological factors, and cultural linguistic factors.
2. Each society incorporates standards of normality, deviation, and abnormality with respect to human behavior, although there may exist pancultural uniformities in each of these forms of qualification.
3. Each society draws its own distinctions regarding which forms of behavioral breakdowns and anomalies are medical in nature (i.e., distinctions that generate labels of illness and bring into play practices of healing). There may exist uniformities in the way certain behavioral forms are qualified.
4. Each society has available systems and traditions of medicine that involve knowledge structures; this knowledge is produced, passed on, and applied by socially appointed experts (who differ as to reputation and authenticity). Expert medical knowledge contains reference to and provides ways of diagnosing and dealing with illness pictures that are psychiatric in nature (i.e., involving behavioral anomalies, breakdowns, deviance, etc.).
5. A society's knowledge structures pertaining to psychiatric illness define, describe, and name these illnesses; the knowledge structures incorporate methods of diagnosis and an inventory of treatment plans or actions for their elimination and/or control.
6. A society's knowledge structures pertaining to psychiatric illness incorporate prevailing and traditional cultural standards and conventions about behavior. The illnesses described, the modes of their diagnosis, and the technologies of their treatment reflect conventions of how people should behave, how they (should or can) misbehave, what meanings are to be ascribed to behavioral alterations, how such aberrations are to be shaped into normal channels of behavior, and how persons showing these behaviors are to be regarded and handled in the event "normal" behavior is reinstated.
7. Western European systems of psychiatric knowledge have always reflected particularities of the history and culture of these societies. The illnesses produced are a function of the special social, political, economic, ecological, biological, and cultural conditions prevailing in the societies. The system of description and diagnosis of psychiatric illness reflects conventions about the normality versus abnormality of behavior and about personhood, social behavior, and the nature of illness. Finally, technologies of treatment, the end points of treatment, and the meanings ascribed to persons and incorporated in the career of a psychiatric patient are all equally imbued with meanings deriving from the culture and history of the societies in question.
8. The contemporary European and Anglo-American system of psychiatric knowledge as incorporated in that system's classification (including DSM-IV) has

shown a progressive tendency to create discourses dominated by the language categories and epistemologies of scientific objectivism. Such discourses minimize reference to symbolic characteristics of persons, such as social standing, prestige, power, spiritualism, motives, intentions, reasons, values, ethics, and ultimate purposes for living. The discourse and language of scientific objectivism handle persons as mechanical objects and eschew or disregard the view that persons are socially, culturally, and morally situated. In effect, the nosologies illustrate a secularization and materialization of behavior and personhood. Despite these considerations, the nosologies reflect a basic dualistic view of the person, and emphasis is given to autonomy, voluntarism, and individualism. These conventions of personhood are implicit in the DSM-IV system.

9. The discourse of contemporary scientific psychiatry as incorporated in its knowledge structures and diagnostic systems has been facilitated and influenced by the role psychiatry has played in helping the state solve its problems regarding medically ill, deviant, marginal, and needy people. Early psychiatric experts were supported by the state and helped its personnel and representatives carry out requirements for the maintenance of social order and control. Contemporary knowledge structures of psychiatry are rational, scientific, and bureaucratic, largely as a consequence of the need to foster this alliance with the state, its apparatus, and its institutions. The state backs scientific research in psychiatry, and the latter feeds back knowledge that is legitimized by the state and used as a basis for rationalizing services and supporting further research.

10. Psychiatric knowledge structures such as those incorporated in DSM-IV have dual functions: they serve the state and its apparatus (i.e., the establishment and the status quo), and they also serve the needs of the population, which is to say, the needs of the people differentiated as to social and cultural characteristics.

11. Psychiatric knowledge structures such as those incorporated in DSM-IV should be rendered valid and useful (i.e., they should reflect scientific objectivist canons as much as possible and in this sense apply across societies). However, these knowledge structures, because they apply to persons in need, should also be sensitive to the cultural realities of such persons.

References

American Psychiatric Association: Diagnostic and Statistical Manual of Mental Disorders, 4th Edition. Washington, DC, American Psychiatric Association, 1994

Butler T: Mental Health Social Policy and the Law. London, Macmillan, 1985

Castel R: The Regulation of Madness. Translated by Halls WE. Berkeley, University of California Press, 1986

Cohen H: The evolution of the concept of disease, in Concepts of Medicine. Edited by Lush B. New York, Pergamon, 1961, pp 159–169

DeSwann A: In the Case of the State. New York, Oxford University Press, 1988

Dube KC: Nosology and therapy of mental illness in Ayurveda. Comp Med East West 6(3):209–228, 1978

Fabrega H, Jr: Disease and Social Behavior: An Interdisciplinary Perspective. Cambridge, MA, MIT Press, 1974

Fabrega H, Jr: An ethnomedical perspective of Anglo-American psychiatry. Am J Psychiatry 146:588–596, 1989

Fabrega H, Jr: Psychiatric stigma in the classical and medieval period: a review of the literature. Compr Psychiatry 31:289–306, 1990a

Fabrega H, Jr: The concept of somatization as a cultural and historical product of Western medicine. Psychosom Med 52:653–672, 1990b

Foucault M: Madness and Civilization, A History of Insanity in the Age of Reason. New York, Random House, 1965

Foucault M: Discipline and Punishment: The Birth of the Prison. Translated by Sheridan A. New York, Random House, 1979

Goldstein J: Console and Classify. Cambridge, England, Cambridge University Press, 1987

Grmek MD: Diseases in the Ancient Greek World. Baltimore, MD, Johns Hopkins University Press, 1989

Haldipur CV: Madness in ancient India: concept of insanity in Charaka Samhita (1st century A.D.). Compr Psychiatry 25:335–344, 1984

Hudson RP: Disease and Its Control: The Shaping of Modern Thought. Westport, CT, Greenwood Press, 1983

Jackson SW: Melancholia and Depression. New Haven, CT, Yale University Press, 1986

Kirmayer LJ: Culture affect and somatization. Transcultural Psychiatric Research Review 21:159–188, 237–262, 1984

Kleinman A: Patients and Healers in the Context of Culture. Berkeley, University of California Press, 1979

Kraupl-Taylor K: The concepts of disease. Psychol Med 10:419–424, 1980

Kraupl-Taylor K: Sydenham's disease entities. Psychol Med 12:243–250, 1982

Lloyd GER: Magic, Reason and Experience. Cambridge, England, Cambridge University Press, 1979

Nutton V: The seeds of disease: an explanation of contagion and infection from the Greeks to the renaissance. Med Hist 27:1–34, 1983

Pagel W: Van Helmont's concept of disease—to be or not to be? the influence of Paracelsus. Bull Hist Med 46:419–445, 1972

Pagel W, Winder M: Harvey and the modern concept of disease. Bull Hist Med 42:496–509, 1968

Porter R: Mind Forg'd Manacles. London, England, Athlone Press, 1987

Rather LJ: Towards a philosophical study of the idea of disease, in The Historical Development of Physiological Thought. Edited by McBrooks C, Cranefield PF. New York, Hafner, 1959, pp 351–373

Rosen G: Madness in Society. Chicago, IL, University of Chicago Press, 1968

Scull AT: Museums of Madness. New York, St. Martin's Press, 1979

Temkin O: The scientific approach to disease: specific entity and individual sickness, in Scientific Change. Edited by Clembie AC. New York, Basic Books, 1963, pp 629–647

Tseng WS: The development of psychiatric concepts in traditional Chinese medicine. Arch Gen Psychiatry 29:569–575, 1973

Veith I: Hysteria: The History of Disease. Chicago, IL, University of Chicago Press, 1965

Chapter 2

How Is Culture Important for DSM-IV?

Arthur Kleinman, M.D.

Before DSM-III-R (American Psychiatric Association 1987) was published, the chair of its task force, Robert Spitzer, asked me to offer some comments that might form part of the Introduction cautioning mental health professionals about the potential for DSM's misuse when applied to members of ethnic minorities and to populations in other, especially non-Western, societies. I drafted a letter of five or six paragraphs in response to his request. To my surprise, I discovered that some of what I wrote had been lifted out and compressed into two paragraphs on pp. xxvi and xxvii of the Introduction.

Those two paragraphs, in spite of Spitzer's good intentions, are symbolic of DSM-III-R's limitations when applied across ethnic, cultural, and international boundaries: namely, they are too little, too late. We have the opportunity to make much more systematic recommendations for inclusions of crucial concepts, methods, and practices that could render the next edition of the DSM more appropriate for use in the United States' multicultural society and in the global context to which it is increasingly being applied. DSM-IV (American Psychiatric Association 1994) needed to be less biased by North American cultural orientations, more open to cross-cultural variation in health and pathology, and more practically useful and valid when applied in the plural contexts of diverse ethnic groups.

Thereby, DSM-IV could have functioned more validly as an international or global diagnostic system, which it is fast becoming in practice. Too little of what we recommended was included in DSM-IV. Our recommendations, which were based on the following understanding of how culture pertains to psychiatric diagnosis and practice, are relevant to the development of DSM-IV.

Changing Conceptions of Culture

In its Victorian usage, culture conveyed the ideas both of the biological basis of racial difference (a strongly racialist meaning) and of higher and lower levels of civilization (a strongly moral message). The Nazis discredited the former, the colonialists the latter.

In its more recent forms, culture has been used in psychiatry as a demographic description of populations, as in the indexical use of respondents' ethnic status. The relationship between ethnicity and particular disease profiles, risk factors, or even disorders culture bound to particular groups continues as a useful avenue for epidemiological research.

In the 1950s, 60s, and 70s, culture was understood more as shared value orientations and beliefs about the body, the self, illness, and treatment. That view of culture is apparent in the large number of studies of the illness beliefs and therapeutic practices of different groups or subgroups. Whereas this approach to culture often fosters "cultural sensitivity," it also suffers from the tendency to superficially stereotype entire groups—for example, "This is the way Hispanics respond to depression!"—and to convey the erroneous sense that cultural orientations are conventions, mistaken beliefs that can be taken off and put back on again at will.

In recent years, a much more sophisticated idea of culture has gained ground in anthropology. This is the notion that culture is constituted by, and in turn constitutes, local worlds of everyday experience. That is to say, culture is built up ("realized") out of the everyday patterns of daily life activities—common sense, communication with others, and the routine rhythms and rituals of community life that are taken for granted—which reciprocally reflect the patterning downward of social relations by shared symbolic apparatuses—language, aesthetic sensibility, and core value orientations conveyed by master metaphors. In these local worlds, experience is an interpersonal flow of communication, interaction, and negotiation—that is, it is social, not individual—which centers on agreement and contestation about what is most at stake and how that which is at stake is to be sought and gained. Gender, age cohort, social role and status, and personal desire all inflect this small moral universe in different ways. The upshot is culture in the making, in the processes that generate action and that justify practices. Thus, the locus of culture is not the mind of the isolated person, but the interconnected body/self of groups: families, work settings, networks, whole communities.

In this new perspective, culture is more than what is meant when we talk of rates, symptoms, or treatment of psychiatric conditions in exotic places or special groups: schizophrenia in China, depression among Puerto Ricans, or the mental health system (or lack thereof) in Tanzania. In addition to these culturally salient phenomena, culture is also an influential aspect of North American psychiatry and society. Cultural processes pattern the diagnostic practices of a psychiatrist in Boston, a psychologist in San Francisco, a psychiatric social worker in Toledo, and a mental health aide in Beijing as much as they do the forms and patterns of disorder and the coping processes in which families engage to deal with afflicted members. DSM-III-R, the official diagnostic system of the American Psychiatric Association, and its application by professionals in particular institutional and societal contexts, then, are cultural phenomena: the former, a document that is clothed with cultural commitments; the latter, forms of interaction that are culturally patterned and socially negotiated (Kleinman 1988a, 1988b). Here are a few examples.

The chief symptom of major depression is said to be the emotion of sadness or depression. That seems obvious. After all, depression is a psychological, emotional problem, is it not? Yet in most societies, most people experiencing clinical depressions do not complain mainly of sadness. Instead they talk about fatigue, headaches, backaches, stomach upset, insomnia, loss of appetite, and so on. For most depressed people this physical experience is most real. As a result, they visit primary care doctors rather than mental health professionals, and usually their depression is neither diagnosed nor effectively treated (Kleinman 1986).

To define emotions as central to the experience of depression is to make a commitment every bit as "cultural" as the beliefs of Chinese businesspersons, Hindu peasants, or ethnic minorities in the United States (Jenkins et al. 1991). It is characteristic of Western culture to separate the emotional and physical components of depression and give primacy to the former. This cultural bias in favor of a mind-body dichotomy is strengthened by another feature of our society and our medicine: the fact that most research on depression involves patients in psychiatric treatment, who are a special, often self-selected minority of all depressed persons (Guarnaccia et al. 1990).

Probably none of us living in Western societies would be surprised to be asked by a mental health worker if we felt "blue" or "down." The terms seem natural as a description of depression. However, all such linguistic categories are derived from cultural models of the world, the person, or the illness. *Down* makes sense to us because Western culture has traditionally regarded depression as a result of the soul moving downward in the body (Jackson 1986). The word *depression* itself is derived from Latin roots meaning to press down. Belief and experience are so intertwined that we consider a downward inner feeling natural and universal. Most of the 80% of our planet's people who live in non-Western societies would be baffled by this. They are more likely to experience depression as a feeling of emptiness—a bodily counterpart to the idea of soul loss (Shweder 1985).

Because illness categories reflect cultural principles, we must be careful not to let our own cultural bias exert a hidden, damaging effect on our scientific research and therapies. For example, many Plains Indians hear the voice of a recently deceased relative calling them from the afterworld. The experience is normative and without psychopathological sequelae for members of these communities and therefore, by definition, cannot be abnormal. In contrast, for an adult white North American such an experience might well be a hallucination with serious mental health consequences.

Of all the adult mental disorders described in DSM-IV, besides the organic brain disorders and substance abuse, convincing evidence supports the case of only four that are distributed worldwide: schizophrenia, manic-depressive (bipolar) disorder, major depression, and a group of anxiety disorders including panic anxiety, obsessive-compulsive disorder, and certain phobias. The rest of our adult mental illness categories are peculiar to North America and Western Europe. An interesting example is anorexia nervosa. This disorder exists in contemporary Western societies that regard slim female bodies as beautiful, sexually desirable, and commercially significant. Except among the Westernized upper middle class of Japan, Taiwan, and Hong Kong, there is no anorexia nervosa in Asia (Littlewood and Lipsedge 1987).

Dissociation in North America presents, increasingly it would seem from the clinical literature, as multiple personality disorder. However, in societies such as India, where the concept and experience of self is more fluid and sociocentric and communal religious idioms of distress receive more cultural legitimation than egocentric psychological ones, dissociation, though common, rarely appears as multiple personality but rather occurs as possession by demons or gods or as meditative states. The former is often pathological; the latter form, however, is usually (though not always) socially normative and personally normal (Castillo 1991). Thus cultural context constructs unique forms of mental states and strongly influences which experiences are normal and which are pathological.

The changing culture of the psychiatric profession and the ethos of contemporary times in North America clearly contribute to the construction of multiple personality by practitioner and patient, whereas a decade ago, this construction was not supported by the cultural context (Hacking 1995). Yet this particular construction is a return to concerns at the turn of our century that animated the work of Pierre Janet and William James as well as the experiences of their patients. Hysteria's reverse history of going out of social fashion as well as out of prevalence during the same 10 decades points to the same cultural process through which psychiatric category, social expectation, and experience constitute each other. Can we interpret chronic fatigue syndrome as a 20th century cultural recycling of 19th century *fin de siècle* neurasthenia? The scientific jury is still out, but the hypothesis is worth considering (Abbey and Garfinkel 1991).

Schizophrenia, in contrast, is nearly ubiquitous. Although the content of hallucinations, delusions, and thought disorder varies, those symptoms as well as negativity, withdrawal, and impaired reality testing can be demonstrated nearly everywhere—proof, it is claimed, of schizophrenia's strong biological roots. Nevertheless, there are also important cultural differences that may be clues to the causes of schizophrenia. Contrary to conventional assumptions, epidemiological and ethnographic studies show that the disorder is not equally common everywhere (Kleinman 1988a). The prevalence ranges from 1 in 1,000 in non-Western societies to more than 1 in 100 in Western societies. Some preliterate hunter-gatherer groups, nomads, and settled horticulturalist societies have no schizophrenia. Economically and technologically advanced, urbanized, and bureaucratized societies have much higher rates of schizophrenia than peasant societies. Indeed, the disorder seems to be relatively uncommon in any society without a system of wage labor (Warner 1985). The reason for this remains unclear.

Furthermore, the symptoms and course of schizophrenia vary geographically. One out of every fourth or fifth schizophrenic patient in Madras, India, is catatonic, but there are hardly any catatonic patients in western Europe or North America. More than half of hospitalized Japanese patients with this diagnosis are hebephrenic. Schizophrenia is more likely to have a rapid onset in Nigeria or China than in the United States. Several major studies by the World Health Organization have shown that schizophrenia, regardless of age at onset, is a less serious illness and has a better outcome in poor countries, despite their limited health services, apparently because families and communities provide better support for schizophrenic patients (Hopper 1991; Jenkins and Karno 1992; Kleinman 1988a). Research is now being conducted to identify these influences more precisely and use the results to improve the treatment of schizophrenia in the United States.

The practice of the psychiatrist is also culturally patterned. A psychiatric diagnosis, after all, is an interpretation of an interpretation. Contrary to the positivism of most academic psychiatry, as Nils Bohr knew in physics, there can be no immediate grasping of reality outside of historically derived categories. What the patient reports is itself an interpretation of experience based on his or her own cultural categories, words, images, and feelings for expressing (and thereby constituting) symptoms. The psychiatrist's interpretation occurs one remove further.

Moreover the psychiatrist is influenced by what is at stake in a particular institutional setting. The diagnosis in a disability evaluation, in a contested courtroom drama, in a military hospital, in a politically oppressive system such as Nazi mental hospitals or Stalin's psychiatric gulag is inseparable from powerful institutional constraints that become a normative order that can change utterly how a diagnosis is applied.

DSM-IV's Theoretical Commitments

Notwithstanding strong protestations to the contrary, DSM-IV makes a number of fundamental theoretical assumptions, conceptual commitments that exert a significant cultural influence. For example, DSM-IV assumes that mental illnesses are phenomena in the natural world that can be verified through objective observation. This theoretical position gives primacy to observation as a means of verification. As I have shown elsewhere, commitment overemphasizes reliability of diagnosis (verification of observations) and underemphasizes validity of diagnosis (verification of the concepts that guide those observations) (Kleinman 1988a, 1988b).

Other theoretical commitments include the conviction that psychiatric disorders are preprogrammed diatheses out of which unfolds a natural course of the disease process. The course of psychiatric disorders, however, has been shown repeatedly and definitively to be inseparable from ongoing social events and coping resources (Moos 1991), from family relationships (Jenkins and Karno 1992; Vaughn and Leff 1976), and from involvement with medical and welfare systems (Katon et al. 1982a; Osterweis 1984, 1987). That is to say, the course of mental illness is social, not natural. The fact that outcome of schizophrenia varies inversely with the social development of the country in which schizophrenia is experienced, which has been replicated on several occasions, is another piece of evidence in support of this argument (Hopper 1991).

The mind-body dichotomy that looms behind the somatoform disorders chapter; the pathogenetic-pathoplastic division implicit in the chapters on major mental disorder; the idea of single, stable personalities as socially normative and personally normal, which underwrites both the dissociative disorders section and Axis II—all are examples of DSM-IV's powerful orientation to Western cultural values. In contrast to the last of these conceptual commitments, the members of many non-Western societies and traditionally oriented ethnic groups regard the person as more sociocentric than egocentric; the boundaries of the ego as permeable; and the self (or soul) as fluid and capable of leaving the body, entering altered states, and becoming possessed (Gaines 1994; Kleinman and Good 1985; Stigler et al. 1990). These alternative ideas are basic to the mental health categories of traditional Chinese, Indians, Southeast Asians, and members of African and South American groups, who together constitute more than three fourths of the world's population. Thus, the cultural influence on DSM-IV is not only apparent but represents a minority bias cross-culturally.

DSM-IV's categories are written in such a way as to make it seem that there can be no major variations in health and human development, yet the empirical record tells exactly the opposite story. Variations are the rule across societies with respect to normal and abnormal psychological processes and child development. So uncommon is dysphoria as a presenting complaint among Chinese patients with depression, for example, and so common are somatic complaints that neurasthenic depression (chronic fatigue syndrome in North America may be an example) can be seen as a major subtype that can hardly be regarded as "atypical." Rather, the classical picture of major depressive disorder is heavily influenced by the study of psychiatric inpatients and outpatients. Because most patients with this disorder worldwide attend primary care rather than psychiatric clinics, where they describe an experience of chronic somatic complaints, DSM-IV diagnostic criteria for this extremely common disorder are inadequate and may even be invalid.

Invalidating Applications

When applied in a narrow, mechanical fashion, DSM-IV is too easily turned into something it was never meant to be: an overly formalistic blueprint that pathologizes ordinary and extraordinary experience and that disaffirms the meaning-oriented subjectivity of suffering in favor of technical diagnoses that often lack personal and collective significance. It is highly appropriate that DSM-III-R cautioned against such mindless application. However, a single paragraph inserted in an Introduction few read more than once was not likely to protect against this high-risk misuse, which is particularly problematic when patient and practitioner come from different cultural, ethnic, religious, or socioeconomic backgrounds and when the diagnostic system is applied in cultural contexts radically different from that in which it was first formulated. Regrettably, even though DSM-IV has many more things to say about culture, few of the really crucial recommendations that our panel made were included. Therefore, much of what DSM-III-R was criticized about holds for DSM-IV too.

Culturally sensitive application of the DSM diagnostic system means that questions in clinical interviews and in other assessment techniques must be translated into terms that are socially meaningful; however, it also means that consideration must be given to indigenous conceptualizations, values, and practices. Cultural sensitivity must be given particular attention when clinical work or research is conducted cross-culturally and internationally.

With this limited review as background, what can be done to improve DSM-IV's cultural validity and therefore cross-cultural utility?

Steps Toward A Culturally Valid DSM-V

1. DSM-IV's introduction includes a longer and more specific set of guidelines concerning the use of DSM with members of ethnic, refugee, and cross-cultural groups in both domestic and international settings. These guidelines discuss expectable problems such as mistranslation, ineffective clinical communication, and potential for cultural bias (causing both over- and under-diagnosis) in the clinical application of diagnostic categories. Practical strategies should be described that can be used to overcome these problems. Also, the section on cultural assessment should be moved out of the Appendix and into the Introduction. Key cultural idioms of distress such as *nervios* or *ataques* among Puerto Ricans should be introduced and it should be pointed out that these are common channels of communication and behavior that may express either normal or pathological states. There is no one-to-one correlation between a specific DSM-IV diagnostic category and a cultural idiom of distress.

   The Introduction should also include a section on culturally appropriate clinical and research use of DSM-IV. This brief section should outline what is meant by culturally sensitive diagnostic interviewing and culturally valid translation and application of DSM-IV–based diagnostic tests and research instruments. To justify and illustrate these and the other additions, the Introduction should give a few illustrations of common cross-cultural problems in DSM's use. Included should be consideration of the cultural blind spot syndrome, which results when patient and practitioner share ethnicity or culture but the practitioner fails to take culture into account (Lin 1984).

2. It should be officially debated whether it is useful and feasible for a cultural axis to be added to assess degree of acculturation, likelihood for cultural obstacles, and particular types of cultural bias. Such an axis, on the one hand, could highlight cultural issues and make their evaluation a routine part of the clinical assessment proceedings. Alternatively, a cultural axis might well not be used, inasmuch as Axes IV and V already are often not addressed in clinical work. For this reason, including a cultural axis runs the risk of being more

window dressing than substance. The section on culture should also be moved forward to a more prominent place in the Introduction.

A cultural axis could take a number of forms. One form would be to ask patients to self-describe their ethnic or cultural identity as well as their perceived degree of acculturation, language fluency, religious affiliation, and any special dietary or other practices that could be used to assess the degree of practicing behavioral ethnicity. Thus patients' or families' explanatory models would be elicited to assess culturally influential beliefs on illness experience by asking them: What do you call your illness? What do you believe to be its cause? Why did it begin when it did? What do you expect to be the course or outcome? What do you fear most about this condition? What treatment do you expect? What do you fear most about the treatment? Are you following the prescribed treatment? If not, can you explain why? (The last two questions are useful because noncompliance is an especially frequent and predictable problem in cross-cultural care.) This approach is part of the cultural assessment in DSM-IV's Appendix. Being part of a new axis could make the approach a part of standard practice.

3.   Under each disease condition or chapter there should be a section on cultural issues in diagnosis that includes specific, culturally relevant inclusion and exclusion criteria and discussion of cultural influence on symptoms, illness behavior, course, and risk factors. At present, most of what DSM-IV says about culture under most diseases is not crucial for diagnosis and treatment. In DSM-V that needs to change.

For example, if an experience or behavior occurs in a culturally authorized setting, such as a ritual, and is regarded by members of the culture as expectable and normative, then the exclusion criteria should state that no mental disorder should be diagnosed. Alternatively, under differential diagnosis, cultural behaviors that are normal could be considered. Disorders such as *taijin kyofusho*—a common phobia in Japan based on a culturally resonant fear of embarrassing others, rather than being criticized by them as in social phobia—which represent special cultural patterns of mental disorders (in this case phobias), should be listed as a special disease state (another phobic disorder that is not a variant of social phobia).

Under Axis II, antisocial personality disorder presents a special problem. If applied to high-crime inner-city neighborhoods where African American and Hispanic adolescents, in particular, are socialized in local worlds where violence is routine and where many of the behaviors listed are normative, albeit brutal and brutalizing, coping styles that aid survival and that can also represent the only available means of resisting authority that is perceived as unresponsive and biased (so-called "weapons of the weak"; Scott 1985), then this category lacks validity and ends up blaming the patient. Surely, just as its "unemployed" criterion is qualified to indicate that suitable employment must be available, the other criteria must be similarly qualified. In the same vein, posttraumatic stress disorder following torture, war, and other forms of political violence requires qualifications that indicate it is an expectable psychophysiological consequence that is not necessarily an indication of personal pathology (Young 1990, 1995).

Thus, the diagnostician must be trained to take the context into account before committing himself or herself and the person being evaluated to a specific diagnosis.

4. For dissociative disorders (as well as other mental disorders that are particularly common and significant cross-culturally), specific examples should be given of common symptoms and behaviors cross-culturally; because dissociation occurs in more than 95% of the world's cultures and is most often normative and normal (though it also can express psychopathology), differentiating normal from abnormal dissociation is crucial (Bourguignon 1976).

5. Appendix to DSM-IV lists the common cultural idioms of distress and culture-bound syndromes for major ethnic minorities and refugee groups in the United States and should be moved to the text itself.

A case could be made for a separate chapter on culture-bound syndromes, and incorporation of at least major culture-bound syndromes of American ethnic groups and the major non-Western societies in Axis I. If properly written, such a chapter could be a significant contribution to DSM-IV-R, and would signal that DSM is intended as an internationally useful classification. However, if improperly handled, such a chapter could create more problems than it resolves. Thus, it would be important to have contributions from both anthropologists and cross-cultural psychiatrists who have studied culture-bound disorders. Alternatively, one could argue that because 90% of DSM categories are culture bound to North America and western Europe, the very idea of culture bound as "exotic" syndromes outside Euro-American culture itself is flawed; therefore, the use of this concept to label *only* non-Western or ethnic syndromes is biased and inappropriate. This could be dealt with by including Euro-American culture bound disorders such as anorexia nervosa.

6. An Appendix should also include a list of expectable problems in working with interpreters and how to prevent them (see Introduction and Conclusion in Harwood 1981).

7. Each section of the *DSM Case Book* should contain illustrative cross-ethnic and cross-cultural cases. Alternatively, an argument could be made for a separate casebook for ethnic and cross-cultural cases, because clinicians learn best from case examples.

8. The Introduction to DSM-IV defines and explains culture and ethnicity so that it is clear that cultural groups are heterogeneous owing to gender, age, subethnic grouping, social class, and lifestyle. In DSM-V emphasis should be extended to the appreciation of how the culture of biomedicine and the institutional cultures of professional practice influence practitioners' own perspectives and actions.

Cultural beliefs for some intellectuals are conventions that can be debated and altered; for most people, however, cultural orientations are deeply held, felt ideas about what is most at stake in experience; they are like natural law, the way things are, and therefore are neither easily negotiated quickly nor abandoned. If the practitioner's focus is on suffering—the felt experience of pain and distress, the enduring or experiencing of trials to the body-self and the network—then taking culture into account does not mean changing unscientific beliefs but rather affirming, witnessing, and engaging the illness in the embodied terms in which it is experienced.

A serious interest in the patient's culture means a more sophisticated and sensitive engagement with religious values than psychiatrists generally demonstrate. Ninety percent of North Americans express a belief in God, and more than 75% pray to God for assistance, so that even in this "secular" society, the perceived teleology of the experience of suffering is likely to be articulated in religious terms that affect the illness and its treatment.

This clinical methodology should allow diagnosticians to go beyond basic cultural sensitivity to culturally valid use of the diagnostic system and its application.

References

Abbey SE, Garfinkel PE: Neurasthenia and chronic fatigue: the role of culture in the making of a diagnosis. Am J Psychiatry 148:1638–1646, 1991

American Psychiatric Association: Diagnostic and Statistical Manual of Mental Disorders, 3rd Edition, Revised. Washington, DC, American Psychiatric Association, 1987

American Psychiatric Association: Diagnostic and Statistical Manual of Mental Disorders, 4th Edition. Washington, DC, American Psychiatric Association, 1994

Bourguignon E: Possession. San Francisco, CA, Chandler and Shark, 1976

Castillo R: Culture, trance and mental illness: divided consciousness in South Asia. Doctoral dissertation, Cambridge, MA, Harvard University, 1991

Gaines A (ed): Ethnopsychiatry. New York, State University of New York Press, 1994

Guarnaccia P, Good B, Kleinman A: A critical review of epidemiological studies of Puerto Rican mental health. Am J Psychiatry 147:1449–1455, 1990

Hacking I: Rewriting the Soul. Princeton, NJ, Princeton University Press, 1995

Harwood A (ed): Ethnicity and Medical Care. Cambridge, MA, Harvard University Press, 1981

Hopper K: Some old questions for the new cross-cultural psychiatry. Med Anthropol 5:299–330, 1991

Jackson S: Melancholia and Depression. New Haven, CT, Yale University Press, 1986

Jenkins J, Karno M: Expressed emotion among Mexican-descent families: cultural adaptation of the method and principal findings. Am J Psychiatry 149:9–21, 1992

Jenkins J, Kleinman A, Good B: Cross-cultural studies of depression, in Psychosocial Aspects of Depression. Edited by Becker J, Kleinman A. Hillsdale, NJ, Erlbaum, 1991

Katon W, Kleinman A, Rosen G: Depression and somatization, I. Am J Med 72:127–135, 1982a

Katon W, Kleinman A, Rosen G: Depression and Somatization, II. Am J Med 72:241–247, 1982b

Kleinman A: Social Origins of Distress and Disease: Depression, Neurasthenia and Pain in Modern China. New Haven, CT, Yale University Press, 1986

Kleinman A: Rethinking Psychiatry. New York, Free Press, 1988a

Kleinman A: The Illness Narratives: Suffering, Healing and the Human Condition. New York, Basic Books, 1988b

Kleinman A, Good B (eds): Culture and Depression. Berkeley, University of California Press, 1985

Lin EHB: Intraethnic characteristics and patient-physician interaction: cultural blind spot syndrome. J Fam Pract 16(1):91–98, 1984

Littlewood R, Lipsedge M: The butterfly and the serpent: culture, psycho-pathology and biomedicine. Cult Med Psychiatry 11:289–336, 1987

Moos R: Life stressors, social resources, and the treatment of depression, in Psychological Aspects of Depression. Edited by Becker J, Kleinman A. Hillsdale, NJ, Erlbaum, 1991, pp 187–214

Osterweis M: Bereavement. Washington, DC, National Academy Press, 1984

Osterweis M: Pain and Disability. Washington, DC, National Academy Press, 1987

Scott J: Weapons of the Weak. New Haven, CT, Yale University Press, 1985

Shweder R: Menstrual pollution, soul loss and the comparative study of emotions, in Culture and Depression. Edited by Kleinman A, Good B. Berkeley, University of California Press, 1985, pp 182–215

Stigler J, et al (eds): Cultural Psychology. Chicago, IL, University of Chicago Press, 1990

Vaughn C, Leff J: The measurement of expressed emotion in the families of psychiatric patients. Br J Soc Clin Psychol 15:157–165, 1976

Warner R: Recovery From Schizophrenia: Psychiatry and Political Economy. New York, Routledge & Kegan Paul, 1985

Young A: Moral conflicts in a psychiatric hospital treating combat-related PTSD, in Social Science Perspectives on Medical Ethics. Edited by Weisz G. Boston, MA, Kluwer, 1990, pp 65–82

Young A: The Harmony of Illusions. Princeton, NJ, Princeton University Press, 1995

Chapter 3

African American Perspectives

Ezra E. H. Griffith, M.D.

A frican American mental health professionals have long had some interest in the question of psychiatric diagnosis, particularly because they have often been struck by the notion that the basic concepts of psychiatry reflect the culture and history of western Europe–influenced societies. Given the history of and interactions between blacks and whites in the United States, application of the psychiatric diagnostic system in this country has understandably evoked suspicion and distrust among some black professionals in some contexts. Nowhere is this more evident than in the diagnosis of schizophrenia and affective disorders among blacks. Jones and Gray (1986) have outlined several reasons for the apparent overdiagnosis of schizophrenia among blacks and the confusion that clinicians seem to experience when confronted with a black patient suffering from depression. Much of the problematic diagnosing seems linked to the preference that clinicians have for attributing a diagnosis of severe, chronic illness to a black patient. Clinicians will sometimes ignore a history of alcoholism in a black patient and attribute the signs of dementia to a schizophrenic illness (F. M. Baker, personal communication). This clinical prejudice is, of course, born of the natural prejudice that is pervasive in the broader culture.

In Chapter 1, Fabrega raises the question about the politicizing of the psychiatric enterprise and suggests that we are often resistant to untangling medical and sociopolitical issues in the context of the diagnosis task. However, in a society such as the United States, which is polarized by the race question, few African American mental health professionals would suggest that the diagnostic system used in this country escapes the charge of commingling the medical and the political. Even Fabrega's reference to the use of the diagnostic system in the Soviet Union to achieve political ends may possibly be amusingly culture bound—that is, if one assumes Fabrega really believes he has to go as far as the Soviet Union to prove his point. Many African American professionals would simply have argued that the diagnostic system in America is ripe for distortion and the achievement of political ends.

The previous statement is the clearest and shortest route to answering Fabrega's question of whether one can have a language of psychiatric illness and psychopathology that is truly culture free. Fabrega, by his own examples, argues convincingly that a culture-free language is hard to design and use. His most impressive examples are in the personality disorders category. Over the years, some African American professionals (S. Okpaku, personal communication) have been routinely concerned that the antisocial personality disorder diagnosis has been too readily applied to blacks. It has been thought that the common use of this diagnosis is part of the overall effort to categorize black males in a way that assures them no help from the mental health system, which in turn then often facilitates the entry of black males into the prison system.

Of course, whites are not the only ones who can politicize the diagnosis process. It is really no surprise that from time to time, black mental health professionals argue that the personality disorders category should encompass the racist personality. Organized psychiatry has not taken well to the suggestion that such an entity deserves serious consideration. However, by implication, Fabrega makes us wonder why American psychiatrists are highly preoccupied with the concept of narcissism and equally afraid of racism. Of course, a part of the dilemma is that white psychiatrists, who control the diagnosis system, can well foresee the ultimate political uses of the racist personality disorder category. At the risk of being provocative, I would suggest some of my black psychiatrist colleagues have been too smugly righteous in their assumption that not very many blacks would deserve the diagnosis of racist personality disorder. Regardless of the side one takes in this political-medical argument, the subject is good proof of Fabrega's view that there are clear cultural bases to the historical foundation of psychiatric diagnosis.

These concepts enunciated by Fabrega obtain further clarification in Chapter 2 from Kleinman, who provides some specific examples that are thought-provoking. I agree readily with Kleinman that establishment of a cultural axis in DSM-IV (American Psychiatric Association 1994) would be a mere curiosity. Few professionals would likely use it anymore than the current axes.

However, Kleinman reminds us also that there are some diagnostic categories or concepts that receive considerable emphasis in the current American diagnostic system. There is a disregard for principles that constantly intrigue those who work with African American patients. For example, anorexia nervosa is a relatively uncommon disorder among blacks, although it is emerging among United States and Caribbean blacks. In contrast, Kleinman's reference to the mind-body dichotomy reminds me that many Caribbean blacks will complain of pain in the head and belly rather than admit straightforwardly to feeling sad or blue because of a separation from a spouse. Similarly, the current diagnostic system does little to contend with the phenomenon of the hex, which is a common framework for voicing discomfort, used by both United States and Caribbean blacks.

Kleinman cogently considers the notion that dissociation is internationally ubiquitous and contradicts the United States view that the boundaries of the ego are relatively impermeable. Ritual spirit possession and altered states of consciousness are common among United States and Caribbean blacks, a fact that can be verified readily across the United States in Sunday church services held in the black community. Indeed, a very intriguing task for a psychiatrist is trying to determine when the spirit possession has become truly pathological and to understand why the patient's possession state is no longer within his or her acceptable boundaries for ritual possession.

Here an additional problem deserves mention: the vocabulary blacks often use to communicate their feelings of despair or simply frustration is so extreme, in comparison to that used by the whites around them, that the behavior is often categorized as severely pathological. This is most evident in relation to the vocabulary of violence. I was struck recently by a black high school student's description of his behavior in the context of his school. He argued that no white student in the school had the right to walk into territory delimited as belonging to the black students, on pain of being beaten. The black student asserted the right to be violent to defend his diplomatic and political rights in a way that clearly saw the use of violence as nothing unusual. Indeed, he was confident of the moral rightness of his position. It is unclear what this vocabulary of violence is all about, but it is evident that deeming it pathological misses the point. The more important question is why many people in the black community see violence as the appropriate vocabulary for resolving conflict and difference.

Carl Bell (personal communication) acknowledges that black children are frequently witnesses to violence in the black community. Apart from the fact that these children may manifest symptoms of a chronic form of posttraumatic stress disorder, they also gradually learn to internalize violence as a means of communication and a way of problem solving. The behavior of violence then progressively becomes not antisociety at all but rather conforms clearly to the culture rampant in certain pockets of the black community. Most troubling, of course, is that it may all just lead to the killing of blacks by blacks, a problematic phenomenon in the black community (Griffith and Bell 1989).

References

American Psychiatric Association: Diagnostic and Statistical Manual of Mental Disorders, 4th Edition. Washington, DC: American Psychiatric Association, 1994

Griffith EEH, Bell CC: Recent trends in suicide and homicide among blacks. JAMA 262:2265–2269, 1989

Jones BE, Gray BA: Problems in diagnosing schizophrenia and affective disorders among blacks. Hosp Community Psychiatry 37:61–65, 1986

Chapter 4

Native American Perspectives

James W. Thompson, M.P.H., M.D.

Although the philosophical and anthropological underpinnings of nosology and their poor application in DSM are important topics, our primary job is to ask whether DSM can be made more culturally relevant in its daily use. A discussion will therefore be offered on improving the cultural relevance of DSM in clinical care, with particular reference to Native Americans, including Alaska Native and Canadian Indians.

Nosological Problems

The first problem is the mistaken tendency to consider all members of a minority group similar. For example, the loss of many traditional ways and intermingling between groups has blurred some of the differences between Indian tribes. However, it would be a great mistake to assume that either the cultures or the psychopathologies of all Indian people are the same. It was recommended that DSM-IV contain a discussion about cultural diversity within minority groups and how a clinician can elicit information on this diversity as it applies to diagnosis.

The second problem is related to assumptions about psychopathology in minority cultures. Clinicians working with Native American people may erroneously assume that mental disorder in Native Americans is identical to that in whites, requiring no deviation at all from Western conceptualizations of psychopathology. Similarly, it may be assumed that mental disorder in Native Americans is so unlike that found in whites that there is little hope for the Western clinician to understand it or deal with it. These are, respectively, an under-determination and an over-determination of the importance of culture. The first assumption leads to culturally insensitive care. The second leads the clinician to ignore psychopathology or to attribute it to cultural or social problems that are seen as outside the purview of health care.

Cultural insensitivity, arising from the assumption that mental disorders in Native Americans are identical to those of the majority culture, is a very real problem, but the larger problem by far is that of ignoring DSM disorders entirely in Native Americans. Given this state of affairs, it is premature to work toward making psychiatric care for Native American people culture sensitive. A preliminary step is to improve the recognition of DSM disorders in Native Americans. Having accomplished this task, sensitivity to Native American cultures can then be addressed.

It is recommended that DSM state that much psychopathology in minority individuals is similar to that found in whites, although social and cultural influences may alter the presentation of these disorders. Such psychopathology should not be ignored in the name of cultural sensitivity. It is also recommended that DSM contain information to help the clinician deal with the interface between the patient's culture and the clinician's culture. This information should not consist of facts about specific groups, but rather should include guidance as to the process one goes through to find explanations of diagnostic terms to which both patient and clinician can relate (Kleinman et al. 1978).

A third problem is that cultural practices appearing strange to the majority culture may be thought of by majority clinicians as pathological. It is recommended that DSM include material that assists the clinician to make the distinction between pathology and cultural difference.

A fourth problem is that some difficulties in minority groups are seen as being normative, and therefore as "normal," although in fact they are pathological. This is cultural sensitivity turned on its head. An example in Native Americans is alcoholism. Alcoholism prevalence rates vary widely by tribe and location (Stratton et al. 1978; Westermeyer 1974). However, when clinicians have observed Native American communities where there is a high prevalence of alcoholism, it has been a common point of view that alcoholism is not deviant, not maladaptive, and therefore not an illness (Heath 1988; Kunitz and Levy 1974). Increasingly, however, Native American people have been speaking out against this point of view, to clarify that alcoholism is clearly deviant and maladaptive. DSM-III-R helped in this regard, as it provided criteria for determining when alcohol use is pathological. It defined heavy drinking as abnormal and never adaptive or healthy, despite the fact that it might be common. It is recommended that DSM clearly state that although cultural factors must be taken into account when diagnosing disease and illness, pathology should not be dismissed simply because it occurs with a high prevalence in a particular community or group.

Finally, it is important to discuss the inclusion of the so-called culture-bound syndromes. This concept has a long history in cross-cultural psychiatry (Hughes 1985).The concept of culture-bound could sequester nonmajority psychopathology and imply that some psychopathology is found only within a single culture. There may be the implication that the culture itself must in some way have caused the psychopathology. The greatest danger of placing culture-bound syndromes in DSM is that the majority clinician may feel that he or she cannot understand or deal with culture-bound conditions and so may miss psychopathology with which he or she can effectively deal. The majority clinician may also believe that trying to apply Western knowledge to a culture-bound syndrome amounts to cultural insensitivity. As previously discussed, DSM mental disorders are often ignored in Native Americans and may be further ignored if clinicians define Native American psychopathology largely as culture bound and outside their purview. The explicit assumption in DSM should be that a patient's condition almost always can be understood with a culturally sensitive application of Western concepts of psychopathology, until this assumption is proved incorrect by treatment failure or other evidence.

Conclusion

Efforts to improve the cultural sensitivity of DSM must be done with the realization that North American minority populations are being treated within the context of a Euro-American majority culture and largely by Euro-American health care personnel. A balance must be struck between a nosology that will help to ensure access of minority people to state-of-the-art psychiatric care and a nosology that is sensitive to a given patient's cultural context as it interfaces with the majority culture. Clinicians must not wear the blinders of ethnocentrism, but neither should they overdetermine the importance of culture such that they despair of providing appropriate care to minority people. A culturally sensitive DSM would greatly assist in achieving that balance.

References

Heath DB: Emerging anthropological theory and models of alcohol use and alcoholism, in Theories on Alcoholism. Edited by Chaudron CD, Wilkinson DA. Toronto, Ontario, Canada, Addiction Research Foundation, 1988

Hughes CC: Culture-bound or construct-bound? The syndromes of DSM-III, in The Culture-Bound Syndromes: Folk Illnesses of Psychiatric and Anthropological Interest. Edited by Simons RC, Hughes CC. Dordrecht, The Netherlands, D Reidel, 1985

Kleinman A, Eisenberg L, Good, B: Culture, illness, and care: clinical lessons from anthropologic and cross-cultural research. Ann Intern Med 88:251–258, 1978

Kunitz SJ, Levy JE: Changing ideas of alcohol use among Navajo Indians. Q J Stud Alcohol 35:243–259, 1974

Stratton R, Zeiner A, Paredes A: Tribal affiliation and prevalence of alcohol problems. Q J Stud Alcohol 39:1166–1177, 1978

Westermeyer J: The drunken Indian: myths and realities. Psychiatric Annals 4(9):29–36, 1974

Chapter 5

Asian American Perspectives

Keh-Ming Lin, M.P.H., M.D.

In the development of the DSM-IV, there were several important reasons to take into consideration the experiences of Asians and Asian Americans. First, Asian Americans represent one of the fastest growing ethnic minority groups in the United States (Fawcett and Carino 1987). The 1990 census counted more than 6.5 million Asians in the country, representing 3% of the total population. With an Asian American growth rate of more than 100% per decade, psychiatrists in this country can no longer afford to ignore the existence of this population. Second, like DSM-III, DSM-III-R, DSM-IV, future DSMs will be widely used in various Asian countries, and thus can ill afford to be provincial. Third, cross-cultural validation is one of the best ways to ensure that current concepts and diagnostic conventions are universal and thus of enduring value. The sharp contrasts in the cultural values and orientations between Asian and Western populations provide an excellent opportunity to search for a common language in psychiatric classification and diagnosis across cultures that will likely lead to significant insights in the field of psychiatric nosology.

In this chapter I briefly discuss three fundamental conceptual issues: 1) the mode of expression of emotion and distress, 2) the concept of self and the nature of social relationships, and 3) the influence of culturally shaped health beliefs.

Mode of Expression

Although there are apparent exceptions, Asians often are thought to be more subdued and inhibited in their emotional expression when compared with other major cultural groups. This is attributable in part to specific influences of the prevailing cultural ideologies emphasizing the virtue of silence and equanimity (Bond 1986; Hsu 1981) and the unique early childhood training and child-rearing experiences (Tobin et al. 1989) associated with the inculcation of these virtues.

However, there have also been some intriguing research findings suggesting the existence of innate cross-ethnic differences in temperament (Kagan 1977) that can be clearly identified within several days of birth. Such cross-ethnic differences may contribute to difficulties for Western-trained psychiatric clinicians in accurately evaluating Asian patients, especially if they are not familiar with Asian cultures and thus not able to "tune in" and detect more subtle, often nonverbal expressions of mood and attitudes. This could lead to an underestimation of the degree of psychopathology and, especially, underdiagnosis of mood disorders, including both mania and depression. When coupled with language difficulties and cultural barriers, such dampening of emotional expression could also easily be mistaken as a sign of emotional withdrawal or flat affect. At the same time, culturally congruent and adaptive traits such as this also could be identified by Western clinicians as evidence of an Axis II disorder, such as avoidant and/or dependent personality disorder.

The Concept of Self and the Nature of Social Relationships

Again, exceptions notwithstanding, it is generally fair to say that Asian cultures are predominantly group oriented. This is in sharp contrast to the heavy emphasis on individualism commonly seen in contemporary Western societies (Kleinman 1986, 1988; K. M. Lin and Kleinman 1988). As eloquently elaborated in Chapters 1 and 2, this fundamental difference in cultural orientation can be expected to profoundly influence the formation and presentation of behavioral problems and, hence, psychiatric diagnosis. As mentioned, the Japanese syndrome *taijin kyofusho* (Kitanishi and Tseng 1989) represents one of the most dramatic examples.

Differences between Asian and Western peoples (Marsella et al. 1985; Roland 1988) in the concept of self and interpersonal relationships should be expected to significantly influence personality structures and the manifestation of Axis II disorders. For example, although dependent personality disorder in some form may occur in Asia, this corresponding category, as formulated in DSM, is completely irrelevant and inapplicable in most Asian cultures. The socialization process of Asians actually encourages behavioral patterns such as allowing others to make most of an individual's important decisions (e.g., Chinese parents choosing a spouse or a career for their offspring) and an individual's not doing things on his or her own (e.g., Japanese company employees preferring collective rather than individual decisions). Similarly, borderline and narcissistic personality disorders, at least as defined according to DSM-IV criteria, are rarely applicable for Asian patient populations. This also has to do with cultural differences in the concept of self, the nature of social structure, and the opportunity for "acting out." Several thought-provoking publications (Adityanjee et al. 1989; Peters 1988) have also suggested that multiple personality disorder may be a Western culture-bound phenomenon and may be exceedingly rare in the Asian setting.

Culturally Shaped Health Beliefs

Culturally shaped health belief systems are of central importance not only in determining the interpretation and communication of symptoms and disabilities but also in influencing how symptoms and disabilities are actually experienced, perceived, and conceptualized by patients and professionals (Kleinman 1988). As elaborated in Chapters 1 and 2, this applies not only to non-Western cultures but also to Western traditions. Indeed, as a product of the Western intellectual legacy, modern psychiatric nosology has been heavily imprinted by European and North American cultural characteristics (Fabrega 1989). One of such unique Western beliefs is the artificial separation between the mind (psychological processes) and the body (physiological processes). This has led to a deep-rooted tendency of psychiatrists to regard the psychological side of the manifestations of conditions such as depression and anxiety disorders as primary and the changes that are more somatic and biological in nature as secondary, despite evidence indicating that the latter are at least equally important, if not more so, in relation to both pathogenesis (Deakin 1986) and treatment responses (Silver 1986). Looking through this Western prism of mind-body dichotomy, Asian and other non-Western patients who fail to make such a distinction run the risk of being labeled as more primitive, not psychologically minded, somatizing, and alexithymic. This fundamental difference in the conceptualization of the mind-body relationship is also one of the major reasons for the current controversy over the meaning and nosological status of some of the so-called culture-bound syndromes, such as *hwa byung* among Koreans (K. M. Lin 1983), *shen-k'uei* in Chinese (K. M. Lin 1981), and the *dhat* syndrome among Indians (Weiss et al., in press). It is possibly for the same reason that the diagnosis of neurasthenia (T. Y. Lin 1989) continues to enjoy high popularity in many contemporary Asian societies.

Summary

This is a very brief discussion of the applicability and problems of DSM-IV in the Asian and Asian American cultural settings. Asians represent more than half of the population on Earth. Any diagnostic system or portion of the system that cannot be meaningfully applied to the majority of the human race deserves careful scrutiny as to its validity and clinical utility.

References

Adityanjee MD, Raju GSP, Khandelwal SK: Current status of multiple personality disorder in India. Am J Psychiatry 146:1607–1610, 1989

Bond MH: The Psychology of the Chinese People. Hong Kong, China, Oxford University Press, 1986

Deakin JFW (ed): The Biology of Depression. London, England, Gaskell, 1986

Fabrega H: An ethnomedical perspective of Anglo-American psychiatry. Am J Psychiatry 146:588–596, 1989

Fawcett JT, Carino B (eds): Pacific Bridges: The New Immigration From Asia and the Pacific Islands. Staten Island, NY, Center for Migration Studies, 1987

Hsu FLK: Americans and Chinese: Passage to Differences, 3rd Edition. Honolulu, University Press of Hawaii, 1981

Kagan J: The use of cross-cultural research in early development, in Culture and Infancy: Variations in the Human. Edited by Leiderman PH, Tulkin SR, Rosenfeld A. New York, Academic Press, 1977

Kitanishi K, Tseng WS: Social phobia among Japanese: clinical, family and cultural exploration. Reviewed by Prince R. Transcultural Psychiatric Research Review 26:137–147, 1989

Kleinman A: Social Origins of Distress and Disease: Depression, Neurasthenia and Pain in Modern China. New Haven, CT, Yale University Press, 1986

Kleinman A: Rethinking Psychiatry. New York: Free Press, 1988

Lin KM: Chinese medical beliefs and their relevance for mental illness and psychiatry, in Normal and Abnormal Behavior in Chinese Culture. Edited by Kleinman A, Lin TY. Dordrecht, The Netherlands, D Reidel, 1981, pp 95–111

Lin KM: Hwa-Byung: a Korean culture-bound syndrome? Am J Psychiatry 240:105–107, 1983

Lin KM, Kleinman A: Psychopathology and clinical course of schizophrenia: a cross-cultural perspective. Schizophr Bull 14:555–567, 1988

Lin TY: Neurasthenia: its place in modern psychiatry. Cult Med Psychiatry 13:105–129, 1989

Marsella AJ, DeVos G, Hsu FLK: Culture and Self: Asian and Western Perspectives. New York, Tavistock, 1985

Peters LG: Borderline personality disorder and the possession syndrome: an ethnopsychoanalytic perspective. Transcultural Psychiatric Research Review 25:5–46, 1988

Roland A: In Search of Self in India and Japan: Toward a Cross-Cultural Psychology. Princeton, NJ, Princeton University Press, 1988

Silver H: Physical complaints correlate better with depression than do dexamethasone suppression test results. J Clin Psychiatry 47:179–181, 1986

Tobin JJ, Wu DYH, Davidson DH: Preschool in Three Cultures: Japan, China, and the United States. New Haven, CT, Yale University Press, 1989

Weiss M, Doongaji DR, Siddhartha S, et al: The Explanatory Model Interview Catalogue (EMIC): contribution to cross-cultural research methods from a study of leprosy and mental health. Br J Psychiatry (in press)

Chapter 6

Hispanic Perspectives

Lloyd H. Rogler, Ph.D.

F or several decades, processes shaping migration streams from Mexico, Central and South America, and the Caribbean have been deploying large numbers of Hispanic immigrants into major urban centers in the United States. Thus, in the 8-year period preceding 1988, the size of the Hispanic population grew by about one-third to 19.4 million as a result of immigration and a birth rate that exceeded the death rate. Currently, the estimated size of the Hispanic population is just over 22 million; this does not include unknown numbers of undocumented migrants and Puerto Rico's population.

Hispanic persons display considerable socioeconomic and demographic diversity. Epidemiological studies indicate that such diversity is relevant to issues of mental health. Hispanic people also vary with respect to cultural elements historically rooted in their respective nationalities. Correlatively, a recent review of research suggests that a Hispanic individual's national culture also is relevant to mental health (Rogler et al. 1991). Thus, we should be careful in our use of the word *Hispanic* so as not to neglect fundamental differences among Hispanic people that are relevant to mental health.

Hispanic people have a rich vocabulary of psychological distresses: *Mal del cerebro o de la mente* (bad in the brain or in the mind); *nerviosidad* (nervousness); *espiritualmente debil* (spiritually weak); *locura* (craziness); *perdiendo control* (losing control of oneself); *ido* (gone, usually accompanied by a gesture pointing to the head). There are many other designations also. The point is that this vocabulary is closely intermeshed with many layers and configurations of important cultural meanings. The meanings influence the experience, the expression, the character, and the projected course of the distress. We know very little about such meanings, and this ignorance is problematic.

When Hispanic individuals—in particular, those who are in the first generation, low in acculturation, and economically disadvantaged—seek mental health
care from practitioners, little attention is likely to be given to the cultural meanings
imbedded in their psychological distress. A few research projects have focused on
this issue. The dominant hypothesis advanced to explain this pattern of neglect
points to the cultural distance between the diagnostician and the Hispanic patient.
Differences in the ethnicity of the patient and the diagnostician are considered to
play a role, as is the language spoken during the diagnostic interview. The predic-
tion is that increases in the cultural distance separating the patient from the diagnostic situation contribute to diagnostic errors. However, the situation is much
more complex and, I believe, more prone to error than is usually assumed. At the
root level, the classificatory system being used may well implicate the so-called
category fallacy.

Good and Good (1985) have published a straightforward definition of the
category fallacy: "the reification of a nosological category developed for a particular cultural population and the application of that category to members of another
culture without establishing its validity to that culture" (p. 10). The fallacy involves
the uncritical imposition on a cultural group of clinical categories not developed
in that group and is likely to be another source of diagnostic error, in addition to
those situational sources of error previously discussed.

Research should play a fundamental role in identifying such errors and in sensitizing clinical assessments. However, advocacy on behalf of culturally sensitive
mental health assessments has had a negligible effect on mental health research
(Rogler 1989). In fact, the measures of mental health status that are used in research continue to be drawn almost exclusively from the existing armamentarium
of psychiatric and psychological assessments; they remain untested in culturally
different populations.

An example is provided from Hispanic mental health research. In an analysis
of 30 studies focusing on the relationship between acculturation and mental health,
Rogler et al. (1991) uncovered only two attempts to inductively derive measures of
psychological distress from the life circumstances of Hispanic people and only one
study that attempted a qualitative assessment of psychological distress by means of
open-ended interviews. Nonetheless, the striking imbalance between advocacy on
behalf of culturally sensitive assessments and the lack of such assessments is due, at
least in part, to a failure to develop research-based approaches that would yield
cultural sensitivity. The ethnographic identification of culture-specific syndromes
such as *ataques de nervios* or *susto* among Hispanic people is necessary, but it is far
from being sufficient. We know the desired objective—culturally sensitive mental
health assessments—but we have not developed systematic procedures to attain it.
Once again, our ignorance is problematic.

How should we proceed with such research? Let me propose one line of development by returning to the previously defined category fallacy. First, the category
fallacy involves the imposition of untested mental health classificatory schemes
on persons. This imposition is logically the opposite of inductively deriving the

classificatory scheme from those persons' cultural group. Philosophically, the problem of imposition can never be eliminated. The mind is not a tabula rasa—certainly not the minds of researchers, cluttered as they are with many theoretical and methodological preoccupations. We can, however, develop procedures that strongly bias the classificatory schemes away from the researchers' presuppositions and toward the subjects' culture. Second, in the category fallacy, what is being neglected in the process of imposition is the person's culture, which provides normative expressions of psychological distress. Queries about the individual patient's views of the illness—its causes, treatments, and trajectories—are helpful. By themselves, however, they do not fulfill the required cultural assessments. Procedures are needed that serve to distill the culturally patterned meanings of psychological distress out of the private, individualized beliefs and behaviors of persons.

Chapters 1 and 2 remind us once again that culture is relevant to mental health assessments in many ways. Its influence is not singular. Culturally sensitive mental health research requires that attention be given to the entire research process. Research is made culturally sensitive through an incessant and continuing finely calibrated interweaving of cultural components and cultural awareness into all phases of the research process. I believe this kind of attention needs to be focused on mental health assessments if we are to have a continuing effect on the evolution of DSM and other classificatory efforts. At present, we need to give immediate attention to DSM-IV. Beyond DSM-IV, we need an ever-expanding research-based sensitivity to the complex role of culture in the assessment of mental health.

References

Good B, Good MJ: The cultural context of diagnosis and therapy: a view from medical anthropology, in Mental Health Research in Minority Communities: Development of Culturally Sensitive Training Programs. Edited by Miranda M, Kitano HHL. Rockville, MD, National Institute of Mental Health, 1985, pp 1–27

Rogler LH: The meaning of culturally sensitive research in mental health. Am J Psychiatry 146:296–303, 1989

Rogler LH, Cortes DE, Malgady RG: Acculturation and mental health status among Hispanics: convergence and new directions for research. Am Psychol 46: 585–597, 1991

Chapter 7

Nosological Perspectives

Allen Frances, M.D.

Because it was important that DSM-IV (American Psychiatric Association 1994) be internationally and cross-culturally relevant even for use solely within the United States, the DSM-IV Task Force decided to explore ways in which to ensure cross-cultural applicability. A cross-cultural advisory group, under the direction of Juan E. Mezzich, has reviewed the literature on the implications of cultural influences on psychiatric diagnosis. A section of the DSM-IV text for each disorder notes particular manifestations that may be emphasized in different cultural settings.

The Task Force has also reviewed and discussed the methods of classifying the so-called culture-bound syndromes within DSM-IV at international meetings to solicit comments and suggestions; the Task Force has received extensive commentary and data from international advisors. The *DSM-IV Options Book*, which compared DSM-III-R (American Psychiatric Association 1987) criteria sets with various proposed alternatives (including several International Classification of Diseases [World Health Organization 1977] criteria), was published in 1991 anddistributed widely to the international psychiatric community for additional comment.

The Development of DSM-IV

A word on the structure and process used for developing DSM-IV may be useful here. The Task Force on DSM-IV consisted of 24 members, most of whom also chaired one of the 13 Work Groups. Each Work Group drew on the expertise of 50–100 advisors and an International Advisory Board. Each Work Group was responsible for conducting a systematic empirical review that resulted in the diagnostic criteria and accompanying text for a specific group of DSM-IV disorders. The emphasis on empirical review and the large number and diversity of advisors were meant to ensure that DSM-IV would be applicable in the wide variety of settings in which it will be used.

Work on DSM-IV was divided into three separate steps. Initially each Work Group agreed on a series of issues requiring review and resolution in DSM-IV. Issues included problems with some aspect of DSM-III (American Psychiatric Association 1980) or DSM-III-R definitions, differences between the DSM system and the ICD-10 (World Health Organization 1991), important developments in the research literature, and input from clinical perspectives (Frances et al. 1989, 1990, 1991). The Work Groups then conducted 150 literature reviews, applying a uniform, systematic, and detailed methodology (Widiger et al. 1990). First drafts of literature reviews were circulated to advisors, whose comments were incorporated into successive drafts of these literature reviews. The literature reviews were useful in developing options for possible alternative resolutions of the issues and are published in the *DSM-IV Source Book* (Widiger et al. 1994) to document the empirical data on which decisions have been based.

Many questions are insufficiently answered by the available published literature and have required the reanalyses of previously collected but unpublished or incompletely analyzed data sets. Approximately 50 reanalytic projects have been undertaken to address particular diagnostic issues clarified through the literature reviews. In some instances, data reanalysis was used to generate empirically derived criteria sets for consideration in DSM-IV. For each issue, a variety of sites, many international, have participated in the reanalysis of existing data sets. This helped to ensure the generalizability and cross-cultural utility of the decisions made in DSM-IV.

Some issues cannot be completely resolved by literature reviews and unpublished data analysis and require testing in field trials. Twelve such issues (antisocial personality, autism, disruptive behavior, mixed anxiety and depression, mood disorders, obsessive-compulsive disorder, panic and agoraphobia, posttraumatic stress disorder, psychotic disorders, sleep disorders, somatization, and substance use) were selected as the focus of field testing sponsored by the U.S. National Institute of Mental Health. These field trials were the most carefully designed and monitored of any field trials conducted to date; several included extensive international participation. The field trials compared DSM-III, DSM-III-R, and ICD-10 and provided data on which to base empirical crosswalks among systems.

DSM-IV and International and Cross-Cultural Communication

What role might DSM-IV play in promoting international conversation among psychiatrists and other mental health professionals? Several possible roles may develop in various parts of the world depending on the heterogeneity of use; setting; tradition; and professional, institutional, and governmental relationships that contribute to the choice of a diagnostic language that best facilitates communication among psychiatrists.

By making psychiatric diagnosis much more interesting and clinically relevant than had been the case with DSM-II (American Psychiatric Association 1968) and ICD-9, DSM-III made a number of positive contributions to international communication. The manual provided a uniform set of diagnostic criteria that could be translated, both linguistically and clinically, across cultural settings. DSM-III-R was translated into nine languages and has been widely used to promote international clinical research, training, and practice. DSM-III and DSM-III-R have become the basic modes in which clinical research findings have been reported in studies conducted and reported all over the world.

In DSM-IV we have endeavored to build up this tradition in a number of ways:

- DSM-IV is totally compatible with the ICD-10 system and has a section in the text explaining the relationship of DSM-IV to other diagnostic systems including the ICD-10.
- Complex or obscure criteria sets in DSM-III-R have been revised to increase user friendliness.
- Translations of DSM-IV will be clinically and idiomatically correct and will include cross-cultural advisory groups to ensure the generalizability of criteria for DSM-IV.
- Work on DSM-IV was presented at several international meetings, and drafts of DSM-IV criteria were widely circulated to international audiences, so that international users of the DSM were apprised of, and involved in, the process of developing DSM-IV.
- A new section of text in DSM-IV titled "Cultural Considerations" systematically considers possible differences in the manifestation of symptoms in each diagnostic category across cultures.

References

American Psychiatric Association: Diagnostic and Statistical Manual of Mental Disorders, 2nd Edition. Washington, DC, American Psychiatric Association, 1968

American Psychiatric Association: Diagnostic and Statistical Manual of Mental Disorders, 3rd Edition. Washington, DC, American Psychiatric Association, 1980

American Psychiatric Association: Diagnostic and Statistical Manual of Mental Disorders, 3rd Edition, Revised. Washington, DC, American Psychiatric Association, 1987

American Psychiatric Association: Diagnostic and Statistical Manual of Mental Disorders, 4th Edition. Washington, DC, American Psychiatric Association, 1994

Frances A, Widiger TA, Pincus HA: The development of DSM-IV. Arch Gen Psychiatry 46:373–375, 1989

Frances A, Pincus HA, Widiger TA, et al: DSM-IV: work in progress. Am J Psychiatry 147:1439–1448, 1990

Frances A, Widiger TA, First MB, et al: DSM-IV: toward a more empirical diagnostic system. Canadian Psychology 32:174–176, 1991

Widiger TA, Frances A, Pincus HA, et al: DSM-IV literature reviews: rationale, process, and limitations. Journal of Psychopathology and Behavioral Assessment 12:189–202, 1990

Widiger TA, Frances A, Pincus HA, et al: DSM-IV Source Book. Washington, DC, American Psychiatric Press, 1994

World Health Organization: International Classification of Diseases, 9th Revision (ICD-9). Geneva, Switzerland, World Health Organization, 1977

World Health Organization: International Classification of Diseases and Health Related Problems (ICD-10). Geneva, Switzerland, World Health Organization, 1991

Section II

Organic and Psychotic Disorders

Chapter 8

Cultural Influences on the Diagnosis of Psychotic and Organic Disorders

Keh-Ming Lin, M.P.H., M.D.

ecause the concepts and diagnostic criteria of psychotic and organic conditions have derived predominantly from clinical experiences with European and North American patients and have been formulated by Western psychiatric thinkers (Fabrega 1989; A. Kleinman 1988; Wittkower and Prince 1974), issues related to their applicability to and utility with non-Western patients have remained controversial since the days of Kraepelin (1904), Freud (1955), and Laufer (1965). Whereas debates focused on the universal existence of schizophrenia have been largely resolved (A. Kleinman 1988; Leff 1981; Leighton et al. 1963; Murphy 1982; Tseng and McDermott 1981), recent research efforts have concentrated more on the potential pathoplastic and pathogenetic influences of cultural and ethnic factors on major psychiatric conditions. These studies have started to examine the prevalence (Murphy 1982; Srole and Fischer 1962), risk factors, symptom manifestations (Sartorius et al. 1977; Wittkower et al. 1960), subtyping (Morrison 1974), prognosis, clinical course (K. M. Lin and Kleinman 1988; Warner 1985; Waxler 1979), and problems of "misdiagnosis" (Adebimpe 1981; Mukherjee et al. 1983) of these conditions in different cultural settings.

In this brief overview, I outline findings derived from this rich and rapidly growing field and discuss their relevance to contemporary psychiatric diagnostic practices, especially in light of DSM-IV (American Psychiatric Association 1994) and ICD-10 (World Health Organization 1991). Because of space limitations, the thrust of this overview is conceptual rather than methodological in nature, and individual studies will not be scrutinized in great detail. Schizophrenia will serve as the main focus of the review, but material relevant to other diagnostic categories will be incorporated in the discussion when available and appropriate. This is not only because relatively more cross-cultural information is available for schizophrenia than for other psychotic and organic conditions but also because cross-cultural issues surrounding schizophrenia and its boundaries are likely to be more subtle and complicated. Thus, conclusions derived from studies involving schizophrenia should have heuristic value for other related conditions as well.

The Universality of Psychotic Experiences and Schizophrenia

Possibly reflecting the prevailing thinking of the Age of Romanticism in Europe, psychiatric pioneers in the 19th century tended to speculate on a relationship between insanity and civilization, and suggested that psychotic conditions might indeed be rare or even nonexistent among non-Western, especially primitive, populations (Jilek and Jilek-Aall 1970; Wittkower and Prince 1974). However, in subsequent decades, psychiatrists and other medical professionals working in non-Western societies convincingly demonstrated that this is not the case. Acute psychotic breakdowns as well as conditions characterized by chronic, often progressively deteriorating, nonorganic psychotic and asocial behavioral patterns have not only been identified in all contemporary Western and non-Western urban societies, but also in tribal villages (Westermeyer 1980) and among hunter-gatherer groups (Burton-Bradley 1985) living in remote mountainous areas (Kinzie and Bolton 1973) or on isolated Pacific islands (Wilson 1980). Since the 1970s the universality of these conditions has been further confirmed by findings from two large-scale, multinational collaborative studies sponsored by the World Health Organization: the International Pilot Study of Schizophrenia (World Health Organization 1973, 1979) and the more recent Determinants of Outcome Study (Jablensky and Sartorius 1988; Jablensky et al. 1986; Sartorius et al. 1986). Both studies utilized cross-culturally validated structured interview instruments to longitudinally assess carefully selected patients from sites representing divergent cultural backgrounds and different levels of urbanization. The results of these studies convincingly demonstrated that schizophrenia and other psychotic conditions can be identified in all parts of the world, ranging from metropolitan American cities to African villages and Indian towns (Jablensky and Sartorius 1975, 1988; Leff 1981).

In addition to the remarkable similarity in the key clinical features of schizophrenia (Jablensky and Sartorius 1988; Leff 1981), important cross-cultural similarities in terms of clinical course (Hsia and Chang 1978; K. M. Lin and Kleinman 1988), sociodemographic characteristics, predictors of outcome (World Health Organization 1973, 1979; von Zerssen et al. 1990), genetic and family study findings (Hsia 1958), and responses to various pharmacological (K. M. Lin et al. 1986) and psychosocial treatment modalities (K. M. Lin 1987; Yeh 1983) have been demonstrated by recent comparative studies. Furthermore, emerging evidence indicates that some of the neurochemical (Chang et al. 1990; Jeste et al. 1980) and morphological findings (Kaiya et al. 1989; McShane and Willenbring 1984) of schizophrenia may also be cross-culturally applicable. These findings further support the universality of the concept of schizophrenia as formulated by Kraepelin (1904), Bleuler (1950), and Schneider (1959).

Ethnicity and the Pathogenesis of Psychotic Disorders

The acceptance of the universality of schizophrenia and related psychotic conditions, and even the assumption of the supremacy of the biological etiology in causing these problems, does not preclude the possibility that cultural factors play an important role in the pathogenesis as well as in the symptom expression of these conditions. This is clearly the case with many medical conditions, whose prevalence and incidence can vary substantially across cultures for genetic and/ or environmental reasons (Cruickshank and Beevers 1989; Goodman 1979; Polednak 1989; Williams 1975). Prominent examples include the significantly higher prevalence of hypertension among black Africans and African Americans; the higher rate of diabetes mellitus among Native Americans; the higher prevalence of atherosclerosis, myocardial infarction, cystic fibrosis, and colon cancer among whites living in industrialized countries; the higher prevalence of hepatoma and nasopharyngeoma among Chinese; and the uneven ethnic and geographic distribution of multiple sclerosis and systematic lupus erythromatosis. Furthermore, certain conditions are genetically determined and occur exclusively in distinct ethnic groups or among people living in certain geographic areas. These include sickle cell anemia among sub-Saharan black Africans and Americans of African descent, Tay-Sachs disease among Ashkenazic Jews, thalassemia and glucose-6-phosphate dehydrogenase deficiency–related hemolytic anemia in Mediterranean and southeast Asian individuals.

In the field of psychiatry, cultural variations as well as historical changes in the prevalence of different types of organic brain syndromes and "organic psychosis" have been well documented. The prevalence of various types of infection, nutritional deficiencies, head injuries, endocrinological abnormalities, cerebrovascular diseases, seizure disorders, brain tumors, and substance abuse vary substantially across cultural groups. For example, organic brain disorders caused by abscesses, head injuries, and malnutrition may still be relatively more prevalent in less urbanized societies, among refugees (K. M. Lin 1986; Westermeyer 1989a), and in certain ethnic minority groups in the United States (Spector 1985; Williams 1975). Acquired immunodeficiency syndrome (AIDS)–related organic mental disorders are expected to be more prevalent in groups with a higher risk for AIDS (Kaslow and Francis 1989). Hypertension and strokes are significantly more prevalent among blacks and in certain Asian groups (Cruickshank and Beevers 1989; Spector 1985), leading one to speculate that multi-infarct dementia also might be more prevalent among these groups (H. N. Lin et al. 1984). At the same time, reports from Taiwan (H. N. Lin et al. 1984), China (Zhang et al. 1990), and New York (Serby et al. 1987) have suggested that dementia of the Alzheimer type may be less prevalent among Chinese and Chinese Americans. Dramatic differences have been found in the rate of alcoholism among different countries and ethnic groups (Agarwal and Goedde 1990). The same is true in terms of the type and prevalence of drug abuse (Adlaf et al. 1989; P. H. Kleinman and Lukoff 1978), which are influenced by a complicated mixture of sociocultural, economic, and geopolitical forces.

Seen in this light, it is of special interest to note that in the cross-cultural epidemiological literature, certain cultural groups have been consistently identified as having unusually high rates of schizophrenia. These include the Irish in Ireland (Cabot 1990; Murphy 1982; Scheper-Hughes 1979; Torrey 1984; Walsh et al. 1980; Warnes 1979), the southwest Croatians (Folnegovic et al. 1990; Murphy 1982), the northern Swedish (Book 1978), the Scandinavian immigrants in the United States (Malzberg 1969; Odegaard 1932; Sanua 1969), and the Caribbean immigrants in England (Cockrane and Bal 1987; Murphy 1982; Ninuallain et al. 1987). Although methodological problems abound in many of these reports (A. Kleinman 1988; Murphy 1982), the fact that the findings have been replicated by independent investigators points to their robustness and further suggests that they should be systematically tested with more vigorously designed studies. Such studies should also aim to identify risk factors that may be responsible for the increased vulnerability of some of these groups.

Furthermore, even assuming that the overall prevalence rates of schizophrenia are cross-culturally comparable, as advocated by most experts in the field of psychiatric epidemiology (Escobar et al. 1988; Jablensky and Sartorius 1988; Karno and Norquist 1989), the significance of cultural factors in affecting the pathogenesis of schizophrenia cannot be ruled out. Recent research indicates that schizophrenia, like many other medical conditions, might be heterogeneous (Tsuang et al. 1990) and caused by divergent genetic (e.g., as suggested by findings from genetic linkage studies) and environmental (e.g., perinatal minimal brain damage) factors. Both genetic and environmental contributions to many diseases have been demonstrated to vary substantially across cultural groups, and conditions with similar clinical manifestations have been known to diverge etiologically in different cultures. For example, liver cirrhosis is predominantly alcohol related in most Western societies but is most often caused by subclinical chronic hepatitis in most Asians countries (Cruickshank and Beevers 1989; Sung and Chen 1978). The possibility that a similar situation exists with regard to schizophrenia and other psychiatric conditions should not be discounted.

Findings of significant ethnic differences in certain biochemical parameters in schizophrenic patients are in congruence with the previously stated hypothesis (Lawson 1986). Compared with their white counterparts, black schizophrenic patients have been consistently reported to have significantly lower lymphocyte monoamine oxidase activity (Bridge et al. 1983; DeLisi et al. 1980), higher serum creatinine phosphokinase activity (Meltzer 1971), elevated platelet serotonin (Jackman et al. 1983), and a greater frequency of the human leukocyte antigen A2 (HLA-A2) (Luchins et al. 1983); interleukin-2 has been shown to be significantly lower in black nonpsychotic volunteers as compared with whites (Ganguli and Rabin 1989). In another series of studies, Asian (Filipino, Thai, and Chinese) schizophrenic patients had significantly higher catechol-O-methyltransferase activity than their white counterparts (Rivera-Calimlim and Reilly 1983). These biological measures have all been proposed as possible "biological markers" for schizophrenia, and the observed ethnic differences in these measures are intriguing and should be pursued further.

The Pathoplastic Effects of Culture

In contrast to the role of cultural and ethnic factors in the pathogenesis of schizophrenia and other psychotic conditions, their importance in influencing symptom manifestation, subtype classification, and clinical course has been much better recognized and documented. Findings highlighting these influences are summarized in the passages that follow.

Symptom Manifestations

Section A of the DSM-IV diagnostic criteria (American Psychiatric Association 1994) for schizophrenia emphasizes the importance of the bizarre nature of deliriums and hallucinations by requiring only one such symptom to meet the criterion. This is in line with the traditions established by phenomenologists such as Jaspers (1963) and Schneider (1959) (Bemporad and Pinsker 1974). However, without an adequate understanding of the patient's sociocultural and religious background, it would be extremely difficult to determine whether certain experiences and behaviors should be considered as delusional, hallucinatory, or otherwise psychotic in nature, and whether they are sufficiently bizarre to be included as possible evidence of the existence of a schizophrenic process (Gaines 1988; K. M. Lin 1990; Westermeyer 1988).

For example, "being controlled by a dead person" would be readily regarded as a "bizarre delusion" by most clinicians trained in Western settings. This, however, may not be universally appropriate, because in many traditional, non-Western societies, the spirits of the deceased are regarded as capable of interacting with and possessing those still alive (K. M. Lin and Masuda 1981; K. M. Lin et al. 1982; Tseng and McDermott 1981). Possession states and trance-induced or related transient psychosis (A. M. Kleinman 1978; T. Y. Lin 1953; Yap 1960, 1974) are frequently seen in these cultural settings, and should not be confused with schizophrenia. For similar reasons, in societies with a more prominent religious and/or spiritual orientation, various forms of delusions and hallucinations may appear to be more prevalent and also more bizarre to eyes unfamiliar with the local culture. The high prevalence in the belief and fear of sorcery and witchcraft in many traditional societies (Landy 1977) serves as another prominent example. The often observed higher prevalence of hallucinations and delusions in the North American black population (Adebimpe 1981; Liss et al. 1973; Sletten et al. 1972; Vitols et al. 1963) probably could also be partially attributed to religious and spiritual factors. Similar arguments may apply to other subcultural groups with less urbanized backgrounds in this country.

The controversies surrounding the diagnosis and classification of some of the most well-known culture-bound syndromes, such as *koro*, *amok*, and *latah*, also clearly demonstrate the importance of cultural forces in shaping the symptom formation and modifying the mode of distress expressed by psychiatric patients. These syndromes (Simons and Hughes 1985; Yap 1965, 1974), involving extreme fear of the shrinking of the penis and imminent death supposedly caused by such shrinkage (*koro*), sudden fits of random killing (*amok*), and repeated

episodes of extreme startle responses often accompanied by echolalia and copro-
lalia (*latah*) among Malays, can appear extremely delusional and bizarre to clinicians unfamiliar with the culturally specific beliefs and behavioral patterns
responsible for these phenomena.

Sociopolitical factors also can significantly influence the symptom formation
of psychiatric patients. Sustained exposure to racism and discrimination may be
partially responsible for a higher level of vigilance and suspiciousness ("healthy
paranoia") among North American blacks (Delgado 1982; Newhill 1990) and may
contribute to a higher propensity for paranoid symptoms among this population.
Paranoid symptoms also have been reported to be substantially more prevalent
among those being forced to live in an unfamiliar cultural milieu (Edwards 1956;
Kino 1961; K. M. Lin et al. 1982). This is especially so with refugees (K. M. Lin
1986; Westermeyer 1989a, 1989b). Fear of political persecution is a reality of life
for people living under totalitarian regimes. Such fear may contribute to higher
prevalence of paranoid delusions among patients living in such societies
(Westermeyer 1985, 1988).

Other cultural traits also may exert a significant impact on the symptom manifestation of psychotic patients. Japanese schizophrenic patients have been found to
have higher ratings of phobia and self-blaming (Rin et al. 1973). As is generally true
with other psychiatric problems, Chinese as well as other Asian psychotic patients
may be more likely to somatize their symptoms (Chen and Rin 1983). Possibly
reflecting a higher level of homophobia in contemporary Western societies, European and North American male schizophrenic patients often express severe doubts
about their gender identity and believe that they have been persecuted because of
their past homosexual experiences and/or fantasies. This has led to a hypothesis pro-
posing "latent homosexuality" as an etiological factor for the development of paranoid schizophrenia (Freud 1955; Kolb 1977). However, such preoccupation is rare in
non-Western patients with comparable diagnosis (K. M. Lin 1987).

Subtyping

Substantial changes in the relative prevalence of different subtypes of schizophrenia
have been well documented in Western societies (Morrison 1974; Murphy 1982).
Over the past century, the prevalences of catatonic and hebephrenic (disorganized)
subtypes in Western societies have progressively declined and are at present seen infrequently. This is especially true with regard to the catatonic subtype (Morrison
1974; Mann et al. 1986). At the same time, the undifferentiated and paranoid subtypes have become more prevalent. The decline of the catatonic subtype appears to
be widespread, although rates tend to remain high in India. In many cultural areas, as
the population becomes more urbanized, this type of schizophrenic presentation
becomes progressively less frequent. The hebephrenic, or disorganized subtype, however, remains a common diagnostic category in Japan (Kitamura et al. 1989; K. M.
Lin 1987) and, to a lesser extent, in other Asian countries. It is at present unclear what
factors might contribute to these differences. The degree of urbanization and modernization is not likely to be the reason, as the contemporary Japanese population is

at least as urbanized as most Western societies, if not more so. Because the hebephrenic (disorganized) subtype is regarded as having a less favorable prognosis (Grebb and Cancro 1989), the question is not without clinical significance and deserves careful cross-cultural investigation of the factors that might be related to the relative preponderance of this particular subtype among the Japanese.

Clinical Course and Outcome

Since the turn of the century, many clinicians working with non-Western patients have reported that the majority of their patients tend to suffer from a disease process that was characterized by an acute-onset, fulminant but typically short clinical course, followed more often than not by complete remission (Berne 1949; Edgerton 1980; Field 1968; Rin and Lin 1962; Seligman 1929; Smartt 1956). More recently, several small-scaled prospective studies conducted in Mauritius (Murphy and Raman 1971), Sri Lanka (Waxler 1979), and other Asian countries (K. M. Lin and Kleinman 1988) with well-defined schizophrenic patients have demonstrated that these patients also appeared to enjoy significantly better outcomes compared with their Western counterparts. Together these observations suggest that psychosis in the less industrialized, non-Western societies was more likely to be acute and self-limited in nature, and even schizophrenic patients fulfilling stringent diagnostic criteria manifested a better prognosis than in the non-Western settings. Often criticized on methodological grounds (Edgerton 1980; K. M. Lin and Kleinman 1988), these provocative findings have been confirmed by two rigorously designed, large-scale, multinational studies. The first of these studies, the International Pilot Study of Schizophrenia (Jablensky and Sartorius 1975; Sartorius et al. 1978; World Health Organization 1973, 1979), demonstrated significantly better outcomes at 2, 5, and 7 years after the index interviews for patients recruited from study sites located in "developing" countries (e.g., Nigeria, India, Colombia) as compared with those located in "developed" countries (e.g., the United States, Denmark, England). Subsequently, the Determinants of Outcome Study (Sartorius et al. 1986), which used a similar design but included only first-break psychotic patients identified from a well-defined community, also confirmed this finding. In addition, this study demonstrated a higher incidence of acute, nonschizophrenic, functional psychosis in the non-Western, developing countries. As indicated by several authors (A. Kleinman 1988; K. M. Lin and Kleinman 1988; Marsella 1988), these findings are of substantial clinical and theoretical significance and deserve vigorous research efforts in the future to explicate the mechanisms responsible for such crucial cross-cultural differences.

Misdiagnosis in Cross-Cultural Settings

As discussed earlier, considerable obstacles and pitfalls exist in the assessment and diagnosis of psychiatric patients in cross-cultural settings (A. Kleinman 1988; K. M. Lin 1990; Westermeyer 1985). Even if the more obvious problems of language and cultural barriers and the overt or covert biases of the clinicians are minimized, the culturally appropriate evaluation of the meaning and bizarreness of delusions, hallucinations, and other psychotic or psychotic-like symptoms often remain a significant challenge for the clinician. This frequently leads to misdiagnosis of schizophrenia in the cross-cultural clinical settings: patients in these situations could be either overdiagnosed or underdiagnosed. Overdiagnosis happens when the clinician ignores or is not aware of the culturally shared beliefs responsible for the apparently bizarre and psychotic symptoms, such as those described earlier. Underdiagnosis, however, could take place if the clinician overinterprets cultural influences and erroneously discounts genuine psychotic symptoms as culturally acceptable behavior or experiences. Of the two, overdiagnosis appears to be a more frequently encountered problem, resulting in the excessive diagnosis of schizophrenia in cross-cultural and cross-ethnic situations. In North America this has been clearly documented in blacks (Fabrega 1988; Marquez et al. 1985; Mukherjee et al. 1983; Roukema et al. 1984), Hispanics (Jones et al. 1983; Mukherjee et al. 1983), and the Amish (Egeland et al. 1983). When carefully evaluated with the use of well-defined criteria and with a structured interview, this overrepresentation of schizophrenia typically disappears, with many of the patients rediagnosed as experiencing bipolar disorder.

Summary

In this chapter I have reviewed some of the major issues surrounding the diagnosis of schizophrenia and other psychotic conditions in relation to cross-cultural issues. It is clear that even though the cross-cultural evaluation of schizophrenia and related phenomena will remain a challenging task, progress in cultural psychiatry as well as psychiatric nosology has made the task less formidable. Cross-cultural diagnosis would not have been possible without the demonstration of the universality of the concepts of schizophrenia and psychosis. At the same time, without the information regarding the pathoplastic effects of cultural forces on symptom manifestation, subtyping, and clinical course, such exercises would be fraught with misdiagnosis and erroneous conclusions. In addition, even though convincing evidence is still lacking, there is good reason to believe that genetic and environmental factors related to the development of schizophrenia may be unevenly distributed among different cultural and ethnic groups. All these are important issues that await further exploration.

References

Adebimpe VR: Overview: white norms and psychiatric diagnosis of black patients. Am J Psychiatry 138:279–285, 1981

Adlaf EM, Smart RG, Tan SH: Ethnicity and drug use: a critical look. Int J Addict 24:1–18, 1989

Agarwal DP, Goedde HW: Alcohol Metabolism, Alcohol Intolerance and Alcoholism. Berlin, Germany, Springer-Verlag, 1990

American Psychiatric Association: Diagnostic and Statistical Manual of Mental Disorders, 3rd Edition, Revised. Washington, DC, American Psychiatric Association, 1987

American Psychiatric Association: Diagnostic and Statistical Manual of Mental Disorders, 4th Edition. Washington, DC, American Psychiatric Association, 1994

Bemporad JR, Pinsker H: Schizophrenia: the manifest symptomatology, in American Handbook of Psychiatry, Vol 3. Edited by Arieti S, Brody E. New York, Basic Books, 1974, pp 524–559

Berne E: Some Oriental mental hospitals. Am J Psychiatry 106:376–383, 1949

Bleuler E: Dementia Praecox or the Group of Schizophrenias. Translated by Zinker J. New York, International Universities Press, 1950

Book JA: Schizophrenia in a north Swedish geographical isolate 1900–1977. Clin Genet 14:373–394, 1978

Bridge P, Jeste DV, Wise CD, et al: Schizophrenic outcome in late life: symptom state and platelet monoamine oxidase activity. Psychiatry Res 11:91–97, 1983

Burton-Bradley BG: Transcultural psychiatry in Papua New Guinea. Transcultural Psychiatric Research Review 22:5–36, 1985

Cabot MR: The incidence and prevalence of schizophrenia in the republic of Ireland. Soc Psychiatry Psychiatr Epidemiol 25:210–215, 1990

Chang WH, Chen TY, Lin SK, et al: Plasma catecholamine metabolites in schizophrenics: evidence for the two-subtype concept. Biol Psychiatry 27:510–518, 1990

Chen JJ, Rin H: Somatic complaints among schizophrenic patients. Bulletin of the Chinese Society of Neurology and Psychiatry 9:156–161, 1983

Cockrane R, Bal S: Migration and schizophrenia: an examination of five hypotheses. Soc Psychiatry 22:181–191, 1987

Cruickshank JK, Beevers DG: Ethnic Factors in Health and Disease. London, England, Wright, 1989

Delgado AK: On Being Black: Effective Psychotherapy for Low-Income and Minority Patients. New York, Plenum, 1982

DeLisi L, Neckers LM, Staub RA, et al: Lymphocyte monoamine oxidase activity and chronic schizophrenia. Psychiatry Res 2:179–186, 1980

Edgerton RB: Traditional treatment for mental illness in Africa: a review. Cult Med Psychiatry 4:167–189, 1980

Edwards AT: Paranoid reactions. Med J Aust 1:778–779, 1956

Egeland JA, Hostetter AM, Eshleman SK III: Amish study, III: the impact of cultural factors on diagnosis of bipolar illness. Am J Psychiatry 140:67–71, 1983

Escobar JI, Karno M, Burnam A, et al: Distribution of major mental disorders in a US metropolis. Acta Psychiatr Scand Suppl 344:45–53, 1988

Fabrega H: Black-white differences in psychopathology in an urban psychiatric population. Compr Psychiatry 29:285–297, 1988

Fabrega H: An ethnomedical perspective of Anglo-American psychiatry. Am J Psychiatry 146:588–596, 1989

Field MJ: Chronic psychosis in rural Ghana. Br J Psychiatry 114:31–33, 1968

Folnegovic Z, Folnegovic-Smalc V, Kulcar Z: The incidence of schizophrenia in Croatia. Br J Psychiatry 156:363–365, 1990

Freud S: Some neurotic mechanisms in jealousy, paranoia, and homosexuality (1922), in Standard Edition of the Complete Psychological Works of Sigmund Freud, Vol 18. Translated and edited by Strachey J. London, England, Hogarth Press, 1955, pp 221–232

Gaines AD: Delusions: culture, psychosis and the problem of meaning, in Delusional Beliefs. Edited by Oltmanns TF, Maher BA. New York, Wiley, 1988

Ganguli R, Rabin BS: Differences in interleukin-2 production in blacks and whites (letter). N Engl J Med 320:399, 1989

Goodman R: Genetic Disorders Among the Jewish People. Baltimore, MD, Johns Hopkins University Press, 1979

Grebb JA, Cancro R: Schizophrenia: clinical features, in Comprehensive Textbook of Psychiatry, Fifth edition. Edited by Kaplan HI, Sadock BJ. Baltimore, MD, Williams & Wilkins, 1989

Hsia CY: Clinical analysis and follow-up study of 2000 cases of schizophrenia. Chinese Journal of Neurology and Psychiatry 4:89–94, 1958

Hsia CY, Chang MY: Long term follow-up study of schizophrenia. Chin Med J 4:266–270, 1978

Jablensky A, Sartorius N: Culture and schizophrenia. Psychol Med 5:113–124, 1975

Jablensky A, Sartorius N: Is schizophrenia universal? Acta Psychiatr Scand Suppl 344:65–70, 1988

Jablensky SN, Ernberg KA, Cooper AM, et al: Early manifestations and first-contact incidence of schizophrenia in different cultures. Psychol Med 16:909–928, 1986

Jackman H, Luchins D, Meltzer HY: Platelet serotonin levels in schizophrenia: relationship to race and psychopathology. Biol Psychiatry 18:887–902, 1983

Jaspers K: General Psychopathology. Manchester, England, Manchester University Press, 1963

Jeste DV, Doongaji DR, Panjwani K, et al: Cross-cultural study of a biochemical abnormality in paranoid schizophrenia. Psychiatry Res 3:341–352, 1980

Jilek WG, Jilek-Aall L: Transient psychoses in Africans. Psychiatr Clin 3:337–364, 1970

Jones BE, Gray BA, Parson EB: Manic-depressive illness among poor urban Hispanics. Am J Psychiatry 140:1208–1210, 1983

Kaiya H, Uematsu M, Ofuji M, et al: Computerized tomography in schizophrenia familial versus non-familial forms of illness. Br J Psychiatry 155:444–450, 1989

Karno M, Norquist GS: Schizophrenia: epidemiology, in Comprehensive Textbook of Psychiatry, Fifth edition. Edited by Kaplan HI, Sadock BJ. Baltimore, MD, Williams & Wilkins, 1989

Kaslow RA, Francis DP: The Epidemiology of AIDS. New York, Oxford University Press, 1989

Kino FF: Aliens' paranoid reactions. J Ment Sci 97:589–594, 1961

Kinzie JD, Bolton JM: Psychiatry with the aborigines of West Malaysia. Am J Psychiatry 130:769–773, 1973

Kitamura T, Shima S, Sakio E, et al: Psychiatric diagnosis in Japan. Psychopathology 22:239–249, 1989

Kleinman A: Rethinking Psychiatry. New York, Free Press, 1988

Kleinman AM: The three faces of culture-bound disorders: an editorial. Cult Med Psychiatry 2:207–208, 1978

Kleinman PH, Lukoff IF: Ethnic differences in factors related to drug use. J Health Soc Behav 19:190–199, 1978

Kolb LC: Modern Clinical Psychiatry. Philadelphia, PA, WB Saunders, 1977

Kraepelin E: Lectures on Clinical Psychiatry. Edited by Johnstone T. New York, William Wood, 1904

Landy D: Culture, Disease, and Healing. New York, Macmillan, 1977

Laufer H: Kraepelin's importance for cultural psychiatry. Transcultural Psychiatric Research Review 2:9–12, 1965

Lawson WB: Racial and ethnic factors in psychiatric research. Hosp Community Psychiatry 37:50–54, 1986

Leff J: Psychiatry Around the Globe: A Transcultural View. New York, Marcel Dekker, 1981

Leighton AH, Lambo TA, Hughes CC, et al: Psychiatric Disorder Among the Yoruba. Ithaca, NY, Cornell University Press, 1963

Lin HN, Tsai MT, Rin H: Psychiatric disorders among rural elderly: the Hun-Tsun study. Bulletin of the Chinese Society of Neurology and Psychiatry 1 (special issue):65–79, 1984

Lin KM: Psychopathology and social disruption in refugees, in Refugee and Mental Health. Edited by Williams CL, Westermeyer J. Washington, DC, Hemisphere, 1986

Lin KM: Experiences on inpatient wards: Taiwan vs Los Angeles. Am J Soc Psychiatry 7:220–225, 1987

Lin KM: Assessment and diagnostic issues in the psychiatric care of refugee patients, in Mental Health of Immigrants and Refugees. Edited by Holzman WH, Bornemann T. Austin, University of Texas Press, 1990

Lin KM, Kleinman AM: Psychopathology and clinical course of schizophrenia: a cross-cultural perspective. Schizophr Bull 14:555–567, 1988

Lin KM, Masuda M: Impact of the refugee experience: mental health issues of the Southeast Asians, in Bridging Cultures: Social Work With Southeast Asian Refugees. Edited by the Asian American Community Mental Health Training Center. Los Angeles, CA, Asian American Community Mental Health Training Center, 1981, pp 32–53

Lin KM, Masuda M, Tazuma L: Adaptational problems of Vietnamese refugees. Part III. Case studies in clinic and field: adaptive and maladaptive. Psychiatr J Univ Ott 7:173–183, 1982

Lin KM, Poland R, Lesser I: Ethnicity and psychopharmacology. Cult Med Psychiatry 10:151–165, 1986

Lin TY: A study of the incidence of mental disorder in Chinese and other cultures. Psychiatry 16:313–336, 1953

Liss JL, Welner A, Robins E, et al: Psychiatric symptoms in white and black inpatients I: record study. Compr Psychiatry 14:475–481, 1973

Luchins D, Torrey EF, Weinberger DR, et al: HLA antigens in schizophrenia: differences between patients with and without evidence of brain atrophy. Br J Psychiatry 136:243–248, 1983

Malzberg B: Are immigrants psychologically disturbed? in Changing Perspectives in Mental Illness, Edited by Plog SC, Edgerton RB. New York, Holt, Rinehart & Winston, 1969

Mann SC, Caroff SN, Bleier HR, et al: Lethal catatonia. Am J Psychiatry 143:1374–1381, 1986

Marquez C, Zebulon T, Schwartz MA: Diagnosis of manic depressive illness in blacks. Compr Psychiatry 26:337–341, 1985

Marsella A: Cross-cultural research on severe mental disorders: issues and findings. Acta Psychiatr Scand 344:7–22, 1988

McShane D, Willenbring ML: Differences in cerebral asymmetries related to drinking history and ethnicity. J Nerv Ment Dis 172:529–532, 1984

Meltzer HY: Factors affecting serum creatine phosphokinase levels in the general population: the role of race, activity and age. Clin Chem Acta 33:165–172, 1971

Morrison JR: Changes in subtype diagnosis of schizophrenia: 1920–1960. Am J Psychiatry 131:654–677, 1974

Mukherjee S, Shukla S, Woodle J, et al: Misdiagnosis of schizophrenia in bipolar patients: a multiethnic comparison. Am J Psychiatry 140:1571–1574, 1983

Murphy HBM: Comparative Psychiatry. Berlin, Germany, Springer-Verlag, 1982

Murphy HBM, Raman AC: The chronicity of schizophrenia in indigenous tropical peoples. Br J Psychiatry 118:489–497, 1971

Newhill CE: The role of culture in the development of paranoid symptomatology. Am J Orthopsychiatry 60:176–185, 1990

Ninuallain M, O'Hare A, Walsh D: Incidence of schizophrenia in Ireland. Psychol Med 17:943–948, 1987

Odegaard O: Emigration and insanity: a study of mental disease among the Norwegian-born population of Minnesota. Acta Psychiatr Scand Suppl 4:1–206, 1932

Polednak AP: Racial & Ethnic Differences in Disease. New York, Oxford University Press, 1989

Rin H, Lin T: Mental illness among Formosan aborigines as compared with the Chinese in Taiwan. J Ment Sci 108:134–146, 1962

Rin H, Schooler C, Caudill W: Symptomatology and hospitalization. J Nerv Ment Dis 157:4, 1973

Rivera-Calimlim L, Reilly DK: Difference in erythrocyte catechol-O-methyl-transferase activity between Orientals and Caucasians: difference in levodopa tolerance. Clin Pharmacol Ther 35:804–809, 1983

Roukema R, Fadem B, James B, et al: Bipolar disorder in a low socioeconomic population: difficulties in diagnosis. J Nerv Ment Dis 172:76–79, 1984

Sanua VD: Immigration, migration and mental illness, in Behavior in New Environments. Edited by Brody EB. Beverly Hills, CA, Sage, 1969

Sartorius N, Jablensky A, Shapiro R: Two-year follow up of the patients included in the WHO International Pilot Study of Schizophrenia. Psychol Med 7:529–541, 1977

Sartorius N, Jablensky A, Shapiro R: Cross-cultural differences in the short-term prognosis of schizophrenic psychoses. Schizophr Bull 4:102–113, 1978

Sartorius N, Jablensky A, Korten A, et al: Early manifestations and first-contact incidence of schizophrenia in different cultures. Psychol Med 16:909–928, 1986

Scheper-Hughes N: Saints, Scholars, and Schizophrenics: Mental Illness in Rural Ireland. Berkeley, University of California Press, 1979

Schneider K: Clinical Psychopathology, 5th Edition. Edited and translated by Hamilton MW. New York, International Universities Press, 1959

Seligman CG: Temperament conflict and psychosis in a stone-age population. Br J Med Psychol 9:187–202, 1929

Serby M, Chou JCY, Franssen E: Dementia in an American-Chinese nursing home population. Am J Psychiatry 144:811–812, 1987

Simons RC, Hughes CC: The Culture-Bound Syndromes. Dordrecht, The Netherlands, D Reidel, 1985

Sletten I, Schuff S, Altman H, et al: A statewide computerized psychiatric system: demographic diagnostic and mental status data. Int J Soc Psychiatry 18:30–40, 1972

Smartt CGF: Mental maladjustment in the East African. J Ment Sci 102:441–466, 1956

Spector RE: Cultural Diversity in Health and Illness. Norwalk, CT, Appleton-Century-Crofts, 1985

Srole L, Fischer AK (eds): Mental Health in the Metropolis: The Midtown Manhattan Study. New York, Harper & Row, 1962

Sung JL, Chen DS: Clustering of different subtypes of hepatitis B surface antigen in families of patients with chronic liver diseases. Am J Gastroenterol 69:559–564, 1978

Torrey EF: Endemic psychosis in western Ireland. Am J Psychiatry 141:966–969, 1984

Tseng WS, McDermott JF Jr: Culture, Mind and Therapy: An Introduction to Culture Psychiatry. New York, Brunner/Mazel, 1981

Tsuang MT, Lyons MJ, Faraone SV: Heterogeneity of schizophrenia conceptual models and analytic strategies. Br J Psychiatry 156:17–26, 1990

Vitols MM, Waters HG, Keeler MH: Hallucinations and delusions in white and Negro schizophrenics. Am J Psychiatry 120:472–476, 1963

von Zerssen D, Lleon CA, Moller HJ, et al: Care strategies for schizophrenic patients in a transcultural comparison. Compr Psychiatry 31:398–408, 1990

Walsh D, O'Hare A, Blake B, et al: The treated prevalence of mental illness in the Republic of Ireland—the three county case register. Psychol Med 19:465–470, 1980

Warner R: Recovery From Schizophrenia: Psychiatry and Political Economy. London, England, Routledge & Kegan Paul, 1985

Warnes H: Cultural factors in Irish psychiatry. Psychiatr J Univ Ott 4:329–335, 1979

Waxler NE: Is outcome for schizophrenia better in nonindustrial societies? The case of Sri Lanka. J Nerv Ment Dis 167:144–158, 1979

Westermeyer J: Psychosis in a peasant society: social outcomes. Am J Psychiatry 137:1390–1394, 1980

Westermeyer J: Psychiatric diagnosis across cultural boundaries. Am J Psychiatry 142:798–805, 1985

Westermeyer J: Some cross-cultural aspects of delusions, in Delusional Beliefs. Edited by Oltmanns TF, Maher BA. New York, Wiley, 1988

Westermeyer J: Mental Health for Refugees and Other Migrants. Springfield, IL, Charles C Thomas, 1989a

Westermeyer J: Paranoid symptoms and disorders among 100 Hmong refugees: a longitudinal study. Acta Psychiatr Scand 80:47–59, 1989b

Williams RA: Textbook of Black-Related Diseases. New York, McGraw-Hill, 1975

Wilson LG: Community psychiatry in Oceania: fifteen months' experience in Micronesia. Soc Psychiatry 15:175–179, 1980

Wittkower ED, Prince R: A review of transcultural psychiatry, in American Handbook of Psychiatry, Vol II: Child and Adolescent Psychiatry, Sociocultural and Community Psychiatry. Edited by Caplan G. New York, Basic Books, 1974

Wittkower ED, Murphy HB, Fried J, et al: A cross-cultural inquiry into the symptomatology of schizophrenia. Ann NY Acad Sci 84:854–863, 1960

World Health Organization: The International Pilot Study of Schizophrenia, Vol 1. Geneva, Switzerland, World Health Organization, 1973

World Health Organization: Schizophrenia: An International Follow-Up Study. Chichester, England and New York, Wiley, 1979

World Health Organization: International Classification of Diseases and Health Related Problems (ICD-10). Geneva, Switzerland, World Health Organization, 1991

Yap PM: The possession syndrome: a comparison of Hong Kong and French findings. J Ment Sci 106:114–137, 1960

Yap PM: The culture-bound reactive syndrome, in Mental Health Research in Asia and the Pacific. Edited by Caudill W, Lin TY. Honolulu, HI, East-West Center Press, 1965, pp 33–53

Yap PM: Comparative Psychiatry. Toronto, Ontario, Canada, University of Toronto Press, 1974

Yeh EK: The chronic mental patients: the most neglected group—problems and recommendations. Bulletin of the Chinese Society of Neurology and Psychiatry 9:1–16, 1983

Zhang M, Katzman R, Salmon D, et al: The prevalence of dementia and Alzheimer's disease in Shanghai, China: impact of age, gender, and education. Ann Neurol 27:428–437, 1990

Chapter 9

Cultural Comments on Organic and Psychotic Disorders: I

Ellen Corin, Ph.D.

C hapter 8 presents a good picture of the various levels of influence of culture on psychotic disorders. One could disagree with Lin's choice of the classic distinction between pathogenic and pathoplastic influences as an organizing thread of his discussion because of its artificial nature and because it tends to minimize the diagnostic significance of pathoplastic variations. The distinction nevertheless enables organization of very complex material.

The main issue arising from cross-cultural research is that of identifying significant differences, their effects, and their underlying causes and defining criteria or principles to guide diagnostic decisions. In discussing the diagnostic significance of cross-cultural data, it is useful to remember that variations affecting prognosis and therapy are considered diagnostically significant by the DSM-IV Psychotic Disorders Work Group (e.g., comments on negative symptoms or on postpsychotic depression in schizophrenia); they therefore deserve attention.

The data presented by Lin in Chapter 8 illustrate different types of cross-cultural variations: variations in incidence or prevalence rates, variations in the clinical presentation of the disorder, and variations related to the person making the diagnosis and to his or her diagnostic frame. One could add a fourth type of variation that Lin does not mention and that involves the boundaries between diagnoses. Lin describes the first type of variation as reflecting the pathogenic effects of culture and the following two types as reflecting pathoplastic effects.

Variations in incidence or prevalence rates have no direct implications for diagnosis. However, it is clear that choices regarding inclusion criteria directly influence the amplitude of reported cross-cultural variation in rates of a disorder (Kleinman 1988; Sartorius et al. 1986). To Lin's comments, I would add here only that hypotheses other than biological heterogeneity have also been formulated to explain cross-cultural epidemiological data. Murphy's (1982) work is certainly one of the most systematic and rigorous attempts to draw social and cultural hypotheses from a thorough examination of cross-cultural variation in incidence or prevalence rates.

Variations in the clinical presentation of the disorders can be of many types, and the implications of such variations for diagnosis vary accordingly. Variations can first concern the relative frequency of specific symptoms that are normally part of the schizophrenic clinical picture. Research suggests that culturally dominant symptoms are related to the conception of the person, the significance of social relationships, or the vision of reality in a particular society, all features that should be taken into account in a global therapeutic project. However, one should be aware that the relationship between dominant symptoms and culture is not a simple one. Studies have suggested that culturally prevalent symptoms either are an extension or an exaggeration of culturally valued beliefs and behaviors or present a counterimage of cultural norms (see, e.g., Katz et al.'s 1988 work, which contrasted schizophrenia patients from Agra, India, and Ibadan, Nigeria). At that level, variation concerns the weight of specific symptoms within the range of schizophrenic symptoms; it gives a special flavor to the clinical picture, more than affecting diagnosis per se. As suggested before, implications concern therapy and follow-up more than diagnosis. In the area of prognosis, one could expect that the fact that the symptoms are more or less familiar in a cultural setting, along with their degree of congruence with cultural values, could affect the rapidity of diagnosis by the entourage, the reaction to the person, and help-seeking behaviors and therefore could influence the further evolution of the disorder.

Variation in clinical presentation can also have more serious implications for the diagnosis and lead to misdiagnosis. A first source of misdiagnosis is related to the fact that symptoms can have a different diagnostic value according to culture. The best documented examples in this area concern cases in which behaviors we would consider to be schizophrenic symptoms are in fact associated with other types of disorders. This suggests that symptoms cannot be reduced to the status of natural or objective correlates of discrete diseases. In the area of schizophrenia, the fact that the content of delusions reflects cultural themes is well-known and accepted; however, studies quoted by Lin in Chapter 8 indicate that cultural influences go beyond the level of "content" and also concern the structure of symptoms. A diagnostic manual should mention the kinds of symptoms more likely to be misdiagnosed in certain ethnic groups: for example, among black or Hispanic patients, auditory hallucinations or certain kinds of grandiose delusions can be associated with affective disorders (Mukherjee et al. 1983), and among blacks, olfactory hallucinations with a specific content can be associated with subcultural delusions and hallucinations (Teggin et al. 1985).

A second source of misdiagnosis related to the clinical presentation depends on the fact that behaviors or beliefs we would consider psychotic may be considered "normal" in a particular culture; by contrast, behaviors we would consider as falling within the range of normality can have a pathological significance when considered within the context of the group's norms and values (Egeland et al. 1983). In the latter case, what appears important at a diagnostic level is to compare the patient's actions and comments with the normal standards of his or her group. In the first case, one must also seek to avoid what Lin denounces as a risk of underdiagnosis. It should be acknowledged that even for the patient's entourage, the degree of normality of a person's belief or behavior is not wholly determined by the existing cultural belief systems but also depends on more subtle and individual indices. Family and kin generally discriminate normal and abnormal references to the cultural idiom. One could say that what distinguishes a delusion from a culturally normal belief or behavior is a matter of "style" as well as a matter of content. Therefore, one should be very cautious regarding well-intentioned attempts to characterize (for example) "bizarre delusions" by the degree of incongruence between their objective content and the local culture. The Present State Examination (PSE) notion of "subcultural" delusion appears useful in front of ambiguous cases; it can at least draw the clinician's attention to the difficulty of deciding whether a belief is delusional.

The anthropological concept of idiom of distress has been developed to account for the cultural dimension of variations in clinical presentation. It means that, to a certain extent, people tend to use cultural signifiers to express their personal distress or emphasize symptoms that possess a cultural value in the context they live in and deemphasize others that are either culturally nonsignificant or stigmatized. This concept does not entail in itself a relativist position regarding the existence of psychiatric disorders; instead, it proposes a dialectic or interactive position in the nature-culture debate. Idioms of distress and their implications have been mainly documented in the area of depression and somatization, but data discussed by Lin indicate that these idioms also appear to be relevant for psychotic disorders.

Variations related to the clinician stem from data that indicate that practitioners may be more prone to attribute a certain diagnosis to a particular group (e.g., paranoid schizophrenia among blacks [Mukherjee et al. 1983]). It would be important in a diagnostic manual to remind clinicians and researchers of the fact that clinical observations and interpretations also bear the marks of the clinician's personal values and expectations. This observation is familiar to semioticians, who know that "signs" are not a direct mirror of reality and result from an encounter between the "object" and the interpretative frame of the observer (Eco 1984).

In the same way, practitioners can misdiagnose as psychotic symptoms those behaviors or beliefs that have developed as a response to influences external to the person. In their study on the Amish, Egeland et al. (1983) explained how self-consciousness regarding a lack of experience about worldly issues can generate a deep discomfort that can be misinterpreted as a sign of formal thought disorder, how awareness of the group's gossiping about "deviant" behaviors or discourses can be misinterpreted as a paranoid feature, and how religious beliefs can be taken for grandiosity and delusion. This remark also applies to less exotic settings. Negative symptoms of schizophrenia, to which DSM-IV (American Psychiatric Association 1994) gives a prominent place, could be seen as a good example of this difficulty; in reality, what remains controversial is the degree to which behaviors and attitudes described as negative symptoms are endogenous to schizophrenia or represent the common end result of a variety of biological, psychological, and social processes (Pogue-Geile and Zubin 1988; Strauss 1985). Cross-cultural variations in negative symptoms have also been documented in international comparisons (World Health Organization 1979), as well as through interethnic comparisons within a given country; whites seem more prone than blacks (Fabrega et al. 1988), and British Canadians seem more prone that French Canadians (Murphy 1983) to present the so-called "negative symptoms" of schizophrenia. Murphy has interpreted this as defensive reactions built partly on the cultural background and partly on the way in which the patient finds himself or herself treated after signs of illness appear. At another level, when dealing with people from developing countries, the possibility that psychotic symptoms are provoked by nonpsychiatric medical problems should be considered with particular care when making a diagnosis.

The fourth kind of variation, *variation in diagnostic boundaries,* is more difficult to document because it is, by definition, ruled out of standardized research designs. If one considers the issue of duration, it is interesting to remember that in developing countries, schizophrenia has been shown to be more likely to present an acute onset and to have a less severe course. One could hypothesize that factors that influence prognosis can have an impact from the very beginning of the disorder and influence the duration of the first episode of disorders such as schizophrenia. Clinicians should be sensitized to this possibility and encouraged to carefully compare clinical, psychosocial, and milieu characteristics of incipient cases according to their remission or their further evolution toward schizophrenia. Another theme of interest regarding the issue of diagnostic boundaries concerns the place of affective symptoms in schizophrenia. Current data suggest that the presence of an affective component is associated with a better prognosis. However, the World Health Organization's comparative study has also provided evidence that affective symptoms are more prominent in developed countries than in developing ones, even if prognosis is worse in the first (Sartorius et al. 1986). This apparent discrepancy suggests that much remains to be learned about the diagnostic significance of affective symptoms.

Drawing the lessons from cross-cultural variation in terms compatible with the DSM philosophy is not a simple matter. Some findings can be translated into concrete warnings or recommendations, whereas others imply that practitioners or researchers adopt a certain stance in the diagnostic process as well as in the interpretation of observed behaviors. In the latter case, recommendations cannot be as precise as in the first case.

Risks of misdiagnosis are pertinent to sections on "Differential Diagnosis." It is also important to distinguish risks caused by a lack of understanding of the notion of cultural idiom of distress and those caused by the possibility that observed behaviors could be a reaction to nonpsychiatric milieu conditions. One could hypothesize that chances of misdiagnosis related to each of these two sources are stronger in certain areas. Risks deriving from lack of consideration for idiom of distress should concern principally, but not exclusively, symptoms such as content of thought and perception. The possibility of misdiagnosing bipolar disorder as schizophrenia among black or Hispanic ethnic communities especially should be mentioned here. A complementary warning should be added regarding the risk of assessing behavior solely in the light of cultural norms while disregarding individual idiosyncrasies in the use of cultural items. The notion of subcultural delusion should be included for doubtful cases. The second kind of risk mainly concerns behaviors related to formal thought disorders, affect, volition, and interpersonal functioning, which are presumably most likely to be affected by environmentally stressful or changing conditions or by other peoples' reactions to the disorder.

The main difficulty in translating cross-cultural findings into DSM instructions is that it is often not possible to define a priori what is normal or abnormal. Therefore, it does not appear desirable or sufficient to draw up a list of additional behaviors that could be declared "normal" or "abnormal" according to the culture and used in a standardized way to correct the diagnosis. Concrete judgment requires a precise knowledge of the culture and subculture to which patients belong and an ability to decide about the degree of "normality" of particular ways of using cultural items. The only available solution appears to involve relying more on the opinion of informants in the patient's natural environment. In cases of uncertainty, clinicians should be encouraged to diversify their sources of information and to investigate the feelings, comments, and interpretations of family and friends. For example, rather then deciding themselves whether beliefs are culturally acceptable, clinicians or researchers could explore various issues with close relatives or friends from the same ethnic community: the degree of congruence between the patient's "delusions" and traditional beliefs, the congruence of such delusions with beliefs and interpretations held by the entourage, the degree of flexibility or rigidity of the patient's use of belief systems, and the function of these beliefs for the patient and for the entourage. The degree of ethnic belonging of the patient should be taken into account to weigh the significance of these comments. These or other examples of inquiries could be integrated as a special paragraph equivalent to impairment, predisposing factors, or familial patterns rubrics.

Reflections about cultural influences on the diagnosis would not be complete without mentioning another debate not alluded to by Lin regarding the cultural relativity of the diagnosis of schizophrenia itself. This questioning has developed from a consideration of peculiar features of symptoms associated with schizophrenia. For example, some authors submit that to attribute a pathological significance to beliefs or behaviors that imply a permeability of boundaries between the self and others is intimately linked to the Western concept of the self as a well-bounded and autonomous reality (Fabrega 1989). Others have drawn attention to the analogy between schizophrenic symptoms and the general mode of being associated with urbanization and modernization (Devereux 1970). The interest of these hypotheses lies in their sensitization of clinicians and researchers to the fact that psychiatric problems are embedded within a larger world of meaning that could contribute to shape the disorder in a certain direction. However, this perspective appears too alien to the psychiatric paradigm to be easily integrated within DSM. It could nevertheless be useful to introduce the section "Characteristic Symptoms

Involving Multiple Psychological Processes" by a general comment indicating that cultures vary in the way they define the boundaries between the self and others, the living and the dead, and the natural and the supernatural worlds. This warning could help determine the degree or the type of pathology involved in seemingly unusual behaviors or beliefs.

A Matter of Perspective

Decisions regarding these or other additions involving diagnostic boundaries depend on the general position adopted toward variation. It is possible to consider it as an unavoidable "noise" to be neutralized as much as possible; from this perspective, additions would be limited to warnings to avoid gross mistakes. It is also possible to consider that variation may have significant implications at the diagnostic and therapeutic levels and that its exploration would improve the understanding of psychiatric disorders as such (Murphy 1982); in this case, additions would be more substantial and encourage clinicians and researchers to systematically document signs and sources of variation. If documenting variation is important, it is mandatory to include this recommendation in the DSM as such, because the grid of observation preconditions what we observe and discuss and because the very phrasing of the manual may discourage or promote a systematic and rigorous exploration of variation at clinical and research levels and give it scientific credibility. Progress in reliability brought about by DSM-III and DSM-III-R (American Psychiatric Association 1980, 1987) makes it possible to more systematically explore and document variation and its significance and to use it to improve the validity of present boundaries and criteria. This could appear paradoxical or contrary to the general philosophy of DSM-IV. Although main decisions are clearly guided by a search for simplicity and for eliminating any source of ambiguity, what is argued here is the importance of developing a parallel attention to cross-cultural variation that could simultaneously reintroduce some sense of the complexity of the diagnostic process. The two approaches might be kept separate so that clinicians and researchers could choose either to confine themselves to standard "safe" (even if questionable) criteria or to complement these criteria by other data that are potentially significant for diagnosis, prognosis, and treatment.

The usefulness of adding a cultural axis appears more dubious, at least for the purpose of opening the diagnostic process to cultural dimensions. Research literature indicates that Axes IV and V have been underutilized and are not a constitutive part of the diagnosis process; a sixth cultural axis used in the same way would have little impact on psychiatric diagnosis in a cross-cultural context. As stated before, it appears to be more useful to indicate how the exploration of specific items described in the diagnostic categories chapter can be enriched and complemented.

References

American Psychiatric Association: Diagnostic and Statistical Manual of Mental Disorders, 3rd Edition. Washington, DC, American Psychiatric Association, 1980

American Psychiatric Association: Diagnostic and Statistical Manual of Mental Disorders, 3rd Edition, Revised. Washington, DC, American Psychiatric Association, 1987

American Psychiatric Association: Diagnostic and Statistical Manual of Mental Disorders, 4th Edition. Washington, DC, American Psychiatric Association, 1994

Devereux G: Basic Problems of Ethnopsychiatry. Chicago, IL, University of Chicago Press, 1970

Eco U: Semiotics and the Philosophy of Language. Bloomington, Indiana University Press, 1984

Egeland JA, Hostetter AM, Eshleman SK: Amish study, III: The impact of cultural factors on diagnosis of bipolar illness. Am J Psychiatry 140:67–71, 1983

Fabrega H: On the significance of an anthropological approach to schizophrenia. Psychiatry 52:45–65, 1989

Fabrega H, Mezzich J, Ulrich RF: Black-white differences in psychopathology in an urban psychiatric population. Compr Psychiatry 29:285–297, 1988

Katz MM, Marsella A, Dub KC, et al: On the expression of psychosis in different cultures: schizophrenia in an Indian and in a Nigerian community. Cult Med Psychiatry 12:331–355, 1988

Kleinman A: Rethinking Psychiatry: From Cultural Category to Personal Experience. New York, Free Press, 1988

Mukherjee S, Shulka S, Woodle J, et al: Misdiagnosis of schizophrenia in bipolar patients: multiethnic comparisons. Am J Psychiatry 140:1571–1574, 1983

Murphy HBM: Comparative Psychiatry. Berlin, Germany, Springer-Verlag, 1982

Murphy HBM: Socio-cultural variations in symptomatology incidence and course of illness, in Handbook of Psychiatry, Vol I: General Psychopathology. Edited by Shepherd M, Zangwill OL. Cambridge, England, Cambridge University Press, 1983, pp 157–172

Pogue-Geile MF, Zubin J: Negative symptomatology and schizophrenia: a conceptual and empirical review. International Journal of Mental Health 16(4):3–45, 1988

Sartorius N, Jablensky A, Corten A, et al: Early manifestations and first contact incidence of schizophrenia. Psychol Med 16:902–928, 1986

Strauss JS: Negative symptoms: future developments of the concept. Schizophr Bull 11:457–460, 1985

Teggin AF, Elk R, Ben-Arie O, et al: A comparison of CATEGO class "S" schizophrenia in three ethnic groups: psychiatric manifestations. Br J Psychiatry 147:683–687, 1985

World Health Organization: Schizophrenia: An International Follow-Up Study. Chichester, England, Wiley, 1979

Chapter 10

Cultural Comments on Organic and Psychotic Disorders: II

Marvin Karno, M.D.

I t is an honor to comment on Lin's excellent chapter, "Cultural Influences on the Diagnosis of Psychotic and Organic Disorders." For those who are unfamiliar with it, I wish to draw attention to the earlier and more elaborate review article authored by Lin and Kleinman (1988), which I regard as the most sophisticated treatment on the research literature concerning the interface of culture and schizophrenia up to the time of its publication.

Lin's presentation here has been, by necessity, conceptual rather than methodological in nature and has focused principally on schizophrenia. He cites recent and current studies supporting the cross-cultural validity of the Euro-American diagnostic concept of schizophrenia but wisely reminds us, by reference to medical diseases at least as biologically grounded as schizophrenia, how cultural as well as historical factors may powerfully influence the presentation and prevalence of disease.

I wish to focus on two points raised by Lin: the apparent decline of the catatonic (and hebephrenic) subtype of schizophrenia in Western nations and sociocultural influences on symptom prevalence.

Briefly and historically in regard to catatonia, a rereading of Karl Kahlbaum's (1973) slender, famous monograph on catatonia is of value. Kahlbaum presented 25 cases of patients he had studied in two German asylums. Most prominent in his clinical and postmortem case descriptions, in addition to the classic symptoms and signs of catatonia, is the consistent and striking evidence of severe organic and affective disease. The former included high fevers; severe, persistent diarrhea; lungs cavitated by tuberculous lesions; and meninges studded with granulomas. The latter included classic descriptions of major depressive and manic symptoms. Kraepelin (1919) subsumed Kahlbaum's catatonia, along with the hebephrenia described by Kahlbaum's student Hecker (1871), within the family of dementia praecox (later known as schizophrenia), and his stature and authority have to this day deflected adequate attention from the originally described catatonic symptom complex. Thus, much of the mysterious worldwide decline in the prevalence of catatonia in recent decades may be due to improved primary health care. In the broadest sense, this, too, reflects the impact of culture on diagnosis.

A report by Chandrasena (1986) comparing catatonic patients hospitalized in Sri Lanka, Ottawa, and London in the 1970s and 1980s strongly suggests another factor that may be influencing the apparent decline in prevalence of the catatonic subtype of schizophrenia. The data cited in that report indicate that the high rate of catatonia among the Sri Lankan patients (21%, compared with the 5% among British whites and 6%–8% among Canadian whites) was associated with both strikingly longer durations of index episodes of illness among the Sri Lankan patients prior to treatment and a very low likelihood of their having received neuroleptic treatment prior to hospital admission, in sharp contrast to the British and Canadian patients. Thus, earliness of intervention and earliness of neuroleptic treatment may also be key factors in the decline of prevalence of the catatonic subtype of schizophrenia. This is consistent with the findings from the International Pilot Study of Schizophrenia (World Health Organization 1973) cited by Chandrasena (1986) concerning the higher rates of catatonic schizophrenia among Indian and African patients compared with British and North American patients.

In regard to the more general symptoms of schizophrenia, Lin refers to life conditions of threat and discrimination as experienced by refugee, minority, and politically persecuted populations as likely contributing to higher prevalence rates of paranoid delusions among such groups. Los Angeles Epidemiologic Catchment Area (ECA) Study data on psychotic symptom and near-symptom prevalence among United States-born and Mexican-born Mexican Americans revealed some significant differences by cultural and immigrant status (Karno and Norquist 1989).

Evolving studies by our group disclose that auditory hallucinations appear to be more prevalent among Mexican-born respondents than among either Euro-Americans and United States-born Mexicans. This same finding holds for more common near symptoms or pseudosymptoms of auditory hallucinations (e.g., self-reported experiences of hearing things others do not hear that were below symptom threshold). For a reported experience to be counted as a true (in this case psychotic) symptom of mental disorder, it had to be carefully queried and found not to be caused by medical illness or injury or by the use of drugs or alcohol. It also had to be clearly experienced and not explicable as other than a hallucination. All such positive symptoms and all uncertain or near-symptom experiences were recorded verbatim and checked by a research psychiatrist. Many near symptoms may also actually have represented psychopathological experiences.

Both the true and near symptoms were elicited from community household residents. The acculturation level (Burnam et al. 1987) was significantly lower for the total subsample of Mexican-born Los Angeles ECA respondents in comparison with the United States-born subsample. This is believed to represent a possible case of direct cultural influence on schizophrenic symptom expression.

It was also found that white Americans reported substantially higher rates of hypersexuality and grandiosity in response to Diagnostic Interview Schedule (Robins et al. 1981) questions concerning manic symptoms, as compared with United States- and Mexican-born respondents of Mexican origin. The Los Angeles ECA study did not find different prevalence rates for schizophrenia and mania per se between Euro-Americans and native or foreign-born Mexican Americans. This evidence supports the value of focusing at the level of discrete symptoms, rather than pathological entities comprising symptom complexes, in assessing the influence of cultural factors on diagnoses.

References

Burnam MA, Hough R, Karno M, et al: Acculturation and lifetime prevalence of psychiatric disorders among Mexican Americans in Los Angeles. J Health Soc Behav 28:89–102, 1987

Chandrasena R: Catatonic schizophrenia: an international comparative study. Can J Psychiatry 31:249–252, 1986

Hecker E: Die Hebephrenie. Archiv für Pathologische Anatomie und Physiologie und für Klinische Medizin 25:202, 1871

Kahlbaum KL: Catatonia. Baltimore, MD, Johns Hopkins University Press, 1973

Karno M, Norquist GS: Schizophrenia: epidemiology, in Comprehensive Textbook of Psychiatry, Fifth edition. Edited by Kaplan HI, Sadock BJ. Baltimore, MD, Williams & Wilkins, 1989

Kraepelin E: Dementia Praecox and Paraphrenia. Edinburgh, Scotland, E & S Livingstone, 1919

Lin KM, Kleinman AM: Psychopathology and clinical course of schizophrenia: a cross-cultural perspective. Schizophr Bull 14:555–567, 1988

Robins LN, Helzer JE, Croughan J, et al: National Institute of Mental Health Diagnostic Interview Schedule: its history, characteristics, and validity. Arch Gen Psychiatry 38:381–389, 1981

World Health Organization: Report of the International Pilot Study on Schizophrenia. Geneva, Switzerland, World Health Organization, 1973

Chapter 11

Nosological Comments on Culture and Organic and Psychotic Disorders

Michael Flaum, M.D.

n the introductory chapter of this section, Lin summarizes many of the issues surrounding the diagnosis and phenomenology of psychotic and organic disorders in the context of cultural heterogeneity. Focusing on schizophrenia, he reviews the major findings that have emerged from cross-cultural studies of this disorder over the years. Among the most important and intriguing findings are the following:

- Schizophrenia appears to be present in virtually every culture in which it has been studied.
- With a few notable exceptions, prevalence appears to be remarkably similar across cultures.
- In terms of symptom presentation, cross-cultural similarities far outweigh differences.
- There appears to be a variation in the course and outcome across cultures, such that acute onset and good outcome appear to be more common in "developing" than in "developed" countries.

Lin describes the various types of pathoplastic and pathogenetic influences that may underlie both the similarities and differences that have been observed across cultures. He suggests that similar prevalence rates do not necessarily imply common underlying mechanisms, nor does marked variation in course and outcome necessarily reflect etiological heterogeneity. He cautions us to regard most of the findings to date as preliminary and indicates that, like most observations in science, these findings ultimately raise more questions than they answer. The challenge faced by the field of cultural psychiatry in this area is to exploit these epidemiological clues toward a further understanding of the phenomenon that we have tentatively agreed to call *schizophrenia*.

The challenge posed by cultural psychiatrists to those involved in the process of developing and/or revising diagnostic classification systems entails the issue of optimally enhancing the cultural sensitivity of these diagnostic criteria. Because these criteria are largely symptom based, one approach to this challenge is to minimize the emphasis placed on those symptoms that appear to be most likely to be confounded by cultural variation and similarly to increase the emphasis on symptoms that appear to be less prone to misinterpretation or poor reliability across cultures.

In terms of criteria for schizophrenia, Lin appropriately points out that the emphasis on "bizarre" delusions may be particularly problematic. Something that may appear to be bizarre when taken out of the context of a particular subculture may in fact be understandable within the generally shared belief system of that subculture. Although the existing criteria stipulate that assessment of bizarre delusions should be considered within the context of the person's culture, it seems likely that the bizarre versus nonbizarre distinction remains prone to poor reliability and misinterpretation when assessed across cultural boundaries. In fact, even within a given culture this distinction may be problematic. We are aware of three studies that have specifically addressed the issue of reliability of bizarre delusions: Flaum et al. (1991a), R. L. Spitzer (unpublished data, 1991), and Goldman et al. (1992). The range of reliability estimates varied markedly across studies, ranging from a low of approximately .30 to a high of .78. To illustrate, the potential for poor reliability of this criterion item has important diagnostic implications because of the emphasis placed on this dimension within the DSM-III-R criteria for psychotic disorders. Bizarre delusions are assigned increased diagnostic weighting relative to most other symptoms in the A criteria for schizophrenia in DSM-III-R; hence, these criteria can be satisfied by the presence of bizarre delusions alone. This reflects a change from DSM-III (American Psychiatric Association 1980), in which the critical distinction regarding delusions was the persecutory versus nonpersecutory dimension (Kendler et al. 1989). Furthermore, in DSM-III-R, the diagnosis of delusional disorder cannot be made in the presence of bizarre delusions and thus the diagnosis of schizophrenia versus delusional disorder often turns on this distinction.

Through the process of literature reviews, data reanalyses, and field trials, DSM-IV Psychotic Disorders Work Group explored various alternatives to this problem, including 1) eliminating the bizarre versus nonbizarre distinction altogether from the criteria; 2) retaining the distinction with alternative definitions; or 3) replacing the distinction with other domains of delusional experience, such as level of severity, conviction, extension, pressure, or systematization (Kendler et al. 1983). Unfortunately, none of the alternative definitions or dimensions resulted in improved reliability, and the elimination of the distinction appeared to substantially narrow caseness of schizophrenia in an apparently nonvalid manner (i.e., those subjects who satisfied the A criteria for schizophrenia on the basis of bizarre delusions alone did not differ in any respect from the remaining cases) (unpublished data from DSM-IV field trial). Given this, along with the long historical tradition of differentiating schizophrenia from delusional disorder on the basis of the "understandability" of the delusions, it would be wise to retain this distinction in the diagnostic manual and to provide examples mindful of cross-cultural misapplication.

A related issue involves the continuing influence of Schneider's concept of "first-rank" symptoms, despite the consensus that these symptoms are not pathognomonic for schizophrenia (Andreasen and Flaum 1991; Carpenter et al. 1973). These symptoms play an especially prominent role in the revision of the International Classification of Diseases (ICD-10) (World Health Organization 1993), in which the A-1 criteria for schizophrenia are essentially a list of first-rank symptoms, each assigned greater diagnostic weighting than all other symptoms. The presence of first-rank symptoms appears to vary markedly across cultures (Carpenter and Strauss 1974; Ndetei 1988). Although this may represent a real cultural variation in phenomenology, it may also reflect difficulties in translating the subtleties of the definition and application of these terms across languages and cultural boundaries. First-rank symptoms are subjective experiences that are inherently difficult to describe and prone to misinterpretation. A study conducted by our group at Iowa found first-rank symptoms to be markedly less reliable than other types of delusions and hallucinations as well as other positive and negative symptoms of schizophrenia (Flaum et al. 1991b). This study was conducted in an ethnically homogeneous sample with raters of the same subculture and suggests that the problem would be magnified across cultural boundaries. Although optimizing concordance between American and international criteria was one of the goals of DSM-IV process, increasing the emphasis on first-rank symptoms in DSM-IV does not appear to be supported by empirical evidence.

In addition to minimizing those items that may have poor reliability across cultures, an attempt should be made to increase the emphasis on symptoms that may be more reliably assessed (i.e., those in which the assessment can be based more on objective and observable phenomena than on subjective report). Interestingly, negative symptoms, which have been deemphasized in modern diagnostic criteria largely because of concerns about their reliability, may indeed fit this model. Concerns about their reliability stem from the fact that they are not clearly discontinuous from normality as are positive symptoms such as hallucinations or delusions. Yet, each of the so-called core negative symptoms (i.e., poverty of speech, affective flattening, and avolition) are actually assessed by more objective parameters, such as the amount and fluency of speech or activity over a given time period, than are positive symptoms. Studies from both Japan and China have found comparably high levels of reliability in rating these symptoms when compared with those reported in similar studies conducted in Western countries such as Spain, Italy, and the United States (reviewed in Andreasen and Flaum 1991). It must be noted that each of these studies employed an assessment instrument specifically designed for negative symptoms (the Scale for the Assessment of Negative Symptoms [Andreasen 1984]) and that these findings cannot be generalized until studies that simulate the clinical situation are completed.

Data from field trials conducted both by the World Health Organization and the American Psychiatric Association are relevant to inform this issue (Flaum and Andreasen 1991). Assessments are being conducted both with and without the use of structured interviews. Sites for the field trials were selected with the aim of optimizing the cultural heterogeneity of the sample in terms of ethnic diversity, socioeconomic status, and urban versus rural populations.

Advancing technology in telecommunications and travel continues to make the world seem smaller, and there is clearly a need for universally accepted and applicable definitions of psychiatric disorders in fostering high-quality clinical research. However, clinicians and researchers alike must keep in mind that current diagnostic criteria in psychiatry still reflect tentative agreements, and their reification must be actively avoided. Cultural variation is only one of the many potentially confounding factors in the application of these criteria, and their validity will continue to rest on the clinical judgment of the user.

References

American Psychiatric Association: Diagnostic and Statistical Manual of Mental Disorders, 3rd Edition. Washington, DC, American Psychiatric Association, 1980

American Psychiatric Association: Diagnostic and Statistical Manual of Mental Disorders, 3rd Edition, Revised. Washington, DC, American Psychiatric Association, 1987

Andreasen NC: The Scale for the Assessment of Negative Symptoms (SANS). Iowa City, University of Iowa, 1984

Andreasen NC, Flaum M: Schizophrenia: the characteristic symptoms. Schizophr Bull 17:25–49, 1991

Carpenter WT, Strauss JS: Cross-cultural evaluation of Schneider's first-rank symptoms of schizophrenia: a report from the International Pilot Study of Schizophrenia. Am J Psychiatry 131:682–687, 1974

Carpenter WT, Strauss JS, Muleh S: Are there pathognomonic symptoms in schizophrenia? An empiric investigation of Schneider's first-rank symptoms. Arch Gen Psychiatry 28:847–852, 1973

Flaum M, Andreasen NC: Diagnostic criteria for schizophrenia and related disorders: options for DSM-IV. Schizophr Bull 17:133–142, 1991

Flaum M, Arndt S, Andreasen NC: Reliability of bizarre delusions. Compr Psychiatry 32:59–65, 1991a

Flaum M, Arndt S, Fleming F, et al: Reliability and frequency of "first-rank" symptoms in schizophrenia: implications for DSM-IV. Poster presented at the International Congress on Schizophrenia Research, Tucson, AZ, April 1991b

Goldman D, Hien DA, Hass GL, et al: Bizarre delusions and DSM-III-R schizophrenia. Am J Psychiatry 149:494–499, 1992

Kendler KS, Glazer WM, Morgenstern H: Dimensions of delusional experience. Am J Psychiatry 140:466–469, 1983

Kendler KS, Spitzer RL, Williams JBL: Psychotic disorders in DSM-III-R. Am J Psychiatry 146:953–962, 1989

Ndetei DM: Psychiatric phenomenology across countries: constitutional, cultural, or environmental? Acta Psychiatr Scand Suppl 344:33–44, 1988

World Health Organization: International Classification of Diseases, 10th Revision. Mental and Behavioral Disorders: Diagnostic Criteria for Research. Geneva, Switzerland, World Health Organization, 1993

Section III

Substance-Related Disorders

Chapter 12

Culture and the Diagnostic Classification of Substance-Related Disorders

Joseph Westermeyer, M.D., Ph.D.

Introduction: The Questions

1. Pathological pattern of use. Most clinicians have little difficulty ascertaining whether a pathological pattern of use is present. There are exceptions, however. Examples are as follows:
    a. Is a pathological pattern of use present if the patient's ethnic group demands abstinence from the substance, or if the patient's ethnic group or subgroup requires a pathological pattern of use?
    b. Is a pathological pattern of use present if the patient's reference group permits use of the substance for certain categories of persons (e.g., adults over age 18, ill persons, dying persons) but not for the patient's category (e.g., youths, certain persons at work)?
    c. Is there an absolute dose frequency of substance that indicates a pathological pattern, or does it vary by demographic groups or comorbid groups (e.g., mentally retarded, young, or elderly persons or persons on psychoactive medication)?
    d. How do physician attitudes toward normative use affect judgment regarding pathological pattern? This question concerns the reliability of this diagnosis.
2. Associated problems or symptoms
    a. How relevant are such sociocultural factors as secretive use, hiding supply, using alone, feeling remorse?
    b. What are the external validators that confirm this diagnosis across cultural boundaries?
3. Miscellaneous considerations
    a. How does culture affect such associated features as laboratory and physical examination findings, course, age at onset, impairment, complications,

predisposing factors, prevalence, sex, familial patterns, problematic differential diagnosis, excessively low or high prevalence, low reliability, and excessive co-occurrence with other diagnoses?

b.   What should be the restrictions regarding certain Axis I and Axis II diagnoses in the presence of a substance-related disorder (SRD) diagnosis (e.g., adjustment disorder, V codes, borderline personality)?

c.   Should the diagnosis, once made, include ethnically related socioeconomic factors that relate to treatment and prognosis? This question concerns the clinical utility of this diagnosis.

d.   For comorbid conditions, does ethnic bias exist in considering "primary-secondary" relationships?

Methodology

Efforts to assess DSM-IV (American Psychiatric Association 1994) criteria for SRD have not been as extensive and intensive as efforts to assess other DSM-IV diagnoses. Nonetheless, past efforts to assess reliability of SRD diagnoses under various categories have tended to show a high reliability (Leonard et al. 1984; Mulford and Fitzgerald 1981). The progressive and chronic/recurrent nature of this disorder probably accounts for this phenomenon. "Mild" cases are more apt to be early cases rather than truly mild cases. Relaxing or tightening the criteria is apt to affect the inclusion/exclusion of these early or preclinical cases, more than inclusion/exclusion based on severity of clinical cases. This strongly overlapping aspect of different SRD diagnostic criteria (e.g., among DSM-II/DSM-III/DSM-III-R [American Psychiatric Association 1968, 1980, 1987], Research Diagnostic Criteria [RDC], ICD-9) thus has the salutary effect of countering the paucity of DSM-III/DSM-III-R studies, as we can use selected studies of earlier classifications and other concurrent classifications.

Literature Review and Comment

Pathological Pattern of Use

Pathological pattern and culturally prescribed abstinence or intoxication.   DSM criteria are not sufficiently specific regarding pathological use vis-à-vis cultural prescriptions and proscriptions. Thus, some American clinicians define any drug use proscribed by law as pathological (e.g., nonprescribed use of legal drugs such as codeine or morphine or any use of illegal drugs such as cannabis or cocaine or heroin). Clinicians may define any use of potentially injurious but widely available intoxicants as pathological (e.g., volatile inhalants such as industrial solvents and lubricants), although subgroups themselves may not view their use as aberrant. At other times, the group may view the use of virtually any psychoactive substance as deviant (e.g., Mormons and the use of alcohol or caffeine), but the clinician may not. Some clinicians and social scientists support the opinion that clinicians should not define a drinking pattern as pathological if the cultural norms support it (e.g., Native American "bottle gang" drinking, coca leaf chewing, opium smoking). This stance is complicated by the fact that the "ideal norm" (i.e., that which people are supposed to do), especially in some cultures with heavy use among subgroups, may support abstinence, whereas the "behavioral norm" (i.e., that which people actually do) may permit clearly pathological use.

To resolve these points, the following recommendations are made:

- Pattern of use should be defined as pathological if it indicates physiological tolerance (e.g., consumption of 10 ounces of alcohol in a 24-hour period) or carries significant risk (e.g., cannabis use and piloting an aircraft), even if it is supported by the patient's cultural group.
- Ethnic or cultural norms for abstinence should be ignored as criteria for pathological use.
- Potentially pathological use of specific types (e.g., volatile inhalants, street drugs of unknown composition, illegal use of prescription drugs, driving when intoxicated, parenteral injection of drugs) could be included as a V code (i.e., pathogenic substance use), even if it has not yet been associated with a particular problem but has persisted over time (e.g., 2 weeks or a month).

Pathological use for particular demographic subgroups or conditions.   Onset of SRD during childhood or adolescence has raised the question of whether any unsupervised childhood use of even licit substances (e.g., alcohol, tobacco, caffeine) might be considered pathological. In some parts of the world, children begin to make these decisions for themselves well before adolescence. Childhood use may not be associated with childhood problems, but intoxication before the age of 15 is strongly associated with later SRD. Any use of sedatives, opiates, cannabis, hallucinogens, stimulants, and volatile inhalants might be considered at least pathogenic in association with certain activities, even if no demonstrable problem ensues. Examples of such activities might include practicing a profession, operating an airplane or other means of transportation, or undertaking tasks requiring judgment or coordination (e.g., operating machinery, sky diving) while using even modest doses of a psychoactive compound.

Certain Axis III biomedical conditions could inveigh against any substance use or against substance use beyond a certain minimum: an example could be being pregnant and taking psychoactive compounds in particular doses. Certain conditions, such as organic mental syndrome or mental retardation, may be exacerbated by small doses of psychoactive compounds.

Recommendations in the preceding section are relevant here.

Absolute (or height-weight) quantity-frequency versus relative quantity-frequency. The absence of specific quantity-frequency or "doses" in the DSM criteria presents certain problems, as many physicians have mistaken notions regarding pathogenic doses. Constant dosages in the range of 3–4 ounces of ethanol per day are associated with pathological organ changes (i.e., brain, liver, pancreas) in vulnerable individuals. The century-old concept of "Anstie's limit" (Baldwin 1977), which refers to an English physician's observation that four or more drinks per day pose a risk when sustained over a decade or more, should be included in diagnostic guidelines to stimulate awareness on this point.

Impairment at doses well below Anstie's limit does exist for particular subgroups. For example, naive users (e.g., young persons), elderly persons, mentally retarded persons, those with organic mental syndromes/disorders, or those on psychotropic medication may be impaired at lower doses. For example, alcohol-induced amnesia or "blackout" may occur with 1 ounce ethanol in mentally retarded persons or those with organic mental disorder (Westermeyer et al. 1988). Again, the preceding recommendations are relevant here. Culturally sanctioned substances and doses may not be safe in particular subgroups of persons. Scientifically derived safe limits, such as Anstie's limit for alcohol, should transcend more liberal cultural limits.

Physician attitude and PSUD diagnosis.   Numerous factors influence the diagnosis of psychoactive substance use disorder (PSUD) by physicians (Chappell 1973). For example, the belief that making the diagnosis may have a beneficial clinical outcome can be influential. Physician consumption of substances may also play a role. For example, a heavily drinking physician may not recognize alcohol abuse in anyone drinking at the same level, or an abstinent physician may see alcoholism in virtually anyone who uses alcohol. These preferences vis-à-vis alcohol (or other drugs) could possibly be related to ethnic factors, such as religion or national origin, although this has not been demonstrated to occur.

Associated Problems or Symptoms

Psychosocial symptoms affected by ethnicity and socioeconomic status.   Certain common SRD symptoms in middle-class, mainstream Americans are seldom found in certain other American ethnic groups. These include secretive use, hiding supply, or using alone. Family repercussions or socioeconomic complications can differ greatly across ethnic boundaries. Use may be seen not as producing problems, but rather as a response to problems (e.g., unemployment, divorce, loss of children to welfare agencies, inability to cope, or "nerves"). Alienation from one's reference group may occur at minimal dosage among ethnic groups who proscribe any use of psychoactive substances, including licit substances (e.g., smoking among Seventh Day Adventists, drinking among members of the Native American Church).

Biomedical correlates of SRD as culture-fair indices.   Unlike for other disorders, numerous biological markers are available to detect abuse or dependence. These include the following:

*   Clinical signs and symptoms of intoxication
*   Clinical signs and symptoms of withdrawal

- Clinical signs and symptoms of other organic mental disorders (e.g., dementia, amnesia)
- Evidence of organic damage (e.g., abnormal liver function tests, increased red blood cell mean corpuscular volume)
- Evidence of consumption of substances (i.e., in blood or urine or on the breath).

These attributes of the disorder improve diagnostic reliability and validity across ethnicity, nations, and cultures to an extent greater than that for many psychiatric disorders.

Miscellaneous Considerations

Cultural effects on SRD pathology and associated characteristics. Some aspects of SRD remain fairly constant across cultural boundaries. For example, the mean time between heroin addiction onset and treatment seeking was about 3 years in groups from Asia and North America (Berger and Westermeyer 1977). Cocaine also appears to run a rapid course prior to treatment seeking, whereas the mean course with alcohol or opium prior to treatment extends to as long as a decade (Volicer et al. 1983; Westermeyer 1983). Males show a greater point prevalence compared with females, but the gender ratio among cultures may vary from 2:1 to 40:1 for the same drug (Heok 1987; Robins et al. 1984; Westermeyer 1980). Greater exposure to the substance use context appears to account for this difference (Westermeyer 1981).

Infrequently, women may consume a substance more than men; *betel-areca* dependence in Southeast Asia is an example (Ahluwalia and Ponnampalam 1968; Westermeyer 1982), although more men consume it in South Asia and Oceania.

Pathophysiological changes from alcohol or parenteral injection of drugs are qualitatively similar across cultures, given the same mode of administration (Baldwin 1977; Ojesjo 1981), although quantitative differences may exist (Orford 1973). For example, some ethnic groups with a "binge" pattern of drinking have more violent deaths (Levy and Kunity 1974; Westermeyer and Brantner 1972) or alcoholic psychoses (Gottheil et al. 1973). However, groups with more controlled drinking manifest more hepatic and gastrointestinal pathology (Kissin and Begleiter 1974). Types of personal and social impairment also tend to be qualitatively similar (e.g., family discord, interpersonal problems, occupational disability, legal offenses, and financial insecurity) (Westermeyer 1983). However, the quantitative distribution of these problems can vary across ethnic groups in association with cultural values and socioeconomic class (Westermeyer 1972).

Beyond these few common themes, the associated features can differ greatly. Physical and laboratory findings of alcohol abuse, such as anemia and plasma protein, can differ considerably (Westermeyer 1972). Although onset of SRD usually occurs during adolescence or early adulthood, mean age at onset of SRD can differ by several years (Westermeyer 1983). Point prevalence can range from being virtually nonexistent to being the first or second most prevalent psychiatric disorder in a population. Familial patterns of SRD may be less meaningful in ethnic groups with very low rates (Heok 1987).

Restrictions regarding Axes I and II diagnoses.   Some psychiatrists may add an adjustment disorder diagnosis to SRD, although others do not. Adjustment disorder symptoms are so common during the first year of sobriety that virtually all recovering persons can be labeled as having an adjustment disorder during that time period. Use of the category during the first year thus usually conveys no further understanding of the case. V codes similarly are frequent, although the types of V codes differ among patients. The mere presence of adjustment symptoms and V codes provides little assistance, although specification of the symptoms and problems could have research utility. Ethnic variation could exist, but it would have to be demonstrated.

Patterns of Axis II personality disorders are also frequent among patients with SRD. However, these patterns may entirely disappear with abstinence and/or a period of recovery. Adolescents and young adults with SRD may meet criteria for antisocial personality (except for the age criterion) but then not persist in this personality pattern when stable sobriety is established. Under these circumstances, it might be best to defer an Axis II diagnosis until 1 year of sobriety has been established. Here, as with Axis I, ethnic variation may exist but would have to be demonstrated.

Relationship of SRD diagnoses to prognosis and treatment.   Diagnosis in medicine serves to group people together who share characteristics with one another and to distinguish these select groups from others. The SRD diagnosis does predict prognosis without treatment and does identify people apt to respond to one or another of the treatments for SRD (Frances 1988). However, the SRD diagnosis is especially poor across ethnic groups in predicting prognosis or specifying treatment approach. For example, Native American alcoholics have shown treatment outcomes varying from 0% to 20% recovery (Cahalan et al. 1985; Westermeyer and Peake 1983), whereas predominantly white executives, airplane pilots, and physicians have demonstrated recovery rates of 80%–90% (Harper 1983; Washton et al. 1984).

Is this difference in prognosis important in the matter of diagnosis? For medical purposes, diagnosis should tell us about recommended treatment and prognosis associated with and without optimal treatment. Is there a means to generate a treatment plan and related prognosis in SRD? Optimal treatment plans and related prognosis can be extrapolated from the literature. These apply across ethnicities and cultures.

Beyond initial detoxification, locus of treatment can be related to current sociodemographic characteristics as follows:

- Occupied at work or school (not exposed to substances) and living with family of origin or family of marriage (with no substance abusers in family): treatment in an outpatient clinic or evening program is warranted
- Not occupied at work or school, or occupational setting is a stimulus to use: treatment in a day program until occupied
- Living alone in a setting not supportive of sobriety and recovery: relocation to residential care, halfway house, "sobriety house" (i.e., group of recovering persons living together without supervision)

- Unable to maintain abstinence for increasingly prolonged periods, with increasingly brief "slips," or in an occupation in which slips cannot be tolerated because of imminent risk to others (e.g., airline pilot, physician, mother with preschool child): hospital or residential care
- Comorbid psychiatric or medical conditions that require hospital care or complex treatment regimen: treatment in hospital, residential facility, halfway house, nursing home

Prognosis with appropriate treatment is largely related to sociodemographic characteristics and "recovery resources" upon entering treatment (Westermeyer 1989). Occupation and residence predict rates of "improved patients" at 1 year after treatment as follows:

- Not occupied at school or work and not living with family committed to patient's recovery: 0%–20% improvement at 1 year
- Occupied or living with family (but not both): 30%–40% improved
- Occupied and living with family or occupied and active in a self-help group, or occupied and being monitored: 60%–80% improved
- Occupied, living with family, high socioeconomic status, and monitored in occupational role (e.g., pilots, physicians): 80%–100% improved

Comorbid conditions: which is primary?   The high prevalence of SRD with other psychiatric disorders has been well established (Myers et al. 1984). These disorders range from posttraumatic stress disorder (Berk et al. 1989) to schizophrenia. Presumably, the assignment of two comorbid conditions to "primary-secondary" status should depend on etiology—that is, the causative disorder should be primary and the resultant disorder should be secondary. If this cannot be ascertained with reasonable validity, then the chronology of the two disorders should be described— that is, the initial occurring disorder should be primary and the subsequent occurring disorder should be secondary. Frequently in substance abuse and other psychiatric dual disorders, the assignment is made on the basis of clinician bias and/or locus of treatment (e.g., a general psychiatric unit versus a substance abuse unit). This situation is unsatisfactory. Some clinicians hold that at least a chronological sequence can usually be determined for SRD in relation to associated psychiatric disorder (Schuckit et al. 1990). In some cross-cultural research the relationship is not so clear (Westermeyer and Peake 1983). The matter becomes even more complex if more than two disorders coexist, as often occurs. The trend for increasing number of psychiatric diagnoses (i.e., "splitting" rather than "lumping") and the trend for complete diagnostic evaluations covering all possible Axis I diagnoses result in frequent listing of two or more comorbid conditions (Maser and Cloninger 1990).

Ideally all active diagnoses could be listed without those at the top of the list assuming the status of the etiological factor, the initially appearing disorder, or the "most important" disorder. ("Most important" here is often related to financial considerations or other bias.) One alternative might be for diagnoses to always be listed by their order of appearance in the diagnostic manual. Clinicians might then describe any possible etiological, chronological, or priority issues in a separate place in the medical record.

References

Ahluwalia HS, Ponnampalam JT: The socioeconomic aspects of betel-nut chewing. J Trop Med Hyg 71:48–50, 1968

American Psychiatric Association: Diagnostic and Statistical Manual of Mental Disorders, 2nd Edition. Washington, DC, American Psychiatric Association, 1968

American Psychiatric Association: Diagnostic and Statistical Manual of Mental Disorders, 3rd Edition. Washington, DC, American Psychiatric Association, 1980

American Psychiatric Association: Diagnostic and Statistical Manual of Mental Disorders, 3rd Edition, Revised. Washington, DC, American Psychiatric Association, 1987

American Psychiatric Association: Diagnostic and Statistical Manual of Mental Disorders, 4th Edition. Washington, DC, American Psychiatric Association, 1994

Baldwin AD: Anstie's alcohol limit. Am J Public Health 67:679–681, 1977

Berger LJ, Westermeyer J: World traveler addicts in Asia, II: Comparison with "stay at home" addicts. American Journal of Drug and Alcohol Abuse 4:495–503, 1977

Berk E, Black J, Locastro J, et al: Traumatogenicity: effects of self-reported noncombat trauma and noncombat veterans treated for substance abuse. J Clin Psychol 45:704–708, 1989

Cahalan D, Walker RD, Donovan DM, et al: Detoxification recidivism among urban American Indian alcoholics. Am J Psychiatry 142:1467–1470, 1985

Chappell JN: Attitudinal barriers to physician involvement with drug abusers. JAMA 224:1011–1013, 1973

Frances R: Update on alcohol and drug disorder treatment. J Clin Psychiatry 49:13–17, 1988

Gottheil E, Alterman AI, Skoloda TE, et al: Alcoholics' pattern of controlled drinking. Am J Psychiatry 130:418–422, 1973

Harper CR: Airline pilot alcoholism: one airline's experience. Aviat Space Environ Med 20:590–591, 1983

Heok KE: A cross-cultural study of alcohol dependence in Singapore. Br J Addict 82:771–773, 1987

Kissin B, Begleiter H: The Biology of Alcoholism. New York, Plenum, 1974

Leonard KE, Bromet EJ, Parkinson DK, et al: Agreement among Feighner, RDC and DSM-III criteria for alcoholism. Addict Behav 9:319–322, 1984

Levy JE, Kunity SJ: Indian Drinking. New York, Wiley Interscience, 1974

Maser JD, Cloninger CR (eds): Comorbidity of Mood and Anxiety Disorders. Washington, DC, American Psychiatric Press, 1990

Mulford HA, Fitzgerald JL: On the validity of the research diagnostic criteria, the Feighner criteria, and the DSM-III for diagnosing alcoholics. J Nerv Ment Dis 169:654–658, 1981

Myers JK, Weissman M, Tischler G, et al: Six-month prevalence of psychiatric disorders in three communities. Arch Gen Psychiatry 41:959–967, 1984

Ojesjo L: Long-term outcome in alcohol abuse and alcoholism among males in the Lumby general population. Br J Addict 76:391–400, 1981

Orford J: A comparison of alcoholics whose drinking is totally uncontrolled and those whose drinking is mainly controlled. Behav Res Ther 11:565–576, 1973

Robins LN, Helzer JE, Weisman MM, et al: Lifetime prevalence of specific psychiatric disorders in three sites. Arch Gen Psychiatry 41:949–958, 1984

Schuckit MA, Irwin M, Brown SA: The history of anxiety symptoms among 17 primary alcoholics. J Studies Alcohol 51:34–41, 1990

Volicer BJ, Volicer L, D'Angelo N: Variation in length of time to development of alcoholism by family history of problem drinking. Drug Alcohol Depend 12:69–83, 1983

Washton AM, Pottash AC, Gold MS: Naltrexone in addicted business executives and physicians. J Clin Psychiatry 45:39–41, 1984

Westermeyer J: Chippewa and majority alcoholism in the Twin Cities: a comparison. J Nerv Ment Dis 42:398–403, 1972

Westermeyer J: Sex ratio among opium addicts in Asia: influences of drug availability and sampling method. Drug Alcohol Depend 6:131–136, 1980

Westermeyer J: Opium availability and prevalence of addiction in Asia. Br J Addict 76:85–90, 1981

Westermeyer J: Betel-nut chewing. JAMA 148:1831–1832, 1982

Westermeyer J: Poppies, Pipes and People: Opium and Its Use in Laos. Berkeley, University of California Press, 1983

Westermeyer J: Nontreatment factors affecting treatment outcome in substance abuse. American Journal of Drug and Alcohol Abuse 15:383–399, 1989

Westermeyer J, Brantner J: Violent death and alcohol use among the Chippewa of Minnesota. Minn Med 55:749–752, 1972

Westermeyer J, Peake E: A ten-year follow-up of alcoholic Native Americans in Minnesota. Am J Psychiatry 140:189–194, 1983

Westermeyer J, Phaobtong T, Neider J: Substance use and abuse among mentally retarded persons. American Journal of Drug and Alcohol Abuse 14:109–123, 1988

Chapter 13

Cultural Comments on Substance-Related Disorders

Victor R. *Adebimpe*, M.D.

estermeyer's recommendations (Chapter 12) are a distillation of his long experience in grappling with the practical consequences of these issues. Much of the strength of his chapter lies in its documentation of those aspects of substance-related disorder (SRD) that remain constant across cultural boundaries (i.e., biological markers to detect abuse or dependence), in contrast to those that vary with ethnicity and socioeconomic status.

Among the latter, the last section of this chapter addresses the new culture of managed care and its impact on psychiatric diagnosis in the 1990s. It is becoming customary to list one diagnosis as primary and another as secondary for reimbursement reasons, when clinical considerations alone might have reversed the order. This maneuver is often necessary to secure more days for inpatient treatment. Furthermore, the chances of a low-socioeconomic-class SRD patient getting appropriate treatment sometimes depends on a contrived presentation by the patient or a slanted portrayal by the referring physician. In other words, the culture of managed care has introduced an era in which expedient diagnostic formulations may become the norm.

A field trial of the Composite International Diagnostic Interview illustrated other culturally relevant issues—namely, the cross-cultural acceptability and reliability of substance abuse items in a diagnostic questionnaire and the ease with which related concepts can be translated, without substantial loss of meaning, into different languages (Cottler et al. 1991).

Accurate translation of concepts is likely to remain an interesting research challenge, but the finding of high acceptance and excellent reliability for the questions is a major landmark in cross-cultural communication about these disorders.

Reference

Cottler LS, Robins LN, Grant BF, et al: The CIDI-Core Substance Abuse and Dependence Questions: cross-cultural and nosological issues. Br J Psychiatry 159:653–658, 1991

Chapter 14

International Comments on Substance-Related Disorders

Enrique Madrigal, M.D.

The International Perspective

A particular challenge for those involved in diagnosis and classification of substance-related disorders is the complex interaction between culturally specific deep-rooted attitudes and beliefs and the upsurge of clinical criteria derived from technical insight on an international perspective. In general, the issue of substance consumption is linked to idiosyncratic practices ranging from overt sanction to actual proscription or stigmatization of these behaviors.

Culturally determined practices or behaviors and the development of diagnostic criteria pose a serious burden for experts, who have been grappling with conceptual and transcultural issues to comply with a demanding multidisciplinary scientific community.

The diversity stemming from such complex biological, behavioral, and ecological factors has called for multiple international advisory collaborative efforts on definitions and the development of diagnostic criteria. The World Health Organization first attempted to define alcoholism in 1951 (World Health Organization 1951), when the dependence formulation was promulgated. More recently, World Health Organization updated its definitions of psychoactive substance use disorders in preparation for the 10th International Classification of Diseases (ICD-10) (World Health Organization 1991). A joint Alcohol, Drug Abuse and Mental Health Administration (ADAMHA)/World Health Organization project made it possible to maintain a parallel course for ICD-10 and DSM-IV (American Psychiatric Association 1994). At the same time, the Composite International Diagnostic Interview (CIDI) (World Health Organization Division of Mental Health 1990), based on ICD-10, DSM-III-R (American Psychiatric Association 1987), and Present State Examination (PSE) criteria, has been field tested in several World Health Organization collaborating centers.

An international consensus has largely been achieved to limit diagnostic categories to the utilization of substances for the purpose of altering mood or behavior. DSM-IV adopted the term *Substance-Related Disorders* to include medication side effects as well as unintentional exposure to substances that affect the central nervous system and may lead to behavioral or cognitive disturbances (e.g., poisons, toxins, industrial solvents).

Both ICD-10 and DSM-IV establish criteria for clinical assessment of certain pathological patterns of use. One main dissenting feature is the distribution of substance-induced disorders (e.g., Substance-Induced Mood Disorder) in the sections for those disorders with which they share phenomenology. ICD-10 would place these categories in the reformulated psychoactive substance abuse disorders section, along with dependence, abuse, intoxication, and withdrawal syndromes.

Obviously, phenomenology must not be considered independently from cultural biases, which is the reason for Westermeyer's (Chapter 12) reflections on potential difficulties that may be encountered by practitioners from different cultures, who are inevitably influenced by attitudes and mores.

The same is true for relevant criteria to ascertain widely accepted categories, such as harmful drinking, which may be disguised in widely accepted consumption practices. An effort should be made to offer the clinician alternatives for diagnosing patients who are not exposed to driving or who have culturally specific norms about discipline at work and others who may be self-employed; such alternatives should help the clinician assess equivalent risks in relation to specific patterns of consumption.

As has been the case with previous diagnostic classifications, there will be some criticisms about lack of comparability, or even incompatibility, with well-established practices of assessment based on rigid parochial criteria. Nevertheless, these instruments are translated into multiple languages both for demand and for normative reasons stemming from resolutions by the World Health Assembly and are endorsed by local health authorities.

One important issue involves seeking convergence between, on the one hand, the relatively frequent utilization of duly validated diagnostic instruments such as the CAGE (Ewin and Rouse 1970), the Michigan Assessment Screening Test (Selzer 1971), and the Addiction Severity Index (McLellan et al. 1980), and on the other, the widely used diagnostic instruments developed by the World Health Organization and the American Psychiatric Association.

A more complicated task that can be envisioned is the matching of lifestyles, social adjustment, and consequences of irrational use and abuse of psychoactive substances to strict Axis I and II criteria. For this purpose, because the diagnosis is currently related more to behavioral indicators than to neuroadaptive phenomena, it may be convenient to establish multiaxial social scales, which will be more helpful tools for diagnosis and for ascertaining severity and prognosis. This initiative may prove more beneficial for the development of treatment plans and longitudinal or follow-up assessments as well.

References

American Psychiatric Association: Diagnostic and Statistical Manual of Mental Disorders, 3rd Edition, Revised. Washington, DC, American Psychiatric Association, 1987

American Psychiatric Association: Diagnostic and Statistical Manual of Mental Disorders, 4th Edition. Washington, DC, American Psychiatric Association, 1994

Ewin J, Rouse B: Identifying the hidden alcoholic. Paper presented at the XXIX International Congress on Alcohol and Drug Dependence, Sydney, New South Wales, Australia, 1970

McLellan AT, Luborsky L, Woody GE, et al: An improved diagnostic instrument for substance abuse patients: the Addiction Severity Index. J Nerv Ment Dis 168:26–33, 1980

Selzer ML: The Michigan Alcoholism Screening Test: the quest for a new diagnostic instrument. Am J Psychiatry 127:89–91, 1971

World Health Organization: Technical report series, No. 42. Geneva, Switzerland, World Health Organization, 1951

World Health Organization Division of Mental Health: Composite International Diagnostic Interview (CIDI). Geneva, Switzerland, World Health Organization, 1990

World Health Organization: International Classification of Diseases, 10th Revision. Geneva, Switzerland, World Health Organization, 1991

Section IV

Mood and Anxiety Disorders

Chapter 15

Culture and DSM-IV: Implications for the Diagnosis of Mood and Anxiety Disorders

Spero M. *Manson, Ph*.D.

DSM-III (American Psychiatric Association 1980) and DSM-III-R (American Psychiatric Association 1987) represented a remarkable departure from their predecessors. These editions attempted to be theoretically neutral, emphasized a descriptive approach to symptomatology, and used a multiaxial perspective on the assessment process. They also embraced a polythetic view of classification. Not all criteria for a given disorder were required to meet diagnosis, nor were the disorders themselves conceptualized as discrete entities, without overlap and mutually exclusive of one another. However, the authors of these editions introduced to the DSM, especially through the casebook, a set of prototypic categories that, in practice, have become a standard or guide for subsequent clinical evaluation. Application of the diagnostic criteria, in turn, tended to further reify these categories as concrete, independent phenomena, despite repeated cautions to the contrary. The same feature is found in DSM-IV (American Psychiatric Association 1994). The consequences of this practice were enormous for work at the interface of cultural boundaries, and continue to be felt in the newest edition of the DSM.

A truly comprehensive overview of the existing literature on culture-specific features of mood and anxiety disorders, with special emphasis on possible biases in and potential misapplication of relevant diagnostic criteria, is beyond the limits of this chapter. Moreover, such overviews, faced with remarkable variability in the observations reported by this literature, frequently retreat to cataloging the rich diversity of experience in ways that support the author's original perspective on some variation

The preparation of this manuscript was supported in part by National Institute of Mental Health Grants MH42473-05 and MH00833-01.

of a constantly recurring question, namely, "Is the disorder of interest universally common to all human beings, or is it specific to the culture of a particular group?" The arguments that follow often move quickly to absolutist or relativist positions that avoid the toughest challenge: the valid comparison of experiences, which includes ascertaining the meaning that each experience holds for the people in question and determining the degree of equivalence of experiences (see Chapters 1 and 2 for more detailed discussions).

The immediate task for this chapter may be defined much more narrowly. Specifically, can the salient features of mood and anxiety disorders, as defined by the DSM nosological system, be discerned in other cultural populations? Do these features combine in the manner required by DSM formulation? Are the implications of meeting diagnostic criteria in these populations the same as those assumed for DSM? Answers to these questions indicate the extent to which a particular diagnostic system can be extended to different cultural populations. They will not provide definitive answers to questions of universality or relativity. Such answers must await not only careful, reciprocating comparison of these phenomena across cultures but the development of biological markers of relevant disease processes that presumably can serve as invariant points of reference.

Taking up the task outlined above, this chapter examines mood and anxiety disorders within a cross-cultural context. It focuses on the operational characteristics of the major diagnostic criteria that 1) encompass specific symptoms and assign greater importance to some than others, 2) reflect different dimensions or clusters of cognitive, affective, behavioral, and somatic experiences, 3) assume critical thresholds by requiring certain minimums in both the number and duration of symptomatology, and 4) define relationships between disorders, particularly in terms of relative priority for subsequent diagnosis. The discussion draws selectively from the available literature to illustrate the manner and extent to which these criteria may be extended to other cultural populations.

The Separation of Mind and Body

The most salient feature of mood disorders is a distinction between psyche and soma that reflects a long Western intellectual history of mind-body dualism. This distinction is particularly evident in the formulation of major and minor depressive episodes, as well as dysthymia, that revolve around particular affects (i.e., dysphoria, represented by depressed mood or loss of interest or pleasure) and associated somatic symptoms, notably appetite and weight change, sleep disturbances, psychomotor agitation or retardation, fatigue, difficulty concentrating, recurrent thoughts of death, motor tension, and autonomic hyperactivity. Somatic symptoms, like many physical experiences, are relatively easy to ascertain across cultures, although their elicitation poses a special set of problems to which we will return in a few moments. The greatest difficulty lies in determining the presence of dysphoria, as defined by Western experience, largely because of the attendant assumptions about emotion and its phenomenology.

Herein arises one of the first junctures for potential polarization in discussions about the cross-cultural applicability of the DSM. To the extent that emotions appear to be shared or common experiences of people from diverse cultural groups, many assume that this similarity is a function of universal, innate human propensities (Ekman 1982; Izard 1977; Wierzbicka 1986). Others argue that they are essentially cultural artifacts (C. Geertz 1973; Rosaldo 1984).

Sidestepping this debate, I find it plausible that culture at least organizes the stimulus, manifestation, and interpretation of emotions such as dysphoria (Myers 1979). This conclusion follows from the rapidly growing body of evidence as to cultural variation in the phenomenology of these experiences (C. Geertz 1980; B. J. Good and Good 1982; B. J. Good and Kleinman 1985; Kinzie et al. 1982; Lutz 1985, 1988; Manson et al. 1985; Marsella et al. 1985; Myers 1979; Rosaldo 1983, 1984; Shweder and LeVine 1984). As Jenkins et al. (1990) have pointed out, key elements to understanding this variation involve definitions of selfhood, indigenous categories of emotion, and emphases on particular aspects of emotional life: patterning of relationships among emotions, precipitating social situations, and ethnophysiological accounts of bodily experiences of emotions.

Definitions of Self and Loci of Emotion

Definitions of the self vary along a continuum between egocentric and sociocentric (Shweder and Bourne 1984). The former, best exemplified in Western, industrialized populations, characterize the person as unique, separate, and autonomous. The latter, found in many non-Western cultural traditions, depict the person in relational terms, as part of an interdependent collective, defined by kinship and myth (C. Geertz 1984). In the United States such differences are thought to distinguish Hispanics (Murillo 1976), Native Americans and Alaska Natives (Trimble et al. 1984), and Asian Americans (Kleinman and Lin 1981; Tseng and Hsu 1969) from white, middle-class Americans. It should not be surprising, then, that the location and experience of emotions vary along similar lines (Lutz 1985, 1988; Toussignant 1984). In other words, they are not necessarily just intrapsychic phenomena. Hence, clinicians who use diagnostic criteria that depend on eliciting individualistically oriented, contextless self-statements of dysphoria (e.g., "*I* feel blue," "These things no longer mean anything to *me*") or worry (e.g., "*I* am bothered by things that usually do not bother *me*," "*I* fear things that *I* do not normally fear") may overlook other ways of feeling and expressing the same affect.

Variation in the Language of Affect

Numerous studies underscore the rich and varied lexicons of emotion in non-Western cultures (H. Geertz 1959; B. J. Good 1977; B. J Good and Good 1982; B. J. Good et al. 1985; Guarnaccia et al. 1990; Kinzie et al. 1982; Lutz 1985, 1988; Marsella and White 1982; White and Kirkpatrick 1985). Establishing the semantic equivalence of the terms by which people from different cultures refer to the same affect typically is approached through a translation/backtranslation process. One bilingual speaker of languages A and B answers the question, "What is the word or phrase for '_____' in language B?" Presented with that answer, another bilingual speaker of the same two languages is asked, "What is the word or phrase for '_____' in language A?" The results are seldom unequivocal, reflecting the indeterminacy of meaning that typifies human language (B. J. Good and Good 1986; Robins 1989). For example, guilt, shame, and sinfulness, which often are closely linked in Western experience—and, indeed, make up a single question on the Diagnostic Interview Schedule intended to assess feelings of worthlessness—can be translated into Hopi but are conceptualized quite differently and evoke attributions that are distinct from one another as well as from those implied by their English counterparts within the Judeo-Christian framework (Manson et al. 1985). In yet another example, Chinese offers a wealth of terms that convey sadness and despair. One, *you-yu* (Cihai 1957), closely approximates the affective aspect of depression. It describes a prevailing sadness, despair, and listlessness combined with a tendency toward crying, much like the statement, "I feel downhearted and blue." However, as Chang has pointed out, this mood is treated and reported quite differently by the Chinese than by their Western counterparts.

Furthermore, the word *depressed* is absent from the languages of some cultures (Marsella 1980), including certain Native Americans and Alaska Natives (Manson et al. 1985; Terminsen and Ryan 1970) and Southeast Asian refugee groups (Kinzie et al. 1982). However, this absence does not, in and of itself, preclude the existence of related affect, or even of analogous categories of illness. Manson et al. (1987) demonstrated that the DSM-III formulation of major depressive disorder does not correspond directly to any of the categories of illness indigenous to the Hopi. Instead, symptoms of the former distribute differentially across the latter, which are characterized by distinct etiologies and treatments. This particular example depicts the problem of category validity described by B. J. Good and Good (1986).

Selective Elaboration of Emotional Experience

Such variation in the phenomenology as well as the language of emotion suggests that cultures selectively emphasize and elaborate these experiential domains. Drawing from the ethnographic literature on anger, Jenkins et al. (1990) illustrated the dramatic degree to which different cultures may contrast with one another in this regard. Whereas Eskimos (Briggs 1970) and Tahitians (Levy 1973) seldom display anger, the Kaluli of New Guinea (Schieffelin 1983, 1985) and the Yanamamo of Brazil (Chagnon 1977) use elaborate and complex means of expressing anger. Likewise, other cultures encourage (e.g., Iranians [B. J. Good and Good 1982; B. J. Good et al. 1985]) or discourage (e.g., Navajos [Miller and Schoenfeld 1971; Witherspoon 1977]) displays of extreme sadness and sorrow.

Within-group differences also are evident along these lines, most notably in terms of social class and gender, especially for dysphoria. This appears to be true among mainstream Americans (Hirschfeld and Cross 1982; Weissman and Klerman 1981) as well as ethnic minorities (Ackerson et al. 1990; Baron et al. 1990; Canino et al.

1987; Manson et al. 1990; Mendes de Leon 1988; Vega et al. 1984, 1986; Zavalla 1984). Similar dynamics have been observed around the world, for example, in Ghana (Field 1960), Kenya (Abbott and Klein 1979; Mitchell and Abbott 1987; Ndetei and Vadher 1982), Uganda (Orley and Wing 1979), and India (Ullrich 1987, 1988).

Culture not only may place differential emphasis on particular emotions but also can assign unique attributions as well as expression to the intensity of an experience. Vietnamese refugees, for instance, distinguish states of sadness by the degree, duration, and frequency of their feelings (Kinzie et al. 1982). Culture also shapes the general tone of emotional life to which a person should aspire, ranging from the tumultuous involvement of the Yanamamo (Chagnon 1977) to the serenity of the Javanese (C. Geertz 1973).

Thus, distinguishing among mood, symptom, and disorder, which are presumed to vary along a continuum, is not as simple as it might seem (B. J. Good and Kleinman 1985). Although there is no empirical evidence to this effect, current diagnostic operations assume that such experiences are unidimensional, linear, and additive in nature, not unlike a ruler. The cross-cultural literature suggests that the "markers" on the ruler may vary from one group to another, akin to the difference between metric and nonmetric systems of measurement. Not only may the scale of measurement differ in terms of minimal units (e.g., millimeter versus $^1/_{32}$ inch, but the significant categories of aggregation may not correspond as well [e.g., centimeter and meter versus inch, foot, and yard]. Assessing the degree to which subjective conditions such as dysphoria and anxiety are present in cross-cultural settings, then, is not straightforward, as elegantly demonstrated by McNabb (1990) in his article on determining the accuracy and meaning of self-reported "satisfaction" among Eskimos and by Iwata et al. (1989) in their report on the Japanese use of Center for Epidemiologic Studies Depression Scale (CES-D) scalar values.

Let us assume that ways are developed to translate from one "ruler" to another—by no means an easy task, even in the simplest form of the problem. This accomplishment does not take into account the normative uncertainty of psychiatric ratings (Chance 1963; B. J. Good and Good 1986; Guarnaccia et al. 1990; Jenkins 1988; Manson et al. 1985; Murphy and Hughes 1965; Robins 1989). Specifically, the literature indicates that the threshold at which "normal" is demarcated from "abnormal" may vary by gender and cultural group. For example, the persistently higher prevalence of depressive symptoms reported among females than males and among Puerto Ricans than white, middle-class Americans (Guarnaccia et al. 1990) may represent culturally patterned variations in the experiential levels of these phenomena and not necessarily higher rates of disorder. Consequently, such normative differences imply different "cutoff points" for distinguishing common, unremarkable episodes of mood from those that are unusual and noteworthy. Returning to the ruler analogy, if such cutoff points were solely a function of intensity or severity, then female and Yanamamo thresholds between normal and abnormal dysphoria, for example, might fall much further along (or "out" or "up," depending on its orientation) the ruler than male and Javanese thresholds. Current DSM debate over the number of symptoms required to meet Criterion C (persistent avoidance or psychic numbing) for posttraumatic stress disorder reflects an analogous struggle to establish a viable cutoff point.

The DSM, however, uses more than just intensity or severity in rendering such judgments. Duration often figures into the diagnostic calculus (e.g., 2 weeks of persistent dysphoria to meet the criterion for major depressive episode or 1 month to meet that for posttraumatic stress disorder). Nevertheless, the same logic applies. For example, among the Hopi, sadness is so common and widespread that periods of 1 month or more may be required to reach a level of significance for the individual and fellow community members that is equivalent to that presupposed by DSM (Manson et al. 1985). Even then, it appears as if duration is but a "proxy" measure of functional impairment: the sadness or worry experienced by a Hopi person becomes a concern when she or he begins to fail to meet deeply ingrained social expectations.

DSM-IV (American Psychiatric Association 1994) recapitulates a similar issue in its attempt to resolve earlier distinctions between major depressive syndrome and major depressive episode as well as between major depression and dysthymia. This may explain, at least in part, why other criteria (i.e., Feighner criteria and research diagnostic criteria) have been discarded only slowly. The very same definitional quandary emerges and multiplies in complexity as one moves across different cultures.

Dimensions of Depression and Anxiety

Further insight into the gender as well as cultural patterning of affect—in this case, symptoms of depression and mania—can be obtained from studies involving the CES-D. The CES-D is a composite measure that includes items from previously established scales and was developed by researchers at the National Institute of Mental Health for use in epidemiological studies of depressive symptomatology (Radloff 1977). The 20-item scale assesses the occurrence and persistence of the following symptoms in the preceding week: depressed mood, feelings of guilt and worthlessness, psychomotor retardation, loss of appetite, and sleep disturbance. The scale has been shown to be psychometrically sound in terms of its reliability across diverse populations: adults (Radloff 1977; Zich et al. 1990), adolescents (Roberts et al. 1990), and racial/ethnic groups (Radloff 1977; Roberts 1980; Ying 1988). Radloff (1977) described factor analyses by gender and ethnicity (white vs. black) that yielded a consistent dimensional structure comprising four factors that she labeled *depressed affect, somatic complaints, positive affect,* and *interpersonal*. Other researchers subsequently have reported important differences in the factor structures across gender and ethnic groups.

Four studies have examined the CES-D factor structure across gender. Clark et al. (1981) performed principal-components factor analysis with varimax rotation on data provided by a sample of mixed ethnicity. The authors reported a factor structure generally consistent with Radloff's when the full sample was included. However, when factor analyses were performed by gender, the factor structure for females was quite different: with the Kaiser criterion, only three factors were indicated in which the items on Radloff's Depressed Affect dimension were split among the other three factors. Guarnaccia et al. (1989) and Garcia and Marks (1989) examined factor structures across gender within Hispanic Health and Nutrition Epidemiological Study (HHANES) samples, and both reported gender differences. Roberts et al. (1990) used confirmatory factor analytic methods to examine differences in an adolescent sample. Although the Radloff model fit the data adequately for the overall sample, analyses across gender indicated that an assumption of factorial invariance was not warranted.

The possibility of different factor structures across ethnic groups has been considered among Chinese Americans and Hispanics. Both Kuo (1984) and Ying (1988) conducted principal-components analyses of CES-D data from samples of Chinese Americans. Using the Kaiser criterion, they reported finding three factors in which Radloff's depressed affect and somatic complaints factors were combined.

The majority of the work in this area has examined the performance of the CES-D among Mexican American subsamples. Although Roberts (1980) reported finding no differences between Mexican American and white samples, others, using exploratory methods, found that the somatic complaints and depressed affect factors formed a single factor (Garcia and Marks 1989; Guarnaccia et al. 1989). In another study, Golding and Aneshensel (1989), using Los Angeles Epidemiologic Catchment Area (ECA) data, first performed a maximum likelihood exploratory factor analysis with the complete sample and found that the four-factor solution closely corresponded to Radloff's and encompassed all 20 items of the CES-D. They then conducted a confirmatory factor analysis across non-Hispanic whites, United States-born Mexican Americans, and Mexican-born Mexican Americans. Their results failed to support an assumption of factorial invariance.

Three studies have examined the performance of the CES-D among Native American samples. Manson et al. (1990) performed factor analyses on data collected from Native American adolescents attending a boarding school. They obtained a three-factor solution with a strong "general" factor that included items from Radloff's depressed affect, somatic complaints, and interpersonal factors. The remaining two factors encompassed additional items from the somatic complaints factor, as well as a distinct positive affect factor. In a study of older chronically physically ill Native Americans, Baron et al. (1990) reported obtaining a four-factor solution, again with a strong general factor that included both depressed affect and somatic complaints. The remaining three factors were not well defined. Beals et al. (1991) examined the viability of the model tested by Golding and Aneshensel (1989) in which all 20 CES-D items were proposed to load on one of four factors. This model is essentially equivalent to the Radloff one if the criteria are relaxed to include each item as an indicator of the factor on which it had the highest loading. Three alternative models were tested for the full sample: the original four-factor model, a three-factor model in which the somatic complaints and depressed affect factors were collapsed, and a single-factor model. The three-factor model was based on the studies of ethnic minority samples described earlier and on a fact that the literature on Native American supports: specifically, that depressed affect and somatic complaints are not as differentiated in these populations as in others. The justification for the single-factor model stemmed from the frequent use of the overall CES-D score rather than the subscales. The fit of these models also was tested across gender to determine whether the factor structure can be assumed to be equivalent. The correlations between the four factors proved to be moderate (.44 to .64), with one exception: the correlation between the depressed affect and somatic complaints factors was .90. Although the four-factor and three-factor models provided comparable fits to the data, it was apparent that the depressed affect and somatic complaints factors correlated so highly that for the purpose of application they should be considered indistinguishable. The three-factor model, therefore, was deemed the most appropriate for these data.

A number of studies have shown that the factor structures for other, similar self-report measures of symptoms of depression and anxiety (Brief Symptom Index, Zung Self-Rating Depression Scale, Beck Depression Inventory) also vary significantly by cultural populations (B. J. Good et al. 1985; Marsella et al. 1973; Tashakkori et al. 1989), although the evidence for the convergence of depressed affect and somatic complaints is not as strong as that which has emerged in the context of the CES-D.

The high correlation between depressed affect and somatic complaints is relevant to the ongoing debate about the somatization of depressed mood (Lipowski 1990), especially in regard to the role of sociocultural factors, and returns us to the discussion about epidemiological differences in the relationship of mind and body. One view holds that non-Western populations are predisposed to report depressive affect in somatic rather than psychological terms. Explanations include communicational style and socialization (Katon et al. 1982). A popular extension of this view is that non-Western populations do not differentiate somatic from affective complaints. However, as noted earlier, many non-Western populations clearly possess elaborate lexicons in regard to emotional states. The levels at which the respondents in the studies cited earlier endorsed the items subsumed under depressed affect confirm their salience for these populations. However, the degree of association between the depressed affect and somatic complaints factors suggests significant overlap that may be either conceptual or artifactual in nature. This issue deserves close attention, especially to determine how the diagnostic criteria for a disorder such as major depression—which emphasizes affective problems over concomitant somatic complaints—can be applied in the absence of similar distinctions and/or priorities (Eysenck et al. 1983).

Differences in Narrative Context

The expression of emotion also varies by the cultural contexts in which such experiences are discussed. Individuals selectively report the elements they believe to be situationally relevant (Beiser 1985; Cheung 1982; Kinzie and Manson 1983; Tseng and Hsu 1969; Wu 1982). Disclosures of physical and psychological states differ in form as well as content between patient and physician, husband and wife, parent and child, men and women (M. J. Good and Good 1988; Jenkins 1988; Kleinman 1986). This dynamic is a specific corollary of the more general observation that cultural systems provide guidelines for matching behavior to social events and circumstances (Cole et al. 1971; Labov 1970; LeVine 1970). Subsequent differences in display rules for emotion in non-Western cultures may frustrate the elicitation of relevant criteria and assignment of diagnosis.

Ethnophysiology of Somatic Experience

Finally, diagnoses of mood and anxiety disorders also hinge on the presence of somatic complaints: rapid, unintended weight loss or gain; significant changes in appetite; marked disturbances of sleep patterns; fatigue; exaggerated startle responses; motor tension; or autonomic hyperactivity. Although more easily observed and ascertained than affective states, such physical experiences are likewise mediated by social and cultural convention. The medical literature recognized early that the manner of describing pain, even potential sites for its occurrence in the body, may vary from one population to another (Kleinman 1986). In cross-cultural settings, it is not unreasonable to inquire about the somatic complaints detailed by DSM. Indeed, the endorsement of these symptoms by the patient should encourage more aggressive investigation of the possible presence of the disorder of interest. At this point, the diagnostic endeavor must broaden to include the discovery and elimination of alternative causes of the complaints in question (e.g., infectious disease, malnutrition, parasites, and other organic conditions that may be common to the local ecology).

The absence of these symptoms, however, is not as informative. Somatic distress can be expressed in diverse ways not anticipated by DSM. Consider, for example, Ebigbo's (1982) observation of such complaints as "heat in the head," "crawling sensation of worms and ants," "heaviness sensation in the head," and "biting sensation all over the body" among Nigerian patients, or Jenkins's (1988) description of *nervios* among Mexican Americans, which includes "brainache," or the sensation that the brain is "exploding" or "uncontrollable." These and other indigenous means of describing bodily experiences may represent the physiological equivalent of the somatic symptom specified by DSM, which would not have been elicited on direct inquiry. They also may represent different bodily experiences that either co-occur with or denote the criterion affect (e.g., dysphoria or excessive worry) and thus are as clinically meaningful as those designated in DSM.

This growing body of evidence in regard to cross-cultural variation in the identification, elicitation, and meaning of the diagnostic criteria for the mood and anxiety disorders poses a major challenge for present day psychiatry. Maser et al. (1991) surveyed 146 mental health professionals, primarily psychiatrists and psychologists, from 42 countries, excluding the United States, as to international uses of and attitudes toward DSM-III and DSM-III-R. Their study revealed that mood disorders, often in conjunction with anxiety and other disorders, were perceived to be problematic and in need of revision by nearly one-fourth of the respondents. Although it was not possible to determine the genesis of these perceptions, Maser et al. concluded by emphasizing the cross-cultural deficiencies of DSM and the need to reflect this broader range of experience in the nosology and diagnostic formulation.

There are no easy means available by which to accomplish this goal. Much more will be required than tinkering with the kind, number, clustering, or duration of symptoms. The focus must be on the process of inquiry, the way in which a clinician elicits the respondent's story of his or her illness (Kleinman 1988). This process should continue to emphasize the careful clinical description that led to the development of DSM-III and DSM-IV; however, in this case, that tradition must be extended beyond the middle and upper classes of American and European society to the remaining, non-Western world that constitutes the vast majority of humankind. A better understanding of the phenomenology of mood and anxiety disorders across these settings will have to encompass much more than simply the symptoms expressed by a patient. It must take into account the social contexts and cultural forces that shape one's everyday world and give meaning to interpersonal relationships and life events. One very important step in this direction will be to render as explicit as possible the decision-making processes—including assumptions and empirical evidence—that underpin the next revision of the DSM.

Maser et al. (1991) speculated that DSM may never reach the point of a fifth edition and soon will be supplanted by the International Classification of Diseases (ICD) (World Health Organization 1991). The latter, however, is no more embracing of cultural variation than the former, undoubtedly a consequence of their shared intellectual legacy. This need not come to pass—indeed, probably will not if the DSM further distinguishes itself by addressing the next frontier in psychiatric nosology: cultural variation. DSM-IV opens the door to this subject, but much of the relevant materials have yet to be included. This would be objective with high priority for the future.

References

Abbott S, Klein R: Depression and anxiety among rural Kikuyu in Kenya. Ethos 7:161–188, 1979

Ackerson LM, Dick RW, Manson SM, Baron AE: Depression among American Indian adolescents: psychometric characteristics of the Inventory to Diagnose Depression. J Am Acad Child Adolesc Psychiatry 29:601–607, 1990

American Psychiatric Association: Diagnostic and Statistical Manual of Mental Disorders, 3rd Edition. Washington, DC, American Psychiatric Association, 1980

American Psychiatric Association: Diagnostic and Statistical Manual of Mental Disorders, 3rd Edition, Revised. Washington, DC, American Psychiatric Association, 1987

American Psychiatric Association: Diagnostic and Statistical Manual of Mental Disorders, 4th Edition. Washington, DC, American Psychiatric Association, 1994

Baron AE, Manson SM, Ackerson LM, Brenneman DL: Depressive symptomatology in older American Indians with chronic disease: some psychometric considerations, in Screening for Depression in Primary Care. Edited by Attkisson C, Zich J. New York, Routledge & Kegan Paul, 1990

Beals J, Manson SM, Keane KM, et al: The factorial structure of the Center for Epidemiologic Studies Depression Scale among American Indian college students. Psychological Assessment 3:623–627, 1991

Beiser M: A study of depression among traditional Africans, urban North Americans, and Southeast Asian refugees, in Culture and Depression: Studies in the Anthropology and Cross-Cultural Psychiatry of Affect and Disorder. Edited by Kleinman A, Good B. Berkeley, University of California Press, 1985

Briggs J: Never in Anger: Portrait of an Eskimo Family. Cambridge, MA, Harvard University Press, 1970

Canino GJ, Bird H, Shrout P, et al: The prevalence of specific psychiatric disorders in Puerto Rico. Arch Gen Psychiatry 38:381–389, 1987

Chagnon N: Yanomamo: The Fierce People. New York, Holt, Rinehart, & Winston, 1977

Chance N: Conceptual and methodological problems in cross-cultural health research. Am J Public Health 52:410–417, 1963

Cheung FM: Psychological symptoms among Chinese in urban Hong Kong. Soc Sci Med 16:1339–1344, 1982

Cihai: Cihai (Ocean of words and terms). Taipei, Japan, Shangwu (Commercial) Printing House, 1957

Clark VA, Aneshensel CS, Frerichs RR, et al: Analysis of effects of sex and age in response to items on the CES-D scale. Psychiatry Res 5:171–181, 1981

Cole M, et al: The Culture Context of Learning and Thinking. New York, Basic Books, 1971

Ebigbo P: Development of a culture specific (Nigeria) screening scale of somatic complaints. Cult Med Psychiatry 6:29–44, 1982

Ekman P: Emotion in the Human Face. Cambridge, England, Cambridge University Press, 1982

Eysenck HJ, Wakefield JA, Friedman AF: Diagnosis and clinical assessment: the DSM-III, Third Edition. Psychol Rev 34:167–194, 1983

Field MJ: Search for Security: An Ethnopsychiatric Study of Rural Ghana. Evanston, IL, Northwestern University Press, 1960

Garcia M, Marks G: Depressive symptomatology among Mexican-American adults: an examination of the CES-D scale. Psychiatry Res 27:137–148, 1989

Geertz C: The Interpretation of Cultures. New York, Basic Books, 1973

Geertz C: Negara: The Theater State in Nineteenth-Century Bali. Princeton, NJ, Princeton University Press, 1980

Geertz C: For the native's point of view: on the nature of anthropological understanding, in Culture Theory: Essays on Mind, Self, and Emotion. Edited by Shweder R, LeVine R. Cambridge, England, Cambridge University Press, 1984

Geertz H: The vocabulary of emotion: a study of Javanese socialization processes. Psychiatry 22:225–237, 1959

Golding JM, Aneshensel CS: Factor structure of the Center for Epidemiologic Studies Depression Scale among Mexican Americans and non-Hispanic whites. Psychological Assessment 1:163–168, 1989

Good BJ: The heart of what's the matter: The semantics of illness in Iran. Cult Med Psychiatry 1:25–38, 1977

Good BJ, Good MJ: Toward a meaning-centered analysis of popular illness: categories "fright illness" and "heart distress" in Iran, in Cultural Conceptions of Mental Health and Therapy. Edited by Marsella A, White G. Boston, MA, D Reidel, 1982

Good BJ, Good MJ: The cultural context or diagnosis and therapy: a view from medical anthropology, in Research and Practice in Minority Communities. Edited by Miranda M, Kitano K. Washington, DC, US Government Printing Office, 1986

Good BJ, Kleinman A: Epilogue: Culture and depression, in Culture and Depression: Studies in the Anthropology and Cross-Cultural Psychiatry of Affect and Disorder. Edited by Kleinman A, Good B. Berkeley, University of California Press, 1985

Good BJ, Good MJ, Moradi R: The interpretation of Iranian depressive illness and dysphoric affect, in Culture and Depression: Studies in the Anthropology and Cross-Cultural Psychiatry of Affect and Disorder. Edited by Kleinman A, Good B. Berkeley, University of California Press, 1985

Good MJ, Good BJ: Ritual, the state, and the transformation of emotional discourse in Iranian society. Cult Med Psychiatry 12:43–63, 1988

Guarnaccia PJ, Angel R, Worobey JL: The factor structure of the CES-D in the Hispanic Health and Nutrition Examination Survey: the influences of ethnicity, gender and language. Soc Sci Med 29:85–94, 1989

Guarnaccia PJ, Good BJ, Kleinman A: A critical review of epidemiological studies of Puerto Rican mental health. Am J Psychiatry 147:1449–1456, 1990

Hirschfeld RM, Cross C: Epidemiology of affective disorders: psychosocial risk factors. Arch Gen Psychiatry 39:35–46, 1982

Iwata N, Okuyama Y, Kawakami Y, et al: Prevalence of depressive symptoms in a Japanese occupational setting: a preliminary study. Am J Public Health 70:1486–1489, 1989

Izard C: Human Emotions. New York, Plenum, 1977

Jenkins JH: Conceptions of schizophrenia as a problem of nerves: a cross-cultural comparison of Mexican-Americans and Anglo-Americans. Soc Sci Med 26:1233–1244, 1988

Jenkins JH, Kleinman A, Good BJ: Cross-cultural studies of depression, in Advances in Mood Disorders. Edited by Becker J, Kleinman A. Hillsdale, NJ, Erlbaum, 1990

Katon W, Kleinman A, Rosen G: Depression and somatization, a review: part I. Am J Med 72:127–135, 1982

Kinzie JD, Manson SM: Five years of experience in the Indochinese Psychiatric Clinic: what have we learned? Journal of Operational Psychiatry 14(2):105–111, 1983

Kinzie JD, Manson SM, Do TV, et al: Development and validation of a Vietnamese-language depression rating scale. Am J Psychiatry 139:1276–1281, 1982

Kleinman A: Social Origins of Distress and Disease: Depression, Neurasthenia, and Pain in Modern China. New Haven, CT, Yale University Press, 1986

Kleinman A: The Illness Narratives. New York, Basic Books, 1988

Kleinman A, Lin TY: Normal and Abnormal Behavior in Chinese Culture. Boston, MA, D Reidel, 1981

Kuo W: Prevalence of depression among Asian Americans. J Nerv Ment Dis 172:449–457, 1984

Labov W: The logic of non-standard English, in Language and Poverty. Edited by Williams F. Chicago, IL, Markam, 1970

LeVine RA: Cross-cultural study in child psychology, in Carmichael's Manual of Child Psychology, Vol II. Edited by Mussen PH. New York, Wiley, 1970, pp 559–614

Levy R: Tahitians: Mind and Experience in the Society Islands. Chicago, IL, University of Chicago Press, 1973

Lipowski ZJ: Somatization and depression. Psychosomatics 31:13–71, 1990

Lutz C: Depression and the translation of emotional worlds, in Culture and Depression: Studies in the Anthropology and Cross-Cultural Psychiatry of Affect and Disorder. Edited by Kleinman A, Good B. Berkeley, University of California Press, 1985

Lutz C: Unnatural Emotions: Everyday Sentiments on a Micronesian Atoll and Their Challenge to Western Theory. Chicago, IL, University of Chicago Press, 1988

Manson SM, Shore JH, Bloom JD: The depressive experience in American Indian communities: a challenge for psychiatric theory and diagnosis, in Culture and Depression: Studies in the Anthropology and Cross-Cultural Psychiatry of Affect and Disorder. Edited by Kleinman A, Good B. Berkeley, University of California Press, 1985

Manson SM, Walker RD, Kivlahan DR: Psychiatric assessment and treatment of American Indians and Alaska Natives. Hosp Community Psychiatry 38:165–173, 1987

Manson SM, Ackerson LM, Dick RW, et al: Depressive symptoms among American Indian adolescents: psychometric characteristics of the Center for Epidemiologic Studies Depression Scale (CES-D). Psychological Assessment 2:231–237, 1990

Marsella AJ: Depressive experience and disorder across cultures, in Handbook of Cross-Cultural Psychology, Vol V: Psychopathology. Edited by Triandis H, Draguns J. Boston, MA, Allyn & Bacon, 1980

Marsella AJ, White GM (eds): Cultural Conceptions of Mental Health and Therapy. Boston, MA, D Reidel, 1982

Marsella AJ, Kinzie JD, Gordon P: Ethnocultural variations in the expression of depression. Journal of Cross-Cultural Psychology 4:453–458, 1973

Marsella AJ, DeVos G, Hsu F: Culture and Self: Asian and Western Perspectives. New York, Tavistock, 1985

Maser JD, Kaelber C, Weise RE: International use and attitudes toward DSM-III and DSM-III-R: growing consensus in psychiatric classification. J Abnorm Psychol 100:271–279, 1991

McNabb SL: Self-reports in cross-cultural contexts. Hum Organ 49:291–299, 1990

Mendes de Leon CF: Depressive symptoms among Mexican Americans: a three-generation study. Am J Epidemiol 127(1):150–160, 1988

Miller SI, Schoenfeld LS: Suicide attempt patterns among the Navajo Indians. Int J Soc Psychiatry 17:189–193, 1971

Mitchell S, Abbott S: Gender and symptoms of depression and anxiety among Kikuyu secondary school students in Kenya. Soc Sci Med 24:303–316, 1987

Murillo N: The Mexican-American family, in Chicanos: Social and Psychological Perspectives. St. Louis, MO, CV Mosby, 1976

Murphy JM, Hughes CC: The use of psychophysiological symptoms as indicators of disorder among Eskimos, in Approaches to Cross-Cultural Psychiatry. Edited by Murphy JM, Leighton, AH. Ithaca, NY, Cornell University Press, 1965

Myers F: Emotions and the self: a theory of personhood and political order among Pintupi aborigines. Ethos 7:343–370, 1979

Ndetei D, Vadher A: A study of some psychological factors in depressed and non-depressed subjects in a Kenyan setting. Br J Med Psychol 55(3):235–239, 1982

Orley J, Wing JK: Psychiatric disorders in two African villages. Arch Gen Psychiatry 36:513–557, 1979

Radloff LS: The CES-D scale: a self-report depression scale for research in the general population. Applied Psychological Measurement 1:385–401, 1977

Roberts RE: Reliability of the CES-D scale in different ethnic contexts. Psychiatry Res 2:125–134, 1980

Roberts RE, Andrews JA, Lewinsohn PM, et al: Assessment of depression in adolescents using the Center for Epidemiologic Studies Depression Scale. Psychological Assessment 2:122–128, 1990

Robins LN: Cross-cultural differences in psychiatric disorder. Am J Public Health 79:1479–1480, 1989

Rosaldo M: The shame of headhunters and the autonomy of self. Ethos 11:135–151, 1983

Rosaldo M: Toward an anthropology of self and feeling, in Culture Theory: Essays on Mind, Self, and Emotion. Edited by Shweder R, LeVine R. Cambridge, England, Cambridge University Press, 1984

Schieffelin EL: Anger and shame in the tropical forest: on affect as a cultural system in Papua, New Guinea. Ethos 11:181–191, 1983

Schieffelin EL: The cultural analysis of depressive affect: an example from New Guinea, in Culture and Depression: Studies in the Anthropology and Cross-Cultural Psychiatry of Affect and Disorder. Edited by Kleinman A, Good B. Berkeley, University of California Press, 1985

Shweder R, Bourne E: Does the concept of the person vary cross-culturally? in Culture Theory: Essays on Mind, Self, and Emotion. Edited by Shweder R, LeVine R. Cambridge, England, Cambridge University Press, 1984

Shweder R, LeVine R (eds): Culture Theory: Essays on Mind, Self, and Emotion. Cambridge, England, Cambridge University Press, 1984

Tashakkori A, Barefoot J, Mehryar AH: What does the Beck Depression Inventory measure in college students? Evidence from a non-Western culture. J Clin Psychol 45:595–602, 1989

Terminsen J, Ryan J: Health and disease in a British Columbian community. Can Psychiatr Assoc J 15:121–127, 1970

Toussignant M: Pena in the Ecuadorian Sierra: a psychoanthropological analysis of sadness. Cult Med Psychiatry 8:381–398, 1984

Trimble JE, Manson SM, Dinges NG, et al: American Indian concepts of mental health: reflections and directions, in Mental Health Services: The Cross-Cultural Context. Edited by Pedersen PB, Sartorius N, Marsella AJ. Beverly Hills, CA, Sage, 1984

Tseng WS, Hsu J: Chinese culture, personality formation, and mental illness. Int J Soc Psychiatry 6:5–14, 1969

Ullrich HE: A study of change and depression among Havik Brahmin women in a south Indian village. Cult Med Psychiatry 11:261–287, 1987

Ullrich HE: Widows in South India society: depression as an appropriate response to cultural factors. Sex Roles 19(3/4):169–188, 1988

Vega W, Warheit G, Buhl-Auth J, et al: The prevalence of depressive symptoms among Mexican Americans and Anglos. Am J Epidemiol 120:592–607, 1984

Vega W, Kolody B, Valle R, et al: Depressive symptoms and their correlates among immigrant Mexican women in the United States. Soc Sci Med 22:645–652, 1986

Weissman M, Klerman G: Sex differences and the epidemiology of depression, in Women and Mental Health. Edited by Howell E, Baynes M. New York, Basic Books, 1981

White GM, Kirkpatrick J: Person, Self, and Experience: Exploring Pacific Ethnopsychologies. Berkeley, University of California Press, 1985

Wierzbicka A: Human emotions: universal or culture-specific? American Anthropologist 88:584–594, 1986

Witherspoon G: Language and Art in the Navajo Universe. Ann Arbor, University of Michigan Press, 1977

World Health Organization: International Classification of Diseases, 10th Revision. Geneva, Switzerland, World Health Organization, 1991

Wu DHY: Psychotherapy and emotion in traditional Chinese medicine, in Cultural Conceptions of Mental Health and Therapy. Edited by Marsella A, White G. Boston, MA, D Reidel, 1982

Ying Y: Depressive symptomatology among Chinese-Americans as measured by the CES-D. J Clin Psychol 44:739–746, 1988

Zavalla I: Depression among women of Mexican descent. Unpublished doctoral dissertation. Department of Psychology, Amherst, University of Massachusetts, 1984

Zich J, Attkisson C, Greenfield T: Screening for depression in primary care clinics: the CES-D and the BDI. Int J Psychiatry Med 20:259–277, 1990

Chapter 16

Cultural Comments on Mood and Anxiety Disorders: I

Wen-Shing Tseng, M.D.

There has been an increased awareness among psychiatrists that cultural factors have significant impact not only on the occurrence and manifestation of psychopathology (Allen 1986; Brown et al. 1990; Foulks 1972; Golding et al. 1990; Good and Kleinman 1985; Karno et al. 1989; Lin 1983; Pfeiffer 1982; Simons and Hughes 1985; Tan 1988) but also on the process of how the disorder is perceived, conceptualized, and diagnosed (Kirmayer 1991; Tseng et al. 1986, 1992a, 1992b; Westermeyer 1985). This is particularly true regarding minor psychiatric disorders that focus primarily on the matter of emotion, mood, and psychology and are very much subject to the influence of sociocultural factors (Tseng and McDermott 1981).

Diagnosis as a "Process" of Multilevel Interactions

No single classification will perfectly fulfill the need for divergent sociocultural groups. Yet in order to discuss how to improve psychiatric classification to make it culturally more relevant and applicable, clinicians must realize that making a diagnosis is not a static operation of categorization but a process of dynamic operation that involves multilevel factors relating to the patient and the clinician. The chain of interaction of five levels that are involved in the outcome of making a diagnosis and are affected by cultural factors are as follows:

1. *Perception* of stress or problems (by the patient). On the basis of the individual's psychology, the nature of the stress, and the reality of the sociocultural environment, the stress or problems may be "perceived" and "reacted" to differently by

patients, resulting in a different form of psychopathology (Hipler and Cawte 1978; Kimura 1983).

2. *Experience* of problems or disorders (by the patient). This refers to how the symptom, problem, or disorder is internally "experienced" by the patient. The manifestation of symptoms or disorders is determined by the nature of stress, the vulnerability of the patient's personality, and the coping pattern of the patient and is also significantly influenced by the socioculturally molded pattern of reaction to stress (Kasahara 1974).

3. *Presentation* of disorder (by the patient or family). How the problem, symptom, or disorder is "presented," "communicated," or "complained about" to the clinician will be based on the patient's (or family's) orientation to the problem, meaning of sickness, nature of service system, and culturally sanctioned presentation style (Tseng 1975).

4. *Perception and understanding* of disorder (by the clinician). This is how the symptom, problem, or pathology is "perceived" and "understood" by the clinician for making a diagnosis. This involves interaction between the patient and the clinician, the style of interview, the clinician's perception of pathology, and familiarity of disorder (Tseng et al. 1982).

5. *Categorization* of disorder (by the clinician). This refers to how the disorder will be categorized by the clinician for clinical usage. This step is influenced by the professional orientation of the clinician, the classification system used by the clinician, and the purpose of making a diagnosis (Cooper et al. 1969; Tseng et al. 1992a, 1992b).

It is very important to realize that for minor disorder of anxiety or mood, the diagnosis is a "process" of interactions of the above described multilevel steps rather than a way to search for the "existence" of distinct entities of disorder (Kleinman 1988). It is desirable to comprehend how cultural factors that influence the outcome of making a diagnosis might contribute to each step of the process. By doing so, we will be able to realize the limitation of each classification on transcultural application.

Problems Existing in Current Classification Systems

There are four problems inherent in current classification systems:

1. Limited scope for the minor emotional disorders. Merely recognizing the minor emotional disorders in subgroups of mood (depression), anxiety, dissociation, and somatoform disorders does not comprehensively cover the total spectrum of emotional disorders that exist or are observed among various cultural groups.

2. Artificial differentiation and separation of mental manifestation into "psyche" and "soma." The present classification system takes the position that the (pathological) emotional reaction will occur discretely "either as somatoform or as moodform." However, there are many cultural groups that have the predominant

tendency to manifest an undifferentiated, syncretic, or combined somato-mood reaction (Chambers et al. 1986; Lin 1985; Morakinyo 1985).

3. A tendency to use arbitrarily defined categories to identify the existence of Specific disorder, leaving many "undifferentiated," "nonspecific," or "proto-type" conditions left over for the Not Otherwise Specified category. This ignores the fact that the emotional or psychological disorder can be manifested as a prototype rather than a specific form.

4. The problem with distinguishing between "non–stress-related" and "stress-related" disorders. In addition to the basic descriptive feature, stress as an etiology is considered as a supplementary way to categorize the (adjustment) disorder. However, there are problems relating to definition and identification of stress from a cultural point of view: namely, because of cultural perception and sensitivity, "stress" may not be readily identified by populations of different cultural backgrounds or may not be identified in a similar way (Aldwin and Greenberger 1987; Kinzie et al. 1984; Manson et al. 1985). Furthermore, stress may be perceived, defined, and identified with great discord between the patient and the clinician if the two have divergent cultural orientations.

Suggestions for Improvement

The following four suggestions for improvement are offered:

1. Broadening the spectrum of psychopathology to be covered by the classification system. This can be approached by considering the nature of human mind and behavior from the viewpoint of the comparative psychology of mental development, by recognizing knowledge about the spectrum of psychology and psychopathology, and by using the information about the existence of variations of mental disturbances observed in various cultural settings as well as emotional disturbances emphasized at different points in history. For example, pathological anger (Westermeyer 1973), intensive fear (Lambo 1962), or possessed state are not covered. Therefore, additional subgroups may be needed to fill in the uncovered areas in the pathology spectrum.

2. Minimizing the "specificity" concept and definition of disorders.
   a. Recognizing the existence of the disorder characterized by a "mixture" of soma and mood/anxiety symptoms prior to making a differentiation into distinct Somatoform, Mood (Depression), and Anxiety disturbances (Prince 1960; Young 1989).
   b. Recognizing the concept of mixed anxiety-depressive disorder, as there are clinical experiences and epidemiological data to support the need for such a mixed category for mood-anxiety disturbances (Breier et al. 1985; Klerman 1988; Weissman 1988).
   c. Recognizing subgroups of disorder even within the concept of somatoform disorder. Ethnic groups from Asia, as well as from other cultural areas, not only have the tendency to present somatic complaints, but also complain of different clusters of somatic symptoms (e.g., digestive, respiratory,

or muscular system) that can be recognized clinically as well as from research surveys (Tseng et al. 1990). Therefore, Somatoform Disorder may have to be differentiated further to encompass various subgroups of organ systems in the future if need is proved.

3. Minimizing arbitrary definition of disorder by restricting the duration of illness (i.e., recognizing "brief" and "chronic/prolonged" forms of disorders for various disorders, including hypochondriasis, somatization disorder, anxiety disorder, or dysthymia).

4. Minimizing the distinction between non–stress-related disorders and stress-related disorders. Recognize that a limited distinction exists between the stress-related disorder group and the non–stress-related disorder group. A more appropriate system is to dismiss the dual application of the descriptive syndromes and etiology-oriented disorder within the same Axis I: Clinical Syndrome, keeping all diagnostic criteria descriptive and distinguishing stress-related disorders by the subphrase, "associated with adjustmental stress" or by the recognition of the presence of psychosocial stress in Axis IV.

Cultural Contribution Existing in the Nature of Stress

The cultural contribution to the disorder of mood or anxiety disorder is not so much in the area of manifestation and categorization of the psychopathology but in the underlying causes or stress that led a subject to react with mood or anxiety disorders. Therefore, for clinical purposes, attention must be focused more on the examination, understanding, and description of the nature of stress.

Problems Existing in Axis IV: Severity of Psychosocial Stressors

From a cultural viewpoint and particularly regarding mood or anxiety disorders, several problems exist in an Axis IV that focus on psychosocial stressors:

1. Identification of stressor by "definition" rather than by relative, "dynamic" consideration. Stress is not considered to be the total effect of stressor, appraisal (perception), vulnerability, availability of resource (for support), and coping (for problems).

2. Only externally identifiable life events/circumstances are recognized as stressors; internal psychological stress and strains, including belief and perception, are not included.

3. Severity of stress is judged by "professional definition" rather than by the "subject's" own perception and experience. Thus, definition of severity can be culturally biased.

Suggestions for Revising Axis IV With Regard to Stress

1. Incorporating the concepts of perception (appraisal), vulnerability, utilization of resources, and coping pattern into an understanding and assessment of the stressors.

2. Expansion of the concept and scope of psychosocial stressors. Adding stressors relating to or derived from socioculturally based internal psychological conditions:
    a. Stressors derived from sociocultural belief, including supernatural concepts (Beiser et al. 1973; Rubel 1964; Tseng et al. 1992a, 1992b) (e.g., belief in sorcery, loss of soul or vitality)
    b. Conflict relating to value systems or cultural differences, such as "generational gap" and "culture shock"
    c. Problems relating to socio-ethnic-cultural identity, including culture displacement phenomena as seen in minority populations, refugees, or immigrants
3. Revising severity to be determined by the patient's individual perception or experience rather than by the clinician's definition. The degree of severity— none, mild, moderate, severe, extreme, or catastrophic—should be described subjectively by the psychological/subjective impact on the patient rather than objectively by the event/circumstance itself or defined by the clinician.

Conclusion

It is necessary for us to realize that heterogeneous and diverse psychopathology, particularly for the minor psychiatric disorders, exists in various sociocultural settings. It is also important for us to recognize that sociocultural factors have significant impact not only on the development and manifestation of disorders but also on the understanding and categorization of the disorders. Making a diagnosis is a product of a process of multilevel interaction between patient and clinician; hence categorization of disorder will result in "variations" rather than "typicality" in classification.

References

Aldwin C, Greenberger E: Cultural differences in the predictors of depression. Am J Community Psychol 15:789–813, 1987

Allen IM: Post-traumatic stress disorder among black Vietnam veterans. Hosp Community Psychiatry 37:55–61, 1986

Beiser M, Burr WA, Ravel JL, et al: Illness of the spirit among the Serer of Sengal. Am J Psychiatry 130:881–886, 1973

Breier A, Charney DS, Heninger GR: The diagnostic validity of anxiety disorders and their relationship to depressive illness. Am J Psychiatry 142:787–797, 1985

Brown D, Eaton WW, Sussman L: Racial differences in prevalence of phobic disorders. J Nerv Ment Dis 178:434–441, 1990

Chambers J, Yeragani VK, Keshavan MS: Phobias in India and the United Kingdom: a transcultural study. Acta Psychiatr Scand 74:388–391, 1986

Cooper JE, Kendal RE, Gurland BJ, et al: Cross-national study of diagnosis of the mental disorders: some results from the first comparative investigation. Am J Psychiatry 125(suppl):21–29, 1969

Foulks EF: The Arctic Hysterias of the North Alaskan Eskimo. Washington, DC, American Anthropological Association, 1972

Golding JM, Karno M, Rutter CM: Symptoms of major depression among Mexican-Americans and non-Hispanic whites. Am J Psychiatry 147:861–866, 1990

Good B, Kleinman A: Culture and anxiety: cross-cultural evidence for the patterning of anxiety disorders, in Anxiety and the Anxiety Disorders. Edited by Tuma H, Maser JD. Hillsdale, NJ, Erlbaum, 1985

Hipler A, Cawte J: The Malgri territorial anxiety syndrome: primitive pattern for agoraphobia. Journal of Operational Psychiatry 9:23–31, 1978

Karno M, Golding JM, Burnam MA, et al: Anxiety disorders among Mexican Americans and non-Hispanic whites in Los Angeles. J Nerv Ment Dis 177:202–209, 1989

Kasahara Y: Fear of eye-to-eye confrontation among neurotic patients in Japan, in Japanese Culture and Behavior. Edited by Lebra TS, Lebra PL. Honolulu, University Press of Hawaii, 1974

Kimura S: Nihonjin To Taijin-Kyofusho (Japanese and Anthrophobia). Tokyo, Japan, Keiso Shobo, 1983

Kinzie JD, Fredrickson RH, Ben R, et al: Posttraumatic stress disorder among survivors of Cambodian concentration camps. Am J Psychiatry 141:649–650, 1984

Kirmayer LJ: The place of culture in psychiatric nosology: Taijin-Kyofusho and DSM-III-R. J Nerv Ment Dis 179:19–28, 1991

Kleinman A: Rethinking Psychiatry: From Cultural Category to Personal Experience. New York, Free Press, 1988

Klerman GL: Relationship between anxiety and depression, in Handbook of Anxiety, Vol I: Biological, Clinical and Cultural Perspectives. Edited by Roth M, Noyes R Jr, Burrows GD. Amsterdam, The Netherlands, Elsevier, 1988

Lambo TA: Malignant anxiety in Africans. Journal of Mental Science 108:256–264, 1962

Lin KM: Hwa-Byung: a Korean culture-bound syndrome? Am J Psychiatry 140:105–107, 1983

Lin TY: Mental disorders and psychiatry in Chinese culture: characteristic features and major issues, in Chinese Culture and Mental Health. Edited by Tseng WS, Wu DYH. Orlando, FL, Academic Press, 1985

Manson SM, Shore JH, Blom JD: The depressive experience in American Indian communities: a challenge for psychiatric theory and diagnosis, in Culture and Depression: Studies in the Anthropology and Cross-Cultural Psychiatry of Affect and Disorder. Edited by Kleinman A, Good B. Berkeley, University of California Press, 1985

Morakinyo O: Phobic states presenting as somatic complaints syndrome in Nigeria: sociocultural factors associated with diagnosis and psychotherapy. Acta Psychiatr Scand 71:356–365, 1985

Pfeiffer WM: Culture-bound syndromes, in Culture and Psychopathology. Edited by Al-Issa. Baltimore, MD, University Park Press, 1982

Prince R: The "brain fag" syndrome in Nigerian students. Journal of Mental Science 106:559–570, 1960

Rubel AJ: The epidemiology of a folk illness: susto in Hispanic America. Ethology 3:268–283, 1964

Simons R, Hughes CC: The Culture-Bound Syndromes. Dordrecht, The Netherlands, D Reidel, 1985

Tan ES: Transcultural Aspects of Anxiety, in Handbook of Anxiety, Vol I: Biological, Clinical and Cultural Perspectives. Edited by Roth M, Noyes R Jr, Burrows GD. Amsterdam, The Netherlands, Elsevier, 1988

Tseng WS: The nature of somatic complaints among psychiatric patients: the Chinese case. Compr Psychiatry 16:237–245, 1975

Tseng WS, McDermott JF Jr: Culture, Mind and Therapy: An Introduction to Cultural Psychiatry. New York, Brunner/Mazel, 1981

Tseng WS, McDermott JF Jr, Ogino K, et al: Cross-cultural differences in parent-child assessment: USA and Japan. Int J Soc Psychiatry 28:305–317, 1982

Tseng WS, Xu D, Ebata K, et al: Diagnostic pattern for neuroses among China, Japan and America. Am J Psychiatry 143:1010–1014, 1986

Tseng WS, Asai M, Liu J, et al: Multi-cultural study of minor psychiatric disorders in Asia: symptom manifestations. Int J Soc Psychiatry 36:252–264, 1990

Tseng WS, Mo KM, Li LS, et al: Koro epidemic in Guangdong, China: a questionnaire survey. J Nerv Ment Dis 180:117–123, 1992a

Tseng WS, Asai M, Chita Nishi K, et al: Social phobia: diagnostic pattern in Tokyo and Hawaii. J Nerv Ment Dis 180:380–385, 1992b

Weissman MM: Anxiety disorders: an epidemiologic perspective, in Handbook of Anxiety, Vol I: Biological, Clinical and Cultural Perspectives. Edited by Roth M, Noyes R Jr, Burrows GD. Amsterdam, The Netherlands, Elsevier, 1988

Westermeyer J: On the epidemicity of amok violence. Arch Gen Psychiatry 28:873–876, 1973

Westermeyer J: Psychiatric diagnosis across cultural boundaries. Am J Psychiatry 142:798–805, 1985

Young D: Neurasthenia and related problems. Cult Med Psychiatry 13:131–138, 1989

Chapter 17

Cultural Comments on Mood and Anxiety Disorders: II

Byron J. Good, Ph.D.

I begin this chapter by highlighting several significant issues raised by Manson in Chapter 15. I then discuss how these issues are relevant to DSM.

First, Manson reminds us that culture plays an important role in the formation and expression of psychiatric symptoms. For a diagnostic system based not on etiology or biological markers but on symptoms, that is a claim of no small import. Much of neo-Kraepelinian psychiatry today assumes that psychiatric diseases or syndromes are constituted by a final common psychophysiological pathway, whatever their social or psychological precursors may be, and that symptoms are the expressions of these underlying physiological conditions. Because these disease constellations are human universals, so, too, we should assume, are their symptoms. Culture enters to shape the attention to and communication of disordered experience, but not at the more basic level of symptom formation. Manson takes the anthropological position that this may be true of some symptoms, but culture and psychobiology interact in a more profound way in constituting distinctive constellations of human experience. Emotions and symptoms are not simply influenced by cultural display rules; instead, cultural idioms and practices often provide a final common pathway—a psychocultural final common pathway—that yields distinctive forms of experience (Carr and Vitaliano 1985).

These issues are critical for the development of valid symptom criteria for anxiety and affective disorders for several reasons. Many culture-specific modes of experience, including those that are distinctive symptoms of psychopathology, are present in other societies or cultural groups but absent among Anglo-Americans. For example, classic research in West Africa indicates that the morbid fear that one is being bewitched or dreams that one has become a witch are closely associated with both depression and anxiety disorders but are not markers of thought disorders (Collis 1966; Field 1958; Jegede 1978; Lambo 1962; Leighton et al. 1966). Such symptoms map poorly onto any symptom (e.g., "loss of self-esteem or self-deprecation") in the

American manual. It is an experience that is not part of our vocabulary, although it may be pathognomonic in many societies. Similarly, and even more problematic, many cultures have rich somatic vocabularies that convey both somatic and affective meanings and experience (Good and Kleinman 1985). The determination of whether complaints of having an "uncomfortable heart" (described by Middle Easterners in very somatic terms) constitute a sign of depressed mood (Good 1977) or which criterion in the anxiety disorders is the equivalent of Hispanic complaints of *nervios* (see Guarnaccia et al. 1990 for a review) is thus extremely difficult. This signals problems not only for the translation or construction of self-report instruments but also for the validity of diagnostic criteria outside the cultural settings in which they were developed.

Second, Manson reminds us that culture and gender play significant roles in determining norms of expressing emotion and distress and thus in locating the boundaries between normal, abnormal, and pathological or between emotion, symptom, and illness. Years of research have failed to determine whether high rates of psychiatric symptoms among Puerto Ricans in the United States reflect modes of expression or elevated levels of pathology (Guarnaccia et al. 1990), and efforts to establish cutoff points that have validity across gender and society almost always fail. However, Manson argues that the same problem is implicit in the binary judgment of whether a particular symptom (e.g., depressed mood or loss of interest or pleasure) is present or absent.

Third, Manson reviews the literature on factor analyses of the Center for Epidemiologic Studies Depression Scale (CES-D) to demonstrate that culture influences the clustering of symptoms. In particular, the separation of somatic and affective symptoms in separate factors, which allows us to identify depressed mood and anxiety as affective states, which in turn are associated with specific somatic symptoms, is highly problematic for many non-Anglo populations. In addition, however, this observation raises serious questions about whether societies have distinctive constellations of symptoms and therefore whether some diagnostic categories not present in Anglo populations may be present or even quite prevalent in others. The popularity of neurasthenia as a professional and popular illness category in China, for example, seems to reflect not simply a theoretical commitment but the presence of an illness form in which symptoms of both major depressive disorder and generalized anxiety disorder are present and in which particular somatic symptoms are seen to be the defining characteristics rather than the presence or absence of depressed or anxious mood (Kleinman 1986, 1988; Kleinman and Good 1985; Lin 1989).

Finally, Manson reminds us that diagnostic categories may map onto popular cultural categories and professional categories in non-Western medical systems in quite varied ways. In some cases there are quite close parallels in descriptive categories across systems; in others the universe is cut up differently. Folk and popular nosological systems include both descriptive and etiological categories, as was particularly true of DSM-II (American Psychiatric Association 1968). When the so-called culture-bound disorders are discussed, it is important that etiological categories, such as susto in Mexico (often rendered in popular culture as an illness caused by some fright or emotional trauma that occurred in the past), not be expected to map onto a descriptive category from the American diagnostic system.

These observations pose a significant challenge for efforts to formulate a standard diagnostic manual in a manner that is less ethnocentric and more cognizant of cultural variation. The fact that this challenge is not merely the rhetorical gesture of the anthropologist is demonstrated by the finding of Maser et al. (1991) that international psychiatrists find special difficulties in applying the DSM-III (American Psychiatric Association 1980) sections on mood disorders and anxiety disorders. So what are we to do in a practical way if we accept Manson's claims? Because the Research Diagnostic Criteria (RDC) and DSM-IV (American Psychiatric Association 1994) grew out of American clinical experience, and because the criteria reflect both cultural assumptions and modes of expression most common in Anglo populations, should there be a separate diagnostic manual for each society? Indeed, it seems only to be expected that local clinical knowledge in China, Japan, India, or Nigeria, for example, would formulate disorders and criteria somewhat differently from the way we do, were they to follow the same inductive course taken in this country since the late 1960s. Yet how far should such a course be pursued? Should there be separate manuals for Puerto Ricans, Cubans, Salvadorans, and Mexicans? What of the second generation, the children of immigrants from these societies to ours? Here efforts to construct culture-specific diagnostic forms surely break up on the shoals of cultural essentialism and the gross stereotyping that accompanies it. What are our options? I suggest several paths that might be pursued, with specific reference to the mood and anxiety disorders.

I begin first, perhaps paradoxically, with a suggestion for the development of a case book that reflects the true social and cultural diversity of American society and the difficult diagnostic problems that grow out of that diversity. Although much of the focus of debate is on formulation of diagnostic criteria and subtypes of course and disorder, in actual practice diagnostic judgments reflect "prototypical" rather than "criterial" reasoning. The establishment of panic disorder as a distinct disorder was accomplished in large measure by the development of a convincing clinical prototype, an image of the prototypical panic disorder patient that patients in real life more or less closely resemble. Development of criteria were in a sense secondary to the development of a consensus about what the prototypical panic disorder patient "looks like." The case manual is a collection of prototypical cases. It conveys knowledge by representing certain clinical phenomena as prototypes (i.e., as cases that serve the clinician in training as the diagnostic "gold standard," given the absence of biological markers). It has, I believe, more central importance than it is usually given credit for having.

Thus, it is startling to read the current case manuals and discover how limited is the social, ethnic, and cultural diversity of the cases represented. When looking through the first *DSM-III Case Book* (Spitzer et al. 1981), I was struck by how many of the cases concerned physicians, lawyers, business executives, and graduate students. A quick count of the 87 case examples of mental disorders in adults shows that 50% of the cases concern professionals, owners of businesses, wealthy widows, or students; another 24% appear to concern the middle class (e.g., white collar workers or homemakers). Only 11% concern members of the working class, and 15% concern prisoners, unemployed individuals, or institutionalized elderly persons. Ethnicity is mentioned explicitly in very few cases: four patients are identified as having come from Europe, and the ethnicity of one individual, a schizophrenia patient, is suggested by the name "Emilio." My point is not that it would be better to have ethnicity gratuitously mentioned, or for psychopathology to be associated primarily with the poor and with minorities, but all of us know that there is a cost to representing the prototype as an upper middle-class Anglo, just as surely as there is a cost to identifying the 70-kg white male as the prototype and all others as deviations, as is typical during the early years of medical education. (Congresswoman Pat Schroeder has made it clear that when this style of thinking carries over into biomedical and pharmacological research, the result is discriminatory toward women as well as toward minorities.) One result is the construction of a view of psychopathology as suddenly erupting in the life of an otherwise healthy and secure individual, a view that reproduces the image of psychiatric disease as primarily biological while simultaneously reproducing cultural and class assumptions about the nature of the normal individual. A further result is that the extremely difficult diagnostic issues facing those who work, for example, with homeless mentally ill persons, with individuals with severe social problems and comorbid mental disorders, or with members of cultural minorities in our country, are not fully addressed. I recall asking (as part of a research protocol) a man who lived largely on the street if he ever experienced episodes of panic or terror in situations when most persons would not feel panic or terror. His response made it clear the extent to which the very question assumed that the respondent is living in a reasonably secure setting, a situation that is as foreign to many traumatized Central American refugees as to American homeless individuals. *My first recommendation is thus that a task force develop a case book that presents prototypical cases that are as diverse as the American community, and that the difficult issues of culture and diagnosis be examined in this context.*

My second point to the importance of including a substantial paragraph in each diagnostic section indicating what we know about significant cultural variation in diagnostic criteria, diagnostic thresholds, or diagnostic categories. For example: A paragraph in the Affective Disorders section should indicate that culturally distinctive somatic complaints are often essential defining criteria for depressive illness. Indeed, a criterion such as "marked increase in somatic complaints or preoccupation" may well be an appropriate criterion for major depression among Chinese Americans, for example, perhaps even in the absence of depressed mood.

A paragraph on cultural issues in diagnosis might also note variations in duration of symptoms (e.g., as noted by Manson for the Hopi) or in markers of severity. For example, expressions of hostility toward family members (rather than depressed affect) often mark the boundaries of depressive illness among, for example, Mexican Americans or Iranians. This paragraph should recognize what we have learned about differences in diagnostic categories appropriate to particular cultural groups. Guarnaccia et al. (1990) argued that *ataques de nervios* is a popular illness category in Puerto Rico, and a diagnosis of *ataques de nervios* rather than of panic or a somatoform disorder resolves a number of the ambiguities in the analysis of the Diagnostic Interview Schedule (DIS) data from Puerto Rico. Even more important, neurasthenia should be recognized as a valid diagnostic category for much of East Asia and probably for many Asian Americans. To recognize in the text of the diagnostic manual that a disorder such as neurasthenia may be valid in China but not among Anglo-Americans would suggest a major reorientation of the manual, indicating an awareness that although depressive and anxiety disorders are no doubt found universally, the particular constellation of symptoms and categories may vary across cultures. Although DSM-IV has added material on culture, by and large it is not sufficient.

It seems inevitable to *consider the development of a cultural axis as an experimental axis designed to foster and stimulate research on the relation of culture to psychiatric diagnosis.* Given that the five axes in DSM-IV (American Psychiatric Association 1994) represent dimensions along which clinicians evaluate and assess the nature and extent of psychopathology, what could a cultural axis mean? In the context of the DSM framework, a cultural axis would best be conceptualized as representing evaluation of the patient's condition from the perspective of the patient, the patient's family, or the patient's primary social group, and thus from the perspective of the patient's culture. It would thus represent what anthropologists have called the "emic" perspective or that from "the native's point of view," in the words of anthropologist Clifford Geertz (1984). Researchers and clinicians using such an axis should record 1) the culture-specific illness category, 2) the explanatory model, 3) the predominant illness idiom, 4) the primary forms of illness behavior, and 5) the perceived level of disability. For example, an Axis VI assessment might record that a juvenile Puerto Rican patient's family interprets the disorder as an ataque de nervios, that they believe it began with the patient's learning suddenly of the death of a friend, that the disorder seriously affects the patient's ability to function in public and work settings, but that the disorder is acute and likely to pass as the patient resolves his grief and matures as an adult. Such information would add significantly to a diagnostic assessment that recorded generalized anxiety disorder, dysthymic disorder, and undiagnosed seizure disorder. Perhaps more to the point, an Axis VI assessment that a major depression is interpreted by one patient and family in somatic terms (as neurasthenia, as undiagnosed medical illness) and by another patient and family in a religious idiom (e.g., as a punishment by God for sins) may turn out to have greater implications for prognosis and treatment than the diagnosis of major depression alone.

There are reasons not to succumb to the temptation to call for a cultural axis. We cannot at this time specify a single dimension or set of categories comparable to the other axes, as my examples illustrate. Indeed, culture does not have its effect in this fashion. Furthermore, such an axis might therefore be largely ignored, and it might also inappropriately stereotype members of a particular cultural, ethnic, national, or minority group. However, establishment of a cultural axis would promote systematic investigation of the nature of culture-specific evaluations of psychiatric disorders and of their effects on phenomenology, illness behavior, prognosis, and appropriate treatment. It would also lend credence to our contention that systematic elicitation of cultural data—of culturally meaningful assessments of the patient's condition—is necessary for sound diagnostic practice and should be taught systematically as part of the education of psychiatric residents. It would thus encourage clinicians to systematically review cultural aspects of patient care often neglected, and it might thus serve to promote cultural competence and to focus research on what constitutes culturally competent assessment and therapy. Thus, if developed in a careful fashion, a cultural axis might demonstrate the hazards of cultural essentialism while promoting efforts to help clinicians make psychiatric diagnoses in a more culturally sensitive and appropriate fashion.

References

American Psychiatric Association: Diagnostic and Statistical Manual of Mental Disorders, 2nd Edition. Washington, DC, American Psychiatric Association, 1968

American Psychiatric Association: Diagnostic and Statistical Manual of Mental Disorders, 3rd Edition. Washington, DC, American Psychiatric Association, 1980

American Psychiatric Association: Diagnostic and Statistical Manual of Mental Disorders, 4th Edition. Washington, DC, American Psychiatric Association, 1994

Carr J, Vitaliano P: The theoretical implications of converging research on depression and the culture-bound syndromes, in Culture and Depression. Edited by Kleinman A, Good B. Los Angeles, University of California Press, 1985

Collis RJM: Physical health and psychiatric disorder in Nigeria. Transactions of the American Philosophical Society 56:145, 1966

Field MJ: Mental disorder in rural Ghana. Journal of Mental Science 104:1043–1051, 1958

Geertz C: "From the native's point of view": on the nature of anthropological understanding, in Culture Theory: Essays on Mind, Self, and Emotion. Edited by Shweder R, LeVine R. Cambridge, England, Cambridge University Press, 1984

Good B: The heart of what's the matter: semantics and illness in Iran. Cult Med Psychiatry 1:25–58, 1977

Good B, Kleinman A: Culture and anxiety: cross-cultural evidence for the patterning of anxiety disorders, in Anxiety and the Anxiety Disorders. Edited by Tuma AH, Maser JD. Hillsdale, NJ, Erlbaum, 1985

Guarnaccia P, Good B, Kleinman A: A critical review of epidemiological studies of Puerto Rican mental health. Am J Psychiatry 147:1149–1156, 1990

Jegede RO: Outpatient psychiatry in an urban clinic in a developing country. Soc Psychiatry 13:93–98, 1978

Kleinman A: Social Origins of Distress and Disease: Depression, Neurasthenia, and Pain in Modern China. New Haven, CT, Yale University Press, 1986

Kleinman A: Rethinking Psychiatry: From Cultural Category to Personal Experience. New York, Free Press, 1988

Kleinman A, Good B (eds): Culture and Depression. Los Angeles, University of California Press, 1985

Lambo T: Malignant anxiety: a syndrome associated with criminal conduct in Africans. Journal of Mental Science 108:256–264, 1962

Leighton A, et al: Psychiatric Disorders Among the Yoruba. Ithaca, NY, Cornell University Press, 1966

Lin TY (ed): Neurasthenia revisited: its place in modern psychiatry. Cult Med Psychiatry 13:105–129, 1989

Maser J, Kaebler C, Weise RE: International use and attitudes towards DSM-III and DSM-III-R: growing consensus in psychiatric classification. J Abnorm Psychol 100:271–279, 1991

Spitzer R, Gibbon M, Skodol AE, et al: DSM-III Case Book. Washington, DC, American Psychiatric Association, 1981

Chapter 18

Nosological Comments on Culture and Mood and Anxiety Disorders

Michael Liebowitz, M.D.
Ester Salman, B.S.
Dora Cárdenas, M.D.
Carlos Jusino, M.D.
Sharon Davies, R.N.

S ome cross-cultural investigators believe that the DSM categories can be validly applied to other cultures if precautions are taken to account for response tendencies, language differences, acculturation effects, and unique symptom patterns and beliefs. Others hold that the validity of transposing DSM categories derived from a particular cultural framework to other cultures has not been established, and that the unique ways that other cultures define emotional distress or mental disorders deserve equal attention and study. As spokespersons for the latter position, Good and Kleinman (1985) have argued that we lack evidence as to whether clinical syndromes such as panic disorder or major depression as defined in DSM-III-R (American Psychiatric Association 1987) are shaped fundamentally by physiological abnormalities or by culturally grounded perceptions and experiences of sickness. A related question posed by Manson (Chapter 15) is whether the implications of meeting diagnostic criteria are the same for all cultures, as is assumed in DSM.

To answer such questions, Carey (1985) suggested that family/genetic studies and biological challenges such as lactate infusions could help distinguish illness from disease by identifying underlying physiological commonalities that may be masked by culturally diverse symptom expression. Similarly, Manson advocates careful, reciprocating comparison of psychopathological phenomena across cultures and the development of biological markers of relevant disease processes that can serve as "invariant points of reference."

To begin to implement such an approach, we decided to focus on the relationship between the "folk" diagnosis of *ataque de nervios* and panic disorder. *Ataque de nervios* is a label given in Puerto Rican and other Latin American cultures to a transient state of severe emotional upset (Guarnaccia et al. 1989b). The typical symptoms of *ataque de nervios* include "shaking, heart palpitations, a sense of heat rising in the head, and numbness of the hands." Behaviorally, the person begins to shout, swear, and strike out at others. The person then falls to the ground and either experiences convulsive body movements or lies as if dead. Such *ataques* often occur at funerals, accidents, or family conflicts and call forth family or other social supports, suggesting they are culturally shaped and sanctioned responses to severe stress. However, they can be unprovoked and recurrent and can result in a fear of going outside of one's home unaccompanied, suggesting an overlap with unexpected panic attacks, panic disorder, and agoraphobia.

Attempts to understand *ataque de nervios* have gone through several phases. The initial approach was medical and focused on extreme emotional reactions seen in Puerto Rican army recruits. Some investigators tried to fit the response with then-prevailing notions of psychopathology, such as psychotic, conversion, or dissociative reactions (Mehlman 1961). Others thought the features made up a culturally unique "Puerto Rican syndrome" (Fernandez-Marina 1959). Following this, more sociocultural views focused on factors that seemed to provoke *ataques* and made particular individuals or groups vulnerable, including the breakdown of extended family structure in Puerto Rico following mass migrations to the U.S. mainland (Rothenberg 1964). Medical anthropologists such as Guarnaccia et al. (1989a) viewed *ataques* as a form of communication, emanating in times of severe stress from individuals otherwise rendered powerless by, for example, social roles, poverty, separation from social supports, and immigrant status.

More recently epidemiological researchers have compared the prevalence of DSM diagnoses among *ataque* positive and *ataque*-negative individuals in Puerto Rican community samples (Guarnaccia et al. 1989b). Of 1,513 people interviewed with the Diagnosis Interview Schedule (DIS) (Robins et al. 1981), 348 (23%) were retrospectively judged to be *ataque* positive. Particularly elevated rates were found in the *ataque*-positive group for major depressive episodes (13% vs. 2% in the non–*ataque*-positive group), dysthymia (13% vs. 3%), agoraphobia (16% vs. 4%), phobic disorder (26% vs. 8%), and panic disorder (4% vs. 0.4%).

Several interpretations are possible: *Ataque de nervios* may be heterogeneous, with subsets representing the symptomatic expressions of different anxiety and affective disorders. Alternatively, *ataques* are distinct from anxiety/affective disorders but the two share risk factors. Having *ataque* or anxiety/affective disorder could also create a reporting bias, spuriously elevating the rates of the other condition. The community survey could also have recorded as *ataque* positive only the serious *ataque* cases that tended to have more psychiatric comorbidity.

Clinical studies with fine-grained phenomenological assessment of both *ataque* features and psychiatric diagnoses are the next logical step. These would allow clearer elucidation of the relationship of *ataque de nervios* to current DSM categories. To further clarify the relationship of *ataques* to panic disorder, *ataque*-positive individuals with and without panic disorder features could be challenged with half-molar sodium lactate or 5% carbon dioxide, both of which are rather specific panicogens in individuals vulnerable to clinical panic attacks. Family study of individuals with *ataque de nervios* would also clarify the familiality of *ataque* and its relationship to various psychiatric disorders, as long as suitable provision is made for proband comorbidity.

References

American Psychiatric Association: Diagnostic and Statistical Manual of Mental Disorders, 3rd Edition, Revised. Washington, DC, American Psychiatric Association, 1987

Carey G: Epidemiology and cross-cultural aspects of anxiety disorders: a commentary, in Anxiety and Anxiety Disorders. Edited by Tuma AH, Maser JD. Hillsdale, NJ, Erlbaum, 1985, pp 325–330

Fernandez-Marina R: The Puerto Rican syndrome: its dynamics and cultural determinants. Psychiatry 24:79–82, 1959

Good BJ, Kleinman A: Culture and anxiety: cross cultural evidence of the patterning of anxiety disorders, in Anxiety and Anxiety Disorders. Edited by Tuma AH, Maser JD. Hillsdale, NJ, Erlbaum, 1985, pp 297–323

Guarnaccia PJ, Rubio-Stipec M, Canino G: Ataques de nervios in the Puerto Rican diagnostic interview schedule: the impact of cultural categories on psychiatric epidemiology. Cult Med Psychiatry 13:275–295, 1989a

Guarnaccia PJ, DeLaCancela V, Carrillo E: The multiple meanings of ataques de nervios in the Latino community. Med Anthropol 11:47–62, 1989b

Mehlman RD: The Puerto Rican syndrome. Am J Psychiatry 118:328–332, 1961

Robins LN, Helzer JE, Croughan J, et al: National Institute of Mental Health Diagnostic Interview Schedule: its history, characteristics, and validity. Arch Gen Psychiatry 38:381–389, 1981

Rothenberg A: Puerto Rico and aggression. Am J Psychiatry 120:962–970, 1964

Section V

Somatoform and Dissociative Disorders

Chapter 19

Culture and the Diagnosis of Somatoform and Dissociative Disorders

Carlos A. González, M.D.
Ezra E. H. Griffith, M.D.

Throughout its existence, the American Psychiatric Association's DSM has received criticism from workers familiar with syndromes that are not readily classifiable by the manual (Bernstein and Gaw 1990; Karp 1985; Kleinman 1977; Yap 1967). Although there has been a clear progression since the inception of the DSM from a theoretically driven (and thus theoretically limited) approach to diagnosis to a more phenomenological view of mental illness, work remains to be done in achieving a truly global perspective. As recent a work as the DSM-III-R warned that its diagnostic categories "are not based on extensive research with non-Western populations" (American Psychiatric Association 1987, p. xxvii), thereby implying the need for a more comprehensive diagnostic system.

A. M. Kleinman (1977) has warned specifically against the "category fallacy," in which a diagnostic system that is based on categories, as the DSM is, can limit the ways of classifying syndromes, as its own classification scheme is limited by the breadth of experience of its originators. The category fallacy is evident whenever a syndrome is found that is totally unclassifiable by the diagnostic system or when a classified syndrome's essence does not seem to be captured by the diagnosis one is forced to make.

Recently, an NIMH-sponsored Work Group on Culture and Diagnosis convened and endeavored to apply a more comprehensive, less culture-dependent approach to such syndromes, considered as "exotic" or "culture bound," with the purpose of expanding and improving the DSM. The discussion that follows reflects some of the current thought regarding the diagnosis of somatoform and

137

dissociative disorders and attempts to provide a framework within which to view some of the changes that have taken place in DSM-IV.

In current psychiatric diagnostic thinking, there appears to be an essential distinction between mental disorders largely determined by biology and heredity and those that are thought to result largely from culture and upbringing. The schizophrenic and mood disorders seem to fall more in the former camp, as they are thought to be biological entities that produce typical, predictable symptoms, irrespective of culture. Even so, an individual's culture will color the expression of symptoms, whether it be the character of hallucinations and delusions in schizophrenia (Yu-Fen and Neng 1981) or the content of mood-congruent complaints in a major depressive episode.

Dissociative and somatoform syndromes are thought to lie on the other side of this dichotomy. DSM-IV names significant environmental predisposing factors for every dissociative disorder listed, and these include severe emotional childhood trauma, severe psychosocial stress, threat of physical injury or death, threats posed by unacceptable impulses or acts, and severe stress resulting from military combat or an equivalent. Similarly, the manual explicitly states that psychological or emotional conflict is associated with somatoform disorders, particularly in Conversion Disorder and Pain Disorder (American Psychiatric Association 1994).

It is therefore expected that somatoform and dissociative disorders will show a great deal of variation across cultural settings. We intend to focus on syndromes that, although often mentioned in the literature of cross-cultural psychiatry, are not easily diagnosable by the DSM. We will use these syndromes to test the clinical diagnostic applicability of the present DSM and, in doing so, also expect to be able to make recommendations for improving the manual's cross-cultural perspective.

As it is not our wish to "find" pathology in behavior that does not exceed the indigenous boundaries of normalcy, we have chosen not to focus on states that are seen as part of a normal individual's usual cultural experience.

There is little evidence that trance or dissociative states that occur as part of culturally sanctioned ceremony or ritual should be regarded as pathological. Griffith et al. (1980) provided rich descriptions of trance states occurring as part of an African American prayer meeting, yet made it quite clear that the phenomenon is not viewed as a sign of a mental problem, nor do the individuals show any significant psychopathology outside of the ceremonial setting. By the same token, many Puerto Ricans may attribute the cause of mental illness or physical symptoms to supernatural causes, such as spirits (Gaviria and Wintrob 1976). However, it is unlikely that "folk" criteria would classify as insane or mentally ill those Puerto Ricans involved in *espiritismo*, despite the fact that trance states are quite common in the context of a spiritist session (Comas-Díaz 1981). There are a number of other instances, such as the *Umbanda* cult of Brazil (Pressel 1973), *Vodun* in Haiti (Métraux 1972), and the *Zar* cult in Ethiopia and Sudan (Constantinides 1985; Kahana 1985), where the entry into states of altered consciousness occurs only secondarily, as part of a culturally sanctioned ritual cure for various illnesses. We will not focus on these phenomena.

It is also not our wish to equate belief in the supernatural with an altered state of consciousness. Individuals from a number of cultures may attribute the cause of mental illness or physical complaints to supernatural causes, such as possession by spirits, without such a possession involving any discernible signs of dissociation (Bourguignon 1968; Gaviria and Wintrob 1976; Saunders 1977). Bourguignon (1976) made the important distinction between "possession belief" (the attribution of various and sundry physical and emotional symptoms to possession by spirits) and "possession trance," stating that it is only in the latter where an alteration in consciousness occurs.

It is for the above mentioned reasons that we have chosen not to focus on syndromes that are culturally sanctioned and produce no major personal or societal disruption.

Review of the Literature

A comprehensive review of the psychiatric and anthropological literature reveals a number of major syndromes from around the world that have dissociation or somatization as a key feature. These syndromes are separable into various groupings by virtue of their symptom patterns.

Dissociative Syndromes

Possession trance.   There are a number of syndromes of possession trance (Akhtar 1988; Peltzer 1989; Salisbury 1968; Suryani 1984; Suwanlert 1976) generally characterized by the belief that the patient's body is taken over by a spirit. This is manifested by an altered state of consciousness, an inability to control one's actions, a temporary change in the personality of the patient, and a placating attitude adopted by people close to the patient. Possessing spirits often ask for favors or presents from relatives or friends. Excepting the account from New Guinea (Salisbury 1968), the patient is often female and is usually facing some interpersonal conflict or has experienced a loss or quarrel. All of these syndromes are reversible, with the longest lasting several days. In many of them, an episode of possession trance makes the patient more likely to be possessed again in the future.

The various accounts of possession syndromes reveal substantial differences between possession trance and multiple personality disorder as described in DSM-III-R. The association with childhood abuse, an important part of the diagnosis of multiple personality disorder, has hardly been mentioned with regard to possession trance. Although the two syndromes are similar in that they involve the coexistence within a person of different personalities, a key phenomenological difference between the two is the presumed origin of this other personality. In multiple personality disorder (dissociative identity disorder), this origin is understood by the patient and by the treater to be within the afflicted person, whereas the possessed person views the phenomenon as the effect of a completely foreign entity. It is also not common to hear of several "spirits" or "personalities" taking control of the possessed person's behavior.

In part because of such perceived differences between possession and dissociative identity disorder, the approach of DSM-IV has been to include the diagnosis of dissociative trance disorder in the appendix titled "Criteria Sets and Axes Provided for Further Study." This is a substantial improvement from the position of DSM-III-R (American Psychiatric Association 1987), which simply stated that a possession syndrome may "occur as a symptom of Multiple Personality Disorder. In such cases the complaint of being 'possessed' is actually the experience of the alternate personality's influence on the person's behavior and mood" (pp. 271–272). It is more important to note that, despite the more accurate description of the syndrome and its inclusion in an appendix, the clinical diagnosis of someone with such a syndrome would still be dissociative disorder not otherwise specified.

"Fleeing" or "running" syndromes.   Another subcategory of dissociative syndromes includes *piblokto* among the polar Eskimos (Gussow 1960), *chakore* in the Ngawbere of Panama (Bletzer 1985), *grisi siknis* among the Miskito of Nicaragua (Dennis 1985), and Navajo "frenzy" witchcraft (Neutra et al. 1977). These are disorders characterized by wandering or fleeing aimlessly, such that the term *running taxon* has been given to some of them by Simons and Hughes (1985) in their attempt to classify them. In *grisi siknis, piblokto,* and *chakore,* there is a documented prodromal period that may last several days and that is characterized by feelings of lethargy, depression, and anxiety. In all four syndromes, there is a sudden onset of a high level of activity; a trancelike state; potentially dangerous behavior in the form of running or fleeing; and ensuing exhaustion, sleep, and amnesia regarding the episode.

Although the syndrome of *amok* (Arboleda-Flores 1979; Burton-Bradley 1968) is somewhat akin to the above, it needs to be mentioned separately, as it is connected with a very real threat to the life of the patient and of others around him or her at the time of the episode. As in the fleeing syndromes, there is a prodromal period, but the syndrome is characterized by brooding after an episode during which the patient has felt slighted or humiliated. Although the phenomenon involves running, it seems that the hallmark of the syndrome is the senseless and seemingly random harming or killing that accompanies the running. Also unlike the fleeing syndromes and spirit possession, amok affects primarily men.

It is difficult to classify these running or fleeing syndromes by using criteria from the Dissociative Disorders section of DSM-IV, although their principal symptoms, as described by those familiar with the syndromes, are clearly dissociative in character. There is an obliviousness to surroundings, an episode of agitated activity, and amnesia for the episode afterward. However, although some degree of locomotion takes place, it would be difficult to call this "travel away from home," such as in dissociative fugue (American Psychiatric Association 1994, p. 484); the only diagnostic possibility is calling this a dissociative disorder not otherwise specified—hardly a fitting description. The syndrome of *amok* would fare no better with this classification, unless one were to presume that a brief reactive psychosis was taking place, but the presence of psychotic features has not been documented consistently (Arboleda-Flores 1979; Burton-Bradley 1968), despite the association of the syndrome with psychiatric comorbidity (Schmidt et al. 1977). The syndrome's classification as a variant of intermittent explosive disorder may indeed be the most adequate diagnosis at present, with the reservation that this would put it in a class of disorders whose unifying theme is that of not being classified elsewhere.

Trance syndromes. Weidman (1979) described a syndrome among southern blacks in the United States and Bahamians that is referred to as *falling out* or *blacking out,* respectively. This characteristically occurs in response to a high degree of emotional excitement, such as may occur in the setting of a religious ceremony, during an argument, in fear-producing situations, or in "profound sexual conflict." It is characterized by the affected individual's falling down in an altered state of consciousness and not being able to move, despite being able to hear and understand what is happening around him or her. Philippe and Romain (1979) described a strikingly similar syndrome in Haitians, known as *indisposition,* also characterized by an altered state of consciousness during which the individual falls to the ground and is not able to understand what he or she hears or sees. (Although a case could be made for the inclusion of *ataques de nervios,* which occurs in peoples of Hispanic descent, under dissociative syndromes, we have chosen to discuss those below, under somatoform syndromes, because of their prominent somatic features.)

Once again, we are looking at phenomena that the current DSM would diagnose as dissociative disorders not otherwise specified. Clearly, the principal symptoms and signs are those of dissociation. Although there is an alteration in the way that the individual senses reality, the falling and the temporary loss of voluntary motion would not be taken into account by a diagnosis of depersonalization disorder. A diagnosis of conversion disorder would seem to ignore the dissociative component. DSM-IV's new diagnosis of acute stress disorder would account for the dissociative symptoms, but would also necessitate a traumatic stressor of greater magnitude than those usually described as triggering these episodes. The available data on prevalence, although somewhat limited, would indicate that these are not uncommon phenomena, and that such a phenomenon's repeated occurrence in an individual is viewed as an illness by other members of that individual's culture. The principal improvement from DSM-III-R to DSM-IV has been the inclusion of dissociative trance disorder among the Criteria Sets for Further Study. It is hoped that this will at least allow for accumulation of additional data on these dissociative phenomena, eventually leading to a more adequate diagnostic entity. In addition, descriptions of *amok* and the "falling-out" syndromes have been included in the DSM's Glossary of Cultural-Bound Syndromes, serving to expand clinicians' consciousness with regard to these syndromes.

Somatoform Syndromes

Koro. Various reports from Asia, including Hong Kong (Yap 1965), Singapore (Ngui 1969), India (Nandi et al. 1983), China (Tseng et al. 1988), and Malaysia

(Adityanjee et al. 1991) have referred to the syndrome of *koro*, or *suo-yang*, occurring either singly or in epidemics, characterized by acute and prominent paniclike symptoms brought about by the sudden onset of fear that one's genitalia are retracting into the abdomen, and that this will result in death. Although similar syndromes have also been described in Western settings, these have always been associated either with major (Axis I) diagnoses, such as schizophrenia (Ede 1976; Edwards 1970), or with neurological/organic etiologies, such as brain tumor (Lapierre 1972). In contrast, reports from Asia suggest that *koro* presents as a generally benign, time-limited illness without association with additional psychopathology and with a good prognosis.

A review of current diagnostic possibilities in DSM-III-R leaves one with the diagnosis of somatoform disorder not otherwise specified, as it involves "nonpsychotic hypochondriacal symptoms of less than six months' duration." Body dysmorphic disorder, which would seem to capture the almost delusional, somatic quality described in *koro*, is apparently meant to be diagnosed in disorders that are much more chronic than what is described for *koro* (American Psychiatric Association 1987). It is important to note, however, that a description of the syndrome is present in DSM-IV, both in its Glossary of Culture-Bound Syndromes and within the discussion of the differential diagnosis of body dysmorphic disorder. These additions have already served to expand the scope of the manual. Alternatively, Bernstein and Gaw (1990) have outlined a classification scheme for *koro* as a genital retraction disorder in the section on somatoform disorders. The proposed criteria would exclude organic factors and Axis I disorders other than somatoform and would require the determination of whether the case occurred within or outside of the cultural context. Given the high degree of detail available about this syndrome and its apparently common occurrence in Asia, adoption of these criteria would improve the scope and acceptance of the DSM and would lead the way toward research aimed at establishing the validity of such criteria and providing data on incidence and prevalence of the disorder.

Generalized somatic syndromes. There are striking similarities between the Nigerian syndromes of "brain-fag," described by Prince (1985) in students, and *Ode Ori*, described by Makanjuola (1987) among the Yoruba. *Ode Ori* consists of a chronic sensation of "an organism crawling through the head," accompanied by complaints of noises heard inside the ears, palpitations, a "peppery" sensation, darkened vision, and dizziness (Makanjuola 1987, p. 222). Patients with *Ode Ori* who were examined with the Present State Examination commonly exhibited depressed mood, "tension pains," complaints of ill health, delayed sleep, anxiety, and low energy. "Brain-fag" is the name given by Prince (1985) to a disorder found in students, characterized by a sensation that "something is walking about in the centre of [the patient's] head," as well as visual difficulties, poor attention and concentration, and "fatigue and sleepiness in spite of adequate rest." Interestingly, while the Yoruba ascribe *Ode Ori* to a wandering, supernatural organism, the younger generation of students who suffer from "brain-fag" attribute the syndrome to overstudy and exhaustion.

In Koreans and Korean Americans, K. M. Lin (1983) has described the chronic syndrome of *hwa-byung*, literally translated as "anger illness" or "fire illness," as it is attributed both by patients and traditional healers to unexpressed anger or painful life circumstances. The principal complaints include a sensation of an epigastric mass, anorexia, anxiety, dyspnea, feelings of "hotness," epigastric pain, and lack of energy. Patients with *hwa-byung* seek help from both traditional and Western healers, although responses to either one are usually transient at best (Pang 1990). Some response to antidepressant medication has been reported (K. M. Lin 1983), although there are no studies on the uniformity of this finding.

Another generalized somatic syndrome with a strong component of mood dysregulation is that of neurasthenia in China (A. Kleinman 1982; T.-Y. Lin 1989; Ming-Yuan 1989), also known in Japan by the name of *shinkeisuijaku*, or "ordinary" *shinkeishitsu* (Russell 1989; Suzuki 1989). *Neurasthenia* has its roots in 19th-century United States, the term having been coined by physician George M. Beard to describe a syndrome of headaches, insomnia, gastrointestinal symptoms, and vague somatic complaints, which Beard believed derived from an exhaustion of the patient's nervous system (Tsung 1989). Although the diagnosis eventually fell into disuse in its country of origin, it quickly caught on in the rest of the world throughout the 20th century, to the point that the DSM-II reinstituted it as a type of neurosis in 1968, after having not listed it in DSM-I (T.-Y. Lin 1989). Of note, A. Kleinman (1982) studied 100 patients diagnosed as neurasthenic in China with the use of a culturally adapted Schedule for Affective Disorders and Schizophrenia (SADS) and determined that the vast majority of them, although complaining primarily of somatic ailments, had "clinical depression" and could benefit from antidepressant medication.

It is possible that the generalized somatic syndromes described above are culturally specific illness behaviors that occur as reactions to the biologically based disorder known in the West as depression, much as A. Kleinman's (1982) work with neurasthenia in China seems to show. Although DSM-IV has added to and improved its discussion of somatic experience and expression of distress in its description of major depression, the question remains as to how to diagnose such common syndromes without resorting to the wastebasket modifier of "not otherwise specified," whether it be major depression, not otherwise specified or somatoform disorder, not otherwise specified. It may be that the present diagnostic schema for major depressive disorder needs to be expanded to allow for the diagnosis in individuals who are culturally disposed to use somatic expressions of low mood, such as nonmedically explainable complaints related to the head, complaints of ill health or malaise, or gastrointestinal symptoms in the absence of substantial anxiety.

Ataques de nervios. It has long been known that Puerto Ricans and other Hispanic Americans, especially those who are female and middle-aged, exhibit more somatic complaints than non-Hispanic whites (Escobar et al. 1987, 1989; Haberman 1976). Guarnaccia et al. (1989) may have been closer to the truth, however, when they discovered a cluster of symptoms in the somatization factor of the Spanish Diagnostic Interview Schedule (DIS) that described the Puerto Rican syndrome known as *ataque de nervios* ("attack of nerves"). In Puerto Rico, an *ataque de nervios* is a socially sanctioned display of grief or great conflict, characterized by "trembling, heart palpitations, a sense of heat in the chest rising into the head, difficulty moving limbs, loss of consciousness or mind going blank, memory loss, a sensation of needles in parts of the body (paresthesia), chest tightness, difficult breathing (dyspnea), dizziness, faintness, and spells . . . the person begins to shout, swear and strike out at others, [then] falls to the ground and either experiences convulsive body movements or lies 'as if dead.'" Through the use of a scale that selected for people exhibiting this *ataque* symptom cluster, it was possible to find a subset of the Puerto Rican Epidemiologic Catchment Area (ECA) sample who had experienced *ataque* and who differed demographically from the Puerto Rican mainstream. Their conclusion was that the reporting of symptoms of this indigenous syndrome may have been at least partly responsible for the elevated ratings of somatization found by the DIS in the Puerto Rican sample.

The work described above is important in two ways. First, it conveys doubt about the separateness of the categories of dissociation and somatization. People who experience *ataques* exhibit both somatic complaints, such as palpitations, flushing, and dyspnea, as well as substantial dissociative symptoms, which usually include falling to the ground, random agitation or purposeless violence, convulsive movements, and appearing to be "dead." Kirmayer (1991) has suggested that dissociative and somatoform syndromes may indeed share the basic component of high hypnotizability, or the ability to narrowly focus one's attention, whether on a bodily sensation or on a sense of un–self-consciousness. Clearly, diagnostic criteria may need to be reexamined when a disorder is found that straddles two seemingly distinct categories.

In addition to the above observation, the work of Guarnaccia et al. (1989) with somatization and *ataques de nervios* illustrates an excellent way to produce research that will expand the diagnostic capacity of the DSM. Guarnaccia et al.'s reassessment of the results of administering the DIS to Puerto Ricans began with empirical phenomenological research that resulted in a reliable, valid way of describing the culturally influenced syndrome of *ataques de nervios*. Out of this work, an instrument was able to be developed that, when added to the DIS, helped to separate those people who were responding with high numbers of somatic complaints because of their experience with *ataques*, from those with a somatization disorder or hypochondriasis.

It is important to remember, however, that most *ataques de nervios* are not signs of psychopathology, but are rather culturally sanctioned expressions of deep emotion, such as acute grief. Although it is suspected that a small but significant proportion of *ataques* stem from a diagnosable psychiatric condition, it is not certain whether this psychiatric condition is a single entity or comprises a number of already established disorders that could be associated with *ataques* in the Hispanic population. It is interesting that the newly developed acute stress disorder/brief reactive dissociative disorder seems to capture some of the flavor of an *ataque*, especially in the mixing of dissociative, somatic, and anxiety symptoms. As was found for the falling-out syndromes, however, the stressor experienced by the patient is not usually of the extraordinary magnitude required to make the diagnosis. Once again, it is important to note that a description of the syndrome of *ataque de nervios* has been included in the Glossary of Culture-Bound Syndromes of DSM-IV. Although it does not resolve the diagnostic questions raised by the existence of this syndrome, this is a step toward allowing clinicians to view the syndrome as such, rather than as an "atypical" form of a more familiar disorder.

Conclusion

A number of mental syndromes exist primarily in parts of the world that are culturally quite different from the DSM's place of origin. When phenomenological descriptions of these syndromes are examined, it is clear that the current DSM's classification scheme applies poorly to them, and this results in unsatisfactory, ill-fitting diagnoses. Much in the same way that Orwell's "newspeak" attempted to limit thinking by limiting the words one could use to describe things and events, institution of the DSM has inadvertently resulted in the exclusion or trivialization of syndromes that cannot be described by its limited language.

A general recommendation to be made with regard to the above is to echo the voices of Guarnaccia et al. (1989) and Simons and Hughes (1985), among many others, who called for more empirical study of syndromes that are indigenous to various cultures. The aim of collecting such data would be to allow for the creation of diagnostic criteria for each of these syndromes. These locally derived criteria would aid in the decision as to whether a given syndrome can be diagnosed reliably and validly from within the culture. This would be an important step toward the decision to include such a syndrome in what would become a truly global diagnostic system.

There is sufficient documentation, however, to allow for some specific recommendations toward improving the scope of future DSMs:

1. We agree with the inclusion of possession trance disorder, as follows:
    a. Possession trance, characterized by all of the following:
        (1) Conviction of having been taken over, or possessed by, a spirit, power, deity, or other person.
        (2) Episodic change in personality, lasting as long as several days.
        (3) Full or partial amnesia for the event.
    b. The syndrome is not authorized as a normal part of a collective cultural or religious practice.
    c. The possession trance causes significant impairment in social or occupational functioning or causes marked distress.
    d. Not occurring exclusively during the course of a psychotic disorder (including mood disorder with psychotic features and brief reactive psychosis) or multiple personality disorder and is not induced by a substance (e.g., intoxication, withdrawal).
2. Pending further research, it may suffice, for the present, to consider the "running" syndromes as variants of dissociative fugue; or they may be classified as

dissociative disorder not otherwise specified. Brief clinical descriptions of the indigenous syndromes should ideally be included in the manual, as part of the Cultural Considerations section for dissociative fugue.

3.   We agree with Spiegel and Cardeña (Chapter 22) that *amok* may be a cultural variant of intermittent explosive disorder, and we therefore recommend the inclusion of a clinical description of *amok* as part of the Cultural Considerations section under intermittent explosive disorder.

4.   The newly developed category of acute stress disorder/brief reactive dissociative disorder could be applicable to the "falling-out" syndromes and to *ataques de nervios*, provided Criterion A is redefined as being of less severity than what is stated for posttraumatic stress disorder. The clinician must then be cautioned not to use the diagnosis indiscriminately for all incidences of these syndromes, as this may result in the "pathologization" of culturally sanctioned (normal) expressions of deep feeling. Each of the syndromes should be described as in the Cultural Considerations section pertaining to acute stress disorder.

5.   Because of *koro's* uniqueness, we agree with its description as a separate somatoform disorder, as proposed by Bernstein and Gaw (1990). Alternatively, a detailed clinical description should be included under somatoform disorder, not otherwise specified.

6.   Owing to the association of neurasthenia and similar disorders with depression, we favor expanding the diagnostic criteria of major depressive disorder to include descriptions of somatic expression of low mood and energy (e.g., nonmedically explainable complaints related to the head, complaints of ill health or malaise, or gastrointestinal symptoms in the absence of substantial anxiety). Alternatively, description of these syndromes under the heading of mood disorders might at least lead to therapeutic trials of antidepressant medications, which have proven to be effective in the treatment of neurasthenia.

References

Adityanjee MD, Zain AM, Subramaniam M: Sporadic koro and marital dysharmony. Psychopathology 24:49–52, 1991

Akhtar S: Four culture-bound psychiatric syndromes in India. Int J Soc Psychiatry 34:70–74, 1988

American Psychiatric Association: Diagnostic and Statistical Manual of Mental Disorders, 3rd Edition, Revised. Washington, DC, American Psychiatric Association, 1987

American Psychiatric Association: Diagnostic and Statistical Manual of Mental Disorders, 4th Edition. Washington, DC, American Psychiatric Association, 1994

Arboleda-Flores J: Amok. Bull Am Acad Psychiatry Law 7:286–295, 1979

Bemporad JR, Ratey JJ, O'Driscoll G, et al: Hysteria, anorexia and the culture of self-denial. Psychiatry 51:96–103, 1988

Bernstein RL, Gaw AC: Koro: proposed classification for DSM-IV. Am J Psychiatry 147:1670–1674, 1990

Bletzer KV: Fleeing hysteria (chakore) among Ngawberg of Northwestern Panama: a preliminary analysis and comparison with similar illness phenomena in other settings. Cult Med Psychiatry 9:297–318, 1985

Bourguignon E: World distribution and patterns of possession states, in Trance and Possession States. Edited by Prince R. Montréal, Québec, Canada, R. M. Bucke Memorial Society, 1968, pp 3–34

Bourguignon E: Possession. San Francisco, CA, Chandler & Sharp, 1976

Burton-Bradley BG: The amok syndrome in Papua and New Guinea. Med J Aust 1:252–256, 1968

Comas-Díaz L: Puerto Rican espiritismo and psychotherapy. Am J Orthopsychiatry 51:636–645, 1981

Constantinides P: Women heal women: spirit possession and sexual segregation in a Muslim society. Soc Sci Med 21:685–692, 1985

Dennis PA: Grisi siknis in Miskito culture, in The Culture-Bound Syndromes: Folk Illnesses of Psychiatric and Anthropological Interest. Edited by Simons RC, Hughes CC. Dordrecht, The Netherlands, D Reidel, 1985, pp 289–306

Ede A: Koro in an Anglo-Saxon Canadian. Can Psychiatr Assoc J 21:389–392, 1976

Edwards JG: The koro pattern of depersonalization in an American schizophrenic patient. Am J Psychiatry 126:1171–1173, 1970

Escobar JI, Burnam MA, Karno M, et al: Somatization in the community. Arch Gen Psychiatry 44:713–718, 1987

Escobar JI, Rubio-Stipec M, Canino G, et al: Somatic Symptom Index (SSI): a new and abridged somatization construct—prevalence and epidemiological correlates in two large community samples. J Nerv Ment Dis 177:140–146, 1989

Gaviria M, Wintrob RM: Supernatural influence in psychopathology—Puerto Rican folk beliefs about mental illness. Can Psychiatr Assoc J 21:361–369, 1976

Griffith EEH, English T, Mayfield V: Possession, prayer, and testimony: therapeutic aspects of the Wednesday night meeting in a black church. Psychiatry 43:120–128, 1980

Guarnaccia PJ, Rubio-Stipec M, Canino G: Ataques de nervios in the Puerto Rican Diagnostic Interview Schedule: the impact of cultural categories on psychiatric epidemiology. Cult Med Psychiatry 13:275–295, 1989

Gussow Z: Pibloktoq (hysteria) among the polar Eskimo. The Psychoanalytic Study of Society 1:218–236, 1960

Haberman PW: Psychiatric symptoms among Puerto Ricans in Puerto Rico and New York City. Ethnicity 3:133–144, 1976

Kahana Y: The Zar spirits, a category of magic in the system of mental health care in Ethiopia. Int J Soc Psychiatry 31:125–143, 1985

Karp I: Deconstructing culture-bound syndromes. Soc Sci Med 21:221–228, 1985

Kirmayer LJ. Pacing the void: concepts and measures of dissociation. Paper presented at the MacArthur Foundation Mind-Body Network Workshop on Dissociation, Stanford, CA, October 1991

Kleinman A: Neurasthenia and depression: a study of somatization and culture in China. Cult Med Psychiatry 6:117–189, 1982

Kleinman AM: Depression, somatization, and the "new cross-cultural psychiatry." Soc Sci Med 11:3–10, 1977

Lapierre YD: Koro in a French Canadian. Can Psychiatry Assoc J 17:333–337, 1972

Lin KM: Hwa-byung: a Korean culture-bound syndrome? Am J Psychiatry 140:105–107, 1983

Lin T-Y: Neurasthenia revisited: its place in modern psychiatry. Cult Med Psychiatry 13:105–130, 1989

Makanjuola ROA: Ode ori: a culture-bound disorder with prominent somatic features in Yoruba Nigerian patients. Acta Psychiatr Scand 75:231–236, 1987

Métraux A: Voodoo in Haiti. New York, Schocken Books, 1972

Ming-Yuan Z: The diagnosis and phenomenology of neurasthenia: a Shanghai study. Cult Med Psychiatry 13:147–161, 1989

Nandi DN, Banerjee G, Saha H, et al: Epidemic koro in West Bengal, India. Int J Soc Psychiatry 29:265–268, 1983

Neutra R, Levy JE, Parker D: Cultural expectations versus reality in Navajo seizure patterns and sick roles. Cult Med Psychiatry 1:255–275, 1977

Ngui PW: The koro epidemic in Singapore. Aust NZ J Psychiatry 3:263–266, 1969

Pang KYC: Hwa-byung: the construction of a Korean popular illness among Korean elderly immigrant women in the United States. Cult Med Psychiatry 14:495–512, 1990

Peltzer K: Nosology and etiology of a spirit disorder (Vimbuza) in Malawi. Psychopathology 22:145–151, 1989

Philippe J, Romain JB: Indisposition in Haiti. Soc Sci Med 13B:129–133, 1979

Pressel E: Umbanda in Sao Paulo: religious innovation in a developing society, in Religion, Altered States of Consciousness, and Social Change. Edited by Bourguignon E. Columbus, Ohio State University Press, 1973, pp 264–318

Prince R: The concept of culture-bound syndromes: anorexia nervosa and brain-fag. Soc Sci Med 21:197–203, 1985

Russell JG: Anxiety disorders in Japan: a review of the Japanese literature on Shinkeishitsu and taijinkyofusho. Cult Med Psychiatry 13:391–403, 1989

Salisbury RF: Possession in the New Guinea highlands. Int J Soc Psychiatry 14:85–94, 1968

Saunders LW: Variants in Zar experience in an Egyptian village, in Case Studies in Spirit Possession. Edited by Crepanzano V, Garrison V. New York, Wiley, 1977

Schmidt K, Hill L, Guthrie G: Running amok. Int J Soc Psychiatry 23:264–274, 1977

Simons RC, Hughes CC (eds): The Culture-Bound Syndromes: Folk Illnesses of Psychiatric and Anthropological Interest. Dordrecht, The Netherlands, D Reidel, 1985

Suryani LK: Culture and mental disorder: the case of bebainan in Bali. Cult Med Psychiatry 8:95–113, 1984

Suwanlert S: Neurotic and psychotic states attributed to Thai "phii pob" spirit possession. Aust NZ J Psychiatry 10:119–123, 1976

Suzuki T: The concept of neurasthenia and its treatment in Japan. Cult Med Psychiatry 13:187–202, 1989

Tseng WS, Kan-Ming M, Hsu J, et al: A sociocultural study of koro epidemics in Guangdong, China. Am J Psychiatry 145:1538–1543, 1988

Tsung YL: Neurasthenia revisited: its place in modern psychiatry. Cult Med Psychiatry 13:105–129, 1989

Weidman HH: Falling-out: a diagnostic and treatment problem viewed from a transcultural perspective. Soc Sci Med 13B:95–112, 1979

Yap PM: Koro—a culture-bound depersonalization syndrome. Br J Psychiatry 111:43–50, 1965

Yap PM: Classification of the culture-bound reactive syndromes. Aust NZ J Psychiatry 1:172–179, 1967

Yu-Fen H, Neng T: Transcultural investigation of recent symptomatology of schizophrenia in China. Am J Psychiatry 138:1484–1487, 1981

Chapter 20

Cultural Comments on Somatoform and Dissociative Disorders: I

Laurence J. Kirmayer, M.D.

G onzález and Griffith (Chapter 19) have assembled some well-described culture-bound syndromes that, they argue, merit being rescued from the nondescript category of "not otherwise specified." They have suggested some additional diagnoses for a standard diagnostic system that would give formal status to these problems and provide criteria to guide subsequent research. By making culture-bound syndromes the focus of their discussion of cultural difference, they emphasize problems that are most obviously discrepant with a standard diagnostic system but at the same time are the easiest to assimilate into its framework—we need only invent new categories or reorganize old ones. Other cultural differences, less striking (or less codified within the culture), could be handled in a similar fashion or through cautionary notes in the text that accompanies the diagnostic criteria.

However, ethnographic accounts describe many patterns of symptoms that may be viewed not as discrete disorders but as local idioms of distress (Nichter 1981). They exist in parallel with other problems. Their "natural history" is inseparable from their social causes and consequences (Kirmayer 1989; Kleinman 1988). This is true of most of the syndromes collected by González and Griffith, which despite being indigenous categories of distress, also serve as languages of suffering and protest (Koss 1990; Lambek 1989; Lock and Wakewich-Dunk 1990; Mirdal 1985). Placing these within a psychiatric nosology may obscure this important fact. This is one strong reason for preferring a cultural axis orthogonal to existing nosology, in which local terms, with their network of meanings, can be acknowledged as influences on the course of other identified psychiatric disorders.

Culture influences all psychiatric diagnoses, not only the exotic but also the familiar and well entrenched (Kleinman 1988). Consequently, the comments in this chapter first concern the role of culture in shaping established diagnoses and then the specific additions proposed by González and Griffith.

Somatization and Somatoform Disorders

Somatization is a concept born of Western mind-body dualism (Kirmayer 1984). Physical symptoms regularly accompany interpersonal conflict and emotional distress. It is only because clinicians expect patients to adopt an exclusively psychological idiom for their distress that they treat the persistent expression of distress in physical symptoms as a special diagnostic category and, indeed, impute unique pathological mechanisms. This is so both for acute forms of somatized depression and anxiety and for the various somatoform disorders.

There are numerous anecdotal clinical reports and ethnographic accounts of culture-bound syndromes of somatic symptoms, but in most cases we do not know the prevalence or coherence of local clusters or syndromes and their natural history. There are also many culture-specific somatic symptoms (e.g., semen in the urine reported in South Asia [Mumford et al. 1991] and hot, peppery, or crawling sensations in the head reported in Africa [Ebigbo 1986]), but again we know little about their true cross-cultural prevalence, as many simply have not been examined outside the cultures where they fit common idioms.

Culturally transmitted illness schemata shape individuals' search for and report of symptoms (Angel and Thoits 1987). The level of reported somatic symptoms is variable cross-culturally, although probably not as much as has been claimed in anecdotal reports (Beiser 1985; Mumford et al. 1991). In cultures where high levels of somatic symptoms are commonly reported, patients are overdiagnosed as having somatoform disorders at levels of symptomatology that are not uncommon in patients with discrete functional somatic syndromes (Kirmayer and Robbins 1991).

In cultures with strongly inculcated traditional beliefs, maintained by strict social sanctions or an obdurate social order, ideas that we expect to be flexible or negotiable may be rigidly held. This may contribute to a blurring of the distinction between anxious preoccupations and delusions. Something of the sort may account for the quasi-delusional cases of monosymptomatic hypochondriasis that may be common in developing countries (Osman 1991). This consideration is also relevant to the diagnosis of hypochondriasis, which includes the criterion that fears of illness do not respond to appropriate medical reassurance. Of course, to be effective, reassurance must be delivered in socially and culturally appropriate ways.

With regard to specific somatoform disorders, González and Griffith suggest that neurasthenia should be subsumed by a set of broadened criteria for depression. Although Kleinman (1986) found that Chinese neurasthenia patients could be diagnosed with major depression and treated with antidepressant medication, many patients persisted in their somatic and social distress. His data could therefore be interpreted as indicating that neurasthenia is a syndrome with a natural history distinct from that of major depression. If, for the sake of argument, neurasthenic and other functional somatic symptoms can be caused by elective deprivation of stage 4 non-rapid eye movement (REM) sleep (Moldofsky 1986), then it is possible to develop such a syndrome from disparate causes. Depending on whether we emphasize this final common pathway or its personal and social antecedents, we might assign neurasthenic syndromes to an independent diagnostic category (Lin 1989).

González and Griffith endorse Bernstein and Gaw's (1990) proposal of placing *koro* within the somatoform disorders. However, acute anxiety plays a much larger role in *koro* than in other somatoform disorders (with the possible exception of hypochondriasis). Furthermore, *koro* may involve beliefs of delusional intensity or dissociative-like distortions in body image (Ilechukwu 1992). Consequently, there remains some measure of arbitrariness in its classification depending on whether we wish to emphasize the somatic symptom focus, the prominence of anxiety, or the quasi-delusional or dissociative aspects of symptomatology.

Of course, if we admit *koro*, many of the other syndromes might also be granted diagnostic status. For example, *dhat* syndrome, which involves a variety of nonspecific somatic complaints, is common on the Indian subcontinent (Bhatia and Malik 1991). *Dhat* often involves not distinctive symptoms but rather the attribution of fatigue and weakness to loss of semen as a vital fluid. So, by Prince and Tcheng-Laroche's (1987) criteria, it ought not to be included as a distinct culture-bound syndrome. However, ethnophysiological ideas that focus attention on the genitourinary system and sexual dysfunction may lead to frequent reports of symptoms unusual in the West, such as semen in the urine (Mumford et al. 1991). Unless these symptoms and concerns are addressed, treatment may be ineffective (Bhatia and Malik 1991).

Dissociation and Dissociative Disorders

Dissociative disorders involve gaps in experience that are recognized or measured against cultural standards for the univocality and rationality of the self (Kirmayer 1994). Cultural concepts of time and memory shape narrative accounts of actions and experience and may make dissociations more or less common. In cultures (or subcultures) where there is less demand for rational self-control and self-explication, dissociative experiences may be sought after or more readily experienced spontaneously with little or no associated psychopathology. Possession is often simply an explanation for illnesses or troubles and does not involve any dissociative behavior or experience. In cultures where dissociation does occur in possession, it may be ritually prescribed and developed as a socially sanctioned mode of helping or coping and hence not be an illness. However, if the individual is distressed, then possession that occurs as part of a socially sanctioned ritual might nevertheless be considered a psychiatric problem, despite its social genesis and promotion. The pathological status of possession must be judged in each case on the basis of the cause and subsequent impairment of normal role functions.

With regard to the many putative dissociative syndromes mentioned by González and Griffith, it is important again to emphasize that most are not illnesses but ways of describing and expressing distress. For example, falling out and indisposition, like *ataques de nervios*, are folk illnesses that also function as idioms of distress. These and other symptoms related to apparent loss of consciousness or paralysis might equally be classified as somatoform or dissociative disorders depending on which aspect of their phenomenology we emphasize. Again, some notion of the underlying mechanism is necessary to confidently classify the disorder. In fact, the most common dissociative disorder diagnosis in India is probably pseudoseizures, which would be classified as a conversion disorder in a standard diagnostic system (Das and Saxena 1991). If conversion disorder is viewed as a dissociative disorder, then this reclassification of other somatoform problems would make sense in terms of both symptomatology and mechanism.

The startle-matching taxon proposed by Simons and Hughes (1985) is cohesive because of the stereotypy of the startle response, but as González and Griffith note, it may not be an illness at all. Individuals with *latah* do not always seem to suffer themselves but may use this disorder as a form of social protest or even play (Doolittle 1991; Kenny 1990; Winzeler 1991). If *latah* does in fact involve an exaggeration of the startle reflex, it is not at all clear why we would put it with the dissociative disorders rather than with other tic or movement disorders or in a separate category.

Finally, it is worth noting that the written records on which many of the classic culture-bound syndromes are based are not always reliable. Initial reports were made by observers who had limited knowledge of language and custom and who often ignored crucial political realities that governed both the deviant behavior and its labeling and outcome. In many cases a very few documented cases were redescribed and reported, creating the illusion of a common problem. For example, *pibloktoq* is unheard of today, having been replaced by other forms of disavowal or dissociation often associated with alcohol or drug use (Foulks 1980). Similarly, *amok* is now uncommon (Kua 1991). Although wild mass killings occur sporadically in many places, they do not constitute a discrete syndrome any more than any other pattern of violence or crime (Winzeler 1990).

The creation of a category of acute stress disorder or brief reactive dissociative disorder focuses on the antecedents and on the notion that dissociation may represent manifestations of a stress response. It would allow for a diagnosis that does not prejudge the current and premorbid psychological characteristics of the patient. At the same time, by its very name, it puts great emphasis on identifying a stressor. Although this is rarely difficult, its actual relevance to the natural history and treatment of the wide range of culture-specific disorders to be subsumed under this diagnosis remains to be established. The notion that dissociative experience is usually the outcome of severe trauma may itself be a culture-bound idea.

Conclusion

In the nosological furor that has overtaken psychiatry, there is the danger of creating a museum of cultural oddities that, however crowded, does little justice to the social reality of human suffering. If we take the descriptive-phenomenological approach of the framers of DSM-III and DSM-IV (American Psychiatric Association 1980, 1994) at their word, then cross-cultural observations would support a field day of proliferating exotic diagnoses (Simons and Hughes 1985). Prince and Tcheng-Laroche (1987) have suggested that we limit this expansion by excluding syndromes that have no distinctive symptomatology but are based entirely on folk theories of causality. For example, various cultural forms of "fright illness" would not warrant a separate diagnostic category because they primarily involve attributing a wide variety of symptoms or diseases to frightening events. However, if attributions or ideas of causality can themselves have pathogenic effects and substantially influence the symptomatology, course, and outcome of psychiatric disorders (as is claimed by cognitive theory), then cultural beliefs and attributions may provide a basis for clinically significant differences in syndromes or disorders that would have to be recognized in nosology (Kirmayer 1991).

Despite claims to the contrary, the classification of DSM-III and DSM-IV is theoretically driven, as our perception of the taxonomic boundaries and hierarchical arrangement of mental disorders is not simply given in nature but depends on sociocultural and pragmatic assumptions about what sorts of phenomenological differences make a difference (Reznek 1987). Indeed, because cognitive psychology makes it clear that perception is guided by theory, our observations of phenomenology are, to a very large degree, the result of theoretical presuppositions. In practice, only differences between disorders that correspond to theoretical differences in mechanism or clinical differences in treatment and prognosis are likely to be viewed as important enough to warrant a diagnostic distinction.

Different nosologies will arise when we focus on symptomatology, treatment response, or underlying pathological process. A good example is provided by the efforts to place a variety of disparate problems together under the umbrella of dissociation. This grouping reflects not so much superficial similarities in phenomenology as the assumption of common underlying mechanisms. Although the somatoform disorders might seem more purely phenomenological (they involve bodily symptoms), this is belied by conflicts over whether conversion disorder belongs with the somatoform or dissociative disorders; whether *koro* belongs with the somatoform, delusional, or anxiety disorders; and whether many functional somatic syndromes belong in a psychiatric nosology at all, as the role of psychological factors in their incitement is highly variable. To reach a consensus about the most useful classification, we have to consider not only phenomenology, but also the implicit theories that lead us to draw certain phenomenological distinctions.

Phenomenology alone then does not account for the arrangement of disorders in official nosology. In fact, the emphasis on "phenomenology" in DSM-III and DSM-IV often results in descriptions of symptoms and behaviors taken out of the social and cultural contexts that give them meaning. This poses a problem for cultural psychiatry, where the situated or contextual meaning of illness is at the center of both theories of psychopathology and theories of clinical practice.

Trying to fit cultural variations into a nosological framework may be counterproductive if it creates the impression that cultural difference is now successfully contained within or subsumed by a complete and consistent diagnostic system.

Ethnographic writing offers us a way of thinking distinct from that provided by diagnostic classification schemes. To do justice to this, changes in nosology must not simply resolve cultural differences into new "boxes" but must encourage sensitivity to social context and attention to the interaction of personal and social history. Cross-cultural studies pose far more substantial challenges to existing nosology (and its underlying theoretical basis) than can be dispensed with by the addition of a few new categories or a rearrangement of diagnostic hierarchies.

References

American Psychiatric Association: Diagnostic and Statistical Manual of Mental Disorders, 3rd Edition. Washington, DC, American Psychiatric Association, 1980

American Psychiatric Association: Diagnostic and Statistical Manual of Mental Disorders, 4th Edition. Washington, DC, American Psychiatric Association, 1994

Angel R, Thoits P: The impact of culture on the cognitive structure of illness. Cult Med Psychiatry 11:465–494, 1987

Beiser M: A study of depression among traditional Africans, urban North Americans, and Southeast Asian refugees, in Culture and Depression. Edited by Kleinman A, Good B. Berkeley, University of Californian Press, 1985, pp 272–298

Bernstein RL, Gaw AC: Koro: proposed classification for DSM-IV. Am J Psychiatry 147:1670–1674, 1990

Bhatia MS, Malik SC: Dhat syndrome—a useful diagnostic entity in Indian culture. Br J Psychiatry 159:691–695, 1991

Das PS, Saxena S: Classification of dissociative states in DSM-III-R and ICD-10 (1989 draft). Br J Psychiatry 159:425–427, 1991

Doolittle AA: Latah behavior by females among the Rungus of Sabah, in Female and Male in Borneo: Contributions and Challenges to Gender Studies. Edited by Sutlive VH Jr. Williamsburg, VA, Borneo Research Council, College of William and Mary, 1991, pp 121–152

Ebigbo PO: A cross-sectional study of somatic complaints of Nigerian females using the Enugu somatization scale. Cult Med Psychiatry 10:167–186, 1986

Foulks EF: Psychological continuities: from dissociative states to alcohol use and suicide in Arctic populations. Journal of Operational Psychiatry 11:156–161, 1980

Ilechukwu STC: Koro-like syndromes in Nigeria: focus on the 1990 epidemic. Transcultural Psychiatric Research Review 29, 1992

Kenny MG: Latah: the logic of fear, in Emotions of Culture: A Malay Perspective. Edited by Karim WJ. New York, Oxford University Press, 1990, pp 123–141

Kirmayer LJ: Culture, affect and somatization. Transcultural Psychiatric Research Review 21:159–188, 1984

Kirmayer LJ: Cultural variations in the response to psychiatric disorders and emotional distress. Soc Sci Med 29:327–339, 1989

Kirmayer LJ: The place of culture in psychiatric nosology: Taijin kyofusho and DSM-III-R. J Nerv Ment Dis 179:19–28, 1991

Kirmayer LJ: Pacing the void: social and cultural dimensions of dissociation, in Dissociation Culture: Mind and Body. Edited by Spiegel D. Washington, DC, American Psychiatric Press, 1994

Kirmayer LJ, Robbins JM: Functional somatic syndromes, in Current Concepts of Somatization: Research and Clinical Perspectives. Edited by Kirmayer LJ, Robbins JM. Washington, DC, American Psychiatric Press, 1991

Kleinman A: Social Origins of Distress and Disease. New Haven, CT, Yale University Press, 1986

Kleinman A: Rethinking Psychiatry. New York: Free Press, 1988

Koss JM: Somatization and somatic complaint syndromes among Hispanics: overview and ethnopsychological perspectives. Transcultural Psychiatric Research Review 27:5–30, 1990

Kua EH: Amok in nineteenth-century British Malaya history. History of Psychiatry 3:429–436, 1991

Lambek M: From disease to discourse: remarks on the conceptualization of trance and spirit possession, in Altered States of Consciousness and Mental Health: A Cross-Cultural Perspective. Edited by Ward CA. London, England, Sage, 1989, pp 36–61

Lin T-Y: Neurasthenia revisited: its place in modern psychiatry. Cult Med Psychiatry 13:105–130, 1989

Lock M, Wakewich-Dunk P: Nerves and nostalgia: expression of loss among Greek immigrants in Montreal. Can Fam Physician 36:253–258, 1990

Mirdal GM: The condition of "tightness": the somatic complaints of Turkish migrant women. Acta Psychiatr Scand 71:287–296, 1985

Moldofsky H: Sleep and musculoskeletal pain. Am J Med 81(suppl 3A):85–89, 1986

Mumford DB, Bavington JT, Bhatnagar KS, et al: The Bradford Somatic Inventory: a multi-ethnic inventory of somatic symptoms reported by anxious and depressed patients in Britain and the Indo-Pakistan subcontinent. Br J Psychiatry 158:379–386, 1991

Nichter M: Idioms of distress: alternatives in the expression of psychosocial distress: a case study from India. Cult Med Psychiatry 5:379–408, 1981

Osman AA: Monosymptomatic hypochondriacal psychosis in developing countries. Br J Psychiatry 159:428–431, 1991

Prince R , Tcheng-Laroche F: Culture-bound syndromes and international disease classification. Cult Med Psychiatry 11:3–20, 1987

Reznek L: The Nature of Disease. London, England, Routledge & Kegan Paul, 1987

Simons RC, Hughes CC (eds): The Culture-Bound Syndromes: Folk Illnesses of Psychiatric and Anthropological Interest. Dordrecht, The Netherlands, D Reidel, 1985

Winzeler R: Amok: historical, psychological, and cultural perspectives, in Emotions of Culture: A Malay Perspective. Edited by Karim WJ. New York, Oxford University Press, 1990, pp 96–122

Winzeler RL: Latah in Sarawak, with special reference to the Iban, in Female and Male in Borneo: Contributions and Challenges to Gender Studies. Edited by Sutlive VH Jr. Williamsburg, VA, Borneo Research Council, College of William and Mary, 1991, pp 317–334

Chapter 21

Cultural Comments on Somatoform and Dissociative Disorders: II

Mitchell Weiss, M.D., Ph.D.

A nalyzing diagnostic dilemmas posed by specific culturally defined disorders, González and Griffith (Chapter 19) have identified limitations of standard diagnostic systems. Their review grapples implicitly with a fundamental dilemma concerning a culturally informed reorganization of the DSM: Too low a threshold for incorporating locally defined, emic categories on their own terms into the professional system will render the nosology idiosyncratic, incoherent, and difficult to use for comparisons across cultural groups. However, a naive attempt to fit local patterns of illness experience into a categorical framework, prefabricated elsewhere, invites distortions that serve the framework but constrain practice and research.

The focus on dissociative and somatoform disorders and whether to include some new categories help organize the discussion according to familiar headings but also constrains it. It is important to rethink assumptions about the structure of the diagnostic framework and the extent to which boundaries among depressive, anxiety, and somatoform in many clinical settings may be culturally inappropriate. A frequent response to my informal poll of psychiatrists in several cities in India about problems that made DSM-III-R (American Psychiatric Association 1987) most difficult for them to use cited its rigidity in forcing a decision between depression and anxiety among patients whose presentation featured both as equally prominent symptoms. Even for patients from majority communities in the West, recent research with the Structured Clinical Interview for DSM-III-R (SCID) (Williams et al. 1992) has used a strategy of ignoring depression as an exclusion for screening generalized anxiety disorder, recognizing that we cannot study co-occurrence if we systematically ignore it. Comorbidity, if frequent, may challenge the validity of the diagnostic system.

Somatoform complaints may be a prominent feature of depression, neurasthenia, anxiety, and panic, but the only standard DSM-IV (American Psychiatric

Association 1994) diagnosis to recognize explicitly the validity of a mixed category of emotional dysphoria is adjustment disorder with mixed emotional features. Only because adjustment disorders have been defined as a separate heading, a "mixed emotional" subtype eludes this constraint. The structure of DSM-III-R and DSM-IV imposes categories that do not fit typical presentations of some culturally defined disorders. For example, the essential feature of koro is intense anxiety associated with a specific somatoform complaint having both a hypochondriacal (imminent death) and dysmorphophobic quality. Perhaps all three of these disorders—*koro*, hypochondriasis, and dysmorphophobia—might be classified more appropriately under a heading that recognizes that they are more a mixed somatoform-anxiety disorder than either a somatoform or an anxiety disorder.

Diagnostic questions arising from unsatisfactory attempts to classify neurasthenia as either a somatoform or mood disorder provide another example. Instead of choosing one category or the other—implying, "it is really depression," and thereby privileging what may be an inappropriate frame of reference—by recognizing it as an essential mix of mood and somatoform features, the classification becomes less arbitrary and better fits clinical experience. Other locally defined conditions may also be classified as acute or chronic mixed somatoform-mood disorder (e.g., brain fag and *ode-ori* are discussed by González and Griffith; *kamzori* and *ashaktapanna* are Hindi and Marathi terms for enduring "weakness," which are the hallmark of conditions akin to neurasthenia in India).

For a diagnostic classification truly to be an international system, it must consider more carefully the implications of diverse clinical and epidemiological patterns. Recognizing multiple personality disorder but failing to recognize a possession disorder, the current DSM clearly favors dissociative conditions that occur more frequently in North America, even though they probably occur less frequently worldwide. In view of the extensive literature and clinical experience with possession states throughout the world, the assertion of González and Griffith that accounts of possession are "not rigorous enough to establish possession outright as a separate dissociative disorder" could just as easily be made for multiple personality disorder if possession were the accepted category of an Asian DSM. The criteria they suggest for a new possession disorder, despite this assertion, should also be considered cautiously, lest they reify the disorder with too rough an approximation of clinical experience. Must amnesia be required even if the disturbance of identity or consciousness is formidable? The criteria they suggest may turn out to be more useful in generating research questions that produce empirical data.

Other recommendations may also be more provocative than useful at this point: Their suggestion to include "dissociative psychomotor disorder" may shift the balance in the nosology toward an esoteric proliferation of categories. Recognizing that somatization, a process that is frequently clinically significant, occurs infrequently enough as a disorder that reliability studies of somatization disorder in a major study with the SCID remain inconclusive (Williams et al. 1992), one must consider whether including new categories that are likely to be used even less frequently might obscure the significance of more common cultural issues.

A three-way tension links 1) efforts to clarify the cultural dimensions of recognized conditions, 2) a need to reconfigure existing categories, and 3) the value of defining new ones. If Axis I categories are essential for epidemiological research, local names, beliefs, and practices associated with cultural concepts of disorder are essential concerns of clinical practice and anthropological inquiry. They not only convey meaning but also help to define the experience, irrespective of distinctions specified by Axis I. A cultural formulation as part of a clinical evaluation should complement other clinical perspectives. What patients think about clinical problems and what they mean constitute important clinical data that complement findings from other aspects of the evaluation. Just as a psychodynamic interview facilitates a psychodynamic formulation, a clinical ethnographic interview facilitates analysis of cultural dynamics, which may be critical for understanding the clinical issues and providing optimal care.

Questions about culture-specific social contexts of specific disorders are inextricably related to questions of nosology. Among dissociative disorders, child abuse is frequently, if not invariably, a concomitant of multiple personality disorder in the West. Similarly, possession states in India are associated with a typical social context: a recently married young woman put upon by a domineering mother-in-law after entering a new joint family household. Research is necessary to specify typical social contexts, such as cultural patterns of family conflict and their clinical implications. Doing so will clarify the clinical significance of social themes and cultural values that psychiatry has not considered adequately in the past (e.g., power relationships [especially gender related] in the household, social justice in the community, the impact of economic stressors, migration, and related issues).

References

American Psychiatric Association: Diagnostic and Statistical Manual of Mental Disorders, 3rd Edition, Revised. Washington, DC, American Psychiatric Association, 1987

American Psychiatric Association: Diagnostic and Statistical Manual of Mental Disorders, 4th Edition. Washington, DC, American Psychiatric Association, 1994

Williams JBW, Gibbon M, First MB, et al: The structured clinical interview for DSM-III-R (SCID), II: multi-site test-retest reliability. Arch Gen Psychiatry 49:630–636, 1992

Chapter 22

Nosological Comments on Cultural Diversity of Dissociative and Somatoform Disorders

David Spiegel, M.D.
Etzel Cardeña, Ph.D.

The role of culture in the interpretation, content, and process of psychological disorders is of course not exclusive to exotic cultures that produce "culture-bound" disorders. As González and Griffith (Chapter 19) point out, Western culture has its own list of "exotic" syndromes, including anorexia nervosa. Nowhere should cultural influences on symptomatology be more noticeable than among the dissociative disorders, which can be understood as extreme and dramatic responses to socially induced trauma. Thus, the content of dissociative symptoms and, to some extent, the process of dissociative disorders reflect the diversity of cultures, although the mental mechanisms underlying these symptoms may be universal. Possession is far more common than multiple personality disorders in India, for example (Adityanjee et al. 1989).

Possession

The descriptions of possession in the literature do indeed differ from those of multiple personality disorders, in terms of both presumed etiology and symptomatology, although there is clearly a common underlying dissociative mechanism (Cardena 1989; Krippner 1987). The phenomenon of possession per se is not pathological but may actually be sought after. In a number of cultures, possession is the expression of the religious and existential perspectives of a particular group and, particularly within a ceremonial setting, may serve a number of positive social and individual needs (Cardena 1989; Stoller 1989). Possession is likely to come to the attention of the clinician when it is a long-lasting condition occurring outside of a structured ceremonial setting and bringing distress to the individual and/or the social milieu. We should point out that this type of apparently unwilled and distressing possession is the exception rather than the rule within cultures that accept possession as a religious event.

Clearly, possession disorder does occur in the West as well, for example, in certain fundamentalist religious groups. We have seen and treated such a case (D. Spiegel and Fink 1979). At the time, we diagnosed the patient as having hysterical psychosis. Currently the patient would be placed in the "dissociative disorders, not otherwise specified" category, which does include reference to trance and possession states. The patient might also be diagnosed as having a brief reactive psychosis. There is need for a more appropriate placement in our nosology for such disorders, rather than as a variant of multiple personality disorder, as González and Griffith argue.

A proposal considered by our Dissociative Disorders Work Group involved the concept of *multiple personality disorder.* The name of this was eventually changed to dissociative identity disorder.

"Fleeing" or "Running" Syndrome

The fleeing syndromes actually seem to have a fair amount in common with psychogenic fugue, especially because in DSM-IV dissociative fugue no longer requires the development of a new identity but rather simply the loss of ordinary identity, usually accompanied by travel.

This syndrome is not, however, similar to *amok,* which usually involves harm to others. That sounds more like what we would classify as intermittent explosive disorder.

Falling Out, Blacking Out, Indisposition

This syndrome involves both classic symptoms, including an altered state of consciousness, and what would be classified as conversion symptoms: falling down and an inability to move. This disorder thus might be classified as a conversion disorder. The discussion pertaining here also applies to the interesting material on *ataques de nervios.* As the authors note, the co-occurrence of dissociative and conversion symptoms in a variety of cultures should indeed call into question the separation of dissociation and conversion, if not somatization altogether. Data about the frequent co-occurrence of alterations in mental state and dramatic and reversible alterations in sensation and motor control argue strongly for the reassociation of conversion disorders with the dissociative disorders. Historically, Freud (1895/1955) described a number of "hysterical" patients who showed somatoform disorders and various alterations of consciousness. More recently, Ross et al. (1989) found that, in comparison with patients diagnosed as having panic disorder, eating disorder, or schizophrenia, multiple personality patients reported significantly more somatic symptoms (an average of 13.5), and 7 out of the 20 multiple personality patients met the criteria for somatization disorder. Also of relevance is Steinberg's (1990) suggestion that multiple personality disorder may be mistakenly diagnosed as *ataques de nervios.*

The suggestion that the acute stress disorder/brief reactive dissociative disorder be modified to include a milder Criterion A—that is, a milder stressor—is quite an interesting one, especially if it would allow for this category to accommodate this group of disorders clearly observed in other cultures. This also seems appropriate given that such dissociative and conversion symptoms as stupor are included in brief reactive dissociative disorder.

Startle Matching

A common startle disorder among Latinos that Gonzáles and Griffith do not mention is *susto* or *espanto*—literally, sudden fright—assumed to be caused by an "evil eye" or black magic. This category of syndromes is interesting in that it is reminiscent of a spontaneous state of hypnosis: an event that suddenly grabs the subject's attention is followed by an excessive immediate reaction and then a state of extreme suggestibility. Indeed, intense absorption, dissociation of information not immediately relevant to this absorbed state, and enhanced suggestibility are all features of hypnosis (Bowers 1990; Hilgard 1965; H. Spiegel and Spiegel 1987; Weitzenhoffer 1980). Although it is not clear whether this phenomenon requires a new diagnostic category, again it is possible that brief reactive dissociative disorder with a milder stress criterion might cover at least some of the more serious examples of this phenomenon: those that qualify as a symptom rather than as normal, nonpathological behavior.

Koro

This syndrome, seen in Western terms, seems to have features of depersonalization—that is, the experience of disconnection from one's body—panic disorder, acute anxiety symptoms, and hypochondriasis, or excessive worry about somatic dysfunction. In addition, somatoform disorder, not otherwise specified, and body dysmorphic disorder are relevant. It may well be that some new category should be developed, especially if the specificity and prevalence of this disorder is considerable. Another interesting thing about this disorder is the predominance of males over females, which is not typical for conversion disorder.

Neurasthenia

It may well be that the overlap between neurasthenia and depression is so pronounced that a diagnosis such as major depression, not otherwise specified, or even dysthymic disorder, might adequately fit.

Creation of a New Dissociative Disorders Category

An alternative approach to the problem of better accommodating the range of dissociative disorders seen in various cultures is the creation of a new category, using but not limited to syndromes that could be categorized as unspecified dissociative disorders.

Although trance and possession states are common and normal components of religious and other ceremonies in many cultures, trance and possession disorder (leading to distress and dysfunction) is also the most common dissociative disorder reported in non-Western cultures. DSM-III (American Psychiatric Association 1980) mentioned trancelike states as an example of atypical dissociative disorder. DSM-III-R (American Psychiatric Association 1987) expanded the example and provided a definition of trance. The *International Classification of Diseases, 10th Revision* (ICD-10), has included a new category, trance and possession disorders (World Health Organization 1991). DSM-IV has incorporated dissociative trance disorder in its appendix of categories requiring further study.

Eventually, trance and possession disorder could be considered for future standard diagnostic systems as outlined below:

A. Either 1) or 2) must be present:
    1) Trance (i.e., temporary alteration in the state of consciousness), as evidenced by two of the following:
        (a) Loss of customary sense of personal identity
        (b) Narrowing of awareness of immediate surroundings, or usually narrow and selective focusing on environmental stimuli
        (c) Stereotyped behaviors or movements that are experienced as being beyond one's control
    2) Possession (i.e., a conviction that the individual has been taken over by a spirit, power, deity, or other person)
B. The trance or possession state is not authorized as a normal part of collective cultural or religious practice.
C. The trance or possession state causes significant impairment in social or occupational functioning or causes marked distress.
D. The trance or possession state does not occur exclusively during the course of a psychotic disorder (including mood disorder with psychotic features and brief reactive psychosis) or multiple personality disorder and is not due to a substance-induced disorder (e.g., substance intoxication) or a secondary dissociative disorder.

Conclusion

This chapter raises a number of important issues in an extremely thoughtful way. Any classification system creates both opportunities and limitations, focusing our attention on certain problems and thereby forcing us to ignore others. It has been said that when you have a hammer, everything starts to look like a nail. Although the inclusion of every cultural variant into standard diagnostic systems would probably make these systems unwieldy, further research into and description of syndromes that might likely come under the purview of a clinician would be useful. Whether the clinician should be alerted to most unusual cultural expressions of pathology through new diagnoses or through examples in the "not otherwise specified" section might be determined by the actual frequency with which these disorders may come to the attention of the clinician. It is hoped that thoughtful revision of our diagnostic nosology coupled with new data about psychiatric syndromes around the world will help us master our classification schemes rather than be mastered by them.

References

Adityanjee MD, Raju GSP, Khandelwal SK: Current status of multiple personality disorder in India. Am J Psychiatry 146:1607–1610, 1989

American Psychiatric Association: Diagnostic and Statistical Manual of Mental Disorders, 3rd Edition. Washington, DC, American Psychiatric Association, 1980

American Psychiatric Association: Diagnostic and Statistical Manual of Mental Disorders, 3rd Edition, Revised. Washington, DC, American Psychiatric Association, 1987

Bowers PG: Examining subjects' experiences during hypnosis, in Hypnosis: Current Theory, Research and Practice. Edited by van Dyck R, Spinhoven PH, van der Does AJW, van Rood YR, de Moor W. Amsterdam, The Netherlands, VU University Press, 1990

Cardeña E: Varieties of possession experience. Association for the Anthropological Study of Consciousness 5:2–3, 1989

Freud S: Studies on hysteria (1895), in The Standard Edition of the Complete Psychological Works of Sigmund Freud, Vol 12. London, England, Hogarth Press, 1955

Hilgard ER: Hypnotic Susceptibility. New York, Harcourt, Brace & World, 1965

Krippner S: Cross-cultural approaches to multiple personality disorder: practices in Brazilian spiritism. Ethos 15:273–295, 1987

Ross CA, Heber S, Norton RG, et al: Somatic symptoms in multiple personality disorder. Psychosomatics 30:154–160, 1989

Spiegel D, Fink R. Hysterical psychosis and hypnotizability. Am J Psychiatry 136:777–781, 1979

Spiegel H, Spiegel D: Trance and Treatment: Clinical Uses of Hypnosis. New York, Basic Books, 1978; reprinted, Washington, DC, American Psychiatric Press, 1987

Steinberg M: Transcultural issues in psychiatry: the ataque and multiple personality disorder. Dissociation 3:1, 1990

Stoller P: Fusion of the Worlds. Chicago, IL, University of Chicago Press, 1989

Weitzenhoffer AM: Hypnotic susceptibility revisited. Am J Clin Hypn 22:130–146, 1980

World Health Organization: International Classification of Diseases, 10th Revision. Geneva, Switzerland, World Health Organization, 1991

Section VI

Eating and Sexual Disorders

Chapter 23

A Cross-Cultural Review of Eating Disorders in Regard to DSM-IV

Cheryl Ritenbaugh, M.P.H., Ph.D.
Catherine Shisslak, Ph.D.
Nicolette Teufel, Ph.D.
Tina K. Leonard-Green, M.S., R.D.

Statement of the Issues

Anorexia nervosa and bulimia nervosa have been considered the prototypical "culture-bound syndromes" of Western society. Both have been examined intensively from psychological, medical anthropological, and feminist theory perspectives, with considerable attention given to the interaction of cultural norms and individual pathology. The pathological fear of fatness is pathognomonic among Western anorexics and is incorporated into DSM-III-R (American Psychiatric Association 1987) definition of anorexia nervosa. If this fear and other assumedly typical disorder characteristics are not fully transcultural, cases of anorexia and bulimia having somewhat different presentations may be consistently underdiagnosed among minority or non-Western populations.

Significance of the Issues

Review of the literature indicates that by the mid-1980s patients with eating disorders had been diagnosed among most United States minority groups—including American blacks, Puerto Ricans, Mexican Americans, Asian Americans, and some Native American groups—and among many Western and non-Western populations. In the United States, some individuals present with features that do not conform to the standard diagnostic criteria for anorexia nervosa or bulimia nervosa (Shisslak et al. 1989). These individuals' disorders are often missed by the health care system. The information presented in this review suggests that practitioners need to be aware that the presentation of eating disorders may vary relative to a patient's ethnicity, age, and sex.

Method

A representative sample of the literature regarding anorexia nervosa and bulimia nervosa among nonwhites in the United States and in other countries has been reviewed, with particular attention paid to reports that include data on specific individuals, whether collected through surveys or case studies. Theoretical or review articles were not considered. The 1985–1992 holdings of *MEDLINE* and *Index Medicus* were searched. Twenty-eight reports meeting these criteria were identified, 13 focusing primarily on United States minority groups and the remainder covering eating disorders among populations in Canada, England, Europe, Africa, and Asia.

This review, summarized in Table 23–1, focuses on information collected from United States minority groups and from non-United States populations that may have relevance to the possible cultural diversity in the United States situation. The review summaries have been organized by ethnicity. In addition, we have included a section on a broader spectrum of individuals such as males and those who were of older age at onset.

Results

Blacks

In three separate studies of American blacks (Anderson and Hay 1985; L. K. G. Hsu 1987; Silber 1986), 2 males and 15 females were identified with eating disorders. Of the 15 females, 8 were anorexic and 6 were bulimic, and 1 was anorexic with bulimic features. Of the 2 males, 1 was anorexic and 1 was anorexic with bulimic features. In the non–United States case reports of eating disorders among individuals of African heritage (Buchan and Gregory 1984; Fahey et al. 1988; Holden and Robinson 1988; Lacey and Dolan 1988; Robinson and Anderson 1985; Thomas and Szmukler 1985), 18 of 24 patients had bulimia or anorexia with bulimic features. This relative rate of bulimia or bulimic features is higher than in white American case series collected in similar ways (e.g., Anderson and Hay 1985). Diagnostic features of the eating disorders, such as fear of fatness, and level of other psychopathology in family members were found to be similar between American blacks and whites. In one United States study (Anderson and Hay 1985), American black eating disorder patients were described as psychiatrically similar to other American black nonpsychotic psychiatric patients in the same institution; however, the eating disorder patients were from a significantly higher social class.

Gray et al. (1987) surveyed American black and white college students using a questionnaire designed to estimate prevalence of components of the DSM-III-R bulimia nervosa criteria. With this tool, 2% and 3% of black males and females and 4% and 13% of white males and females, respectively, were found to conform to DSM-III-R bulimia criteria. American black women were significantly less likely than white women to indicate fear and discouragement regarding weight and control of food intake. This may be consistent with higher prevalences of obesity among American black females.

Table 23–1. Summary of studies on anorexia and bulimia among U.S. minorities and among patients in other countries, 1980–1991

Reference	Country	No. by ethnic group	No. with anorexia	No. with bulimia	No. of other	Survey	Case study	Measures
Anderson and Hay 1985	United States	7 Black females 1 Black male 110 White females 10 White males	4 1 }98	3 }22			X	
Buchan and Gregory 1984	Zimbabwe	1 Black Zimbabwean female	1				X	DSM-III
Buhrich 1981	Malaysia	Females: 19 Chinese 7 Indians 1 Malaysian 1 Eurasian Males: 1 Indian 1 Eurasian	28 Females 2 Males				X	Questionnaire
Fahey et al. 1988	England	1 African female	1				X	Psychometric assessment
Faltus 1986	Czechoslovakia	22 Czechoslovakian females 2 Czechoslovakian males	22 2			X		Criteria from Faltus (1979)

(continued)

Table 23–1. Summary of studies on anorexia and bulimia *(continued)*

Reference	Country	No. by ethnic group	No. with anorexia	No. with bulimia	No. of other	Survey	Case study	Measures
Fichter and Daser 1987	Germany	65 Germans	29 Males (most also had bulimic symptoms) 23 Females		7 Atypical anorexia males 6 Secondary anorexia males	X		Interview (SIAN) and six questionnaires (ANIS, PDS, FPI, EPI, somatic complaints, general well-being)
Furnham and Alibhai 1983	England	15 Kenyan Asian females resident in Kenya 15 Kenyan Asian females resident in Britain 15 White British females resident in Britain				X		Kelly Triadic Method and Questionnaire
Garner and Garfinkel 1980	Canada	423 Canadian females	84			X		EAT and HSCL
Gray et al. 1987	United States	341 Black females 166 Black males 220 White females 119 White males		10 (3%) 3 (2%) 29 (13%) 5 (4%)		X		Questionnaire (designed to DSM-III)

Study	Country	Sample		Diagnosis		Notes
Hiebert et al. 1988	United States	19 White females 1 White male 9 Hispanic females 1 Hispanic male	19 1 9 1		X	Chart review (outcome comparison)
Holden and Robinson 1988	England	13 Black females	2	11	X	Criteria from Russell 1970
Hsu 1987	United States	6 Black females 1 Black male	2	3	1 Anorexia with/bulimia 1 Anorexia with/bulimia	X	
Kope and Slack (1987)	Canada	3 Vietnamese refugee females	1	1	1 Anorexia with/bulimia	X	
Lacey and Dolan (1988)	England	1 Pakistanian female 1 Jamaican female 2 Afro-Caribbean/English females 1 African/Indian female			5 Normal body weight with bulimia	X	DSM-III
Lee 1991	China (Hong Kong)	16 Chinese females (lower social class)	16 (few had bulimic symptoms)			X	

(continued)

Table 23–1. Summary of studies on anorexia and bulimia (*continued*)

Reference	Country	No. by ethnic group	No. with anorexia	No. with bulimia	No. of other	Survey	Case study	Measures
Lee et al. 1989	China (Hong Kong)	3 Chinese females	1		1 Bulimic anorexia case; 1 Atypical anorexia case		X	
Lee et al. 1991	China (Hong Kong)	35 Chinese females	32	3			X	
Mumford and Whitehouse 1988	United States	204 Asian females	1	7 (3.4%)		X		EAT, BSQI
		355 White females	0	2 (0.6%)				
Nasser 1986	Egypt	50 Arab females at universities in London		6		X		
		60 Arab females at universities in Cairo (reported in previous 1986 study by author)		0		X		
Nwaefuna 1981	Liberia	1 Nigerian female	1			X		Physical examination
Robinson and Anderson 1985	United States and England	3 Black females	2		1 Anorexia with/bulimia		X	EAT-26
		2 Black males	2					

Study	Country	Sample	Findings	Prevalence			Criteria/Method
Rosen et al. 1988	United States	85 Native American females		>50% were dieting and using potentially hazardous methods; 24% used one or more purging methods	X		Questionnaire (not designed to DSM-III diagnoses)
Silber 1986	United States	5 Hispanic females 2 Black females	5 2			X	DSM-II criteria
Snow and Harris 1989	United States	56 Native Americans (51 females, 7 males) 37 Hispanics (31 females, 6 males)		5 Females (10%) 4 Females (13%)	X		Questionnaire (DSM-III based)
Steinhausen 1985	Germany	30 Germans	17 with restrictor anorexia 5 with bulimic anorexia		X		EAT, EDI, OSIQ
Suematsu et al. 1985	Japan	1,011 Japanese (970 females, 41 males)			X		DSM-III
Thomas and Szmukler 1985	England	1 Jamaican female 2 Black females	1 1	1 Anorexia with/bulimia	X	X	DSM-III

Hispanics

Information on eating disorders among Hispanics in the United States comes from three regional subpopulations in New Mexico (Snow and Harris 1989), California (Hiebert et al. 1988), and Washington, D.C. (Silber 1986). In the last two groups, most were first-generation immigrants (4 of 10 and 5 of 5, respectively). In the New Mexico survey, most individuals surveyed were from families who had resided in the United States for many generations.

In her Washington, D.C., study, Silber (1986) identified hospital-based cases that could be considered classic. All were from upper income families who had relatively recently emigrated from Latin America to the United States. The daughters were attempting to cope with the loss of social support associated with leaving their home countries and with the new pressures associated with rapid acculturation. Notably, the diagnoses of anorexia had been unusually delayed, given the degree of wasting reported at the time of diagnosis. Silber attributed this delayed diagnosis to the low index of suspicion for anorexia resulting from the ethnicity of the patients. Hiebert et al. (1988), in a California treatment outcome study, compared Hispanic with white eating disorder patients. They detected no differences attributable to ethnic group when patients were matched on demographic factors.

Snow and Harris (1989), using a questionnaire designed to identify behaviors included in DSM-III-R criteria for bulimia, surveyed 31 Hispanic females in a rural New Mexico high school. Four (13%) met the questionnaire criteria for bulimia; these girls were significantly heavier than those who did not meet the criteria (65.3 kg, vs. 56.9 kg). Increased weight was related to indications of disordered eating and use of potentially harmful weight control techniques. Affirmative responses to questions regarding concerns about weight, body shape, and dieting were considered by the authors to be similar to responses seen in white populations, although risk for anorexia appeared to be low.

Native Americans

Two surveys of Native American high school and college students provide some insight into the prevalence of disordered eating behaviors in this culturally diverse minority population. The New Mexico study by Snow and Harris (1989) also included 51 Pueblo Indian high school girls; the Pueblo girls did not differ significantly from the Hispanic sample. Fifty-three percent indicated feeling "depressed or down on themselves" after a binge, and 20% indicated that they had also used vomiting or laxatives after a binge. Ten percent of the girls met the questionnaire criteria for bulimia; as with the Hispanic girls, the Native American girls who met the criteria were heavier than those who did not (67.0 kg vs. 59.8 kg). Again, risk for anorexia appeared to be low, but risk for bulimia appeared at least comparable to that in white populations.

A second survey (Rosen et al. 1988) of 85 Michigan Chippewa women ages 12–55 years was undertaken on the basis of anecdotal comments from Native American college students indicating that disordered eating behaviors were not uncommon in their communities. The questionnaire was designed to elicit information about dieting behavior but was not designed specifically with regard to DSM-III-R criteria for bulimia. The results indicated widespread use of purging and other deleterious weight loss strategies associated with eating disorders. Seventy-four percent had dieted, 55% had used pathogenic weight loss techniques (fasting, purging, etc.), 12% reported vomiting, and 6% reported use of laxatives and diuretics. As with the Snow and Harris (1989) survey, women reporting dieting were significantly heavier than those not reporting dieting behaviors, and among the dieters, those using pathogenic dieting techniques were heavier than those not using such techniques. Women reporting more severe dieting tended to be older than the sample average, with 10 of the 13 subjects in their 30s and the only woman in her 40s using pathogenic techniques. As with the Pueblo high school group, anorexia did not seem to be a problem.

Immigrant Studies

Several studies have examined disordered eating among immigrants to Western countries. Published reports include the study of Hispanics mentioned earlier, as well as studies of Vietnamese in Canada (Kope and Slack 1987), Egyptians in England (Nasser 1988a, 1988b), Arab Muslims in England (Lieberman 1989), and Asians in England (Mumford and Whitehouse 1988). In each of these reports except for one, the immigrants appeared to be adopting the fear of fatness and other normative values associated with the country to which they were immigrating. Kope and Slack (1987) present case studies of three Vietnamese female refugees with anorexia nervosa in which onset of the illness appeared to be related to the trauma of leaving family behind, traumatic escapes, and coping with the problems of living under the control of older siblings. The classic features of the condition, including disturbed body image and fear of fatness, were all present.

Nasser's (1986) survey of 50 Egyptian females at London universities and 60 Egyptian females at Cairo universities showed no evidence of eating disorders in the Cairo sample, but 12% of the England sample met DSM-III-R criteria by questionnaire. Mumford and Whitehouse (1988) reported administration of the Eating Attitudes Test (EAT) and a body shape questionnaire to 205 Asian and 355 white girls ages 14–16 in a school in England. Asian girls scored significantly higher than white girls on the EAT, suggesting greater concern with food intake and weight. Girls whose scores suggested eating disorders were interviewed; 3.6% of the Asian and 0.6% of the white girls met the criteria for bulimia nervosa on interview; one Asian girl but no white girls met the criteria for anorexia nervosa. A significant difference in eating disorder rates was found between the two groups. The authors attribute the high rate of bulimia nervosa among the Asian girls in part to acculturation.

Lieberman (1989) reported on the case of an Arab Muslim family in England with four bulimic children, two males and two females, which illustrates some of the variability seen in these case studies. Each of the children presented with binging and vomiting. The children were involved in the parental conflict, as each parent reportedly attempted to get the children to take sides against the other parent. The eldest son reported that his behavior served to release tension. As first-generation immigrants, the parental generation remained isolated from their new cultural setting. The author did not provide information relating to the children's body images or fears of fatness.

Furnham and Alibhai (1983), in research related to eating disorders, reported on a three-group study of the relative valuation of thin versus fat body shapes among Kenyan Asian females living in Britain, Kenyan Asians living in Kenya, and British females in Britain. Results showed that the Kenyan Asians living in Kenya valued fatness more and slimness less than either group in Britain. However, between the groups in Britain, the Kenyan Asians had more extreme positive valuation of slimness and negative valuation of fatness, appearing to magnify the Western cultural values as they integrate into a new situation. This is consistent with the findings presented earlier of immigration presenting a high-risk situation for eating disorders.

Non-Western Countries

China (Hong Kong).   The papers from Hong Kong are included because they provide a description of eating disorders with quite different cultural components. Three papers (Lee 1991; Lee et al. 1989, 1991) described persons with anorexia from the lower socioeconomic classes in Hong Kong. In these cases, all DSM-III-R criteria were met except for the fear of fatness. In traditional Chinese culture, some degree of fatness is highly valued, and cultural prescriptions of beauty focus on the face rather than the body. Appropriate to this concern, acne was reported as a precipitant of anorexia nervosa among some of these patients (Lee et al. 1991). Social emphasis is on the importance of eating for health; the patients described here overtly accepted this cultural norm in the extreme by taking control of their eating in an exaggerated attempt to eat only pure or healthful foods. The resulting emaciation was regarded by the patients as unimportant, and attempts directed toward increasing food intake to restore body weight failed. The patients in this series explained their lack of food consumption as secondary to feelings of fullness or epigastric pain. Family dynamics conformed to patterns seen in anorexic families in the United States.

Japan.   Suematsu et al. (1985) surveyed physicians at more than 1,000 institutions regarding the number and types of anorexia cases seen in 1981 and 1983. They received responses from 315 institutions, who reported on a total of about 2,400 cases. Their criteria for diagnosis included distorted body image and denial of illness, in addition to the biological criteria, but they did not specify "intense fear of gaining weight" as one of the criteria. The surveys suggested a 30% increase in the number of cases between 1981 and 1983, but no further data are available regarding whether this apparent trend has continued. By the diagnostic criteria used in this study, the Chinese anorexic persons described by Lee would be considered "typical."

Other Often Overlooked Groups

Because of the widespread knowledge that eating disorders are common among young white American women, it appears that eating disorders may be underrecognized among females older than age 30 and among males. A brief overview of the literature for these groups follows.

Females with older age at onset. In more recent years, cases of eating disorders have been reported among females with a later age at onset (Price et al. 1985). McGlynn and Tinker (1989) described four such cases, two anorexic women and two bulimic women; all were between the ages of 34 and 49 and were married; three had children. The patients had interpersonal conflicts with parents or spouses and self-image distortion. One of the anorexic women had a history of previous intervention for her eating disorder.

L. Hsu and Zimmer (1988) reported five cases of eating disorders in women first diagnosed between the ages of 57 and 72 years old; one presented with anorexia nervosa and four with bulimia. Onset of the eating disorders had occurred 2–6 years prior to the onset of treatment. The four patients with bulimia also had been diagnosed with major depression. Events precipitating the onset of the eating disorder ranged from significant life events such as retirement, marriage, or death of a significant other to a friend's commenting on the patient's weight or suggesting vomiting to control weight. Although all patients had been under a physician's care, their eating disorder had remained undiagnosed. Patients' weights ranged from 30.9 to 72.7 kg, with three patients presenting with weights of less than 36.4 kg. The clinical picture presented by these cases was very similar to that found in younger patients; however, patients who were older at onset did not appear to have the sexual conflicts that often precipitate the onset of eating disorders in the young.

Males. Males are present in many of the case studies presented earlier, making up about 10%–15% of the groups studied. Although represented in many series (Fichter and Daser 1987), few studies have been designed specifically to compare and contrast males and females. Oyebode et al. (1988) studied a matched sample of 13 male and 13 female eating disorder patients and found the clinical features to be similar in both groups. However, the long-term outcome in the males was somewhat worse and was associated with continued preoccupation with food intake and body composition.

Discussion

Much has been written about the extreme cultural value that Western society places on thinness and the concurrent negative valuation of fatness (Callaway 1990; Nichter and Nichter 1991; Ritenbaugh 1982; Seid 1989). High rates of anorexia nervosa in Western societies and increasing rates of anorexia nervosa found among their immigrant groups and rapidly acculturating ethnic minorities attest to this cultural obsession with thinness. Individuals from groups that traditionally had a low prevalence of eating disorders (e.g., U.S. minorities, immigrants, and developing country populations) may be particularly vulnerable to the development of such disorders when faced with the stresses of rapid Westernization, acculturation, and social assimilation (Root 1990). The studies reviewed here point to the need for clinicians to have a heightened suspicion of anorexia nervosa when dealing with underweight patients from virtually any population having contact with or adapting to Western society.

The review presented here also points toward the association of Western cultural values with bulimia nervosa. Bulimic behaviors and bulimia nervosa are found among persons of all body sizes. Among heavier women, the development of these disorders may represent the negative value placed on fatness by Western society. Long-term maintenance of a thin body is extremely difficult once obesity has become established (Bjorntorp and Brodoff 1992; Ritenbaugh 1991); therefore, it is to be expected that pathogenic attempts at weight loss are not uncommon among heavy women. Three of the articles reviewed here suggest that clinicians should be alerted to these types of behaviors among older and heavier Hispanic, Native American, and American black women; all of these populations have a high prevalence of obesity. With growing attention in these populations to the negative consequences of obesity, an increasing incidence of pathogenic attempts at weight loss would not be surprising. Closer examination of the traditions of these groups may show that such behaviors are understood and accepted within these cultures, whereas self-starvation is not. Further research into the etiology and prevalence of bulimia in these minority populations is desirable.

Whereas the criteria for diagnosis of bulimia nervosa focus on behaviors (binging, purging), the criteria for anorexia nervosa include components that are biological (absence of at least three menstrual cycles), behavioral (refusal to maintain body weight above 15% below minimum), and cognitive (fear of fatness). Anorexia nervosa is the only diagnostic category in the DSM in which an ideation is specified (i.e., fear of fatness). This ideation is shared by many nonanorexic Western women, raising the possibility that although fear of fatness is a major feature in the overwhelming majority of anorexic patients, it may be a presenting condition descriptive of Western culture, rather than a requirement for the diagnosis of anorexia. Studies by Lee and colleagues among Hong Kong Chinese (Lee 1991; Lee et al. 1989, 1991) provide an opportunity to gain some distance from our own cultural context. Anorexia among these patients is associated with an exaggeration of cultural values in support of beauty and healthful eating but not fear of fatness, suggesting that cultural norms may influence a patient's rationale for the behavior.

The cross-cultural studies presented here suggest that atypical anorexia may be more widespread than previously recognized and may be the category of choice when dealing with some cultural groups. Shisslak et al. (1989) have described a series of 15 individuals from the United States atypical anorexic in which only 3 had distorted body image. Publication of more case series of atypical anorexia from varied cultural contexts could provide important insights into the roles of cultural norms in the chosen idioms of distress (Nichter 1981). An alternative, and more international, approach comes from Lee (1991), who argued that diagnostic criteria for anorexia nervosa that allow a level of cultural variability may be particularly useful in encouraging cross-cultural and multiethnic studies. Lee proposed replacing "intense fear of gaining weight" with "use of rigid complaints such as fear of fatness, abdominal fullness, or distaste for food to account for the severe restriction of food intake or other weight-losing behaviors." This recommendation does not deny the higher rates of eating disorders in cultures where fear of fatness is the norm but rather suggests the use of diagnostic criteria that lend themselves more readily to international and cross-cultural situations. With rapid cultural transitions under way in many parts of the world, the available international studies in the literature are rapidly becoming out of date. Careful international and cross-cultural studies that address the characteristics of anorexic and bulimic individuals are needed to move these issues toward resolution.

Conclusion

Prior to 1980, there were relatively few case reports of anorexia nervosa or bulimia nervosa outside the developed Western countries or among individuals of non-European descent. By the mid-1980s, the literature suggests that rates of anorexia nervosa and bulimia were on the rise among minority groups in the United States and among immigrant groups and non-Europeans worldwide. Among these groups, most features of the two conditions are similar to the standard Western configuration, with those individuals undergoing rapid acculturation being particularly at risk. However, there is some suggestion of differences in the presentation of the disorders. Chinese anorexic individuals differ in features of body image distortion. Bulimia among minorities from the United States not only may be more common than anorexia but also may be associated with older age and heavier body weights.

A major step toward the development of a truly international diagnostic approach to bulimia nervosa and anorexia nervosa is a heightened awareness among practitioners of the possibility of both bulimia nervosa and anorexia nervosa among minority and non-Western populations. Currently, diagnosis of bulimia nervosa does not require attribution of "fear of fatness"; future research in non-European populations may show that the role of fear of fatness in the anorexia nervosa diagnostic criteria may be specific to the West. It may not be necessary in international classification systems, where it may be replaced instead by terms such as "distorted body image," "refusal to gain weight," and so forth. Although researchers such as Arya (1991) have argued that it is important to maintain the distinction between "true" anorexia and atypical anorexia, such distinctions unfortunately focus the argument on the "true" diagnosis of individual patients, rather than on natural history and appropriate treatment of the condition within and among cultures and may impede understanding of the role of culture in patient attributions. Broader diagnostic criteria and increased emphasis on the prevalence of atypical anorexia will reinforce the message to health professionals that individuals of all backgrounds are potentially at risk.

References

American Psychiatric Association: Diagnostic and Statistical Manual of Mental Disorder, 3rd Edition. Washington, DC, American Psychiatric Association, 1980

American Psychiatric Association: Diagnostic and Statistical Manual of Mental Disorder, 3rd Edition, Revised. Washington, DC, American Psychiatric Association, 1987

Anderson AE, Hay A: Racial and socioeconomic influences in anorexia nervosa and bulimia. Int J Eat Disord 4:479–487, 1985

Arya DK: Anorexia nervosa across cultures (letter). Br J Psychiatry 158:285–286, 1991

Bjorntorp P, Brodoff B: Obesity. Philadelphia, PA, Lippincott, 1992

Buchan T, Gregory L: Anorexia nervosa in a black Zimbabwean. Br J Psychiatry 145:326–330, 1984

Buhrich N: Frequency of presentation of anorexia nervosa in Malaysia. Aust NZ J Psychiatry 15:153–155, 1981

Callaway CW: The Callaway Diet: Successful Permanent Weight Control for Starvers, Stuffers, and Skippers. New York, Bantam Books, 1990

Fahey T, Robinson P, Russell G, et al: Anorexia nervosa following torture in a young African woman. Br J Psychiatry 153:385–387, 1988

Faltus F: Anorexia nervosa in Czechoslovakia. Int J Eat Disord 5:581–585, 1986

Fichter MM, Daser C: Symptomatology, psychosexual development, and gender identity in 42 anorexic males. Psychol Med 17:409–418, 1987

Furnham A, Alibhai N: Cross-cultural differences in the perception of female body shapes. Psychol Med 13:829–837, 1983

Garner DM, Garfinkel PE: Sociocultural factors in the development of anorexia nervosa. Psychol Med 10:647–656, 1980

Gray JJ, Ford K, Kelly LM: The prevalence of bulimia in a black college population. Int J Eat Disord 6:733–740, 1987

Hiebert KA, Felice ME, Wingard DL, et al: Comparison of outcome in Hispanic and Caucasian patients with anorexia nervosa. Int J Eat Disord 7(5):693–696, 1988

Holden N, Robinson P: Anorexia nervosa and bulimia nervosa in British blacks. Br J Psychiatry 152:544–549, 1988

Hsu L, Zimmer B: Eating disorders in old age. Int J Eat Disord 7:133–138, 1988

Hsu LKG: Are the eating disorders becoming more common in blacks? Int J Eat Disord 6:113–124, 1987

Kope TM, Slack WH: Anorexia nervosa in Southeast Asian refugees: a report on three cases. J Am Acad Child Adolesc Psychiatry 26:795–797, 1987

Lacey JH, Dolan B: Bulimia in British blacks and Asians: a catchment area study. Br J Psychiatry 152:73–79, 1988

Lee S: Anorexia nervosa in Hong Kong: a Chinese perspective. Psychol Med 21:703–711, 1991

Lee S, Chiu HFK, Chen C: Anorexia nervosa in Hong Kong: why not more in Chinese? Br J Psychiatry 154:683–688, 1989

Lee S, Leung CM, Wing YK, et al: Acne as a risk factor for anorexia nervosa in Chinese. Aust NZ J Psychiatry 25:134–137, 1991

Lieberman S: A family with four bulimic children. Int J Eat Disord 8:101–104, 1989

McGlynn T, Tinker D: Anorexia nervosa in adulthood. Am Fam Physician 39:173–178, 1989

Mumford D, Whitehouse A: Increased prevalence of bulimia nervosa among Asian schoolgirls. Br Med J 297:718, 1988

Nasser M: Comparative study of the prevalence of abnormal eating attitudes among Arab female students of both London and Cairo universities. Psychol Med 16:621–625, 1986

Nasser M: Culture and weight consciousness. J Psychosom Res 32:573–577, 1988a

Nasser M: Eating disorders: the cultural dimension. Soc Psychiatry Psychiatr Epidemiol 23:184–187, 1988b

Nichter M: Idioms of distress: alternatives in the expression of psychosocial distress: a case study from South India. Cult Med Psychiatry 5:379–408, 1981

Nichter M, Nichter M: Hype and weight. Med Anthropol 13:249–284, 1991

Oyebode F, Boodhoo J, Schapira K: Anorexia nervosa in males: clinical features and outcome. Int J Eat Disord 7:121–124, 1988

Price W, Giannini A, Colella J: Anorexia nervosa in the elderly. J Am Geriatr Soc 33:213–215, 1985

Ritenbaugh C: Obesity as a culture-bound syndrome. Cult Med Psychiatry 6:347–361, 1982

Ritenbaugh C: Body size and shape: a dialogue of culture and biology. Med Anthropol 13:173–180, 1991

Robinson P, Anderson A: Anorexia nervosa in American blacks. J Psychiatr Res 19:183–188, 1985

Root MPP: Disordered eating in women of color. Sex Roles 22:525–536, 1990

Rosen LW, Shafer CL, Dummer GM, et al: Prevalence of pathogenic weight-control behaviors among Native American women and girls. Int J Eat Disord 7:807–811, 1988

Seid R: Never Too Thin: Why Women Are at War With Their Bodies. New York, Prentice Hall, 1989

Shisslak CM, Crago M, Yates A: Typical patterns in atypical anorexia nervosa. Psychosomatics 30:307–311, 1989

Silber TJ: Anorexia nervosa in blacks and Hispanics. Int J Eat Disord 5:121–128, 1986

Snow JR, Harris MB: Brief report: disordered eating in Southwestern Pueblo Indians and Hispanics. J Adolesc 12:329–336, 1989

Steinhausen HC: Anorexia nervosa: transcultural comparisons. Pediatrician 12:157–163, 1985

Suematsu H, Ishikawa H, Kuboki T, et al: Statistical studies on anorexia nervosa in Japan: detailed clinical data on 1,011 patients. Psychother Psychosom 43:96–103, 1985

Thomas J, Szmukler G: Anorexia nervosa in patients of Afro-Caribbean extraction. Br J Psychiatry 146:653–656, 1985

Chapter 24

Cultural Comments on Eating Disorders

Raymond Prince, M.D.

The chapter by Ritenbaugh et al. (Chapter 23) is a useful review of the cross-cultural literature on anorexia nervosa and bulimia. It is clear that these disorders do occur in non-Western immigrants to the United States, Canada, and Europe—that is, among those who might have been expected to be immune from them in their native country. The review also emphasizes that anorexia nervosa is relatively common among Japanese in their homeland and also occurs among the overseas Han Chinese of Singapore, Malaysia, and Hong Kong. The authors make the interesting point that although most of the 35 studies they surveyed found symptom patterns identical with those in DSM-III-R (American Psychiatric Association 1987), there were discrepancies in some reports of Chinese patients. Both Ong et al. (1992) in Singapore and Lee et al. (1989) in Hong Kong found that the anorexia nervosa patients' quasi-delusional belief that they were too fat (a required feature for the diagnosis in DSM-III-R) could not be elicited from some Chinese who otherwise demonstrated characteristic signs and symptoms. It should be noted, of course, that there is a recognized overlap between depressive disorders and anorexia nervosa; DSM-III-R specifically states, "In depressive disorders . . . , weight loss can occur, but there is no disturbance of body image or intense fear of obesity" (p. 66). However, if this Chinese finding receives significant confirmation and does not simply represent anorexia and weight loss as part of a depressive reaction or other illness, a reexamination of the DSM criteria may be called for. Ritenbaugh et al. also caution that because American psychiatrists expect to find these eating disorders only in affluent populations of European descent, the diagnosis may be missed in some of their non-Western immigrant patients.

From my own point of view, the most interesting aspect of these eating disorders is more theoretical than practical. They are, after all, quite rare even in Western cultures. In general community surveys, even a very large sample will yield only a few cases. The Epidemiologic Catchment Area study in the United States, with a total sample size of 20,862 (which included representative samples of five widely dispersed community mental health center catchment areas), found only 11 cases. The authors of the final summary report noted that they did not include anorexia nervosa in their analysis because there were too few cases (i.e., considerably fewer than 1 per 1,000 population) (Robins and Regier 1991).

However, for American psychiatrists, anorexia nervosa is a particularly instructive example of a culture-bound syndrome. We have a clearly defined psychiatric syndrome that seems to be restricted to certain cultures around the world on the basis of differing attitudes, values, and beliefs; a psychiatric disorder that is generated out of thin air as it were. Eating disorders are particularly instructive, because unlike other culture-bound syndromes such as *latah* and *taijin kyofusho*, for the Euro-American psychiatrist anorexia nervosa is "homegrown." The Western psychiatrist shares the cultural pressures toward thinness that seem at the heart of the genesis of the disorder; we all understand that in our contemporary world, thinness is healthy, beautiful, and effective, and fatness is unhealthy, ugly, and slovenly. Western psychiatrists can readily grasp at least the potential of such beliefs and values to create a psychiatric disturbance without the need of an organic basis.

This interesting link between eating disorders and cultural values was first remarked by the Western-trained Chinese psychiatrist Pow Meng Yap, who indeed coined the expression "culture-bound syndrome." Although previously such syndromes had only been described in exotic or non-Western cultures, in 1969 Yap suggested that the Western world might harbor culture-bound syndromes as well and specifically referred to anorexia nervosa as one possibility: "typical culture-bound variations of psychogenic reactions in European and American countries include homosexual-panic and perhaps school-phobia and anorexia nervosa" (Yap 1969, p. 40). Since that time, a considerable literature has emerged supporting the view that anorexia nervosa and bulimia are found primarily in Western cultures or in cultures undergoing rapid and significant Westernization (DiNicola 1990; Prince 1985; Swartz 1985). According to that literature, the following points should be noted:

- In general, anorexia nervosa and bulimia seem to be rare or absent outside of Western or Westernizing cultures.
- Although these disorders have been said to be absent from some cultures, most reports on the matter are merely anecdotal; furthermore, the majority of the thousands of world cultures lack even anecdotal comment. Reports of the type, "I have never seen or heard of a case," include the cultures of New Guinea (Burton-Bradley 1984), southern Nigeria, and the Middle East (Prince 1985).
- In multiethnic communities where studies have been conducted, differential frequencies according to culture have been reported. As Ritenbaugh et al. mention, in Malaysia there is a reported difference in prevalence, with cases being more common among the Chinese, the most affluent of the three major ethnic groups in Malaysia (19 cases); less common among Indians (7 cases); and much less common among Malays (only 1 reported case). The proportions of these three

ethnic groups in the Malaysian peninsula at the time of the study were: Chinese, 36%; Indians, 11%; and Malays, 53%. Thus, on the basis of population we would have expected a much higher proportion of Malays than of the other two ethnic groups among the anorexia cases (Buhrich 1981). Similarly, in South Africa, cases are said to be significantly more common among those of European descent than among blacks (Nash 1984). Still, the methodology of these two studies leaves much to be desired, and even the most basic data such as the differential utilization of health care facilities according to ethnic groups is not presented. It must also be realized that Ritenbaugh et al. were hampered in their review of studies of American ethnic groups, because very often key data were not provided in the available reports. Authors who were not very sensitive to cultural matters referred to, for example, American blacks or African Americans without realizing the very considerable cultural differences between recent Haitian immigrants, newly arrived African ethnic groups (such as Ewe and Yoruba), and blacks who had lived in the United States for many generations. Significant advances in the transcultural psychiatry field will require much greater sensitivity to cultural differences, particularly among non-Western groups; Ewe and Yoruba are as different as French and Norwegians.

References

American Psychiatric Association: Diagnostic and Statistical Manual of Mental Disorders, 3rd Edition, Revised. Washington, DC, American Psychiatric Association, 1987

Buhrich N: Frequency of presentation of anorexia nervosa in Malaysia. Aust NZ J Psychiatry 15:153-155, 1981

Burton-Bradley BG: Letter to the editor. Am J Soc Psychiatry 2:58, 1984

DiNicola VF: Anorexia multiforme: self-starvation in historical and cultural context, II. anorexia nervosa as a culture-reactive syndrome. Transcultural Psychiatric Research Review 27:245–286, 1990

Lee S, Chiu H, Chen C: Anorexia nervosa in Hong Kong: why not more in the Chinese? Br J Psychiatry 154:683–688, 1989

Nash ES: Letter to the editor. Transcultural Psychiatric Research Review 21:227, 1984

Ong YL, Tsoi WF, Cheah JS: A clinical and psychosocial study of seven cases of anorexia nervosa in Singapore. Singapore Med J 23:255–261, 1992

Prince R: The concept of culture-bound syndromes: anorexia nervosa and brain-fag. Soc Sci Med 21:197–203, 1985

Robins LN, Regier DA: Psychiatric Disorders in America: The Epidemiologic Catchment Area Study. New York, Free Press, 1991

Swartz L: Anorexia nervosa as a culture-bound syndrome. Soc Sci Med 20:725–730, 1985

Yap PM: The culture bound reactive syndromes, in Mental Health Research in Asia and the Pacific. Edited by Caudill W, Lin TY. Honolulu, HI, East-West Center Press, 1969

Chapter 25

Cultural Sensitivity and the Sexual Disorders of DSM-IV: Review and Assessment

Dona L. Davis, Ph.D.

The sexual disorders of DSM-IV (American Psychiatric Association 1994) are divided into three groups: paraphilias, sexual dysfunctions, and other. Paraphilias are arousal in response to sexual objects or situations that are not a part of normative arousal patterns and may interfere with the capacity for reciprocal, affectionate sexual activity. Sexual dysfunctions are inhibitions of desire or psychophysiological changes that occur in the sexual response cycle. Other sexual disorders may include feelings of inadequacy of physical type, sexual performance, or personal standards of masculinity or femininity; distress over sexual orientation; distress over repeated sexual conquests; and other forms of nonparaphilic sexual addiction. The purpose of this chapter is to review the literature on the potential roles that cultural factors may play regarding the epidemiology, nosology, diagnosis, and treatment of the DSM sexual disorders.

The cross-cultural and ethnic studies of sexual disorder reviewed in this chapter are drawn from two bodies of literature. The first concerns assessment, diagnosis, and/or treatment of sexual disorders among ethnic clinical populations. The second, a more theoretical body of literature, critiques the cross-cultural appropriateness of the sexual disorder categories themselves. Specific attention, where information is available, is paid to Native Americans, African Americans, Asian Americans, and Latin Americans. Issues concerning the culture-bound syndromes and gender identity disorders are also discussed.

The Paraphilias

The Paraphilias is a medical legacy that can be traced back to Krafft-Ebing's (1886) *Psychopathia Sexualis* and the works of other 19th-century scholars (Weeks 1985). With their encyclopedic approach to cataloging behavior, early cross-cultural reviews often included discussions of sex and the paraphilias. These studies also focused on homosexuality (Brown 1952; Carstairs 1964; Ford and Beach 1951; Gebhard 1971; Jones and Frei 1979; Laubscher 1937; Meikle 1982; Rooth 1973; Suggs and Marshall 1971). Although the presence or absence of specific paraphilias was noted across the evolutionary and ethnographic spectrums (Brown 1952; Carstairs 1964; Ford and Beach 1951; Suggs and Marshall 1971), the cultural relativity of norms and values associated with these behaviors, rather than their similarity to Western categories, is the primary point of discussion.

Ethnographic examples of paraphilias are not usually equivalent to standard diagnostic meanings. For example, exposure of genitals as a form of sexual invitation has been called exhibitionism (Rooth 1973), and biting during lovemaking has been labeled sadomasochism (Ford and Beach 1951). DSM-III-R, however, characterizes paraphilias as habitual, recurrent, compelling, and intense sexual urges and sexually arousing fantasies (American Psychiatric Association 1987; Stoller 1977). Gebhard (1971) cautioned that although some practices, such as adult-child sexual contacts (pedophilia), may be common in a particular society, they are not a matter of preference and so technically are not a paraphilia. In addition, DSM-III-R states that it is common for more than one paraphilia to be found in a single person (Stoller 1977). This issue is totally overlooked in the cross-cultural literature.

The sexual disorders (along with the eating disorders) are frequently cited as examples of DSM disorders that have no parallel in other countries (Kendell 1991). Contemporary anthropologists tend to agree that most standard paraphilias are unique to Western society. Meikle (1982) and Weatherford (1986) both related the Western paraphilias to nonavailability of partners and the primacy of masturbating activities as sexual outlets in North American sex styles. Gebhard (1971) has suggested that paraphilias are unique to complex societies, where individuals can evade social sanctions through anonymity. Yet not all cross-cultural commentators agree with this perspective. Gregersen (1992) and Rhoads and Borjes (1981) have argued that the paraphilia lies not in the cultural acceptance or rejection of a behavior, but in the nature of the specificity of the sexual impulse or interest. In their discussion of love maps, Money and Lamacz (1989) viewed paraphilias as encoded in cultural custom but argued that they are interpsychically, not culturally, determined. In another universalist vein, Ames and Houston (1990) argued that the cross-cultural meaning of pedophilia would be clearer if culture-bound legal definitions were replaced by a universal biologically based definition of *child* as one who lacks secondary sex characteristics.

Clinical studies of ethnicity and paraphilia are rare. A few accounts of the incidence and variation of pedophilia among American ethnic groups do exist, but the focus is on the patients rather than the paraphiliacs and their arousal patterns. Comparisons of age, sex, and sexual acts performed on patients of child abuse indicate that Latin American patients are more likely to be boys and the acts more likely to include anal intercourse (DeJong et al. 1982). Comparison of African American and white patients show that the age at initial abuse for African American females is higher (DeJong et al. 1982). The difference could be attributable to family form and values characteristic of Latin American and African American ethnic groups, but this is not clear (DeJong et al. 1982; French and Wailes 1982). Although Wyatt (1985) found little difference in child sexual abuse rates among white and African American women, she has suggested that stepfathers and cousins are slightly more likely to be perpetrators of abuse among the latter group. Again, family form may play a role. Fischler (1985) has noted that although sexual abuse cases are increasingly recognized in Native American communities, little is known about frequency, characteristics of the perpetrators or the patients, or family dynamics.

Drawing on cross-cultural data to add to the list of paraphilias, Dewaraja and Money (1986) suggested including additional erotic acts such as formicophilia, the practice observed in a Buddhist male of placing small creatures such as insects and snails on his genitals. Asphyxiophilia or desire for a state of oxygen deficiency brought on by hanging, in order to enhance orgasm, has also been reviewed (Innala and Ennulf 1989) as a cross-culturally occurring phenomenon deserving DSM status. Gregersen (1992), a linguist, shows how the listing of paraphilias can go on ad infinitum (i.e., gerontophilia, homocidophilia, narratophilia, raptophilia), yet the notion of paraphilias bound to any culture but the dominant Western culture remains unexplored.

In conclusion, there are clear difficulties with the category of paraphilias. Wholesale critiques of the paraphilias as legalistic, moralistic, and culture bound have come from a variety of sources: social scientists (Pineroba 1988; Reiss 1986), feminists (Irvine 1990a; Pollis 1988; Tiefer 1988a, 1988b), historians (D'Emilio and Freedman 1988; Weeks 1985), and members of the so-called sexual minorities, or oppressed or stigmatized erotic populations (Kirk 1977; Ullerstam 1966). This last group has radically politicized sexuality. DSM medicalization of paraphilias as unfit or unhealthy forms of desire have been equated by such groups with "erotic injustice and sexual oppression" (Christensen 1988; Gochros and Schultz 1972; Kirk 1977; Rubin 1984; Ullerstam 1966; Weeks 1985); these groups politicize themselves as "erotic dissidents" who "keep marching out of the Diagnostic and Statistical Manual and on to the pages of social history" (Rubin 1984, p. 287). Finally, equating sexual labeling with racism, Gochros and Schultz (1972) stated that the phrase "sexually oppressed populations" in North American society should include all those whose sexual needs are ignored, distorted, or suppressed by the dominant Anglo-Saxon values and standards.

Sexual Dysfunctions

This class of sexual disorder is characterized by inhibition of desire or psychophysiological problems encountered in the sexual response cycle. The categories in this section have largely derived from the work of Masters and Johnson (Masters 1987) and Helen Singer Kaplan (1974) and are characterized by a biological, essentialist approach to sexual functions/dysfunctions (Irvine 1990a, 1990b; Tiefer 1988a). This view suggests that sexual response is unaffected by ethnicity and culture

(Christopher 1982; Hong 1984; Ndetei and Wazome 1986). A few clinical reports on ethnicity and sexual dysfunction do exist and suggest that there is a relationship. It must be cautioned, however, that any discussion of sexual dysfunction among American ethnic groups is conducted in light of an abysmally sparse body of literature on ethnicity and normal sexual behavior and beliefs in contemporary American society.

For the United States there are no standard data on the incidence or prevalence of dysfunctions among ethnic groups, the number of minorities who seek sexual therapies, or ethnic attitudes toward therapy or its effectiveness. Nor is there much data on each group's understandings of the nature and prevalence of sexual dysfunctions. This may be the result of several factors. First, in the United States ethnic minorities do not tend to go to sex clinics or to seek treatment for their sexual disorders (Irvine 1990a; Mokuau 1986). Second, when studies do include ethnic variables, apparent similarities among ethnic groups rather than differences are found. Third, the sexual dysfunction theories assume that the dysfunctions are biologically universal and unmediated by ethnicity or culture. Finally, the categorization of American ethnic groups is extremely problematic. For example, Native Americans represent a quite diverse spectrum of cultures. The labels Asian Americans and Latin Americans may likewise refer to individuals who trace their heritage to quite diverse original cultural settings. Social class, education, region, length of residence in the United States, and gender are all variables that affect internal cultural beliefs and practices within the major American ethnic groups.

In a critical review on incidence and prevalence of sexual dysfunctions, Spector and Carey (1990) cited only one reference that dealt with ethnicity. There are, however, a few more sources. For instance, Levine and Yost (1976) studied the frequency of orgasm among a clinical sample of poor African American women in Detroit and concluded that their data supported the hypothesis (Rainwater 1969) that lower class women seem to enjoy sex less than upper class women. The Levine and Yost data, however, were used by Frank et al. (1978) to argue for equally high levels of orgasmic dysfunction among a sample of white middle-class women. They then claimed that comparison of the two sets of data showed that race and class do not appear to make a difference. Similarly, Fischer (1980) found little difference across a series of sexual and psychological variables for African American and white middle-class women in Syracuse, New York. The African Americans, however, did report slightly higher preference rates for intercourse. In a comparison of white, African American, and Asian men who were treated by a urologist for sexual impotency from 1954–1972, Finkle and Finkle (1978) concluded that ethnic origin did not predispose a person to potency problems or directly influence response to counseling.

African Americans

Attempts to describe sexual behavior among African Americans are at best very scarce (Belcastro 1985; Houston 1989; Wyatt 1989), and studies are limited owing to age, regional, educational, class, and other sampling restrictions. Most studies have focused on indigent populations and key issues such as age at first intercourse and use of contraceptive methods or acquired immunodeficiency syndrome (AIDS) prevention (Fullilove et al. 1990; Weinberg and Williams 1988; Wyatt 1989). Other sources have focused on the African American family (e.g., Boyd-Franklin 1989; Gutman 1976; Lawrence 1971; Scanzoni 1971; Stack 1974).

Although Staples (1982) and Herton (1971) presented a controversial assessment of African American male sexuality, they did not directly deal with issues related to clinical assessment of sexual dysfunctions. Johnson (1977) and Mokuau (1986), however, dealt with African American sexuality in terms of the clinical setting. Both authors presented their discussions in terms of "ethnosexual oppression." Sexual oppression, according to Johnson, stems from a belief that blacks are sexually liberated to the point of obscenity. According to Mokuau, the belief is wedded to racism and for African Americans manifests itself in stereotypes of male hypersexuality and female hyposexuality. Mokuau argued that despite the lack of truth to these stereotypes, they may be internalized by both black males and black females. Johnson has suggested that an African American man's obsession with sexual prowess keeps him from understanding the sexuality of women. True to stereotype, Wyatt et al. (1976) provided a case study of an African American couple who had sexual difficulties because both partners expected the male to be sexually aggressive and skilled; when he failed, he felt inadequate, and she felt disappointed.

Asian Americans

As with African Americans, there are very few data on sexual dysfunctions among Asian Americans. Mollica et al. (1987) concluded that loss of sexual interest or pleasure is actually an indicator of depression among Indochinese refugees in Massachusetts. Mollica et al. also reminded potential therapists that such refugees may well have histories of trauma from torture and/or rape. Studies by Lieh-Mak and Ng (1981) and Tseng and Hsu (1970) of Chinese men and ejaculation have mentioned the tendency of Chinese men with sexual problems to somatize their problems and manifest stress as sexual impotence.

Lieh-Mak and Ng (1981) also reported on ejaculatory incompetence—inability or delay of intravaginal ejaculation—among a clinical sample of 12 Chinese men who presented with fertility complaints. Ten of these patients believed that retention of semen was healthy. The authors related this to Taoist beliefs that regulation of ejaculation and female satisfaction are important and that ejaculation and male sexual satisfaction are not always the same thing. The importance of semen retention among Asian men for robust health has been mentioned by several authors (Dewaraja and Sasaki 1991; Money et al. 1991) (see also the discussion of culture-bound syndromes at the end of this chapter).

More sophisticated assessment of sexual dysfunction among Asian migrants comes from two British reports that critiqued Masters and Johnson's work as ethnocentric and stereotyped. Bhugra and Cordle (1988) and d'Ardenne (1986a, 1986b) both reported that for Asians originating on the Indian subcontinent, ejaculatory problems were a primary presenting complaint (d'Ardenne 1986a, 1986b; Bhugra and Cordle 1988), and women tended to complain of vaginal discharge (d'Ardenne 1986a, 1986b) rather than painful intercourse. Problems in conception were the major reason for the clinic visit. According to Ballard (cited in d'Ardenne 1986a, 1986b), concerns about potency also loom larger in Asian men: first, because potency is related to a comprehensive cosmology, and second, because Asian men expect to exert a greater degree of personal dominance over their wives. Bhugra and Cordle have cited the enormous social pressure on young couples to conceive as a primary factor bringing younger couples into treatment.

For Asian Americans in the United States, ethnosexual oppression, according to Mokuau (1986) and Ogawa (1977), can take the form of feelings of physical inadequacy and low sexual self-image gained from living with a dominant culture that values tall, muscular men and tall, blonde women.

Latin Americans

The study of sexuality among Latin Americans is also problematic. Issues of gender ideology such as machismo can border on dangerous stereotypes. Just as hypersexuality (Mokuau 1986) or "super-stud" ability (Johnson 1977) can become damaging stereotypes among African Americans, Mokuau (1986, p. 146) asserted that machismo and mariasmo are forms of ethnosexual oppression that can lock males into "actions of sexual expertise and domination, and [a man] may develop unrealistic expectations of his sexual performance and role." Espin (1984) discussed how the sexual expression of machismo as multiple, uncommitted sexual contacts from adolescence on can make understanding and communication between couples almost impossible.

According to Reiss (1986), premature ejaculation should not be viewed as a problem but as a desired trait among Latin American males. With the exception of Espin (1984), however, little attempt has been made to assess sexual dysfunction in this ethnic population. Certainly the madonna/whore complex (Alarcon 1989; Carrier 1976), machismo and the conquest orientation of males (Giraldo 1972), and the eroticism of forbidden acts (Arnold 1977; Parker 1991) play an important role in Latin American sexuality, which in turn has relevance to the clinical setting.

Treatment Issues

Treatment issues for the various ethnic groups are usually presented in terms of "minority" rather than specific ethnic group issues. Yet each group presents its own special treatment challenges. For instance, in a case study of a psychosexual problem experienced by a Latin American refugee couple in Denmark, Agger and Jensen (1989) discussed the couple's problems in terms of both the severe traumas (including rape) experienced in the homeland and the readjustment from a patriarchal culture in which a woman is an object of conquest and must resist male sexuality to a cultural setting that is not as overtly sexually repressive. Again, Hawton (1985) cautioned against therapy for Asians that assumes women should have an equal opportunity (i.e., equal to men) to initiate sexual activity. Much is made of the relationship of semen loss and sexual dysfunction among some Asian groups. According to the ethnosexual oppression models, ethnic minorities need culturally appropriate counseling. Mokuau (1986) recommended that a therapist should have knowledge of the impact of racism on sexual oppression of individuals, knowledge of cultural coping and folk healing resources, an awareness of cultural stereotypes (for self and other) that the patient may bring into the counseling relationship, and a realization that the ethnic minority client is often bicultural and holds simultaneous membership in two different cultures.

d'Ardenne (1986a) suggested 10 modifications to Masters and Johnson's therapy agenda, including the following: use of drawings and diagrams, avoidance of the use of medical terms or "sick" language, repeated and authoritative instructions, and emphasis on performance objectives rather than discussion.

According to Johnson (1977), African Americans do not go to clinics because they associate sexual therapy with the white middle class, believe that their more permissive subculture frees them from problems of repressed sexuality, and associate sex therapy with experimentalism (e.g., being watched while having sex in a laboratory). Christensen (1988) remarked that minorities usually seek help only in times of crisis and tend to have very negative views toward the therapist.

Treatment effectiveness for minorities remains relatively unevaluated. At best, it is seen as marginally beneficial, especially over the long run (DeAmicas et al. 1985; Irvine 1990a; Margolin and Witztum 1989). d'Ardenne (1986b) stated that success rates for Asians in Britain are approximately the same as for other groups. She also noted that Asians prefer physical treatment methods such as aphrodisiacs, testosterone ingestion, and penile splinting. G. Davis and Cross (1979) described folk treatments for sexual disorder as nonstigmatizing and preferable to medical treatments.

Finally, a word should also be said about sexual dysfunctions and the dominant ethnic group. Some critics regard the sexual dysfunctions as based on culture-bound, masculinist, middle-class, Western values and standards (Christensen 1988). Gregersen (1992) has suggested that religious orthodoxy (strict conservative Judaism or Christianity) is of major importance in almost every form of male sexual dysfunction, with the possible exception of premature ejaculation. Sex therapists Leiblum and Rosen (1988) have asked whether, by applying a diagnostic label to the behavior, we inadvertently create new sexual performance standards of technical competence and sexual enthusiasm. Have we created a major iatrogenic disorder? Alternatively, to ask the question from another perspective, to what degree is the high prevalence for or vulnerability to sexual problems in Western society related to cultural inhibitions or restrictiveness (Welch and Kartub 1978) and unrealistic expectations or ignorance and anxiety about performance that characterize the Euro-American tradition (Golden 1983)?

Cultural Construction and the Critique of Sexology

Historians (Bullough 1976; D'Emilio and Freedman 1988; Duggan 1990; Meyerowitz 1988; Padgug 1979; Peiss 1986; Weeks 1985), social scientists (Abrahmson and Herdt 1990; Bryne and Kelly 1986; Caplan 1987; Herdt and Stoller 1990; Kemnitzer 1977; Leavitt 1991; Miller and Fowlkes 1975; Pollis 1988; Reiss 1986; W. Simons and

Gagnon 1973; Vance 1983, 1991), feminists, and a small group of sexologists or sexual therapists (Abrahmson 1991; Irvine 1990a, 1990b; LoPiccolo and Heiman 1977; Spector and Carey 1990; Szasz 1980; Tiefer 1986, 1987, 1988a, 1988b, 1991) have come to criticize medical concepts of sexuality, including the paraphilias and sexual dysfunctions. Cultural constructionists insist that to develop culturally sensitive understandings of human sexuality and sexual behavior, we must move beyond the simple assessment of how select features of the sexuality of other cultural or ethnic groups fit into or vary from those of Western society (particularly of Western medicine). Constructionists propose that we depart from an emphasis on categorizing and classifying sexual behavior to an emphasis on questioning and analyzing the constructions of the categories themselves as culture bound. Sophisticated cultural constructionist criticisms of DSM categories of the sexual disorders challenge medical professionals to reassess the nature and applicability of these categories across the historical ethnic and ethnographic spectrum. Here, sexuality is not viewed as a fixed or given biological or psychic entity; instead, sexualities are constantly practiced, changed, and modified as are the categories and meanings associated with them (Foucault 1978).

Many authors have critiqued the paraphilias, as a whole or individually, as culture-bound, out-dated constructs of Western medicine—the zeitgeist of a former era. Herdt and Stoller (1989) stated that the concept of pedophilia has no relevance to man-boy sexual relations in New Guinea. Rubin (1984) critiqued the DSM paraphilias as a culture-bound moral hierarchy that reflects Western cultural views of sex as a matter of personal responsibility; as biologically ordained; and as a negative, dangerous, and disruptive force. According to Rubin, Western sexualities are structured with an extremely punitive social framework, where an excess of significance is associated with differences in sexual acts and "unfit" forms of sexual desire (especially those that deviate from practices with reproductive potential).

The sexual dysfunctions have also come in for their share of criticism from the cultural constructionists. Irvine (1990a) critiqued the DSM-III-R sexual dysfunctions for their ignorance of sociocultural factors, their biological essentialism, and their implied focus on correcting bad habits and salvaging marriage by solving sexual troubles. According to Irvine (1990a, 1990b), the Masters and Johnson legacy to the DSM overlooks sources of more intractable sexual problems in heterosexuals such as fear, anger, boredom, overwork, lack of time, inequality in relationships, prior sexual assault on women, and differential socialization of males and females. In sex therapy, according to Irvine, social change, rather than orgasm, should be the cure.

Tiefer (1987) critiqued sex therapy for its "work language" of skills, practice, scheduling, and mastering; for its equation of sexual expression with genital sex; and for its emphasis on penile erections for males. Where inorgasmia was once viewed as a potential to be developed in some cultures and not others, it has become a sexual disorder of females. Marmor's (1971) characterization of healthy sex as tender and affectionate, seeking to give and receive pleasure, discriminating as to partner, and triggered by erotic needs would have limited applicability across ethnic and cultural groups.

Disorders of desire have also come in for their share of criticism. Irvine (1990a) viewed inhibited sexual desire disorder as the medicalization of a simple, nonpathological product of sexual boredom or indifference, owing to the widespread problem of flagging sexual interest in marriage. Irvine critiqued low sexual desire and inhibited female orgasm as an unnecessary hypothetical and mythical construct that is dependent on self-diagnosis, is biologically reductionistic, and is subject to very high treatment failure (close to 50%) rates. In Irvine's feminist analysis, permission for any individual woman to experience desire, discuss sexuality, initiate a sexual encounter, or present herself as passionate varies historically and cross-culturally. Irvine sees desire disorders as embedded, not just in biology, but in power relations between males and females, where power, authority, and active sexual desire are the prerogatives of men.

Although the authors mentioned above critiqued the DSM sexual disorder categories for their emphasis on the physical body and their oversight of issues related to gender, age, race, and ethnicity, they failed to elaborate on the last two conditions. When it comes to the category of other disorders, psychiatrists address a more culturally sophisticated but inconclusive body of literature.

Other Sexual Disorders

This category includes a number of different behaviors such as sexual addiction, dissatisfaction with physical self or sexual competence, and problematic sexual orientation; as a group, these disorders have suffered the greatest criticism and commentary from the cultural constructionists. According to Levine and Yost (1976), for instance, categorizing sexual addiction as a sexual desire disorder is moralistic and subjective and represents a pseudoscientific codification of prevailing cultural values rather than valid clinical diagnosis. It is simply the medicalization of "erotic deviance" that is considered perfectly normal in other cultures (D. L. Davis and Whitten 1987; Marshall 1971). Marked feelings of inadequacy concerning body size, shape of sex organs, and so forth, have been related to American mass media emphasis on narrow, difficult-to-achieve standards of physical attractiveness. Hence, minorities may be more prone to this "disorder" than whites just as a natural part of being different. Critics have even charged that Masters and Johnson's standards for sexual competence and performance result in distorted sexual expectations and are themselves iatrogenic (Irvine 1990a; Tiefer 1988a).

The Culture-Bound Sex Syndromes

A number of so-called culture-bound syndromes can be found in the ethnographic and medical literature (R. C. Simons 1985). These include *koro* (India, Southeast Asia, Malaysia, China); *shen-k'uei* (China); *D'hat, Danidani, Prameha, Bangladeshi* syndrome (Bangladesh); *edani, jryan* (India); and *Tira* (Polynesia). A spate of articles on *koro* and *D'hat* illustrate the nature of controversy between universalists and constructionists point of view. *Koro* refers to a sudden and intense anxiety that the penis will recede into the body. *D'hat* refers to marked obsession with or anxiety over excessive loss of semen (Wen and Wang 1980). In a useful review of the literature, Bernstein and Gaw (1990) have proposed that *koro*, as a genital retraction syndrome, be designated a culture-specific syndrome in DSM-IV and classified under the somatoform disorders. However, others have objected to the culture-specific status, claiming that genital retraction syndrome is more universally experienced (Edwards 1985; Fishbain 1991; Hughes 1985). The same arguments have been cited for *D'hat* (Bhatia and Maslik 1991; Bottero 1991; Chadda and Ahuja 1990). There is also a considerable lack of agreement on what symptoms define these syndromes. For example, Bernstein and Gaw's (1990) argument that fear of death is a defining feature of *koro* has been challenged (Chadda and Shome 1991). Despite the controversy, there is substantial agreement that *koro* and *D'hat* should not be overdiagnosed as schizophrenia or a delusional disorder. Several clinical studies have suggested that a more appropriate diagnosis would be mood disorder—depression or anxiety—(Bhatia and Malik 1991; Bottero 1991) or somatoform disorder (Bernstein and Gaw 1990; Fishbain 1991) and have been reluctant to categorize *koro* and *D'hat* as sexual dysfunctions, even though premature ejaculation or impotence may be involved.

Despite the problems of classification, these exotic syndromes certainly may have ramifications for understanding fertility concerns, concerns with sexual performance among certain ethnic groups, and recognition that not all sexual cosmologies are similar to those of Western medicine. There is a danger inherent in the psychiatric fascination with these exotic syndromes; this danger concerns the temptation to reduce a consideration of cultural sensitivity and the sexual disorders to these colorful, high-profile syndromes and to overlook the extent to which all the sexual disorders of DSM-IV are culture bound.

Gender Identity Disorders

The anthropological literature has made a strong contribution to the understanding of gender identity (see Blackwood 1986; Caplan 1987; Herdt 1990b; Herdt and Stoller 1990), and a brief overview of this contribution is in order.

Anthropological sources show that intersexes may or may not be discomforted by issues of sex and gender identity, however (D. L. Davis and Whitten 1987; Herdt 1990b). Nevertheless, their identity may not necessarily coincide with the Western, binary mode of gender assignment (male vs. female). Herdt (1990a) has described two cultural approaches to gender definition relevant to intersexes and to cross-gender behavior in general. The Anglo-Saxon tradition of two-category classification defines persons primarily by biological or deeper psychological essence. The two categories are thought to be invariant through life. The greater the emphasis on dimorphism, the more negatively stigmatized are those with gender "anomalies." "Polymorphous cultures," such as those in Melanesia, define persons as more fluid and as relatively male or female according to a variety of social and developmental characteristics such as stage of life span, socioeconomic status, and body ritual. Called three-sex or three sex-code systems by Herdt (1990b), these societies are more flexible about the fit between gender identity and gender classification and emphasize the social (rather than individual) context of ideology, socialization, and gender development. The person in this cultural milieu is not a man, a woman, a man who wants to be a woman (or vice versa), or a person with confused sexual orientation; instead, the person is placed in a third gender category.

Indeed, the anthropological literature also includes plentiful discussion of third gender or cross-gender categories that are not made up of biological intersexes but are socially constructed (D. L. Davis and Whitten 1987). For instance, Williams (1986) has described how many Native American societies tolerate sexual diversity. Certain Native American individuals are viewed as neither strictly men or women but as belonging to an alternate gender. In such societies, a person's spirit or character is more important than biology in determining social gender identity.

In an anthropological review article on sex, sexuality, gender, and gender variance, Jacobs and Roberts (1989) suggested that three genders are not enough and fail to capture the complexity of the ethnographic record. For example, the Siberian Chuckchee have seven recognized genders, and the Mohave Indians (California) have four genders. Jacobs and Roberts also suggested that most English-speaking countries recognize four genders: woman, lesbian, man, and gay male. In Latin America, the distinction of insertor/insertee, as applied to men who engage in same-sex activities (Parker 1991), reflects different gender designations according to this model.

In many cases, gender identity may or may not have anything to do with sexual arousal. In the anthropological record, gender identity, cross-dressing, and sexual orientation do not exist on a continuum but are discrete and independent categories (Callender and Kochems 1986; D. L. Davis and Whitten 1987). Even in America, transsexual informants (Bolin 1988) regard themselves as qualitatively distinct from transvestites. Irvine (1990b) hypothesized that surgery has created a third American sex rather than making "males" into "females" or vice versa. Critics such as Bolin (1988) and Irvine (1990a, 1990b) have suggested that prior to surgery, transsexual surgery candidates are forced to conform to the physician's idea of a "real" woman or man and what arouses such candidates.

Conclusion

The various categories of the sexual disorders pose some interesting issues for anthropology and psychiatry. There is a much larger body of literature on ethnicity and the treatment of sexual disorders than there is on nosology and diagnosis. Criticisms of the DSM's sexual disorders echo criticism of sexology in general, which is disparaged for its lack of "rigor" and construct validity (Abrahmson 1991; Tiefer 1991; Vance 1991). Researchers have speculated that the vast majority of ethnic minorities who seek treatment of sexual dysfunction turn to folk practitioners and folk cures (Bourne 1985; d'Ardenne 1986b; Rack 1982; Wyatt 1982). This not only reflects the politics of research and the alienation of these people from modern medicine but must also be viewed as reflecting the cultural essence of their problems.

The notion that self-conceived "marked distress" must be a condition for a sexual desire disorder implies cultural sensitivity as does the consideration of "the context of a person's life" (Schover et al. 1982). If anything, this review demonstrates the need for further study on this topic. At present the following three statements best address the nature of the relationship between cultural issues and the sexual disorders:

1. Cultural features can and do affect the experience and diagnosis of the gender identity disorders and all three categories of the sexual disorders.
2. These categories are themselves so culture bound that they are problematic when applied cross-culturally.
3. The so-called culture-bound sexual disorders such as *koro* and *D'hat* are best subsumed under other diagnostic categories.

References

Abrahmson P: I think she doth protest too much: reply to Tiefer. J Sex Res 28:603–606, 1991

Abrahmson P, Herdt G: The assessment of sexual practices relevant to the transmission of AIDS. J Sex Res 27:215–232, 1990

Agger I, Jensen S: Couples in exile: psychosexual dynamics of a Latin American refugee couple. Sexual and Marital Therapy 4:101–108, 1989

Alarcon N: Third Woman: The Sexuality of Latinas. Berkeley, CA, Third Woman Press, 1989

American Psychiatric Association: Diagnostic and Statistical Manual of Mental Disorders, 3rd Edition, Revised. Washington, DC, American Psychiatric Association, 1987

American Psychiatric Association: Diagnostic and Statistical Manual of Mental Disorders, 4th Edition. Washington, DC, American Psychiatric Association, 1994

Ames AM, Houston DA: Legal, social, and biological definitions of pedophilia. Arch Sex Behav 19:333–345, 1990

Arnold K: The introduction of poses to a Peruvian brothel and changing images of male and female, in The Anthropology of the Body. Edited by Blacking J. New York, Academic Press, 1977, pp 179–197

Belcastro PA: Sexual behavior differences between black and white students. J Sex Res 21:56–67, 1985

Bernstein R, Gaw A: Koro: proposed classification for DSM IV. Am J Psychiatry 147:1670–1674, 1990

Bhatia MS, Malik SC: Dhat syndrome: a useful diagnostic entity in Indian culture. Br J Psychiatry 159:691–695, 1991

Bhugra D, Cordle C: A case control study of sexual dysfunction in Asian and non-Asian couples 1981–1985. Sexual and Marital Therapy 3:71–76, 1988

Blackwood E (ed): Anthropology and Homosexual Behavior. New York, Haworth, 1986

Bolin A: In Search of Eve: Transsexual Rites of Passage. South Hadley, MA, Bergin and Garvey, 1988

Bottero A: Consumption by semen loss in India and elsewhere. Cult Med Psychiatry 15:303–320, 1991

Bourne S: Asian medicine: traditional remedies or health risks? The Listener 114:8–10, 1985

Boyd-Franklin N: Black Families in Therapy: A Multisystems Approach. New York, Guilford, 1989

Brown J: A comparative study of deviations from sexual mores. Am Sociol Rev 17:135–146, 1952

Bryne D, Kelly K: Alternative Approaches to the Study of Sexual Behavior. Hillsdale, NJ, Erlbaum, 1986

Bullough V: Sexual Variance in Society and History. New York, Wiley, 1976

Callender C, Kochems l: Men and non-men: male gender mixing statuses and homosexuality, in Anthropology and Homosexual Behavior. Edited by Blackwood E. New York, Haworth, 1986, pp 178–179

Caplan P (ed): The Cultural Construction of Sexuality. London, England, Tavistock, 1987

Carrier JM: Cultural factors affecting male Mexican homosexual behavior. Arch Sex Behav 5:103–124, 1976

Carstairs MG: Cultural differences in sexual deviation, in The Pathology and Treatment of Sexual Deviation: A Methodological Approach. Edited by Rosen I. London, England, Oxford University Press, 1964, pp 419–434

Chadda RK, Ahuja N: Dhat syndrome. Br J Psychiatry 156:577–579, 1990

Chadda RK, Shome RL: Koro: classification and case reports (letter). Am J Psychiatry 148:1766–1767, 1991

Christensen CP: Issues in sex therapy with ethnic and racial minority women, in Women and Sex Therapy. Edited by Cole E, Rothblum ED. New York, Haworth, 1988, pp 187–205

Christopher E: Psychosexual medicine in a mixed racial community. British Journal of Family Planning 7:115–119, 1982

d'Ardenne P: Behavior therapy and ethnic minorities, in Behavior Therapy in Primary Care: A Practical Guide. Edited by France R, Robson M. London, England, Croom Helm, 1986a, pp 23–32

d'Ardenne P: Sexual dysfunction in a transcultural setting: assessment, treatment and research. Sexual and Marital Therapy 1:23–34, 1986b

Davis DL, Whitten RG: The cross-cultural study of human sexuality. Annual Review of Anthropology 16:69–98, 1987

Davis G, Cross H: Sexual stereotyping of black males. Arch Sex Behav 8:269–279, 1979

DeAmicas L, Goldberg D, LoPiccolo J, et al: Clinical follow-up of couples treated for sexual dysfunction. Arch Sex Behav 14:467–489, 1985

DeJong AR, Emmett EA, Hervada AR: Sexual abuse of children: sex-, race-, and age-dependent variations. Am J Dis Child 136:129–134, 1982

D'Emilio J, Freedman EB: Intimate Matters: A History of Sexuality in America. New York, Harper & Row, 1988

Dewaraja R, Money J: Transcultural sexology: formicophilia, a newly named paraphilia in a young Buddhist male. J Sex Marital Ther 12:139–145, 1986

Dewaraja R, Sasaki J: Semen-loss syndrome: a comparison between Sri Lanka and Japan. Am J Psychother 45:14–20, 1991

Duggan L: Review essay from instincts to politics: writing the history of sexuality in the US. J Sex Res 27:95–109, 1990

Edwards JW: Indigenous koro, a genital retraction syndrome of insular Southeast Asia: a critical review, in The Culture-Bound Syndromes. Edited by Simons RC, Hughes CC. Dordrecht, Holland, D Reidel, 1985, pp 169–191

Espin OM: Cultural and historical influences on sexuality in Hispanic/Latin women: implications for psychotherapy, in Pleasure and Danger: Exploring Female Sexuality. Edited by Vance C. Boston, MA, Routledge & Kegan Paul, 1984, pp 149–164

Finkle A, Finkle C: Sexual impotency: counseling of 388 private patients by urologist from 1954 to 1982. Urology 23:25–30, 1978

Fischer S: Personality correlates of sexual behavior in black women. Arch Sex Behav 9:27–35, 1980

Fischler R: Child abuse and neglect in American Indian communities. Child Abuse Negl 9:95–106, 1985

Fishbain D: Koro: classification and case reports (letter). Am J Psychiatry 148:1765–1766, 1991

Ford CS, Beach FA: Patterns of Sexual Behavior. New York, Harper, 1951

Foucault, M: The History of Sexuality, Vol I. New York, Pantheon, 1978

Frank E, Anderson C, Rubenstein D: Frequency of sexual dysfunction in "normal couples." N Engl J Med 299:111–115, 1978

French LA, Wailes SN: Perceptions of sexual deviance: a bi-racial analysis. International Journal of Offender Therapy and Comparative Criminology 26:242–249, 1982

Fullilove MT, Fullilove RE, Haynes K, et al: Black women and AIDS prevention: a view towards understanding the gender rules. J Sex Res 27:47–64, 1990

Gebhard PH: Human sexual behavior: a summary statement, in Human Sexual Behavior. Edited by Marshall DS, Suggs RC. New York, Basic Books, 1971, pp 206–217

Giraldo O: Machismo as a psychocultural phenomenon. Revista Latino Americana de Psicologia 4:295–309, 1972

Gochros HL, Schultz LG: Human Sexuality and Social Work. New York, Association Press, 1972

Golden J: Psychiatric aspects of male sexual dysfunction. Postgrad Med 74:221–229, 1983

Gregersen E: The World of Sexuality. New York, Irvington, 1992

Gutman HG: The Black Family in Slavery and Freedom, 1750–1925. New York, Pantheon, 1976

Hawton K: Sex Therapy: A Practical Guide. London, England, Oxford University Press, 1985

Herdt GH: Development discontinuities and sexual orientation across cultures, in Homosexuality/Heterosexuality. Edited by McWhirter D. New York, Oxford University Press, 1990a

Herdt GH: Mistaken gender. American Anthropologist 92:433–446, 1990b

Herdt GH, Stoller RJ: Commentary to "The socialization of homosexuality and heterosexuality in a non-Western society." Arch Sex Behav 18:31–34, 1989

Herdt GH, Stoller RJ: Intimate Communications. New York, Columbia University Press, 1990

Herton C: Social struggle and sexual conflict: black sexuality and the contemporary ideology of black power in Sexuality: a Search for Perspective. Edited by Grummon D, Barclay A. New York, Van Nostrand Reinhold, 1971, pp 126–139

Hong L: Survival of the fastest. J Sex Res 20:109–122, 1984

Houston LN: Romanticism and eroticism among black and white college students. Adolescence 26:261–272, 1989

Hughes CC: The genital retraction taxon: commentary, in The Culture-Bound Syndromes. Edited by Simons RC, Hughes CC. Dordrecht, The Netherlands, D Reidel, 1985, pp 193–194

Innala SM, Ennulf KE: Asphyxiophilia in Scandinavia. Arch Sex Behav 3:181–189, 1989

Irvine JM: Disorders of Desire: Sex and Gender in Modern American Sexology. Philadelphia, PA, Temple University Press, 1990a

Irvine JM: From difference to sameness: gender ideology in sexual science. J Sex Res 27:7–24, 1990b

Jacobs S, Roberts C: Sex, sexuality and gender variance, in Gender and Anthropology: Critical Reviews for Research and Teaching. Edited by Morgan S. Washington, DC, American Anthropological Association, 1989, pp 438–462

Johnson LB: Blacks, in The Sexually Oppressed. Edited by Gochros HL, Gochros J. New York, Association Press, 1977, pp 173–191

Jones H, Frei D: Exhibitionism—a biological hypothesis. Br J Med Psychol 52:63–70, 1979

Kaplan HS: The New Sex Therapy. New York, Brunner/Mazel, 1974

Kemnitzer, D: Sexuality as social form: performance and anxiety in America, in Symbolic Anthropology. Edited by Dolgin J, Kemnitzer D, Schneider D. New York, Columbia University Press, 1977, pp 292–309

Kendell R: Relationship between DSM IV and ICD 10. J Abnorm Psychol 100:297–301, 1991

Kirk SA: Society and sexual deviance, in The Sexually Oppressed. Edited by Gochros HL, Gochros J. New York, Association Press, 1977, pp 173–191

Krafft-Ebing R: Psychopathia Sexualis. Stuttgart, Germany, FJ Rebman, 1886

Laubscher JF: Sex, Custom and Psychopathology. London, England, George Routledge & Sons, 1937

Lawrence C: Color, class, and a minority view, in Sexuality: A Search for Perspective. Edited by Grimmon D, Barclay AM. New York, Van Nostrand Reinhold, 1971, pp 109–125

Leavitt S: Sexual ideology and experience in a Papua New Guinea society. Soc Sci Med 33:897–907, 1991

Leiblum SR, Rosen RC: Introduction: changing perspectives on sexual desire, in Sexual Desire Disorders. Edited by Leiblum SR, Rosen RC. New York, Guilford, 1988, pp 1–17

Levine S, Yost M: Frequency of sexual dysfunction in a general gynecological clinic. Arch Sex Behav 5:229–239, 1976

Lieh-Mak F, Ng ML: Ejaculatory incompetence in Chinese men. Am J Psychiatry 138:685–686, 1981

LoPiccolo J, Heiman J: Cultural values and therapeutic definition of sexual dysfunction. Journal of Social Issues 33:166–183, 1977

Margolin J, Witztum E: Supernatural impotence. Br J Med Psychol 63:333–342, 1989

Marmor J: "Normal" and "deviant" sexual behavior. JAMA 217:165–170, 1971

Marshall DS: Sexual behavior on Mangaia, in Human Sexual Behavior. Edited by Marshall DS, Suggs RC. New York, Basic Books, 1971, pp 103–162

Masters W: Sexuality in perspective. Trans Stud Coll Physicians Phila 9:45–57, 1987

Meikle S: Culture and sexual deviation, in Culture and Psychopathology. Edited by Al-Issa I. Baltimore, MD, University Park Press, 1982, pp 339–358

Meyerowitz J: Women Adrift. Chicago, IL, University of Chicago Press, 1988

Miller P, Fowlkes M: Social and behavioral constructions of female sexuality, in Sex and Scientific Inquiry. Edited by Harding S, O'Barr J. Chicago, IL, University of Chicago Press, 1975, pp 147–164

Mokuau N: Ethnic minorities, in Helping the Sexually Oppressed. Edited by Gochros HL, Gochros JS, Fischer J. Englewood Cliffs, NJ, Prentice Hall, 1986, pp 141–161

Mollica RF, Wyshak G, deMarneffe D, et al: Indochinese versions of the Hopkins Symptom Checklist-25: a screening instrument for the psychiatric care of refugees. Am J Psychiatry 144:497–500, 1987

Money J, Lamacz M: Vandalized Love Maps. Buffalo, NY, Prometheus, 1989

Money J, Prakasam K, Joshi VN: Semen-conservation doctrine from ancient Ayurvedic to modern sexological theory. Am J Psychother 45:9–13, 1991

Ndetei DM, Wazome EG: Experiences from a marital-sex therapy clinic in Nairobi. Acta Psychiatr Scand 74:479–484, 1986

Ogawa D: Asian Americans, in The Sexually Oppressed. Edited by Gochros HL, Gochros J. New York, Association Press, 1977, pp 192–201

Padgug R: Sexual matters: on conceptualizing sexuality in history. Radical History Review 20:3–23, 1979

Parker R: Bodies, Pleasures and Passions: Sexual Culture in Contemporary Brazil. Boston, MA, Beacon Press, 1991

Peiss K: Cheap Amusements. Philadelphia, PA, Temple University Press, 1986

Pineroba JA: Antropologia Sexual: Lecturas de Antropologia Sexual. Madrid, Spain, Universidad Nacional de Educacion a Distancia, 1988

Pollis CA: An assessment of the impacts of feminism on sexual science. J Sex Res 25:85–105, 1988

Rack P: Race, Culture and Mental Disorder. London, England, Tavistock, 1982

Rainwater L: Sex in the culture of poverty, in The Individual, Sex and Society. Edited by Broderick C, Bernard J. Baltimore, MD, Johns Hopkins University Press, 1969, pp 129–140

Reiss IL: Journey into Sexuality. Englewood Cliffs, NJ, Prentice Hall, 1986

Rhoads J, Borjes E: Incidence of exhibitionism in Guatemala and the United States. Br J Psychiatry 139:242–244, 1981

Rooth G: Exhibitionism outside Europe and America. Arch Sex Behav 2:351–363, 1973

Rubin G: Thinking sex: notes for a radical theory of the politics of sexuality, in Pleasure and Danger: Exploring Female Sexuality. Edited by Vance C. Boston, MA, Routledge & Kegan Paul, 1984, pp 267–319

Scanzoni JH: The Black Family in Modern Society. Boston, MA, Allyn & Bacon, 1971

Schover LR, Friedman J, Weiler S, et al: The multiaxial problem-oriented diagnostic system for the sexual dysfunctions: an alternative to DSM III. Arch Gen Psychiatry 39:614–619, 1982

Simons RC: Introduction: the genital retraction taxon, in The Culture-Bound Syndromes. Edited by Simons RC, Hughes CC. Dordrecht, The Netherlands, D Reidel, 1985, pp 151–153

Simons W, Gagnon J: Sexual Conduct. Chicago, IL, Aldine, 1973

Spector I, Carey M: Incidence and prevalence of the sexual dysfunction literature: a critical review of the empirical literature. Arch Sex Behav 19:389–408, 1990

Stack CB: All Our Kin. New York, Harper & Row, 1974

Staples R: Black Masculinity. San Francisco, CA, Black Scholar Press, 1982

Stoller RJ: Sexual deviations, in Human Sexuality in Four Perspectives. Edited by Beach FA. Baltimore, MD, Johns Hopkins University Press, 1977

Suggs RC, Marshall DS: Anthropological perspectives on human sexual behavior, in Human Sexual Behavior. Edited by Marshall DS, Suggs RC. New York, Basic Books, 1971, pp 218–243

Szasz T: Sex by Prescription. Garden City, NY, Anchor/Doubleday, 1980

Tiefer L: In pursuit of the perfect penis. Am Behav Sci 29:579–599, 1986

Tiefer L: Social constructionism and the study of human sexuality, in Sex and Gender. Edited by Shaver P, Hendrick C. Newbury Park, CA, Sage, 1987, pp 70–94

Tiefer L: A feminist critique of the sexual dysfunction nomenclature, in Women and Sex Therapy. Edited by Cole E, Rothblum ED. New York, Haworth, 1988a, pp 5–21

Tiefer L: A feminist perspective on sexology and sexuality, in Feminist Thought and the Structure of Knowledge. Edited by Gergen MM. New York, New York University Press, 1988b, pp 16–26

Tiefer L: New perspectives in sexology: from rigor (mortis) to richness. J Sex Res 28:593–602, 1991

Tseng W, Hsu J: Chinese culture, personality formation, and mental illness. Int J Soc Psychiatry 16:5–14, 1970

Ullerstam L: The Erotic Minorities. New York, Grove Press, 1966

Vance C: Gender systems, ideology, and sex research, in Powers of Desire: The Politics of Sexuality. Edited by Snitow A, Stansell C, Thompson S. New York, Monthly Review Press, 1983, pp 371–384

Vance C: Anthropology rediscovers sexuality: a theoretical comment. Soc Sci Med 33:875–884, 1991

Weatherford JM: Porn Row. New York, Arbor House, 1986

Weeks J: Sexuality and Its Discontents: Meanings, Myths, and Modern Sexualities. London, England, Routledge & Kegan Paul, 1985

Weinberg MS, Williams CJ: Black sexuality: a test of two theories. J Sex Res 25:197–218, 1988

Welch MR, Kartub P: Socio-cultural correlates of incidence of impotence: a cross-cultural study. J Sex Res 4:218–230, 1978

Wen JK, Wang C: Shen-k'uei syndrome. Normal and Abnormal Behavior in Chinese Culture 18:357–369, 1980

Williams W: The Spirit and the Flesh: Sexual Diversity in American Indian Culture. Boston, MA, Beacon Press, 1986

Wyatt GE: Identifying stereotypes of Afro-American sexuality and their impact on sexual behavior, in The Afro-American Family. Edited by Bass BA, Wyatt GE, Powell G. New York, Grune & Stratton, 1982, pp 334–339

Wyatt GE: The sexual abuse of Afro-American and white-American women in childhood. Child Abuse Negl 9:507–519, 1985

Wyatt GE: Reexamining factors predicting Afro-American and white American women's age at first coitus. Arch Sex Behav 18:271–298, 1989

Wyatt GE, Strayer R, Lobitz W: Issues in treatment of sexually dysfunctioning couples of Afro-American descent. Psychotherapy: Theory, Research and Practice 13:44–50, 1976

Chapter 26

Nosological Comments on Eating and Sexual Disorders

Michael B. *First,* M.D.

These two sections in DSM describe disturbances in the appetitive physiological functions of sex and eating. Because these disorders entail a deviation from "normal" patterns of eating and sexual behavior, the boundary between the presence and absence of disorder is inherently problematic and highly subject to cultural influences. DSM will continue to rely on the clinician's judgment of "clinical significance" in setting this boundary, which includes a consideration of the cultural context of the presenting symptoms.

Few changes have been made in the eating disorders section of DSM-IV (American Psychiatric Association 1994). From an organizational standpoint, pica and rumination disorder have been moved into the feeding disorders section in the childhood disorders part of the classification. Anorexia nervosa and bulimia nervosa remain in the eating disorders section but are placed after the sexual disorders in the classification, as many individuals experience onset of these disorders in early adulthood.

The rules for making a comorbid diagnosis of anorexia nervosa and bulimia nervosa have been changed in DSM-IV. In DSM-III-R (American Psychiatric Association 1987), individuals who meet criteria for both anorexia nervosa and bulimia nervosa receive both diagnoses, resulting in the potentially misleading implication that the individual has two separate disorders. In DSM-IV, a diagnosis of anorexia nervosa takes precedence over that of bulimia nervosa, so that individuals with persistently low weight who binge and purge frequently are to be diagnosed only with anorexia nervosa. To allow the clinician to note that presence of bulimic behavior, two subtypes for anorexia nervosa are included: binge eating/purging type (for individuals who regularly binge) and restricting type (for individuals who do not regularly binge).

The definition of a binge in DSM-IV has been modified in two ways: 1) the requirement that the consumption of food in a binge be "rapid" has been removed; and 2) the sense of lack of control over the eating behavior has been highlighted by separating it into a separate criterion. In DSM-III-R, the definition of bulimia nervosa allowed for a variety of compensatory mechanisms to counteract the effects of the binge, including purging, use of laxatives or diuretics, exercise, and fasting. Because of concerns that this definition resulted in excessive heterogeneity and a definition of bulimia nervosa that was at variance with common usage, it was proposed that the diagnosis of bulimia be restricted to those individuals who engage in purging behavior. Ultimately, this narrow definition was rejected in favor of adopting a subtyping scheme that indicated the regular use of purging versus nonpurging behavior.

Finally, in reviewing the literature on individuals who binge eat, there appeared to be a significant number of individuals who engage in binge eating behavior but who do not use any inappropriate compensatory mechanisms to avoid gaining weight. A new disorder, binge eating disorder, was proposed to cover such individuals who would otherwise have been diagnosed with eating disorder, not otherwise specified. Because of limited data about how best to define it, a proposed set of diagnostic criteria appears in the DSM-IV Appendix for Categories Needing Further Study.

For the sexual dysfunctions, there are several small changes in the criteria sets. Because of the inherent difficulty in knowing the boundary between "normal" sexual functioning and a diagnosable sexual dysfunction, a diagnostic criterion has been added to require the sexual dysfunction to be clinically significant (i.e., the disturbance must cause "marked distress or interpersonal difficulty"). This sense of marked distress is often related to the individual's expectations about sexual performance and functioning, which are established by the individual's subculture. The specific changes in the diagnostic criteria for female orgasmic disorder partly stem from an attempt to correct for our society's overvaluing of the ability to reach orgasm during intercourse. Rather than focus on the site of stimulation necessary to produce orgasm, the DSM-IV criteria instruct the clinician to base his or her judgment on the "woman's orgasmic capacity being less than would be reasonable for her age, sexual experience, and adequacy of sexual stimulation she receives."

To facilitate the differential diagnosis of sexual dysfunctions, two changes have been made in this section. First, two new disorders have been added: secondary sexual dysfunction, for those conditions that are judged to be etiologically related to a general medical condition (e.g., erectile disorder due to diabetes mellitus), and substance-induced sexual dysfunction, for those conditions that are judged to be etiologically related to the use of a substance or medication (e.g., cocaine-related orgasmic dysfunction). Second, a diagnostic criterion is being added to each of the sexual dysfunctions to alert the clinician to consider substance-induced and secondary etiologies.

In summary, the changes in DSM-IV for these sections are relatively minor and serve to improve diagnostic clarity and differential diagnosis. A number of useful and relevant suggestions to increase cultural sensitivity have been suggested (see Chapter 25) and have informed the preparation of the DSM-IV text for these disorders.

References

American Psychiatric Association: Diagnostic and Statistical Manual of Mental Disorders, 3rd Edition, Revised. Washington, DC, American Psychiatric Association, 1987

American Psychiatric Association: Diagnostic and Statistical Manual of Mental Disorders, 4th Edition. Washington, DC, American Psychiatric Association, 1994

Section VII

Adjustment and Stress Disorders

Chapter 27

Adjustment Disorder in DSM-IV: Cultural Considerations

Morton Beiser, M.D.

DSM-IV (American Psychiatric Association 1994) describes adjustment disorder as the development of emotional or behavioral symptoms in response to an identifiable psychosocial stressor (or multiple stressors) occurring within 3 months of the onset of the stressor. Unlike other diagnoses in DSM-IV, this category is not defined by specific psychopathological behaviors. Conditions gain their designation as adjustment disorders by exclusion (i.e., "This category should not be used if the disturbance meets the criteria for another specific Axis I disorder... or is merely an exacerbation of a preexisting Axis I or Axis II disorder [criterion C]") (American Psychiatric Association 1994, p. 623). The etiological tie to a specific stressor and the differentiation from other forms of disorder are highlighted by the requirement that the disorder "... must resolve within 6 months of the termination of the stressor (or its consequences) (Criterion E)" (American Psychiatric Association 1994, p. 623). Finally, the exclusion of uncomplicated bereavement and the imposition of inclusion criteria such as 1) that "marked significant distress that is in excess of what would be expected given the nature of the stressor" and 2) that "there is significant impairment in social or occupational (academic) functioning" presumably ensures the differentiation between adjustment disorder and more mundane distress (American Psychiatric Association 1994, p. 623).

Attempts to use this construct as a framework for a literature review highlight its limited nosological utility, at least as presently defined. First, the fact that this is a diagnosis by exclusion indirectly implies that disorders that are clearly reactive to external stressors occupy a lower hierarchical rung than other DSM-IV categories. Second, a judgment about whether a disorder fulfills one of the major criteria—that symptoms cease after stress is alleviated—can be made only in retrospect. A diagnosis should offer a forecast, not a retrospective: inaccurate diagnosis can lead to such consequences as inappropriate treatment and stigmatization. Finally, although a skilled clinician operating with sufficient information might be able to distinguish adjustment disorder from a syndrome that fulfills the criteria for an affective disorder, such differentiations will not be possible in many clinical settings, let alone in field research. For example, epidemiological research reports are consistent in suggesting that depressive disorder is highly prevalent, affecting between 4% and 8% of the general population (Regier et al. 1988; Robins et al. 1984). Investigations of the correlates of depression implicate factors such as job loss in the precipitation of disorder and strongly suggest that people who regain their jobs also regain their mental health (Iversen and Sabroe 1988). At the same time, validation studies of instruments such as the National Institute of Mental Health Diagnostic Interview Schedule (DIS) (Robins et al. 1981), routinely used in epidemiological surveys, reveal that although there is considerable overlap between epidemiological and clinical assessment, slippage occurs among so-called borderline cases—people whose burden of symptoms does not quite fulfill diagnostic criteria (Robins 1985). In other words, depending on cut-points employed, some of the phenomena counted among depressive disorders in population surveys may represent what DSM-IV classifies as emotional or behavioral disturbance in reaction to stress that ceases when stress is alleviated. These observations stimulate the speculation that if instruments capable of assessing adjustment disorder according to DSM-IV guidelines were available, some of the very high community prevalence figures for disorders such as major depression might be attenuated by reclassifying them into adjustment disorder. The current guidelines, insufficient for diagnosing adjustment disorder, make such differentiations impossible.

Toward a Taxonomy of Antecedents

In an important methodological review, Dohrenwend and Dohrenwend (1982) reported that "distress," as measured by commonly used psychiatric epidemiological screening scales, overlaps but does not completely coincide with psychiatric diagnosis. According to the Dohrenwends, well-known instruments such as the Center for Epidemiologic Studies Depression Scale (CES-D) (Radloff 1977) and the Psychiatric Epidemiology Research Interview (PERI) (Dohrenwend et al. 1980) do not measure disorder; instead, analogous to body thermometer readings, elevated scores signal psychological fever but not its significance. "When it [a score] is elevated, you know that something is wrong but you do not know what specific thing is wrong until you learn more about the context" (Dohrenwend and Dohrenwend 1982, p. 1272).

Basing their argument on the Dohrenwend review as well as the results from many community surveys that use nonspecific measures of psychological upset, Carr and Vitaliano (1985) proposed a model in which distress is defined as a complex of biobehavioral responses to antecedent stressors (perceived as well as real) mediated by vulnerability to stress (demographic factors; genetic, physiological and psychological predisposition), and psychological and social resources (coping strategies, social supports).

Carr and Vitaliano's formulation suggests a way to make the adjustment reaction category more meaningful. Because antecedents rather than description lie at the heart of the adjustment disorder concept, the nosological goal for this category should be to construct a taxonomy of antecedents by identifying stressors that regularly and predictably place mental health in jeopardy. In this connection, a report from a World Health Organization working group, containing preliminary descriptions of *abnormal psychosocial situations* which, there is good reason to believe, play a role in various psychiatric conditions is of particular interest (Goor-Lambo et al. 1990).

One challenge to developing a taxonomy of antecedents is to ensure the relevance of identified stressors by recourse to a level of abstraction sufficient to guarantee their universal applicability. At the same time, stressors must not be so abstract that they lose clinical meaningfulness.

The balance of this presentation is devoted to describing migrant adjustment disorder, a prototype for a taxonomy based on antecedents.

Migrant Adjustment Disorder

People all over the world are on the move. In developing countries, large-scale population shifts are depleting rural villages and swelling already glutted cities. Economically developed countries, concerned about population decline, admit large numbers of immigrants from their industrialized neighbors but also from poor, threatened, or politically repressive countries.

A body of literature suggests that during the first 2 years of resettlement, migrants suffer an elevated risk of developing emotional distress. Early reports were based on studies of migrants in treatment, the results of which were inappropriately generalized (Grinberg 1984; Mathers 1974; Tyhurst 1951, 1977). However, more recent surveys of representative community samples support the concept that migration and resettlement set in motion a phase-related mental health risk (Beiser 1988; Rumbaut 1985; Westermeyer et al. 1984).

The University of Toronto Department of Psychiatry (Clarke Institute) Refugee Resettlement Project, a study of Southeast Asian refugees admitted to Canada in the early 1980s, demonstrated that 10–12 months after arrival, new settlers experienced higher rates of distress than refugees who had come to Canada earlier or than they themselves displayed 2 years later (Beiser 1988). Using similar methods, Rumbaut (1985) observed the same overall pattern albeit a slightly later period of maximum risk (12–18 months after arrival).

Using structured questionnaires containing culturally specific idioms of distress together with the DIS (Robins et al. 1981, 1985), Self Report Questionnaire (SRQ) (Harding et al. 1980), and Senegal Health Scales (Beiser et al. 1976) items, as well as questions based on DSM-III criteria for affective disorders, bilingual interviewers surveyed the entire cohort in 1981 and then repeated the survey in 1983. Symptom responses were subjected to grade of membership (GOM) analysis. A variant of cluster analysis, GOM analysis differs from other techniques of this type in at least two important ways. Unlike approaches such as factor analysis and other forms of cluster analysis that assume that diagnostic categories must be mutually distinct, GOM analysis rests on "fuzzy" set theory. Classification, which relies on loose associations among definitional characteristics, produces diagnostic prototypes that may have overlapping or fuzzy boundaries. Furthermore, GOM analysis does not assume that individuals belong to one and only one category. Instead, in fuzzy set nosology, an individual may exhibit more than one symptom profile, each of which may be manifested to greater or lesser degree. Each individual in the sample then receives a numerical value for each GOM category describing the degree to which he or she approximates each of the diagnostic prototypes (Beiser et al. 1994; Blazer et al. 1988; George et al. 1989).

One of the categories produced by the GOM analysis of the Refugee Resettlement Project mental health data was a complex of depressive and somatic symptoms resembling the DSM-IV description of depressive disorder. The greater the number of symptoms belonging to this particular aggregate reported by an individual, the closer he or she was to being a "classic case" or prototype of depression and the closer his or her score approached 1.0. People with few or none of the symptoms making up this complex received scores approaching 0. In a general population sample, one would expect to find few, if any, subjects with a score of 1.0, indicating the presence of the full-blown syndrome. This was also the case among the refugee sample, which did, however, contain a number of individuals with partial manifestations of the prototype.

A second symptom profile emerged that was similar to that describing depressive disorder. However, by contrast, the second category had even more intense depressive and somatic symptoms accompanied by panic (Beiser et al. 1994). Although not an official DSM-IV diagnosis, depression with panic has been a frequent product of empirical analysis of clinical and population-based symptom data (Blazer et al. 1988; Paykel 1971). Some research results suggest that depression together with panic disorder has a higher familial loading than depression alone (Leckman et al. 1983; Weissman et al. 1984).

The two symptom complexes—depression and depression with panic—were replicated in a sample of resident Canadians interviewed with a questionnaire during the Refugee Resettlement Project. Identical to the instrument administered to the refugees, the Canadian questionnaire contained distress items from well-known instruments frequently used in mental health surveys, as well as the symptom responses based on a Southeast Asian lexicon of idioms of distress suitably translated into English. In both the Canadian and refugee samples, culture-specific items contributed in the same way to defining the two types of depression. In other words, a refugee endorsing a culture-specific distress item was as likely to respond positively to one of the DIS, SRQ, or Senegal Health Scale items as the average resident Canadian.

Partial manifestations of both symptom complexes were prevalent among refugees who had been in Canada less than 1 year at the time of original interview. The longer people stayed in Canada, the less distress they reported. However, refugees with high GOM scores on the depression plus panic profile at time 1 were highly likely to be still experiencing symptoms 2 years later.

Although immigrant and refugee studies suggest that these syndromes can be usefully thought of as predictable biobehavioral responses to the stresses of resettlement, the temptation to "overpsychiatrize" must be avoided. Only a minority of newcomers experience overwhelming distress, become "cases" for community prevalence counts, or end up in treatment. A taxonomy based on antecedents must specify not only those factors that make some people more vulnerable to distress than others but also the psychological and social shock absorbers that protect others.

Vulnerability Factors

Convergent research evidence suggests that young, poorly educated, unemployed males who do not speak the host country language are at particular risk for developing distress during the early years of resettlement (Beiser 1983; Beiser et al. 1993; Krupinski et al. 1973).

Sociocultural factors help explain demographic relationships. In the early years of resettlement, young males, more than other groups, are forced into contact with the host society as they and their families grapple with the immediate problems of shelter and sustenance. Work, which is critical both for livelihood and for maintaining mental health, is difficult to find if one is poorly educated or cannot speak the language of the dominant society. Regardless of whether one is a migrant or a member of the receiving society, unemployment creates a risk for emotional distress (Beiser et al. 1993; Hurh and Kim 1990; Stein 1986; Westermeyer et al. 1984). Establishing that two factors correlate in the same way in two different populations does not guarantee that the etiological links are identical. Data from the Refugee Resettlement Project support the concept that for resident North Americans, the symbolic significance of work has mental health implications as powerful as its importance in guaranteeing security. Settled Canadians, like their United States and European counterparts, value work as a source of self-esteem and social contact (Warr 1982). For refugees, however, the mental health impact of unemployment may not result from threats to self-concept or social network. For sociocentrically oriented people such as Southeast Asian refugees, joblessness jeopardizes mental health, because unemployed people cannot fulfill familial obligations (Beiser et al. 1993; Stein 1986).

Finally, the symptom complex itself seems to have prognostic significance: the presence of panic in addition to depression may suggest genetic vulnerability.

Protective Factors

Psychological and social factors mitigate the impact of resettlement stress. The way in which individuals attend to time is an important, if seldom studied, adaptive mechanism. In daily life, most people maintain a balance in their focus on past, present, and future. Data from the Refugee Resettlement Project demonstrate that, in contrast to people living under ordinary, expectable circumstances, refugees isolate past percepts from consciousness to selectively attend to the present and a foreshortened future. The minority of refugees who, in a departure from this pattern, focus on the past experience an elevated risk of depression. Although it is true that people who are depressed are also frequently preoccupied with the past, there is evidence that this mode of thought is more than a depressive concomitant. Refugee nostalgia for the past frequently precedes the onset of depression (Beiser 1987; Beiser et al. 1989). Refugee Resettlement Project data suggest that those refugees displaying the depression with panic syndrome were much more preoccupied with past percepts, to the exclusion of present and future, than those in the general population or in the depressed-only group.

Social support from family, friends, and community provide important mental health resources as well as defenses against stress.

Research has repeatedly demonstrated that marital partners, family, and a like-ethnic community provide crucial social support for newcomers. Married people with extended connections living in or near a like-ethnic community of significant size have a mental health advantage over nonmarried, isolated immigrants and refugees (Beiser 1983; Beiser et al. 1989; Hitch and Rack 1980; Hurh and Kim 1990; Murphy 1973; Saxena 1989; Stein 1986; Westermeyer et al. 1983).

Does It Fit With DSM-IV?

Although migrant adjustment disorder satisfies many of the DSM-IV criteria, symptom stabilization in the depression plus panic subgroup violates the DSM-IV criterion specifying that distress must disappear within 6 months of removal of the stressor. Studies from different countries confirming the recalcitrance of migration-induced psychological upset argue against the usefulness of an arbitrary 6-month cutoff point (Hitch and Rack 1980; Saxena 1989).

Data about a migration adjustment syndrome illustrate how research results should modify criteria to make them conform more closely to empirical reality. The model underlying adjustment disorder specifying that when stress is removed, distress disappears fails to do justice to the complexity of person-environment interactions. For example, among newcomers struggling to find their way in a new country, emotional distress probably jeopardizes one's chances of staying employed, and losing a job creates a further risk for developing a disorder (Kessler et al. 1987a; Westermeyer et al. 1990). Unemployment and emotional upset thus interact to create a mutually reinforcing spiral of maladaptation.

Migrant Adjustment Disorder: A Prototype

A World Health Organization working group has proposed a classification of psychosocial situations for which there is evidence to adduce an etiological role in psychiatric disorder (Goor-Lambo et al. 1990; Jacob and Tannenbaum 1988). "Migration or social transplantation" appears as item 71 in this list under a general category of societal stressors.

Migration admittedly creates a risk for mental disorder (Canadian Task Force on Mental Health Issues Affecting Immigrants and Refugees 1988). A proportion of newcomers, albeit a small number relative to the population of migrants, develop an Axis I condition or symptoms of a severity sufficient to be categorized under migrant adjustment disorder. Because Canada and the United States continue to be major immigrant-receiving countries, each admitting newcomers at a rate roughly equal to 0.6% of their respective populations, it behooves mental health professionals in North America to be familiar with this stressor, its potential consequences, and the factors that may help explain why some people with adjustment disorder may experience a resolution of symptoms and others a more chronic course.

Clinical and population-based research reports about migration and its consequences help make it a model for a taxonomy of antecedents. Although they are conceptually far less well developed than migration syndrome, the research literature suggests at least two other candidates for inclusion in a taxonomy of antecedents: loss of face and marginalization.

Loss of Face

A behavioral construct that New Zealand Maori call *whakama* (Sachdev 1990) and that Samoans refer to as *musu* (Gluckman 1977) denotes a complex of behaviors including shame, self-abasement, feelings of inferiority, gloominess, and social withdrawal. In a discussion in which the author pointed out the dangers of medicalizing concepts such as *whakama*, Sachdev (1990) described its societal regulatory functions. The shame of failing to live up to prescribed expectations may give rise to the distressing symptoms of *whakama* and *musu*. In industrialized societies, where work determines status, unemployed people suffer "inferred inadequacy," a reaction involving shame, isolation, and depressed mood (Kessler et al. 1987a, 1987b). Among village Serer in Senegal, West Africa, people afflicted with *pobouh lang* experience a shameful compulsion to eat sand. Although the geophagic disorder itself may have a physiological base—perhaps sickle cell anemia (Prince 1989)—the associated symptoms of depression, guilty feelings, and withdrawnness are based on shame and the need for concealment (Beiser et al. 1974). Phenomena as seemingly disparate as *whakama*, *musu*, inferred inadequacy, and *pobouh lang* may be conceptually linked individual reactions to the stress of loss of face. Although culture determines the context for loss of face, the cross-cultural similarity of biobehavioral response to its threat or actualization seems remarkable.

Marginalization

A few days after a cloth mill in the southern United States received a shipment of fibers from an exotic foreign country, one of the employees left work complaining of nausea, vague pains, and fainting. During the ensuing week of June in the early 1960s, almost half of the mill workers either entered the hospital or became bedridden. Medical and public health authorities failed to uncover the unusual microorganisms they had expected to find, and shortly afterward everyone recovered and returned to work. Kerckhoff and Back explained what they call the "June bug" epidemic as a psychological strike by the female mill employees who felt powerless to change working conditions that were making them unhappy and excessively burdened by responsibilities at home and on the job (Kerckhoff and Back 1968).

Basing her argument on data from a different part of the continent and at another point in time, Dunk (1989) discussed the phenomenon of *nevra*, or broken nerves, among the Greek community of Montreal. According to Dunk, *nevra* can be a normal expression of social distress related to family or work problems. Greek women do, however, seek medical care with exaggerated forms of *nevra* including such symptoms as headaches, dizziness, vague pains, and fear of loss of control. Dunk asserted, "The more frequent reasons for women presenting with *nevra* in a medical settings are: the conditions of factory and homework; gender-roles ascribed to women and their limited options for expressing distress; changes in family structure upon migration and their implications for increasing women's work and isolation; and the few social support networks available for women" (p. 42). In an analysis of neurasthenia and depression in China, Kleinman (1982) reported that three-fourths of the patients he studied used somatization, a culturally sanctioned idiom of distress, to negotiate a way out of intolerable work situations.

Despite differences of time, place, and culture, the June bug, *nevra*, and neurasthenia phenomena share certain features in common. All are vague symptomatic states exhibited by people whom social structural constraints have rendered relatively impotent to effect changes in their difficult life situations. Their symptoms, which assume culturally acceptable forms, offer a way out, sometimes only temporary and sometimes more permanent, as well as a sanctioned outlet to express resentment.

Should Adjustment Disorders Be in a Standard Diagnostic Manual?

Does a recommendation to include in a DSM adjustment reactions or disorders such as migration syndrome, loss of face, or marginalization run the risk of medicalizing problems that have their roots in depriving, traumatizing, or constraining social structures? Arguments over what is medical and what is social are probably specious. Forced with the stress of living in a fragmenting, changing world, people have less and less recourse to traditional forms of support to alleviate or buffer socially induced stresses. Medical care is often sought when no other avenue of help seems to be available. Like it or not, mental health providers are called on by a public with a variety of needs, some of them disorders that are products of stress emanating from social disequilibrium, many of which may be relatively short-lived. Differentiation of conditions that, in the main, are reactions to stress from those in which biological and psychological predispositional vulnerability may play larger etiological roles is important for clinical care and for planning services.

The research base for a taxonomy of antecedents is fragmentary, suggestive rather than definitive. It will be important to develop the category of adjustment disorder so that health providers know what they are being called on to treat: epidemiologists, what they are counting and nosologists, what they are naming.

References

American Psychiatric Association: Diagnostic and Statistical Manual of Mental Disorders, 4th Edition. Washington, DC, American Psychiatric Association, 1994

Beiser M: Changing time perspective and mental health among southeast Asian refugees. Cult Med Psychiatry 11:437–464, 1987

Beiser M: Influences of time, ethnicity, and attachment on depression in southeast Asian refugees. Am J Psychiatry 145:46–51, 1983

Beiser M, Burr WA, Collomb H, et al: Pobouh lang in Senegal. Soc Psychiatry 9:123–129, 1974

Beiser M, Benfari RC, Collomb H, et al: Measuring psychoneurotic behavior in cross-cultural surveys. J Nerv Ment Dis 163:10–23, 1976

Beiser M, Turner RJ, Ganesan S: Catastrophic stress and its effects on the mental health of southeast Asian refugees. Soc Sci Med 28:183–195, 1989

Beiser M, Johnson PJ, Turner RJ: Unemployment, underemployment and depressive affect among southeast Asian refugees. Psychol Med 23:731–743, 1993

Beiser M, Cargo M, Woodbury MA: A comparison of psychiatric disorder in different cultures: depressive typologies in southeast Asian refugees and resident Canadians. International Journal of Methods in Psychiatric Research 4:157–172, 1994

Blazer DG, Swartz M, Woodbury MA, et al: Depressive symptoms and depressive diagnoses in a community population: use of a new procedure for analysis of psychiatric classification. Arch Gen Psychiatry 45:1078–1084, 1988

Canadian Task Force on Mental Health Issues Affecting Immigrants and Refugees: After the door has been opened: mental health issues affecting immigrants and refugees in Canada. Canada, Ministry of Supplies and Services, 1988

Carr JE, Vitaliano PP: The theoretical implications of converging research on depression and the culture-bound syndromes, in Culture and Depression: Studies in the Anthropology and Cross-Cultural Psychiatry of Affect and Disorder. Edited by Kleinman A, Good B. Berkeley, University of California Press, 1985, pp 244–266

Dohrenwend BP, Shrout PE, Egri G, et al: Nonspecific psychological distress and other dimensions of psychopathology. Arch Gen Psychiatry 37:1229–1236, 1980

Dohrenwend BS, Dohrenwend BP: Perspectives on the past and future of psychiatric epidemiology. Am J Public Health 72:1271–1279, 1982

Dunk P: Greek women and broken nerves in Montreal. Med Anthropol 1:29–45, 1989

George LK, Blazer DG, Woodbury MA, Manton KG: Internal consistency of DSM-III diagnoses, in the Validity of Psychiatric Diagnoses. Edited by Robins LN, Barrett JE. New York, Raven, 1989, pp 99–126

Gluckman LK: Clinical experience with Samoans in Auckland, New Zealand. Aust NZ J Psychiatry 11:101–107, 1977

Goor-Lambo G, Orley J, Poustka F, et al: Classification of abnormal psychosocial situations: preliminary report of a revision of a WHO scheme. J Child Psychol Psychiatry 31:229–241, 1990

Grinberg L: A psychoanalytic study of migration: its normal and pathological aspects. J Am Psychoanal 32:13–38, 1984

Harding TW, de Arango MV, Baltazar J, et al: Mental disorders in primary health care: a study of their frequency and diagnosis in four developing countries. Psychol Med 10:231–241, 1980

Hitch PJ, Rack PH: Mental illness among Polish and Russian refugees in Bradford. Br J Psychiatry 137:206–211, 1980

Hurh WM, Kim KC: Correlates of Korean immigrants' mental health. J Nerv Ment Dis 178:703–711, 1990

Iversen L, Sabroe S: Psychological well-being among unemployed and employed people after a company close-down: a longitudinal study. Journal of Social Issues 44:141–152, 1988

Jacob T, Tannenbaum DL: Family assessment methods, in Assessment and Diagnosis in Child Psychopathology. Edited by Rather M, Tuma AH, Lann IS. New York, Guilford, 1988, pp 196–231

Kerckhoff AC, Back KW: The June Bug. New York, Appleton-Century-Crofts, 1968

Kessler RC, Turner JB, House JA: Intervening processes in the relationship between unemployment and health. Psychol Med 17:949–961, 1987a

Kessler RC, House JS, Turner JB: Unemployment and health in a community sample. J Health Soc Behav 28:51–59, 1987b

Kleinman A: Neurasthenia and depression: a study of somatization and culture in China. Cult Med Psychiatry 6:117–190, 1982

Krupinski J, Stoller A, Wallace L: Psychiatric disorders in eastern European refugees now in Australia. Soc Sci Med 7:31–45, 1973

Leckman JF, Merikangas KR, Pauls DL, et al: Anxiety disorders and depression: contradictions between family study data and DSM-III conventions. Am J Psychiatry 140:880–882, 1983

Mathers J: The gestation period of identity change. Br J Psychiatry 125:472–474, 1974

Murphy HBM: Migration and mental disorders: an appraisal, in Uprooting and After. Edited by Zwingmann C, Pfister-Amande M. New York, Springer-Verlag, 1973

Paykel ES: Classification of depressed patients: a cluster analysis derived grouping. Br J Psychiatry 118:275–288, 1971

Prince I: Pica and geophagia in cross-cultural perspective. Transcultural Psychiatric Research Review 26:167–197, 1989

Radloff L: The CES-D Scale: a self-report depression scale for research in the general population. Applied Psychological Measurement 1:388–401, 1977

Regier DA, Boyd JHF, Burke JD Jr, et al: One-month prevalence of mental disorders in the United States based on five epidemiologic catchment area sites. Arch Gen Psychiatry 45:977–986, 1988

Robins LN: Epidemiology: reflections on testing the validity of psychiatric interviews. Arch Gen Psychiatry 42:918–924, 1985

Robins LN, Helzer JE, Crougham J, et al: National Institute of Mental Health Diagnostic Interview Schedule: its history, characteristics and validity. Arch Gen Psychiatry 38:381–389, 1981

Robins LN, Helzer DE, Weissman MM, et al: Lifetime prevalence of specific psychiatric disorders in three sites. Arch Gen Psychiatry 41:949–958, 1984

Robins LN, Helzer JE, Orvaschel H, et al: The Diagnostic Interview Schedule epidemiologic field methods in psychiatry, in The NIMH Epidemiologic Catchment Area Program. Edited by Eaton WW, Kessler LG. Orlando, FL, Academic Press, 1985, pp 143–170

Rumbaut RD: Mental health and the refugee experience: a comparative study of Southeast Asian refugees, in Southeast Asian Mental Health: Treatment Prevention Services and Research (DDHS Publication ADM-1399). Edited by Owan T, Bliatout B, Lin K-M, et al. Rockville, MD, National Institute of Mental Health, 1985

Sachdev PS: Whakama: culturally determined behavior in the New Zealand Maori. Psychol Med 120:433–444, 1990

Saxena S: Diagnosis of refugees. Am J Psychiatry 146:410–411, 1989

Stein BN: The experience of being a refugee: insights from the literature, in Refugee Mental Health in Resettlement Countries. Edited by Williams C, Westermeyer J. Washington, DC, Hemisphere, 1986, pp 5–23

Tyhurst L: Displacement and migration: a study in social psychiatry. Am J Psychiatry 107:561–568, 1951

Tyhurst L: Psychosocial first aid for refugees. Mental Health and Society 4:319–343, 1977

Warr P: Psychological aspects of employment and unemployment. Psychol Med 11:437–464, 1982

Weissman MM, Gershon ES, Kidd KK, et al: Psychiatric disorders in the relatives of probands with affective disorders. Arch Gen Psychiatry 41:13–21, 1984

Westermeyer J, Vang TF, Neider J: Migration and mental health among Hmong refugees: association of pre- and post-migration factors with self-rating scales. J Nerv Ment Dis 171:92–96, 1983

Westermeyer J, Neider J, Vang TF: Acculturation and mental health: a study of Hmong refugees at 15 and 35 years post-migration. Soc Sci Med 18:87–93, 1984

Westermeyer J, Callies A, Neider J: Welfare status and psychosocial adjustment among 100 Hmong refugees. J Nerv Ment Dis 178:300–306, 1990

Chapter 28

Cultural Comments on Adjustment and Stress Disorders

Janis H. Jenkins, Ph.D.

lthough my commentary addresses cultural dimensions of stress and adjustment disorders, I begin by noting that the apparent importance of culture in adjustment and stress disorders should not cloud our vision of the importance of culture in more biogenetically regarded disorders such as schizophrenia. Even though psychosocial factors are not specific components of standard diagnostic criteria for schizophrenic and affective disorders, these should not be regarded as less "cultural," less "stress-related," or less responsive to psychosocial features of the cultural environment. At issue here is an apparent willingness to construct a diagnostic category that explicitly acknowledges the importance of cultural and psychosocial factors in the case of stress and adjustment disorders, but not in the case of other major mental disorders.

On the (Non)Specificity of Adjustment Disorder

Perhaps no greater contrast can be drawn than that between the diagnostic criteria for schizophrenia and those for adjustment disorders. Symptom criteria for schizophrenic disorders are relatively specific and rarely employed; adjustment disorders have few, if any, specific behavioral symptom criteria and are commonly applied to scores of outpatients (Fabrega et al. 1987). Schizophrenia is often regarded as the most serious and exotic of psychiatric disorders, whereas adjustment disorders are perhaps the least serious and most quotidian of DSM listings. Indeed, adjustment disorders, with their nonspecific symptom criteria and broad-ranging set of psychosocial etiological factors, are analogous to the common cold. An apparent contradiction exists in the frequency and ease with which this diagnostic category is assigned, on the one hand, and the degree of nonspecificity of the category, on the other. This lack of clarity will surely be compounded when attempting to extend this diagnostic category cross-culturally.

A prevalent clinical attitude surrounding adjustment disorders is to regard adjustment disorder as a nonstigmatizing diagnosis for clinically significant—albeit divergent—behavioral and emotional symptoms. As summarized by Beiser in Chapter 27, this diagnosis is made by clinicians only after all other Axis I and Axis II disorders have been ruled out. Adjustment disorder is then a diagnosis of default, insufficient severity, and relatively little stigma.

Cultural Orientations

I cannot share in Beiser's endorsement of Carr and Vitaliano's (1985) model of distress as a complex of biobehavioral responses to a stressor that is mediated by demographic, biogenetic, and psychosocial resources. Explicit notions of culture are nowhere to be found in this formulation. The problem of fleshing out a theoretical orientation to culture is crucial. One conceptualization of culture is as follows:

A generalized, coherent context of shared symbols and meanings that persons dynamically create and recreate for themselves in the process of social interaction. In everyday life, culture is something people come to take for granted; it is their way of feeling, thinking, and being in the world—the un-self-conscious medium of experience, interpretation, and action. Culture is thus the most generalized baseline from which individuals may deviate and hence is invaluable for comparative studies of psychopathology (Jenkins and Karno 1992)

Beiser's call for a taxonomy of antecedent stressors that regularly and predictably place mental health in jeopardy is important, as little systematic comparative research has been carried out that could provide an empirical basis for such a task. A great many of the items in an "inventory of stressors" can be expected to be culturally specific, although there may also be common cross-cultural contexts that evoke significant distress in most of their members. Certainly we can anticipate some of the kinds of psychosocial and environmental stressors that would be included in such a listing of antecedent stressors. These stressors include acute life events such as loss of a job or loved one, sexual abuse or assault, serious accident or injury, natural disaster, eviction from a home, and a frightening or life-threatening experience. However, some of these stressful "events" can co-occur or recur, as in the case of civil warfare, abusive relationships, or political persecution. One question concerns whether we would consider exposure to war-related horrors as a "psychosocial stressor" of etiological significance or whether the apparent severity of such a stressor is to be reserved for posttraumatic stress disorder. In either case, a cautionary note is in order to avoid inappropriately pathologizing normal human response to what, by any culture's standards, can only be regarded as intolerable and horrific conditions (e.g., torture, massacres, and so forth).

The available repertoire of affective and behavioral response to a distressing event or circumstance would also be substantially culturally shaped. The judgment of what constitutes "excessive" must be made relative to the normative assumptions of the bounds of how one's colleagues might otherwise construe and respond in a more functional, less maladaptive manner to a similar psychosocial stressor.

Psychiatric Disability Among Refugees

I now turn my comments to Beiser's discussion of the concept of migrant adjustment disorder. Migrants are usefully distinguished into the categories of immigrants and refugees. The term *immigrant* implies some degree of choice concerning the decision to leave one's natal country, whereas the designation of *refugee* is meant to signal that departure is involuntary and repatriation, often impossible. Clinical and cultural knowledge concerning refugee mental health has emerged only relatively recently. For Southeast Asian refugees, we have a quite excellent set of studies (Beiser 1989; Kinzie et al. 1984; Mollica et al. 1987; Westermeyer 1988), and a few studies have emerged for Central Americans (Guarnaccia and Farias 1988; Jenkins 1991; Jenkins and Valiente, in press; Suarez-Orozco 1990). Many common features of refugee experience have been identified for the Southeast Asian and Latin American refugees in North America. These include lack of contact with kin in the home country; linguistic barriers; acculturation, family, and gender conflicts; poverty; inadequate housing; legal status; and prejudice and discrimination.

Clinical conceptualizations of the life situations of refugees must take into consideration those problems previously engendered in one's natal country and those encountered as new arrivals in a foreign nation. The mental health sequelae of past and current stressors (e.g., chronic fear, anxiety, and terror related to war experiences and the current threat of deportation) are commonly seen in clinical settings, where refugees frequently present with full or partial syndromes of depressive and posttraumatic stress disorders (Jenkins 1991; Kinzie et al. 1984; Mollica et al. 1987; Westermeyer 1989). Other commonly observed mood and anxiety disorders include dysthymia, somatization, and panic disorders. Careful evaluation of diagnostic criteria is necessary if these disorders are to be distinguished from the proposed migrant adjustment disorder. In addition, there appear to be culturally specific symptoms in relation to refugee experience. Among Salvadoran psychiatric outpatients, culturally distinctive symptoms include pronounced bodily sensations of heat (*"el calor"*), electric shocks, and other somatic complaints associated with the condition of *nervios* (Jenkins 1988, 1991; Jenkins and Valiente, in press).

As currently proposed, there appear to be conceptual difficulties with Beiser's "marginalization" category, as it includes diverse indigenous categories such as *nevra*, neurasthenia, and "June bug." Of theoretical concern is the equation of the cultural work of professional psychiatric diagnosis with the cultural work of the folk sector illness categories based on family and community conceptions and categories of illness. The purpose of professional psychiatric categories is to describe and operationalize particular syndromes for classification and treatment. The purpose of folk categories, particularly at the family level of analysis, can be quite different. Indigenously defined folk categories reflect moral standing, social relations, role functioning, and emotional and physical well-being of not only the ill person but also their kin (Fabrega 1970; Jenkins 1988). The cultural meanings of folk categories of illness represent a complex set of interrelations, as Good and DelVecchio-Good (1982) have written in their article on "heart distress" in Iran.

In cultural-psychiatric research with Latin American immigrants and refugees, families and patients alike employ the term *nervios* for everyday upsets, major depression, and schizophrenia. The purposively vague and fluid boundaries of this folk category are maintained for the management of stigma, family bonds, and culturally preferred styles of affective communication. Thus, the "cultural work" of folk categories is different from the "cultural work" of psychiatric diagnostic classification (Fabrega 1970; Good 1977; Jenkins 1988). If, as Kleinman (1988) has argued, it is a "category fallacy" to unquestioningly apply psychiatric diagnostic categories across cultures, it may equally be a category fallacy to incorporate certain folk categories into psychiatric nosology.

References

Beiser M: Catastrophic stress and factors affecting its consequences among southeast Asian refugees. Soc Sci Med 28:183–195, 1989

Carr JE, Vitaliano P: The theoretical implications of converging research on depression and the culture bound syndromes, in Culture and Depression. Edited by Kleinman A, Good B. Berkeley, University of California Press, 1985

Fabrega H: On the specificity of folk illnesses. Southeastern Journal of Anthropology 26:305–314, 1970

Fabrega H, Mezzich J, Mezzich A: Adjustment disorder as a marginal or transitional illness category in DSM-III. Arch Gen Psychiatry 44:567–572, 1987

Good B: The heart of what's the matter: The semantics of illness in Iran. Cult Med Psychiatry 1:25–28, 1977

Good B, DelVecchio-Good MJ: Toward a meaning centered analysis of popular illness categories: "fright illness" and "heart distress" in Iran, in Cultural Conceptions of Mental Health and Therapy. Edited by Marsella AJ, White G. Dordrecht, The Netherlands, D Reidel, 1982

Guarnaccia P, Farias P: The social meanings of nervios: a case study of a Central American woman. Soc Sci Med 26:1233–1241, 1988

Jenkins JH: Ethnopsychiatric interpretations of schizophrenic illness: the problem of nervios within Mexican-American families. Cult Med Psychiatry 12:1233–1331, 1988

Jenkins JH: The state construction of affect: political ethos and mental health among Salvadoran refugees. Cult Med Psychiatry 15:139–165, 1991

Jenkins JH, Karno M: The meaning of expressed emotion: theoretical issues raised by cross-cultural research. Am J Psychiatry 149:9–21, 1992

Jenkins JH, Valiente M: Bodily transactions of the passions: el calor among Salvadoran women refugees, in The Body as Existential Ground. Edited by Csordas TJ. Cambridge, England, Cambridge University Press (in press)

Kinzie JD, Frederickson B, Fleck J, et al: Posttraumatic stress disorder among survivors of Cambodian concentration camps. Am J Psychiatry 141:645–650, 1984

Kleinman A: Rethinking Psychiatry. New York, Free Press, 1988

Mollica R, Wyshak G, Lavelle J: The psychosocial impact of war trauma and torture on southeast Asian refugees. Am J Psychiatry 144:1567–1572, 1987

Suarez-Orozco M: Speaking of the unspeakable: toward psychosocial understanding of responses to terror. Ethos 18:353–383, 1990

Westermeyer J: DSM-III psychiatric disorders among Hmong refugees in the United States: a point prevalence study. Am J Psychiatry 145:197–202, 1988

Westermeyer J: Psychiatric Care of Migrants: A Clinical Guide. Washington, DC, American Psychiatric Press, 1989

Chapter 29

Cultural Comments on Adjustment Disorders

J. David Kinzie, M.D.

Responding to the issues raised by Beiser in Chapter 27 is not easy. There are very little empirical data by trained clinicians, either in clinical or field studies, that give information on adjustment disorders. I believe that, most of the studies that have been reported by Beiser and others have used self-rating scales or lay interviewers in the field. The last two studies on epidemiology that I conducted with Cambodian refugees and Native Americans did not even include the adjustment reaction or adjustment disorders as part of the diagnosis. My colleagues and I have found that this diagnosis is quite unreliable, even when made by experienced transcultural psychiatrists. Also, we have found that it is of little clinical utility. If individuals had several or more symptoms, they almost always met other Axis I diagnosis criteria (i.e., for depression, generalized anxiety, or dysthymic disorder). This was especially true if the symptoms led to some clinical impairment as currently required by DSM-IV (American Psychiatric Association 1994). In the study that Beiser quotes, subjects evaluated by a computer analysis had symptom patterns of depression or depression with panic disorder. These are both Axis I diagnoses, and by the exclusion criteria of adjustment reaction, I think such patterns would not qualify for adjustment disorder.

Beiser's chapter gives a great deal of thought and comment to the role of antecedents or psychosocial stressors involved in a specific disorder—say, an adjustment disorder. As he points out, this is unusual in the current diagnostic nomenclature. With the exception of posttraumatic stress disorder, no other disorders are defined by their antecedents. I find that Beiser's concept of enlarging the role of antecedents in defining a medical disorder quite intriguing. It has a great deal of appeal, on the one hand, as many people throughout the world are undergoing cultural and social changes that are indeed quite stressful. On the other hand,

233

adjustment disorder really is not comparable to other medical disorders. We do not define the physical trauma a patient suffers by describing how big the car was that hit him or her; we concentrate instead on the actual injuries suffered by the patient. Furthermore, small cars could produce a severe injury and big cars could produce a minor injury. Similarly, the reactions to a major psychosocial stress are quite variable.

As physicians we are concerned, or ought to be, with an individual's psychological and biological symptoms that define a disorder. This does not mean that we are not concerned about the psychological stresses or, indeed, the social-cultural matrix in which this disorder occurred.

Another problem with the emphasis on antecedents is that many psychiatric residents, and even experienced clinicians, confuse the antecedent and the disorder. We have had several residents who diagnosed an adjustment disorder reaction simply because there was an event to which the patient was adjusting. They ignore the fact that there are many symptoms that may lead clearly to more specific Axis I diagnosis (i.e., major depression).

Beiser has given us a model of an adjustment reaction to a psychosocial stress called the *migrant* type. This is quite interesting, and I have operationalized in Table 29–1 my perspective on Beiser's concepts. This makes it analogous to other types of adjustment disorders. Exclusion Criterion C is very important. The patient must not meet the criteria for any other major diagnostic disorder. I agree with Beiser that a 6-month limit for this disorder is far too short. If we followed the analogy of other disorders, we should have both acute and chronic forms, depending on whether the symptoms remit within 6 months.

I believe that in view of the little empirical data from cross-cultural studies of adjustment disorders, we should take something such as the migrant type of adjustment disorders, as Beiser suggests, and then begin the necessary field and clinical

---

Table 29–1.   Adjustment disorder, migrant type (after Beiser, Chapter 27, this volume)

A.   The development of emotional or behavioral symptoms in response to a geographic move that results in significant changes in culture, language, or social relations and occurring within 3 months of the onset of the move.

B.   These symptoms or behaviors are clinically significant, as evidenced by either of the following:
   1.   There is significant distress that is in excess of what is usually expected from the migration.
   2.   There is significant impairment in social or occupational (academic) functioning.

C.   This disturbance does not meet the criteria for any Axis I disorder and is not merely an exacerbation of a preexisting Axis I or Axis II disorder.

Specific Type

Acute type: If the symptoms or behaviors that have developed in response to the migration have persisted no longer than 6 months.

Chronic type: If the symptoms or behaviors that have developed in response to the migration have persisted for longer than 6 months.

studies by experienced clinicians. We need data to determine whether such an entity exists and if so, its characteristics, its clinical utility, and response to treatment.

Reference

American Psychiatric Association: Diagnostic and Statistical Manual of Mental Disorders, 4th Edition. Washington, DC, American Psychiatric Association, 1994

Chapter 30

Nosological Comments on Culture and Adjustment Disorders

David Spiegel, M.D.

In Chapter 27 Beiser raises some provocative questions about the nature of mental disorder and the structure of our classification system. There are several fundamental dimensions that are always present in discussions about diagnostic nosology. One of them is the "normal" versus the "pathological." As Beiser notes, the adjustment disorder category straddles that boundary. Being among the mildest of mental disorders and presumably related to normal stressors in the environment, the adjustment disorders clearly combine elements of normal and maladaptive reaction to stress. The more stressful the precipitant, the less maladaptive the presumed response to it—that is, the more it can be expected that there will be some cognitive and emotional reaction to the stressor. As Beiser notes, we do not want to unduly pathologize responses that are highly prevalent in the population; at the same time, we do not want to ignore diagnosable and treatable entities.

Another major issue raised by Beiser in his chapter is the prevalence of symptoms in relation to a stressful event. On the one hand, there is no point in describing as a separate category an adjustment reaction whose prevalence is extremely low. On the other hand, if the prevalence is extremely high, it enters the domain of normal response. As Beiser notes, only a minority of newcomers suffer overwhelming distress. The question becomes a somewhat empirical one of what constitutes a substantial minority: one big enough to be taken seriously, but small enough not to be considered normative.

The second major dimension addressed in Chapter 27 is the problem inherent in any classification system: the need to cull from individual cases common features in order to provide some simplification of the phenomena observed. The price of doing this is losing individual characteristics at the expense of data reduction. There have been a variety of approaches to this problem, and disagreement about it goes at least as far back as the philosophical debate between Plato and

Aristotle. The Platonic approach places more emphasis on the primacy of the realm of ideas and views real cases as imperfect approximations of the truth, which is the structure or category. The Aristotelian approach is more empirical, viewing categories as emergent properties of individual instances. Beiser seems to be more Aristotelian than Platonic, suggesting that we rethink the adjustment disorders categories in terms of specific stressors, such as migration, loss of face, and marginalization. Such an approach clearly flies in the face of one of the underlying premises of DSM-III, DSM-III-R, and DSM-IV (American Psychiatric Association 1980, 1987, 1994), which is to focus on phenomenology and remove etiology. This is mainly a reaction against the psychoanalytic predominance in DSM-II (American Psychiatric Association 1968). At the same time, the purely phenomenological approach cannot completely work: witness posttraumatic stress disorders, which clearly presume an etiology and are more extreme variants of the phenomena of interest to Beiser.

Although clearly it is of use to be able to identify specific and widespread syndromes, one concern that confronts me in reading this chapter is that the range of possible "unique" stressors is almost infinite. We could have an unwieldy nosology, based on an array of stressors leading to myriad adjustment disorders.

My second concern with this perspective involves Axes IV and V. Clearly these are meant to take into account the nature and severity of psychosocial stressors and resiliency and adaptation. These axes do less well in assessing social support, which is an extremely important measure. Conceptually, Axes IV and V are very important, although in reality their utilization and application in psychiatric treatment and research has been quite disappointing. In essence, Beiser is suggesting that Axis IV be incorporated into Axis I, which is a major change.

Another problem that emerges is the overlap between the adjustment disorders and more traditional psychiatric diagnostic categories. For example, in his discussion of the relationship between affective disorder and adjustment disorder, Beiser notes that many patients with the potential for developing major depression might wind up in the adjustment disorder category. It is important to note that dysthymic disorder is a less severe form of depression, albeit chronic, that may likewise be commingled with adjustment disorder or mistaken for it.

One of the other problems with the adjustment disorder diagnoses is misuse for other purposes (e.g., not stigmatizing patients). It is my impression that the majority of adjustment disorder diagnoses are made to present to insurance carriers and other third-party payers who have no respect for confidentiality of patient data; such diagnoses are of sufficient severity to warrant treatment but are mild enough to minimize damage to the record and reputation of the patient. Our diagnostic categories are used for purposes other than the best possible description of the problem.

For Beiser's perspective to be taken seriously, it will be necessary to resolve questions about the relationship between Axis I and Axis IV diagnoses and to examine the domain of potential adjustment disorder diagnoses, which are focused more on etiology than phenomenology.

References

American Psychiatric Association: Diagnostic and Statistical Manual of Mental Disorders, 2nd Edition. Washington, DC, American Psychiatric Association, 1968

American Psychiatric Association: Diagnostic and Statistical Manual of Mental Disorders, 3rd Edition. Washington, DC, American Psychiatric Association, 1980

American Psychiatric Association: Diagnostic and Statistical Manual of Mental Disorders, 3rd Edition, Revised. Washington, DC, American Psychiatric Association, 1987

American Psychiatric Association: Diagnostic and Statistical Manual of Mental Disorders, 4th Edition. Washington, DC, American Psychiatric Association, 1994

Section VIII

Personality Disorders

Chapter 31

Culture and Personality Disorders

Edward F. Foulks, M.D., Ph.D.

In this chapter, I discuss DSM Axis II personality disorders (PDs) from the perspective of cultural psychiatry for the purpose of rendering this classificatory system more sensitive and relevant for use in diverse ethnic communities. The authors of the DSM, illustratively in DSM-III-R (American Psychiatric Association 1987), have been careful to offer several caveats that must be applied when considering diagnosis across cultural groups:

1. "It is important that the clinician not employ DSM in a mechanical fashion, insensitive to differences in language, values, behavioral norms, and idiomatic expressions of distress" (p. xxvi).
2. "Neither deviant behavior, e.g., political, religious, or sexual, nor conflicts that are primarily between the individual and society are mental disorders unless the deviance or conflict is a symptom of a dysfunction in the person" (p. xxii).
3. "There is no assumption that each mental disorder is a discrete entity with sharp boundaries (discontinuity) between it and other mental disorders, or between it and no mental disorder . . . This does not imply a resolution of the controversy concerning whether these conditions are in fact quantitatively or qualitatively different" (p. xxii). (This caveat should be applied to the observation that thresholds of recognition and tolerance for monthly disordered behavior vary tremendously across cultural groups.)

The diagnostic categories of the DSM were, however, developed from the experiences of psychiatrists in the United States, and the system has in fact been intended for use in "American" society. Some clinicians have assumed, therefore, that the DSM need not be concerned with the manifestations of psychiatric disorders in foreign societies nor require considerations of cultural sensitivity. American society, however, is not a homogeneous melting pot of cultures. There are many ethnic subcultures, and it is evident that there are often real barriers to communication and understanding across these distinctly differing groups within American society.

All people, diagnosticians included, are implicitly, unconsciously, and perhaps inevitably guided in their discriminations by categories acquired from the subculture of their origin. Many anthropologists, in fact, question whether it is even possible to actually transcend cultural barriers and gain a true understanding of a person from a different ethnic group. Diagnosticians need to be sensitive, therefore, to potential cultural variations in behavior and perceptions of behavior when applying the descriptions contained in the DSM to individuals from ethnic or social class groups other than their own.

Another consideration in this regard is the fact that despite original intentions, the DSM has become de facto international in its application. For example, DSM-III-R has been translated into Chinese, Japanese, Danish, Dutch, Finnish, French, German, Greek, Italian, Spanish, Portuguese, Swedish, and Norwegian.

The World Health Organization has traditionally maintained the position that mental health problems are strikingly similar across cultures and that the psychiatric disorders described in DSM-III-R, as well as their required diagnostic criteria, are "real entities" rather than culturally relative behaviors, and they are potentially discoverable in certain proportions in all human groups worldwide. This position deemphasizes the importance of culture in shaping behavior and instead focuses on universal behaviors that all human groups have in common. Such universalist assumptions are supported by increasing evidence that some psychiatric disorders have a genetic predisposition and by large-scale surveys that have reported similar symptom clusters in patients from widely divergent cultural and societal areas (World Health Organization 1973).

Giving additional impetus to this perspective are the many recent discoveries of the biological basis of behavior and emotion. These discoveries have provided the expectation that ultimately psychiatric disorders will be defined not only with phenomenological precision but also by measurable deviations from normal neurophysiology. Questions remain, however, as to whether these deviations are marked by definable boundaries from the "normal," as seen from examples in such genetic disorders as trisomy 21, or whether psychopathology represents the extreme ends of Gaussian distributions of normal human traits. In spite of the caveats announced in DSM-III-R's introduction, the diagnostic precision that is sought by the DSM is more compatible with the former notion (i.e., of defining discrete categories for behavior that have clear demarcation from normal behavior and do not overlap with other diagnostic categories) than with the latter.

The quest for diagnostic precision in this regard has been particularly problematic when considering the Axis II PDs. As pointed out by Kendell (1982) and by Cloninger (1987), past research on personality traits indicates little or no evidence of bimodality or multimodality, as would be expected if personality variation were influenced by discrete processes. Rather, their research shows that personality traits follow a normal Gaussian distribution in general population samples. Evidence of such a continuous spectrum between normal personality traits and PDs presents a number of major dilemmas in applying DSM diagnoses across ethnic and national groups. For example, DSM-III-R defines personality traits as "enduring patterns of perceiving, relating to, and thinking about the environment and oneself, and are exhibited in a wide range of important social and personal contexts. It is only when personality traits are inflexible and maladaptive and cause either significant functional impairment or subjective distress that they constitute Personality Disorders" (American Psychiatric Association 1987, p. 335).

Issues of whether a personality trait is maladaptive or causes functional impairment or subjective distress are obviously related to the cultural context. Defining or labeling deviances from "normal personality" is clearly a culture-relative exercise, and its boundaries are reflective of the specific values, ideals, worldview, resources, and social structures of the society. Raybeck (1988), for example, has pointed out that labeling a person who does not conform to the norm as "abnormal" is less likely to occur in small societies than in larger societies, and this factor may account for better rates of remission for severe mental disorders in such societies. Personally well-integrated values characterize smaller societies and stabilize their definitions of social life. In contrast, larger societies often contain multiple competing values that in themselves can contribute conflict to personal integration. The interdependence and equality among members of small-scale societies inhibits the labeling of individuals as deviant, and, when such labeling does occur, it is less likely to result in loss of power or status as it does in larger societies. A nonconforming person is often still able to be a contributor to a small community and is often linked to other people through a variety of interpersonal and kinship ties. The nonconforming person in a larger community is less likely to be an essential contributor and often has weakened family and social network ties to others. In such cases, labeling such a person as deviant costs others in the community very little in terms of social contributors and in terms of risk to social cohesiveness. Indeed, the labeling of deviants in large-scale societies may actually enhance social integration of others by scapegoating the misfits and thereby reaffirming the acceptable norms of behavior. It should be noted, however, that although smaller societies may tend to use deviant labels in public less frequently, they nevertheless recognize deviances of severe mental disorders; they attempt to differentiate them categorically from mystical status and other normal culturally patterned behaviors, and they have developed nomenclatures for behavioral and mental aberrations (Murphy 1976; Westermeyer and Wintrob 1979).

Another factor complicating development of a universal standard for demarcating abnormality from normality across ethnic groups is the observation that different cultures have tended to emphasize different traits of personality as ideal. The traits of novelty seeking, quick-temperedness, and extravagance may be ideals of behavior for males in a certain society, where child-rearing patterns, sanctions, rituals, and institutions are also seen to educate and reinforce these values. Furthermore, given evidence that there are genetic factors involved in the expression of these traits, a society valuing such traits may promote marital and mating patterns that would select for such traits. Therefore, because of cultural learning factors as well as perhaps the more controversial, genetic selective breeding factors, it might be expected that each society would not only idealize but actually realize its own unique dimension and patterns of personality, which would establish unique standards of normality. It is apparent that even in the absence of such extreme development of valued traits, there would still be considerable qualitative difference among societies regarding the demarcation of abnormality from normality on the Gaussian distributions of traits. We would therefore expect from this perspective that the variation in personality and in PDs would be identical in degree to the differences between the various cultures that generate them.

A similar perspective is provided by studies of personality development across cultures. Rearing patterns and socialization practices vary considerably across cultures and result in profound differences in experiences during important periods of development in childhood. Parenting in any society is determined in part by learned beliefs, values, and practices that are for the most part historically derived. The uniqueness of childhood experiences across cultures may play an important role in shaping certain traits of personality, emphasizing some while suppressing others. In this process, ideal versus deviant traits would be implicitly or explicitly defined within any cultural context.

A major issue for the diagnostician working across cultures is the requirement of differentiating the ideal personality type, the typical personality, and the atypical personality from the standpoint of cultural functionality. Ideal personality types are most often revealed when questioning individuals in a society about what they are like and how one should raise children and conduct life. In any society, the "typical personality" and its behavioral correlates may differ considerably from the ideal, yet be considered normal and expectable from the perspective of that society. Likewise, the atypical personality may be neither ideal nor average in behavior and still not be considered abnormal. Such atypical individuals may be found in the ranks of mystics, priests, ministers, artists, and others who transcend typical and ideal social roles and are considered to make major overall contributions to their societies. In these cases, the definitions of PD resting on determinations of functionality relative to the culture of origin may assume a different dimension when such an individual is displaced to the context of another culture. The Vietnamese refugee who is a highly developed Buddhist may exhibit traits that are a religious inspiration to others in his home country but that lead to a diagnosis of schizoid PD in the American clinic.

Cloninger (1987) has discussed basic personality traits from the perspective of acquired adaptive capabilities that all humans possess to varying degrees. It is the innate variation in the relative quantity of each trait in interaction with environmental demands that, he believes, results in those enduring qualities that define personality. He proposed that PDs such as those listed in DSM represent the outcomes of extreme strength or extreme weakness of one or more traits interacting with the strength and weakness of others.

Evidence based on the relatively fixed nature of certain trait categories on test-retest reliability indices indicates the presence of three basic interacting predispositions in reacting to environmental stimuli. The first trait, harm avoidance, is revealed by the observation that some individuals are predisposed to react to changes in their environment with apprehensive cautiousness; others react in a fearless, uninhibited way; but most are somewhere between the two. The second basic trait, reward dependence, is evidenced in the tendency of some people to be detached and emotionally tough-minded in evaluating situations and other people; others are sentimental and moody; and again, most are somewhere in between. The third fundamental trait dimension is novelty seeking, with some individuals impulsively driven toward novelty to the point of risk taking and personal pain; others are more cautious, reflective, and conservative; and most are somewhere in between. There is evidence that the harm avoidance axis derives its regulation from the serotonergic system of the brain; the novelty seeking axis, from the dopaminergic system; and the reward dependence axis, by the norepinephrine system. It is the relative strength and weakness of each of these systems interacting with each other vis-à-vis the environment that determines personality. Cloninger (1987) and Siever et al. (1990) proposed further that genetic factors may be related to the expression of these three neurotemperamental systems, and the exaggeration of any of them may relate the Axis II personality disorders to Axis I disorders. Thus, schizophrenia would represent a further exaggeration of the traits that determined the schizotypal personality, and these disorders would be seen in genetically related individuals (Frangos et al. 1985; Siever et al. 1990).

Investigating spectrum disorders from a phenomenological and psychobiological perspective, Siever and Davis (1991) proposed that four major categories of Axis I disorders can be related systematically to four clusters of Axis II disorders. They argued that dysfunction in the cognitive/perceptual dimension results in odd cluster disorders and, if extreme, schizophrenic disorders. Dysfunction in the impulsivity/aggression dimension results in borderline-antisocial personality disorders and, if severe, impulse control disorders. Dysfunction in the affective stabilizing dimension results in dramatic cluster disorders and, if severe, major affective disorder. Finally, dysfunction in the anxiety/inhibition dimension results in anxious cluster disorders and, if severe, anxiety disorders.

These models suggest that PDs may represent the nonadaptive extreme of basic trait expression, although the extent of convergence of normal and pathological traits remains to be determined (Siever and Davis 1991). According to Cloninger (1987), the optimum of overall flexibility in social adaptation might be found in the range of intermediate or nearly average trait values. Variants at either extreme may excel or have advantage in certain social roles or cultural configurations but are less flexible in their ability to adapt socially overall. Cloninger proposed that balanced selection for intermediate adaptive optima may explain the persistence of the extreme variants in populations. Each three-way combination of extreme trait expression has a 2% chance of accuracy in any normal population. Interestingly, the lifetime prevalence of antisocial personality (the only PD investigated in the Epidemiologic Catchment Area [ECA] Study 1984) was found to be 2.1% in New Haven, Connecticut; 2.6% in Baltimore, Maryland; 3.3% in St. Louis, Missouri (Robbins et al. 1984); and 3.0% and 3.6% in whites and Mexican Americans, respectively, in Los Angeles, California (Karno et al. 1987). Examining the Canino et al. ECA-related, Puerto Rico Island study, one also finds that there is no major difference between rates in Puerto Rico and those in the five sites of the ECA study in the mainland United States (Guarnaccia et al. 1990).

These findings are remarkable from two perspectives:

1. They are close to rates (2%–3%) predicted in Cloninger's model of PDs.
2. They indicate that culturally unique factors play a negligible role in the formation of antisocial PD among such ethnically diverse groups as Mexican Americans, Puerto Ricans, and non-Hispanic Americans and that social class may be the more important determinant.

Prevalence studies of other PDs in general populations have not been done. However, Zimmerman and Coryell (1989) reported results of interviews with first-degree relatives of normal controls and patients with a variety of psychiatric disorders using the Diagnostic Interview Schedule (DIS) and the Structured Interview from DSM-III PDs (SIDP). They found that even given the high risk of the sample, the overall point (5-year) prevalence rate for any PD was low (antisocial PD = 3.3%; passive-aggressive PD = 3.3%; histrionic PD = 3%; schizotypal PD = 2.9%; compulsive PD = 2%; dependent PD = 1.8%; borderline PD = 2.9%; avoidant PD = 1.3%; paranoid-schizoid PDs = 1.8%). It should be noted that once again, these figures are within the range of PD rates predicted by Cloninger's model. Hyler et al. (1990) suggested that these PDs may have accounted for a considerable portion of the population in the ECA study who sought mental health services but had no disorder according to the DIS.

Paris (1991) has reported that the World Health Organization has conducted a cross-cultural survey of the incidence of PDs using the Personality Disorder Examination (PDE) designed according to the criteria for PDs in the *International Classification of Diseases,* 10th Revision (ICD-10) (World Health Organization 1991). Clinical populations at 15 sites in North America, Asia, Africa, and Europe were evaluated, and findings suggest that most of the PDs recognizable in the West could be identified at the other sites as well. Because the study populations were all urban, the general community prevalence rates of PDs, especially in rural, underdeveloped countries, has yet to be determined.

Cultural Relativism and the DSM Personality Disorders

Many traits that are included as diagnostic criteria for various personality disorders may be considered normal in other cultures. In these cases, traits may be perceived as both ego-syntonic by the patient and socially syntonic by the patient's reference group. It is therefore important to consider the cultural context to differentiate normal role behavior from the extremes that might indicate a PD. Impairments in the cross-cultural context, however, may be the result of maladjustment to a majority or new cultural perspective that is dominant or related to dysfunction of the reference group itself. We believe that traits that do not result in impairment and are not considered to be undesirable by the patient or his or her reference group should not be included on the list of traits essential to meeting diagnostic criteria for a PD. Such cautions may avoid mislabeling and unnecessarily stigmatizing people from other ethnic groups or social classes. The following are examples of how culturally prescribed behaviors may confound evaluations for PDs:

1. *Paranoid PD.* Many Mediterranean peoples who have beliefs in the power of the "evil eye" also bear grudges and are unforgiving of insults; read hidden, threatening meanings into benign events; expect without sufficient basis to be harmed by others; and are reluctant to confide in others for fear that the information would be used against them. Such individuals would rate the diagnosis of this PD unless examined in context of their beliefs (Maloney 1976).
2. *Schizoid PD.* Essential traits, including solitary activities, lack of emotion, lack of sexual desire, indifference to praise or criticism, and constricted affect, would also characterize the enlightened Buddhist priest (Roland 1988).
3. *Schizotypal PD.* Traits essential for this diagnosis are magical thinking, unusual perceptual experiences, odd or eccentric behavior and appearances, inappropriate abstract speech, and few close friends or confidants; these traits are also commonly manifested by the shaman or mystic in many small societies (Michael 1972).
4. *Antisocial PD.* This disorder has been found to be more prevalent among the urban poor than elsewhere, suggesting some degree of conformity to alienated, disenfranchised, sociocultural conditions (Myers et al. 1984).
5. *Histrionic PD.* Many successful actresses, fashion models, and show girls demonstrate the traits of being overly concerned with physical attractiveness and are emotionally overexpressive, self-centered, and uncomfortable in situations where she or he is not the center of attraction. Tchambuli males also demonstrate these traits (Mead 1972).
6. *Narcissistic PD.* Many successful business and political leaders take advantage of others to achieve their own ends, have a grandiose sense of their self-importance, are preoccupied with fantasies of unlimited success and power, have a sense of entitlement, require constant attention, and lack empathy with how others feel—all traits that would render this diagnosis unless considered within the context of valued roles in societies (Lasswell 1977).
7. *Avoidant PD.* Many individuals in severely oppressed, minority groups are reluctant in social situations because of fear of saying something inappropriate; they show anxiety in front of others, are unwilling to get involved with people unless certain of being liked, are easily hurt by criticism, and often exaggerate potential difficulties or risks in doing something ordinary but outside their

routines. Labeling such individuals as having a mental disorder may mask their real problems of acculturation.

8. *Dependent PD.* Essential traits for this diagnosis are found in individuals who agree with others, even when they believe others are wrong, because of fear of rejection; they allow others to make most of their important decisions, volunteer to do things that are unpleasant in order to get other people to like them, feel devastated or helpless when close relationships end, fear being abandoned, and are easily hurt by criticism. Such traits also correspond well to the culturally ideal personality traits admired by the traditional Inuit (Briggs 1970; Foulks 1973).

9. *Obsessive-Compulsive PD.* Talmudic scholars, priests, ministers, some academic scholars, and scientists manifest a preoccupation with details, rules, and lists and have an excessive devotion to work to the exclusion of leisure activities and friendships. Such people are often overconscientious and scrupulous about matters of morality, ethics, and values beyond those dictated by their religion. They often have restricted expression of affection and a reluctance to let others do things because of a conviction that they will not do them correctly—all traits essential to this PD diagnosis.

10. *Passive-Aggressive PD.* These traits are witnessed commonly in populations that are coerced into tasks by higher authority or that have no apparent activity alternatives offering them more freedom of choice, as witnessed in discussions of workers in communist countries. Here, scaling for degree of sociocultural dystonicity becomes complex in societies where values on such traits are changing.

Summary and Conclusion

In light of the implications of these studies, it is perhaps too early to pass judgment on whether the DSM-III-R or DSM-IV PD categories can be validly and usefully applied to diverse ethnic populations. Important preliminary field studies are required to answer questions that may eventually render DSM more cross-culturally applicable. Such studies might include

1. Emic research to discover PDs defined in certain ethnic groups that are not contained in a standard diagnostic system list of PDs. Personality traits unique to individuals in other cultures may at times result in impairment in those cultural contexts but not meet full criteria for any specified DSM PD. Such traits might be classified as personality disorders, not otherwise specified, or as a culture-bound syndrome.

2. Emic research to discover whether a core group of DSM PDs are seen as pathological or dysfunctional in diverse ethnic groups.

3. Etic research conducted with the SIDP or a comparable culturally and linguistically adapted instrument across ethnic groups in the United States and abroad to verify previous findings of constant lifetime prevalence rates for each PD.

4. Research to discover the cultural variability along a Gaussian personality trait continuum that indicates unique points of pathology demarcation for each ethnic group.

Results of such studies might provide some scientific basis to justify the inclusion of additions to a standard diagnostic system and make it more adaptable for use across diverse ethnic groups. Studies reviewed here suggest that consideration be given to the following three possibilities in the construction of future diagnostic systems:

1. An additional rating requirement could be established for each PD diagnosis that would include a cutoff point on a Likert scale of 1–10, for degree of
    a. Ego dystonicity for the personality traits required to diagnose a PD.
    b. Sociocultural dystonicity for the personality traits required to diagnose a PD. This scaling could be required to score an essential trait as present for each diagnostic category and to establish "caseness." Another less exacting approach might be to incorporate the notions of ego dystonicity score into a global functioning axis. The current Axis V in DSM-IV (American Psychiatric Association 1994) rates level of functioning without considering cultural factors.
2. An additional category of potential PDs based on extreme trait expressions could perhaps be included in the "not otherwise specified" category. For example, extreme trait expressions of self-assertiveness, punctuality, and independent decision making are symptoms of a severe PD, glossed over as "immaturity" by the Inuit of North Alaska, but are adaptive and nonpathological for non-Native Alaskans.
3. Expansion of the DSM's Introduction and section on PD categories to include cultural relativism and emic perspectives.

References

American Psychiatric Association: Diagnostic and Statistical Manual of Mental Disorders, 3rd Edition, Revised. Washington, DC, American Psychiatric Association, 1987

American Psychiatric Association: Diagnostic and Statistical Manual of Mental Disorders, 4th Edition. Washington, DC, American Psychiatric Association, 1994

Briggs J: Never in Anger: Portrait of an Eskimo Family. Cambridge, MA, Harvard University Press, 1970

Canino G, Bird H, Shrout P: The prevalence of specific psychiatric disorders in Puerto Rico. Arch Gen Psychiatry 44:727–735, 1987

Cloninger CR: A systematic method for clinical description and classification of personality variants. Arch Gen Psychiatry 44:573–588, 1987

Foulks E: The Arctic hysterias, in Anthropological Studies No. 10. Edited by Maybury-Lewis D. Washington, DC, American Anthropological Association Press, 1973

Frangos E, Athanassenas G, Tsitourides S, et al: Prevalence of DSM-III schizophrenia among the first-degree relatives of schizophrenic probands. Acta Psychiatr Scand 72:382–386, 1985

Guarnaccia P, Good B, Kleinman A: A critical review of epidemiological studies of Puerto Rican mental health. Am J Psychiatry 147:1449–1455, 1990

Hyler S, Skodal A, Kellman D, et al: Validity of the Personality Diagnostic Questionnaire Revised: comparison with two structured interviews. Am J Psychiatry 147:1043–1047, 1990

Karno M, Hough R, Burnham M, et al: Lifetime prevalence of specific psychiatric disorders among Mexican Americans and non-Hispanic whites in Los Angeles. Arch Gen Psychiatry 44:695–701, 1987

Kendell R: The choice of diagnostic criteria for biological research. Arch Gen Psychiatry 39:1334–1339, 1982

Lasswell H: Psychopathology and Politics. Chicago, IL, University of Chicago Press, 1977

Maloney C: The Evil Eye. New York, Columbia University Press, 1976

Mead M: Sex and temperament in three primitive societies, in Studies in Siberian Shamanism. Edited by Michael H. Toronto, Ontario, Canada, University of Toronto Press, 1972

Michael H: Studies in Siberian Shamanism. Toronto, Ontario, Canada, University of Toronto Press, 1972

Murphy J: Psychiatric labeling in cross-cultural perspective. Science 19:1019–1028, 1976

Myers K, Weissman M, Tischler G: Epidemiological Catchment Area Program (ECAP). Arch Gen Psychiatry 41:959–967, 1984

Paris J: Personality disorders, parasuicide and culture. Transcultural Psychiatric Research Review 28:25–39, 1991

Raybeck D: Anthropology and labeling theory: a constructive critique. Ethos 16:371–397, 1988

Robbins L, Helzer J, Weissman M, et al: Lifetime prevalence of specific psychiatric disorders in three sites. Arch Gen Psychiatry 41:949–958, 1984

Roland A: In Search of Self in India and Japan. Princeton, NJ, Princeton University Press, 1988

Siever L, Davis K: A psychobiological perspective on the personality disorders. Am J Psychiatry 148:1647–1658, 1991

Siever L, Keefe R, Bernstein D, et al: Eye tracking impairment in clinically identified patients with schizotypal personality disorder. Am J Psychiatry 147:740–745, 1990

Westermeyer J, Wintrob R: Folk criterion for diagnosis of mental illness in rural Laos; on being insane in sane places. Am J Psychopathy 136:755–761, 1979

World Health Organization: The International Pilot Study of Schizophrenia. Geneva, Switzerland, World Health Organization, 1973

World Health Organization: International Classification of Diseases, 10th Revision. Geneva, Switzerland, World Health Organization, 1991

Zimmerman M, Coryell W: DSM-III personality disorder diagnosis in a non-patient sample. Arch Gen Psychiatry 46:682–689, 1989

Chapter 32

Cultural Comments on Personality Disorders: I

Renato D. Alarcón, M.P.H., M.D.

None of the existing definitions of personality thoroughly covers the complex array of its characteristics and features, and the conceptualization of personality disorders (PDs) is considerably less elaborated and much more difficult. Current diagnostic systems define personality as the way in which a given individual perceives, relates, and thinks about himself or herself and his or her environment. Personalities emerge as a result of genetic, environmental, and experiential factors, with only the first being biological sensu stricto. The experiential component derives from the individual's unique interaction with the environmental forces traditionally represented by family and society. In that sense, the social, or perhaps more appropriately, the sociocultural roots of personality are fundamentally relevant. It follows that any distortion (i.e., inflexibility or maladaptiveness, to use DSM-IV's parameters) of the individual's experienced perception of such factors may result in any of the clinical entities that we call personality disorders (Dunham 1976; Haldipur 1980).

Culture embodies a complex set of notions, from the ethnic to the religious, from values and morals to artistic or scientific expressions, from child-rearing practices to funeral rituals (Fabrega 1987). Sociologists and anthropologists have struggled with the notions of basic or collective personalities to describe the intricacies of the individual-culture interactions (Greenley 1984; Kleinman 1977; Landy 1977). As culture molds many of the styles and strategies that constitute a given personality, it seems legitimate to assume that some individuals will experience the formative influence of culture in ways that emphasize the strongest, but not necessarily the best, features of their cultural milieu and may consequently develop the maladaptive, inflexible, dysfunctional, pervasive, and distressing traits of a PD. A PD, it has been said, in tacit recognition of the value of the dimensional model (Widiger and Rogers 1989), can be seen as a caricature of the normal personality, much in the same way as it can reflect the distorted aspects of the individual's culture.

Critique of the Overview Chapter

In Chapter 31, Foulks recognizes the increasing volume of biological contributions that would tend to homogenize symptomatological clusters of PDs in different sociocultural areas. In fact, he almost seems to endorse the assumption that if deviations from normal neurophysiology could be clearly demarcated (thus eliminating overlap), then the entire problem of cultural factors in PDs (and indeed in all psychopathological conditions) would be a moot one. Later he moves away from this position, of course, but such statements reflect well the current ambivalence in the field of cultural psychiatry with regard to facing the overwhelming literature on biological etiopathogenic documentation (Odejide 1979; Singer et al. 1978; Westermeyer 1985).

Although defining or labeling a PD is certainly a culturally relative exercise, the question here is whether these actions (i.e., defining and labeling) are all that is "cultural" in the field of PDs. Some would argue that PDs are not only culturally definable but are, at least partly, culturally determined.

The most provocative suggestion in Chapter 31 is that the three PD clusters in DSM-III (American Psychiatric Association 1980) and DSM-IV (American Psychiatric Association 1994) represent a "folk taxonomy" of American psychiatrists, in contrast to "the scientifically based system of Cloninger" (1987). The advantages with the latter are "a more accurate account of the pattern of overlap of traits" and the "balanced selection" for intermediate adaptive optima ("normal personalities") and for the persistence of "extreme variants" (PDs). Although Cloninger's contribution is indeed a considerable advance, there are still a number of problems in such a conceptualization that make it inapplicable even for DSM-IV, and much less for a culturally sensitive and relevant consideration of PDs. Some of these problems are the following:

- Innate variations of "acquired adaptive capabilities" and the "interaction of each trait with environmental demands" are time-honored, hardly new theoretical assumptions.
- The three basic interacting predispositions in reacting to environmental stimuli are by no means the final or even the only ones; they could be seen rather as related to the instruments used in the specific research design. Furthermore, their dimensional nature has not yet covered the numerous interacting possibilities beyond the correlation (already attempted) with the existing DSM-IV categories.
- The ascription of neurotransmitter systems regulating in a specific manner each of the three basic predispositions is simplistic at best, and to say that "genetic factors may be related to the expression of these three neuro-temperamental systems" is quite a predictable yet unproved proposition.

- The prevalence findings cited in Chapter 31 refer in some cases to specific PDs (e.g., antisocial) and in other cases to several of the DSM-III types, so that the percentage figures can be construed ambiguously as reflecting one (antisocial) or all personality types; therefore, one cannot conclude that "these figures are within the range of PDs predicted by Cloninger's model."

One cannot argue with Foulks's statement that the main role of the psychiatrist is to differentiate within a cultural context normal role behaviors from the extremes that would indicate PDs. His examples of the types of dilemmas posed by such a task are, for the most part, adequate. Thus, his comment on antisocial PD recognizes sociocultural factors that go against the genetic basis postulated by Cloninger (1987) and Siever and Davis (1991). He does not mention, however, the political implications of the antisocial PD diagnosis as he does with the avoidant type. The issue of violence as a personality trait is enormously ambiguous and culturally relevant in this respect (Alarcon 1983; Levav et al. 1989; Montero 1988). Clinicians would say that "fear of rejection" is seen more in avoidant than in dependent PDs. The "coercion by higher authority" that he sees as generating passive-aggressive PD could also be invoked for the antisocial and dependent types. Anomie and its different outcomes are a pervasive yet little studied factor vis-à-vis PDs.

Cultural Diagnosis of PDs: A Proposal

A PD needs to be culturally dissected so that a culture's value as a predisposing, correlating, complicating, or therapeutic factor in the patient's overall clinical context can be duly assessed. Such cultural assessment can be carried out both instrumentally and clinically through:

- The study of basic cultural parameters in the description of the personality along the normal-pathological continuum;
- The evaluation of opinions and background data gathered from the patient's family or reference group;
- The exploration of the individual patient's own perceptions of his or her cultural context sampling, for instance, his views on religious values or about conceptions of mental illness.

Precise measurements of these cultural elements or components are difficult but highly desirable. Perhaps as Abroms (1981) has pointed out, we should abandon the attempt to quantitate the relative contributions of genotype versus environment (the latter including psychological and social factors) to psychiatric conditions and instead assign a complementary role to each in the diagnosis and treatment of such conditions. Perhaps, as Littlewood (1990) and Leff (1990) have proposed, we should attempt to explain (or understand) each psychiatric condition vis-à-vis a theoretical bipolar spectrum ranging from the biological to the sociological (or sociocultural), adding an estimation of the cultural distance between populations being studied or individual patients being compared. This is consonant with the postulates of universality and contextualization advocated by the "new cross-cultural psychiatry" (Kleinman 1977).

Another approach could be to globally assign a cultural profile to each PD category, rather than "dissecting" individual criteria, and then proceed with the examination of each type from the different cultural perspectives. For instance, let us assume first that as a result of a literature review of available evidence, the 11 usually recognized personality types are ranked in the following order, from the "most biologically based" to the "most psychosocioculturally based": schizotypal, paranoid, schizoid, antisocial, borderline, obsessive-compulsive, narcissistic, histrionic, passive-aggressive, avoidant, and dependent.

A first look at the above gradation suggests that the more biologically based a personality type is, the more vulnerable it will be to psychosocial stressors. Independent from this, however, a second assumption has to do with a cultural profile assignable to each of the PDs. Such a profile can result from conventional social and cultural criteria, a general assessment of the DSM operational criteria for each category, and clinical experience in the study of PDs. To some extent, we could use Millon's (1981) biosocial approach to aid in the characterization of such profiles.

Some of the traits included in such profiles might reflect cultural characteristics of the patient's social group, so it would be incumbent on the clinician to sort them out (Leff's assessment of the "cultural distance") and assign to them a diagnostic as well as a therapeutic value (Caplan 1981; Henderson 1980). It is here that our third assumption could be used: the analysis of the "symptoms" present in the above sets from the perspectives provided by different ethnic and cultural groups.

It is possible to see, through the identified "symptoms," some of these cultural influences, which then can help to weight the clinical evidence more objectively. It should not be forgotten that even within seemingly homogeneous cultural groups, there are subgroups or variations resulting from correlative cultural differences based on regional, religious, or other social parameters. Such is the case among Anglo patients in the South and the Northeast, or among Mexicans and Puerto Ricans in the Hispanic community. Nevertheless, some general rules can be applicable, in the manner hypothesized here, and can no doubt be enriched by research findings.

Can the cultural perspective allow the eventual identification of new PD types? The answer is definitely yes, provided that steps toward "cultural dissection" are followed. However, the consideration of "personal dispositions," in Dohrenwend's terms (1986), as mediators of psychopathology and the cultural factors leading to chronicity in mental pathology (Lefley 1990) are concepts still awaiting heuristic documentation. The cultural approach to diagnosis is flexible and adaptable, open to research and a degree of quantification (Leighton 1986), and relevant to every and all classificatory systems.

Additional Comments

The aforementioned proposal in no way conflicts with Foulks's well-conceived suggestions. In fact, I see the "cultural dissection" approach as complementary to the two emic research proposals made in Chapter 31. There is a significant body of literature offering at least sketches of not always recognized PDs, and determining a core group of ethnically detectable PDs or PD symptoms is a feasible task (Murphy 1982; Sachdev-Perminder 1990; Spitzer et al. 1989).

The question of dimensional versus categorical approaches will not be solved any time soon in the field of PDs. The typological approach is clinically more desirable, and Foulks's fourth suggestion implies just that. In contrast, the "cultural profiling" proposed above fits more with the prototypical philosophy explored as part of the DSM-IV development process (Frances et al. 1990).

The notions of ego-dystonicity and sociocultural dystonicity are precisely the kind of parameters encompassed by the "cultural dissection" approach. Perhaps the only difference is whether a scale or a more qualitative (i.e., clinical) assessment should be used, the latter being favored by my review of the existing literature. Foulks himself does not advocate scaling as a definitive approach, according to his alternative suggestion of incorporating ego dystonicity into Axis V.

References

Abroms GM: Psychiatric serialism. Compr Psychiatry 22:371–378, 1981

Alarcon RD: A Latin American perspective on DSM III. Am J Psychiatry 140:102–105, 1983

American Psychiatric Association: Diagnostic and Statistical Manual on Mental Disorders, 3rd Edition. Washington, DC, American Psychiatric Association, 1980

American Psychiatric Association: Diagnostic and Statistical Manual on Mental Disorders, 4th Edition. Washington, DC, American Psychiatric Association, 1994

Caplan G: Mastery of stress: psycho-social aspects. Am J Psychiatry 138:413–420, 1981

Cloninger CR: A systematic method for clinical description and classification of personality variants. A proposal. Arch Gen Psychiatry 44:573–588, 1987

Dohrenwend BP: Social stress and psychopathology, in A Decade of Progress in Primary Prevention. Edited by Kessler M, Goldston SE. Hanover, NH, University Press of New England, 1986, pp 87–114

Dunham HW: Society, culture and mental disorder. Arch Gen Psychiatry 33:155–157, 1976

Fabrega H: Psychiatric diagnosis. A cultural perspective. J Nerv Ment Dis 175:383–394, 1987

Frances A, Pincus HA, Widiger TA, et al: DSM-IV: work in progress. Am J Psychiatry 147:1439–1448, 1990

Greenley JR: Social factors, mental illness, and psychiatry care: recent advances from a sociological perspective. Hosp Community Psychiatry 35:813–820, 1984

Haldipur CV: The idea of "cultural" psychiatry: a comment on the foundations of cultural psychiatry. Compr Psychiatry 21:206–211, 1980

Henderson S: A development in social psychiatry. The systematic study of social bonds. J Nerv Ment Dis 168:63–69, 1980

Kleinman A: Rethinking the social and cultural context of psychopathology and psychiatric care, in Renewal in Psychiatry. Edited by Manschreck T, Kleinman A. New York, Wiley, 1977

Landy V: Culture, Disease and Healing. New York, Macmillan, 1977

Leff J: The "new cross-cultural psychiatry." A case of the baby and the bathwater. Br J Psychiatry 156:305–307, 1990

Lefley HP: Culture and chronic mental illness. Hosp Community Psychiatry 41:277–286, 1990

Leighton AH: Psychiatric epidemiology and social psychiatry. Am J Soc Psychiatry 6:221–226, 1986

Levav I, Lima BR, Somoza Lennon M, et al: Salud mental para todos en America Latina y el Caribe. Bases epidemiologicas para la acción. Bol Of Sanit Panam 107:196–219, 1989

Littlewood R: From categories to contexts: a decade of the "new cross-cultural psychiatry." Br J Psychiatry 156:308–327, 1990

Millon P: Disorders of Personality. DSM III: Axis II. New York, Wiley, 1981

Montero M: Understanding behavior in conditions of economic and cultural dependency. Int J Psychol 23:597–617, 1988

Murphy HBM: Comparative Psychiatry: The International and Intercultural Distribution of Mental Illness. New York, Springer-Verlag, 1982

Odejide AO: Cross cultural psychiatry: a myth or reality. Compr Psychiatry 20:103–109, 1979

Sachdev-Perminder LV: Whakama: culturally determined behavior in the New Zealand Maori. Psychol Med 20:443–444, 1990

Siever L, Davis K: A psychobiological perspective on the personality disorders. Am J Psychiatry 148:1647–1658, 1991

Singer K, Ney PG, Lieh-Mak F: A cultural perspective on child psychiatric disorders. Compr Psychiatry 19:533–540, 1978

Spitzer RL, Gibbon M, Skodol AE, et al (eds): DSM-III-R Case Book. Washington, DC, American Psychiatric Press, 1989

Westermeyer J: Psychiatric diagnosis across cultural boundaries. Am J Psychiatry 142:798–805, 1985

Widiger TA, Rogers JH: Prevalence and comorbidity of personality disorders. Psychiatric Annals 19:132–136, 1989

Chapter 33

Cultural Comments on Personality Disorders: II

Robert F. Kraus, M.D.

Since the 1970s progressive development and revitalization have taken place in psychiatry. Intensive research has resulted in significant and sophisticated progress in the area of psychiatric classification. López and Núñez (1987) have surveyed a range of diagnostic criteria and interview schedules and have noted that cultural influences in the definition and expression of psychopathology are largely ignored. The preparation of DSM-IV (American Psychiatric Association 1994) offered an opportunity to address this problem. The integration of cultural factors into the diagnostic equation would enrich our theory and practice. Intercultural variations in the etiology, phenomenology, treatment course, and outcome of the various mental illnesses mirror the true nature of mankind as it has evolved. These variations reflect the variations in human nature. The endlessly diverse (or heterozygous, to use the biological term) quality of human beings is at the core of their capacity for change, growth, and adaptation. The lack of consideration of sociocultural factors by current American psychiatry practitioners obscures the fact that consideration of such factors has been very much in the mainstream of psychiatric and medical thought for more than 200 years. Emil Kraepelin, who continues to exert a significant influence on psychiatry nosology, advocated the development of a comparative psychiatry (Vergleichende Psychiatrie) to study intercultural variation in the incidence and content of mental disorders. Rudolf Virchow, a giant in the development of Western biomedicine, described medicine as a social and political phenomenon.

In this response to Chapter 31, I address two issues. First, I discuss Western biomedicine and DSM-IV as cultural phenomena. Second, I propose a model for the understanding of human pathology.

Biomedicine and DSM-IV as Cultural Phenomena

Galtung (1981) has written about the intellectual styles that characterize various scientific traditions and intellectual communities of the world. He noted how little awareness members of a given intellectual community seem to have regarding the peculiarities of their community. Each scientific tradition has a version of "truth" that is more or less equated with what is intersubjectively acceptable within a network of acceptable colleagues. Western biomedical tradition and DSM-IV, which is very much a part of that tradition, are, in certain essential respects, products of culture. Western biomedical knowledge is defined, communicated, and modified through a nerve-ending process of disease classification. It would be well for us to remember that in an increasingly international world, 80% of the world population does not share in Western culture. Moreover, in the United States it is projected that by the year 2000, one-third of Americans will be black, Asian, Hispanic, or Native American. Our biomedicine, unlike the rest of science, continues to some degree in the tradition of the Platonic concept of types. A type, in Plato's world, was an animal that, when bred with another animal of the same type, would always breed true. In psychiatry this persists as prototypic categorization, a process by which patients are assigned diagnoses on the basis of the degree to which they resemble a prototype of the category. The assignment of diagnostic categories is a useful and necessary exercise in a clinical science, but it causes real mischief when the fact of continuous variation and changing adaptation in human populations must be taken into account. It is apparent that in some quarters the diagnostic categories have been reified and the diagnostic manual has been turned into something it was never intended to be. This probably relates in part to our cultural preoccupation with precise description and quantification.

A Concept Model for Psychopathology

Although as stated earlier, the knowledge of the relationships between sociocultural factors and psychopathology has been with us for years, cultural psychiatry—as a discipline with a distinctive body of knowledge; paradigms to organize that knowledge; and methodologies, techniques, and research questions—is a fairly recent development. The limited knowledge base, the rapid evolution of the field, the incomplete theoretical systems, and the sheer breadth and complexity of the task—to understand humans in all aspects—are daunting. At this point, there is no grand unifying paradigm. In terms of the contribution of cultural psychiatry to DSM-IV, it would be prudent to remember that the discipline is in the early middle ground in terms of paradigm development.

The model underlying a classification system in psychiatry must be comprehensive and allow for expansion and revision of our nosology as new research findings become available. Human psychopathology should be seen as the resultant of biological, psychological, interpersonal, social, and cultural factors acting in concert and in reciprocal relationship with one another and evolving in their relationship over time, both in the individual sense in terms of the life cycle and in the evolutionary sense in terms of human populations. Psychiatric diagnosis must deal with reality on various levels. On the physical/biological level, genetic and epidemiological studies, as noted by Foulks, suggest that there are biological commonalities underlying psychopathology and behavior shared by all human groups. Cloninger's proposed classification of personality disorders on the basis of relative activities of the adrenergic, serotonergic, and dopaminergic systems is representative of new research in the area of biological characterization of psychopathology and illustrates the integrative function of the central nervous system in organizing historic, social, and psychological data as well as in mediating biological subsystems. On the psychological level one deals with complex, experiential, subjective, phenomenal reality—the illness as experienced by the person. Social reality deals with social facts, actions, or judgments by an authority that have the impact of fact. The social world in which we live rises out of the interaction among these three orders of reality.

References

American Psychiatric Association: Diagnostic and Statistical Manual of Mental Disorders, 4th Edition. Washington, DC, American Psychiatric Association, 1994

Galtung J: Structure, culture and intellectual style: an essay comparing Saxonic, Teutonic, Gallic and Nepponic approaches. Social Science Information 20:817–856, 1981

López S, Núñez J: Cultural factors considered in selected diagnostic criteria and interview schedules. J Abnorm Psychol 96:270–272, 1987

Chapter 34

Nosological Comments on Culture and Personality Disorders

Bruce Pfohl, M.D.

As Foulks points out in Chapter 31, the personality disorders present some special concerns with respect to cultural issues. The personality disorders involve traits that are on a continuum with normal personality traits and require a higher level of inference in their assessment. Inferential interpretation of behavior may be influenced by the cultural background of both the individual and the clinician making the judgment.

Key questions for those reviewing the DSM criteria for the personality disorders are Do general caveats in the diagnostic manual sufficiently alert the clinicians to cultural concerns, and do the data exist to support more specific modifications to the criteria?

It is not trivial to determine how the theoretical concerns illuminated by Foulks are played out when the diagnostic criteria are actually applied in different clinical settings. For example, Foulks points out that many Mediterranean peoples believe in the "evil eye," and that cultural norms may include a tendency to bear grudges, a tendency to read hidden threats into benign events, and a reluctance to confide in others. He is concerned that people from such a cultural background are at higher risk for being diagnosed as having paranoid personality disorder even though the behavior is not abnormal or problematic within the culture. However, it could be argued that culturally sensitive yardsticks already exist in the criteria for paranoid personality disorder. For example, the first criteria is "expects, without sufficient basis, to be exploited or harmed by others." If one really does live in a culture where people frequently "bear grudges," then that individual would have sufficient basis for expecting harm, and this would exclude the individual from meeting the criterion.

The criterion for schizotypal personality disorder involving odd beliefs and magical thinking contains the caveat that the beliefs must be "inconsistent with cultural norms." A clinician who was raised in a different culture might be slower to appreciate that a given belief is culturally normal, but the criterion clearly indicates that knowledge of the individual's cultural background is necessary to make the decision.

The issue involving occupational or cultural subgroups raises an additional level of complexity. For example, what if an empirical study did indeed confirm that successful actors, actresses, and models were more likely to meet criteria for histrionic personality disorder? The reason for the finding would still be ambiguous. It is possible that the diagnosis represents a false positive, but it is also possible that there is a process of self-selection such that individuals with histrionic personality disorder are attracted to professions such as acting and modeling because such professions provide an opportunity for these individuals to be the center of attention and take advantage of emotional expressiveness. The issue might be resolved by comparing individuals in the acting profession with and without criteria for histrionic personality disorder. If the individuals with histrionic personality disorder were more likely to experience problems such as subjective distress over interpersonal relationships, divorce, and difficulty getting along with others in work settings, then the diagnosis could be useful and valid.

Perhaps the clinician's best tool for dealing with cultural variation in traits is the requirement that a disorder cause either significant functional impairment or subjective distress for the individual. This component of the definition can also be used to determine when clinical intervention is indicated. In a military state where citizens are encouraged to report on the behavior of others, paranoid personality traits might be quite adaptive, and treatment aimed at reducing the level of hypervigilance might actually put the individual at risk. In contrast, the same type of behaviors in a different society might alienate others and be maladaptive. Similarly, compulsive personality traits may be adaptive in some settings and maladaptive in others.

In contrast, knowledge about predisposing biological factors for personality traits may not provide much help in defining what constitutes a disorder. For example, fair skin may not be a particular problem in some climates, but in other climates, risk for skin cancer may be considerably increased in such individuals. In this case, the need for special intervention is determined not by the biological trait, but by the interaction of the trait with a particular environment. Likewise, if a gene predisposing toward compulsive personality traits were discovered, the presence of a disorder might be determined by the interaction of the trait with the occupational and cultural milieu of the individual.

I believe that Foulks's observations have at least two implications for the immediate future. First, more cross-cultural empirical data are needed. Such studies must not only compare rates of different personality traits across cultures but also incorporate methodology to determine whether the differences are as a result of actual differences in behavior, differences in attributions assigned to the behavior, or differences in whether the behavior leads to distress or disability in a given cultural setting. Answering these questions is likely to take a long time.

Second, it may be much more important to incorporate the insights of Foulks and others into the training of clinicians than into the diagnostic criteria themselves. It is critical that psychiatry residents be exposed to patients from a variety of cultures and that consideration of the cultural and subcultural context of psychiatric symptoms be routinely considered when cases are presented for teaching purposes. The value of conferences should be measured by the effect they have on psychiatric education and practice in general. Unless cultural issues are a key component of psychiatric training, cautions or caveats in the diagnostic manual will not be sufficient to ensure valid diagnoses and appropriate psychiatric intervention.

Section IX

Childhood-Onset Disorders

Chapter 35

Cultural and Ethnic Considerations in the DSM-IV Diagnosis and Classification of Childhood-Onset Disorders

Gloria Johnson-Powell, M.D.

ocial and behavioral epidemiology has begun to provide a rich source of data for advancing epidemiological theories on mental health of racial/ethnic minority populations in the United States. However, what gains have been achieved have been made primarily for culturally diverse and/or minority group adults, with fewer comparable advances for similar populations of children (Comas-Diaz and Griffith 1988; Kiev 1972).

Although social scientists have long noted child-rearing practices and the variations in child development in many countries and cultures throughout the world, rarely have such studies focused on disordered behavior of children or childhood psychopathology (Gibbs and Huang 1990; Powell et al. 1983; Werner 1979; Werner et al. 1971). With the growing prominence of adult psychiatric epidemiology, many epidemiological studies of children have also been undertaken, but few in culturally or ethnically diverse populations. Indeed, a determination of the role of psychosocial and cultural factors in childhood psychiatric disorders is limited by the fact that it has not been a priority area of research in child psychiatry. Although ethnically diverse children represent a significant percentage of the 9 million children who are in need of psychiatric services in this country, the concerns of cultural, racial, ethnic, and linguistically diverse youths have been invisible in child psychiatric research and training programs (Dougherty et al. 1987).

In his review of developmental psychopathology, Kazdin (1989) found that the prevalence rates of childhood dysfunction not only differed as a function of the type of disorder but also were influenced by age, sex, ethnic background, geographical region, socioeconomic status, and family structure. He noted that "tracking behavior can be more problematic with children than with adults because the progression of behaviors are not well charted" (Kazdin 1989, p. 182). The special characteristics of children and adolescents that have created obstacles to the advancement of clinical research on childhood dysfunction are as follows:

- Early signs of problems may not necessarily be clinically significant.
- Problem behaviors appear and disappear because children develop rapidly.
- A problem may appear and disappear at one age and be replaced by another problem at a different age (Kazdin 1989).

Social and Cultural Factors in Childhood Diagnosis: An Overview

Human social and mental development is increasingly seen as the confluence of many interrelated changing systems and subsystems, including the biological, social, cultural, and historical (Hinkle 1974; Levine 1969). An individual's responses, whether normal or not, are greatly influenced by the cultural milieu. Thus, crucial to understanding the observed behavior of a child is an understanding of the child-rearing practices that are embedded in the cultural values, beliefs, and attitudes of the child's parents and extended family, as well as of the community in which he or she lives, and the relationship of the child to the parent or caregiver and the caregiver's transmission of sociocultural values of the country of origin (Giordano and Giordano 1977; Levine 1977). If the socialization process of children is preparation to face the complexities of life in adulthood, then psychopathology may be considered a consequence of problems or complications in this process (Jacoby 1967; Levine 1977).

Every culture induces stress during the process of socialization (Wittkower and Dubreil 1973). Some elements of cultural content may create tensions such as taboos that frustrate essential human needs. In addition, the social organization in which children and families are embedded may not be structured or integrated, thus creating social disorganization such as unemployment, poverty, migration, immigration, rapid urbanization, and lack of education (Holtzman et al. 1975). These social disorganizational factors become sources of tension and stress. In contrast to social disorganization, social rigidity, or social patterns of domination and extreme conformity, should be considered in this same category. All of these factors may impair the necessary expansion of role definition during social change and migration, which often results in cultural lag. A third major cause of psychocultural stress is sociocultural change, particularly problems in acculturation (Powell et al. 1983). All three causes of psychocultural stress are interrelated and combine to cause such stresses as alienation, value polymorphism, and role deprivation.

Children from cultural backgrounds that are different from those in the dominant society may demonstrate symptomatic differentiation as a result of culturally determined aspects of family structure, family interaction, and role conflicts. McGolderick et al. (1982) evaluated the way in which the family must be able to adapt to the changing needs of a changing society. When families keep their old traditions in a changing society—even their own society and not one outside their social setting—conflict between generations is frequent, and personality problems are more prominent (Wittkower and Dubreil 1973). Factors such as immigration, mobility, acculturation, detribalization, social rejection, and poverty have been found to be related to psychiatric problems in children because of problems in adaptation (Gibbs and Huang 1990; Powell et al. 1983).

Studies of familial and sociocultural antecedents of psychopathology provide convincing evidence that sociofamilial characteristics affect child-rearing practices and child-parent relationships (Levine 1969, 1977; LeVine 1980). For example, there are differences in communication, interaction, socialization of children, expectations, and emotional expressions among ethnic and cultural groups (McGolderick et al. 1982). Acculturation brings stresses of cultural conflict, role conflict, deprivation, and alienation. Alienation is often experienced as feelings of powerlessness, meaningless, normlessness, cultural estrangement, social isolation, and rejection, which result from barriers to interaction, communication, and learning. Such feelings of alienation are a sign of impaired socialization, which may present itself differently in the behavior of a particular child, depending on the culture, degree of acculturation, socioeconomic status, and resources of the family.

When socialization occurs in a society in which the culture of the child and family is different from that of the dominant society, the socialization process may become increasingly stressful for both children and their families (Gibbs and Huang 1990). For clinicians, knowledge of the normal response to stress among culturally diverse children is a necessary tool for adequate diagnosis. An understanding of the stress of acculturation and the behavioral manifestations thereof must be incorporated into the differential diagnosis. Murphy and Moriarty (1978) described the coping style and strategies of some children, which are probably very similar to those of the culturally different child trying to cope with a new way of living and being in a culturally different milieu:

> Some children developed self-protective preventive devices or compensatory measures to manage such problems: timing rest; ability to limit or fend off excessive stimulation; ability to control the impact of the environment through strategic withdrawal, delay, and caution; and the ability to select and to restructure the environment. Involved here as prerequisites were realistic appraisal of the environment, acceptance of people, clear differentiation of fantasy from reality, and many cognitive coping capacities. (Even) tolerance of temporary regression protects against stress by reducing tension. (p. 338)

However, often these processes that are adopted by culturally different children to try to cope with stress and decrease the vulnerability are given psychopathological labels.

Self-Concept and Mental Health Among Minority Group Children

What children think or feel about themselves is largely determined by what they perceive other people think or feel about them. Very early in children's lives, self-perception is mediated by their primary caretakers or family members. As children increase their social network beyond the home, self-perception is mediated by society at large. Children learn to distinguish differences in skin color and other physical characteristics by age 3, and by age 6 or 7, all children are able to make such distinctions, with the most crucial period being between ages 4 and 5. Awareness of religious and national ethnic groups also occurs during early childhood but comes later than racial awareness. The development of racial and ethnic identification is an integral part of minority group children's total development of self. However, the self-differentiation process occurs in a continuing context of social interactions in which others both distinguish and evaluate them by means of their racial category and label them in affectively-laden terms that refer to their race (or ethnicity) (Proshansky and Newton 1968).

Because of the importance that race or ethnicity may have in their acceptance or rejection by their peers, it is clear that the psychic energy minority group children must use to sort out the complexity of an ethnic or racial identity may take its toll in other important areas of development. Research data indicate that there is a direct relationship between problems in the development of self and the degree to which children's ethnic or racial group is socially unacceptable and exposed to discrimination and deprivation (Powell 1973; Powell et al. 1983). The early studies of Clark and Clark (1947), Goodman (1952), and Radke and Trager (1950) showed that the self-awareness of minority group children evolved in a race-conscious, ethnocentric sociocultural milieu that assigned negative values to racially and culturally different people. More recent studies have revealed that this process still exists for minority group children (Gibbs and Huang 1990).

The available theoretical literature on psychosocial stress as a heuristic model for the analysis of the epidemiological findings on the physical and mental health of the poor and ethnic/racial minorities is a combination of many models of the stress-adaptation process as precursors to disease and systems malfunctions. Much of the research on the effects of psychosocial stress on health emphasizes the importance of episodic, major social stress events that have a disruptive effect on daily functioning (B. P. Dohrenwend and Dohrenwend 1974; B. S. Dohrenwend and Dohrenwend 1970; B. S. Dohrenwend 1973; Holmes and Rahe 1967). The literature has consistently reported that individuals from low-income backgrounds experience more major stresses in their lives and that these events are more disruptive for them than for their more affluent counterparts (Myers and King 1983). The urban stress model proposed by Myers and King suggests that individuals who belong to ethnic/racial groups and/or who are also poor are exposed to a greater amount of stress and are often exposed to stress over an extended period of time. Consequently, the severity of the impact of that stress on their lives is substantially greater. *There is no life events scale that includes racial/ethnic discrimination as a major and/or continuous stressor for minority group children or adults.* In this respect minority group children are invisible in the DSMs, and the psychosocial stress that impinges on their development and their mental health is rarely considered in the diagnostic process. The consequences of this oversight are many and include erroneous diagnoses and inadequate treatment.

Classification Issues and Sociocultural Factors: Some Recommendations

Rutter and Gould (1985) advanced the following four principles germane to sociocultural factors with regard to classification of child psychiatric disorders:

1. Classification must be based on facts that have an operational definition.
2. The purpose should be to classify problems and not to classify children as problems.
3. It must be broad based to ensure that important disorders are not overlooked.
4. Relevant information must be conveyed so that the classification is suitable or applicable to the clinical situation.

In examining multiaxial approaches, Rutter and Gould (1985) noted that the DSM-III (American Psychiatric Association 1980) multiaxial framework differs from the World Health Organization's multiaxial scheme for child psychiatric disorders (Rutter et al. 1975) in the important area of psychosocial factors. The major criticisms of DSM-III have included the following:

1. The assumption that all forms of stress are mediated by the same process is incorrect.
2. The criteria for the assessment of the severity of stressors are highly speculative.
3. The axis for psychiatric syndromes is not inclusive for psychosocial factors that may have played a major etiological role (Rutter and Shaffer 1980).

The third criticism prevails in DSM-III-R in spite of the fact that *there is compelling evidence that psychosocial factors contribute to causation and prognosis for children and adolescents* (Rutter 1981).

The major unresolved problems are that 1) most psychosocial factors are not adequately coded, and 2) improvement is needed in the conceptualization and definition. Rutter and Gould (1985) emphasized the importance of improving the systematic acquisition of reliable and valid data on psychosocial factors. Cantwell's (1988) critique of DSM-III noted that Axis IV was unreliable and provided information in a way that was not consistent with current concepts and research data on psychosocial stressors that affect children and adolescents.

These critiques emphasize the need for greater efforts toward making an axis on psychosocial stressors more valid and reliable. Improvements on Axis IV would require modification in data collection instruments; attention to diagnostic reliability as determined by criterion variance; and, most importantly, information, observation, and interpretation of variances. To reflect the unique experiences of culturally diverse children, Axis IV must be updated or the World Health Organization's Axis V for psychosocial factors should be considered for the development of future modifications of DSM. Axis V should record the level of adaptive functioning, incorporating a global assessment of impairment to offset the overinclusiveness of pathological disorders that is prevalent in the current methodologies used. To more accurately reflect the population of children from diverse sociocultural backgrounds, major research studies must include culturally appropriate diagnostic scales to collect the data.

Summary and Conclusion

In 1983 the American Academy of Child Psychiatry addressed the psychiatric needs of children, noting that children with complex problems do not receive the comprehensive and continuous care they need and identifying the groups of children at risk for psychiatric disorder. Among the 16 categories listed were children of ethnic/racial minority groups, children from low-income families, and children of immigrants. Minority group children and children of immigrants are often poor and also are found in high percentages in other at-risk categories as well (American Academy of Child Psychiatry 1983). Thus, their plight must be viewed with great concern.

Kazdin (1989) astutely reminded us of the fact that studies of psychopathology among children must have a developmental framework. Studies on the development of culturally diverse children in different ecological settings remain suspect because differences are often interpreted as deficits. Such interpretations are a result of the ethnocentrism of the clinician/observer. However, as long as psychiatric training programs do not include information on cross-cultural child development or offer exposure to culturally diverse children in community-based settings, ethnocentrism will continue to hamper the process.

The U.S. Office of Technology Assessment has estimated that only 2 million of the 9.5 million children who need mental health treatment are receiving it (Dougherty et al. 1987). Within most major metropolitan areas, the underserved children are frequently from the inner city, are immigrants, and are culturally different and/or minority group children who have multiple problems and few resources. As the numbers of such children increase, there must be an urgency about making improvements in the diagnostic process. Although we must be arduous and earnest, careful and precise, we must also proceed with all deliberate speed.

References

American Academy of Child Psychiatry: Project Future. Washington, DC, American Psychiatric Press, 1983

American Psychiatric Association: Diagnostic and Statistical Manual of Mental Disorders, 3rd Edition. Washington, DC, American Psychiatric Association, 1980

Cantwell D: DSM III studies, in Assessment and Diagnosis in Child Psychopathology. Edited by Rutter M, Tuma AH, Lann IS. New York, Guilford, 1988

Clark KB, Clark MP: Racial identification and preference in Negro children, in Readings in Social Psychology. Edited by Newcomb T, Hartley E. New York, Holt, 1947

Comas-Diaz L, Griffith EEH: Clinical Guidelines in Cross-Cultural Mental Health. New York, Wiley, 1988

Dohrenwend BP, Dohrenwend BS: Stressful Life Events: Their Nature and Effects. New York, Wiley, 1974

Dohrenwend BS: Life events and stresses: a methodological inquiry. J Health Soc Behav 14:167–175, 1973

Dohrenwend BS, Dohrenwend BP: Class and race as status-related sources of stress, in Social Stress. Edited by Levine S, Scotch NA. Chicago, IL, Aldine, 1970

Dougherty DM, Saxe L, Cross T, et al: Children's mental health: problems and services (a report by the U.S. Office of Technology Assessment). Durham, NC, Duke University Press, 1987

Gibbs J, Huang A: Children of Color. San Francisco, CA, Jossey-Bass, 1990

Giordano J, Giordano GJ: The Ethno-Cultural Factor in Mental Health: A Literature Review and Bibliography. New York, Institute on Pluralism and Group Identity, 1977

Goodman M: Race Awareness in Young Children. Reading, MA, Addison-Wesley, 1952

Hinkle LE: The effects of exposure to culture change, social change and changes in interpersonal relationships on health, in Stressful Life Events: Their Nature and Effects. Edited by Dohrenwend BS, Dohrenwend BP. New York, Wiley, 1974

Holmes TH, Rahe RH: The social readjustment rating scale. J Psychosom Res 11:213–218, 1967

Holtzman WH, Diaz-Guerrero R, Swartz JD: Personality Development in Two Cultures. Austin, University of Texas Press, 1975

Jacoby J: The construct of abnormality: some cross-cultural considerations. Journal of Experimental Research in Personality 2:1–15, 1967

Kazdin AE: Developmental psychopathology: current research, issues, and directions. Am Psychol 44(2):180–187, 1989

Kiev A: Transcultural Psychiatry. New York, Free Press, 1972

Levine IL: Culture, personality, and socialization: An evolutionary view, in Handbook of Socialization: Theory and Research. Edited by Goslin DA. New York, Rand McNally, 1969

Levine IL: Child rearing as cultural adaptation, in Culture and Infancy: Variations in the Human Experience. Edited by Leiderman PH, Tulkin SR, Rosenfield A. New York, Academic Press, 1977

LeVine RA: Anthropology and child development. New Dir Child Dev 8:71–86, 1980

McGolderick M, Pearce JK, Giordano J: Ethnicity and Family Therapy. New York, Guilford, 1982

Murphy LB, Moriarty AE: Vulnerability, Coping and Growth: From Infancy to Adolescence, 2nd Edition. New Haven, CT, Yale University Press, 1978

Myers HF, King LM: Mental health issues in the development of the Afro-American child, in The Psycho-Social Development of Minority Group Children. Edited by Powell GJ, Yamamoto J, Morales A, et al. New York, Brunner/Mazel, 1983

Powell GJ: Black Monday's Children: A Study of the Psychological Effects of School Desegregation on Southern School Children. New York, Appleton, 1973

Powell GJ, Yamamoto J, Romero A, et al: The Psycho-Social Development of Minority Group Children. New York, Brunner/Mazel, 1983

Proshansky H, Newton P: The nature and meaning of the Negro self-identity, in Social Class, Race, and Psychological Development. Edited by Deutsch M, Katz I, Jensen A. New York, Holt, 1968

Radke M, Trager H: Children's perceptions of the social roles of Negroes and whites. J Psychol 29:3–33, 1950

Rutter M: Stress, coping, and development: some questions and some answers. J Child Psychol Psychiatry 22:323–353, 1981

Rutter M, Gould MS: Classification, in Clinical Psychiatry: Modern Approaches, 2nd Edition. Edited by Rutter M, Hersov A. New York, Wiley, 1985

Rutter M, Shaffer D: DSM III: a step forward or back in terms of classification of child psychiatric disorders. J Am Acad Child Adolesc Psychiatry 19:371–394, 1980

Rutter M, Shaffer D, Shepard M: A Multiaxial Classification of Child Psychiatric Disorders. Geneva, Switzerland, World Health Organization, 1975

Werner EE: Cross-Cultural Child Development: A View From the Planet Earth. Monterey, CA, Brooks/Cole, 1979

Werner EE, Bierman JM, French D: The Children of Kauai: A Longitudinal Study from the Prenatal Period to Age Ten. Honolulu, University of Hawaii Press, 1971

Wittkower ED, Dubreil G: Psychocultural stress in relation to mental illness. Soc Sci Med 7:691–704, 1973

Chapter 36

Cultural Comments on Childhood-Onset Disorders: I

William H. *Sack*, M.D.

J ohnson-Powell's discussion in Chapter 35 of the need to highlight sociocultural factors as important contributions to understanding diagnostic nosology resonates with our ideas from clinical and research experience with Cambodian youths this past decade. We also agree with Johnson-Powell that Axis IV as it currently stands is inadequate to reflect cultural factors in understanding minority children. In reading existing presentations of Axis IV, one finds minimal references to cultural stress or resettlement stress as contributing psychosocial stressors. However, this axis seems to be a logical place for accommodating transcultural issues. For children, the "distance" between Axis IV and Axis I is shorter than for adults— that is, children are in general more vulnerable to the effects of external stressors. Thus, this issue gains particular salience for minority youths.

We have been carrying out research on Cambodian youths that reflects the importance of gaining a clear understanding about prior and current stress as it relates to an Axis I diagnosis. In 1990 we interviewed 69 Cambodian teenagers (average age, 14 years) who as children had survived the horrors of the Pol Pot regime from 1975 to 1979. We constructed measures of their prior war trauma, their resettlement stressors during the first year in this country, and their stressors during the preceding year (Sack et al., in press). We found that there was a strong correlation between prior war trauma and a current diagnosis of posttraumatic stress disorder (PTSD). We also found that having suffered war trauma left one more vulnerable to the vicissitudes of resettlement stressors. Resettlement stress appears to be independent of current stressor experiences. Past stressor experiences make stronger contributions to current PTSD diagnoses than do more recent stressors.

These findings echo Johnson-Powell's emphasis on the importance and magnitude of cultural stress as an important contributor to psychopathology. Minority youths as refugees often have a history of severe trauma as well as the stress of repatriation with which to contend.

Reference

Sack W, Clarke G, Him C, et al: A six-year follow-up study of Cambodian refugee adolescents traumatized as children. J Am Acad Child Adolesc Psychiatry (in press)

Chapter 37

Cultural Comments on Childhood-Onset Disorders: II

Glorisa Canino, Ph.D.

Johnson-Powell in Chapter 35 stresses the importance of cultural experiences in shaping emotional expression and the overt behavior of individuals with mental illness. She states that investigations of psychopathology "need a corrective factor to balance the implicit assumption that abnormal behavior everywhere is similar in scope and in kind" and that to accomplish this corrective factor, one should examine the characteristics of the individual in the context of the family and the community. Johnson-Powell ends her chapter by emphasizing the need for revision and for giving more emphasis to psychosocial factors in Axis IV in the classification of mental disorders for children and adolescents. She provides evidence from Rutter's studies that suggest that psychosocial factors contribute to causation and prognosis of mental disorders in children and makes a strong call for a psychosocial stressors axis that takes into consideration various forms of abnormal psychosocial situations. Johnson-Powell concludes her presentation by stressing the need for cross-cultural epidemiological research and for the cross-cultural testing of nosological categories from the diagnostic classification of children and adolescents.

The veracity of Johnson-Powell's statements regarding *the importance of culture in shaping psychopathology can be more fully understood if we consider that childhood disorders, even within a given culture, cannot be made on the basis of observations of only one environment.* Within a particular culture, comprehensive assessment of a child requires multiple sources of data—from the school, the parent, and the child—each of which contributes a different picture of the child's functioning. If contextual variations are important in childhood assessment within a culture, they may be even more important when we are comparing children from different cultural contexts. However, the task of comparing rates of disorder in children across cultures is greatly hampered by a lack of consensus as to the most valid definitions of childhood psychopathology.

Several child psychiatric epidemiological surveys have been conducted in different regions of the world, such as Canada (Offord et al. 1987), New Zealand (Anderson et al. 1987), the United States (Costello et al. 1988; Vélez et al. 1989), and Puerto Rico (Bird et al. 1987). All of these population studies have revealed rates of psychiatric disorders for children and adolescents that are much higher than those reported in previous studies (Gould et al. 1980). It is nevertheless difficult to ascertain whether these higher rates are a result of a true increase in psychiatric disorders in children over time or to changes in the nosology from DSM-II to DSM-III (American Psychiatric Association 1968, 1980; Bird et al. 1990).

Although the similarities in prevalence rates across regions are striking, it is important to note that in Puerto Rico, DSM-III diagnostic criteria as applied by child psychiatrists yielded a prevalence rate of psychiatric disorder of 49.5%. It was only when the severity criteria of the Children's Global Assessment Scale (C-GAS) was applied that prevalence rates were lowered to 18.2%. If we were to view as cases all the children who met DSM-III criteria, we would be impelled toward the implausible conclusion that nearly half of the children of Puerto Rico are psychiatrically disturbed (Bird et al. 1990). Further analysis of this data bank has revealed that many children who met diagnostic criteria were not severely impaired and were not considered to be in need of mental health services by the same psychiatrists who diagnosed them, suggesting that DSM-III is overinclusive, particularly for measuring psychiatric disorder in the Puerto Rican population. Unfortunately, because of the differences in method of ascertainment of cases and differences in the age range studied and in the type of populations studied across the psychiatric epidemiology studies, it cannot be determined whether DSM-III categories are also overinclusive in other cultures. We therefore add to Johnson-Powell's presentation that there is a need to emphasize not only Axis IV but also Axis V, which codes the highest level of adaptive functioning. The importance of this axis does not apply only to minority children. Costello and Shugart (1990) have provided evidence that demonstrates that many patients with subthreshold disorders, particularly in the disruptive disorders domain, are in need of mental health services and are functionally impaired, whereas many children meeting criteria for either anxiety or depressive disorders are not impaired or in need of care. What use is a classification system if it is not related to the need for treatment, to psychosocial dysfunction, or to some degree of personal well-being?

There is definitely a need for cross-cultural epidemiological studies of mental disorders in children and adolescents in which the instrumentation and methodology used are similar, to determine more precisely whether there are some specific disorders of children that may be more prone to be affected by cultural variations.

References

American Psychiatric Association: Diagnostic and Statistical Manual of Mental Disorders, 2nd Edition. Washington, DC, American Psychiatric Association, 1968

American Psychiatric Association: Diagnostic and Statistical Manual of Mental Disorders, 3rd Edition. Washington, DC, American Psychiatric Association, 1980

Anderson JC, Williams S, McGee R, et al: DSM-III disorders in preadolescent children. Arch Gen Psychiatry 44:69–80, 1987

Bird HR, Canino G, Rubio-Stipec M, et al: Estimates of the prevalence of childhood maladjustment in a community survey in Puerto Rico. Arch Gen Psychiatry 45:1120–1126, 1987

Bird HR, Yager TJ, Staghezza B, et al: Impairment in the epidemiological measurement of childhood psychopathology in the community. J Am Acad Child Adolesc Psychiatry 29:796–803, 1990

Costello EJ, Shugart M: Above and below threshold: severity of psychiatric symptoms and functional impairment in a pediatric sample. Paper presented at the Annual Meeting of the American Academy of Child and Adolescent Psychiatry, Chicago, IL, 1990

Costello EJ, Costello AJ, Edelbrock C, et al: Psychiatric disorders in pediatric primary care: prevalence and risk factors. Arch Gen Psychiatry 45:1107–1116, 1988

Gould MS, Wunsch-Hitzag R, Dohrenwend BP: Formulation of hypotheses about the prevalence, treatment and prognostic significance of psychiatric disorders in children in the U.S., in Mental Illness in the US: Epidemiological Estimates. Edited by Dohrenwend BP, Gould MS, Link B. New York, Praeger, 1980, pp 9–44

Offord DR, Boyle MH, Szatmari P, et al: Ontario child health study: II. Six month prevalence of disorder and rates of services utilization. Arch Gen Psychiatry 44:832–836, 1987

Vélez CM, Johnson J, Cohen P: A longitudinal analysis of selected risk factors for childhood psychopathology. J Am Acad Child Adolesc Psychiatry 28:861–864, 1989

Chapter 38

Nosological Comments on Culture and Childhood-Onset Disorders

Magda Campbell, M.D.

There is an ever increasing number of non–English-speaking immigrants, refugees, and minorities in the United States. During the 1980s, 8.6 million people entered this country (U.S. Census Bureau 1993). During this same period, the percentage of people who spoke a language other than English at home increased from 6.6% to 13.8%, representing almost 32 million persons (U.S. Census Bureau 1992). Particularly fast growing is the Hispanic population (Marcos 1988), which numbered 22.3 million in 1992 (U.S. Census Bureau 1992). Among the states in which 15%–40% of people do not speak English as a primary language are New York, California, and Texas (U.S. Census Bureau 1992). Thus, language, ethnic, and cultural factors must be taken into account in evaluating psychiatric patients.

Cultural influences may alter or modify the symptoms of a psychiatric disorder or the expression of some symptoms or even result in a psychiatric disorder not usually seen in this country. Furthermore, the prevalence rates of certain disorders in the United States may be different from those in other cultures, including Puerto Rico (Canino et al. 1987). When the patient is a child, cultural identity and degree of acculturation in both child and parent should be considered.

The Obvious Barrier of Language

A careful evaluation of the child is not possible without communication with the parent. If an interpreter is required, he or she must be fluent both in English and in the family's primary language. This issue was substantially addressed by Vázquez and Javier (1991). The interviewer or the interpreter may introduce distortions (Marcos 1979; Vásquez and Javier 1991); the interview language may affect diagnosis (Del Castillo 1970), and the degree of fluency or lack thereof may influence the degree and type of psychopathology displayed by the patient (Marcos et al. 1973). In all children, but especially in the case of a very young and/or retarded or

283

severely disturbed child, the clinician relies heavily on the history obtained from the parent. When language poses a barrier and the child's interview must be carried out through an interpreter, the use of a pictorial instrument, such as the "Dominique" in Canada, may be helpful (J. P. Vala, personal communication). A variation of this is being used at the National Institute of Mental Health, and another is currently under development (Ernst and Vingiano 1989; Ernst et al. 1990).

Diagnosis and Phenomenology

The diagnosis itself, the clinical picture, and the prevalence rate of a disorder all may be influenced by culture. Although the major mental disorders seem to have a similar appearance across cultures, their expressions may differ. Severe disorders such as autism are seen on all continents with the same clinical (behavioral) manifestations. Little is known about major depression in children and adolescents across cultures; in adults there are differences in content of symptoms or forms in which depressive disorder is displayed (Fabrega 1974; Singer 1975) as well as in prevalence rate (Singer 1975). Expressed emotion seems to be influenced by culture (Jenkins and Karno 1992). With regard to differences in prevalence rate, hysteria is very rarely seen in children in this country, but in India it is a relatively common condition (S. Srinath, personal communication). Catatonia, rarely seen in the United States at the present time, may be more common in adolescents who have recently immigrated from India, Korea, Hong Kong, or Taiwan. Dissociative disorder, suicidality, IQ, and learning disorders should also be given specific attention. Native American adolescents have a higher rate of psychiatric problems than the general population (Blum et al. 1992). For Native Americans, suicide peaks at between 15 and 24 years of age, and in this group cluster suicide has a culturally specific pattern (Bechtold 1988).

A distinction between a disorder and (age-related) behavioral deviations is not always clear (Bird et al. 1990). For example, all symptoms of conduct disorder, when of low frequency and transient, may be present as part of the normal developmental process (Kazdin 1987). The prevalence of conduct disorder may be affected by cultural variables and the uprootedness that is associated with migration. Certainly the child of a new immigrant or refugee, once in school, may be reacting to his or her parents' immigrant status, to ways of living that differ from that of the mainstream, or to being of a different race.

Language, cultural differences, and obstacles and problems related to acculturation are all important considerations for the development and revision of diagnostic classification systems. Differences in clinical manifestation and in prevalence rates of psychiatric disorders of children and adolescents are key research areas. Their results may usefully inform the development of classification systems.

The development of a cultural axis, as outlined in Chapters 2 and 43, is an interesting concept. By attending to ethnic identity; language fluency and preferences;

and the cultural framework of illness, assessment, and care, such an axis may have a significant impact on the quality of diagnostic classification.

References

Bechtold DW: Cluster suicide in American Indian adolescents. Am Indian Alsk Native Ment Health Res 1:26–35, 1988

Bird HR, Yager TJ, Staghezza B, et al: Impairment in the epidemiological measurement of childhood psychopathology in the community. J Am Acad Child Adolesc Psychiatry 29:796–803, 1990

Blum RW, Harmon B, Harris L, et al: American Indian-Alaska native youth health. JAMA 267:1637–1644, 1992

Canino G, Bird H, Shrout P, et al: The prevalence of specific psychiatric disorders in Puerto Rico. Arch Gen Psychiatry 44:727–733, 1987

Del Castillo JC: The influence of language upon symptomatology in foreign-born patients. Am J Psychiatry 127:242–244, 1970

Ernst M, Vingiano W: Development of a graphic psychiatric self-rating scale. Compr Psychiatry 30:189–194, 1989

Ernst M, Godfrey KA, Alpert M, et al: Development of a pictorial-based interview for children and adolescents, in American Academy of Child and Adolescent Psychiatry Annual Meeting Proceedings, 1990, p 67

Fabrega J Jr: Problems implicit in the cultural and social study of depression. Psychosom Med 36:377–398, 1974

Jenkins JH, Karno M: The meaning of expressed emotion: theoretical issues raised by cross-cultural research. Am J Psychiatry 149:9–21, 1992

Kazdin AE: Conduct Disorders in Childhood and Adolescence. London, England, Sage, 1987

Marcos LR: Effects of interpreters on the evaluation of psychopathology in non-English-speaking patients. Am J Psychiatry 136:171–174, 1979

Marcos LR: Understanding ethnicity in psychotherapy with Hispanic patients. Am J Psychoanal 48:35–42, 1988

Marcos LR, Urcuyo L, Kesselman M, et al: The language barrier in evaluating Spanish-American patients. Arch Gen Psychiatry 29:655–659, 1973

Singer K: Depressive disorders from a transcultural perspective. Soc Sci Med 9:289–301, 1975

U.S. Census Bureau. Statistical Abstract of the United States. Washington, DC, U.S. Government Printing Office, 1992

U.S. Census Bureau. Statistical Abstract of the United States. Washington, DC, U.S. Government Printing Office, 1993

Vázquez C, Javier R: The problem with interpreters: communicating with Spanish-speaking patients. Hosp Community Psychiatry 42:163–165, 1991

Section X

Culture-Bound Syndromes

Chapter 39

The Culture-Bound Syndromes and Psychiatric Diagnosis

Charles C. Hughes, Ph.D.

T he so-called "culture-bound syndromes" have been discussed under a variety of covering terms, such as *psychogenic psychoses, ethnic psychoses, ethnic neu- roses, hysterical psychoses, exotic psychoses, atypical psychoses, culture-reactive syndromes,* and the like (Hughes 1985a). Sometimes they are offered as examples of "transcultural psychiatry," "cross-cultural psychiatry," or even "culturogenic stress." A more discursive definition refers to "episodic and dramatic reactions, specific to a particular community . . . locally identified as discrete patterns of behavior" (Littlewood and Lipsedge 1985, p. 105). Other definitions include "a collection of signs and symptoms (excluding notions of cause) which is restricted to a limited number of cultures primarily by reason of certain of their psychosocial features" (Prince and Tcheng-Laroche 1987, p. 3) and Cassidy and Ritenbaugh's "constella- tion of symptoms which has been categorized as a dysfunction or disease" (quoted in Swartz 1985, p. 726).

This chapter is not a review of the diverse symptomatic content of the phrase "culture-bound syndromes." Such a review can be found elsewhere (e.g., Simons and Hughes 1985). More to the point, productive discussion of the generic mean- ing and formulation of a useful definition has suffered as a result of bemusement with the exotic symptomatic nature of the syndromes. Here, initially taking a meta- analytic stance toward the phrase "culture-bound syndromes," I direct attention toward a core meaning and critique the label's indiscriminant application to what often turn out to be incomparable phenomena. The need for the phrase's transla- tion into familiar terms and conceptual structures is reviewed as a basis for dis- cussing its relevance to a standard classification system such as the American Psychiatric Association's series of DSMs. Finally, comments are directed toward the uses of the phrase's basic insight in the clinical setting as a significant and all- too-often overlooked element in patient assessment and management.

When discussed at all in a psychiatric text, the culture-bound syndromes receive only perfunctory recognition. Rarely even indexed, their discussion typically consists of only a page or two—so slight as to be useless for either research or clinical applications (see, for example, Freedman et al. 1975, 1976; Hill et al. 1986; Kaplan and Sadock 1985, 1988; Kendell and Zealley 1983; Kolb 1977; Lazare 1989; Nicholi 1988). Unfortunately—the medium being a large part of any message—such treatment institutionalizes the subject matter as an afterthought, extraneous to the main (i.e., conventional) work of the text. A cogent example is found in an otherwise useful discussion of the topic in a general text published by the American Psychiatric Press (Talbott et al. 1988). Of the 38 chapters in this book of more than 1,300 pages, "Psychiatry and Culture" is Chapter 35 (Griffith 1988).

The short shrift given such an important idea as culture probably means that its generic conceptual character and the empirical pervasiveness of its referents are not well understood—or certainly at least not firmly established—in the diagnostic process. "Culture" is commonly treated as simply another variable of restricted segmental dimensions, as if it were comparable, for example, to age or gender (Hughes 1991).

In any case, when in mainstream psychiatry the culture-bound syndromes are thus separated and set aside and given special, restricted status, they are vulnerable and easily at risk of being dismissed as marginal, irrelevant to serious consideration (except perhaps as an annoying conceptual gadfly that has to be explained away!).

These syndromes have sometimes been included in discussions of cultural psychiatry (Haldipur 1980; Hill et al. 1986). However, for an anthropologist (as well as for the late H. B. M. Murphy 1977), this raises questions of why the "psychiatry" institutionalized in DSM-III-R and DSM-IV (American Psychiatric Association 1987, 1994) is not itself also considered "cultural psychiatry," in this instance a psychiatry having a Eurocentric heritage. Why are these particular syndromes thus differentiated, they alone being set apart as examples of "cultural psychiatry"? Indeed, which is the "set" and which the "subset" in the relationship between "psychiatry" and "cultural psychiatry"? Is "psychiatry" (by which is implicitly meant Euro-American biomedically based psychiatry) an empirically transcendent, constant, fixed point of reference against which all other conceptualizations of disorder and aberrancy must be measured? Or is that set of conceptualizations and techniques itself the product of a particular set of cultural events?

Bruner (1990) has spoken of theoretical enrichment provided by an emerging recognition of the importance of perspectives drawn from cross-cultural psychology and a reflexive "cultural psychology," which acknowledges that in any human activity, cultural context deeply structures both the interpretation of findings as well as the very parameters of the search for understanding. Obviously psychiatry should do no less and should examine its own culturally structured roots, not only when the issue is that of assessing a patient from a different cultural background, but in all instances. In a "social psychiatric" frame, the need for a contextual understanding of the patient's life-situation applies equally well even when no major cultural boundary is being crossed (as, for example, in the clinical encounter with patients from a socioeconomic status lower than the clinician's). In Murphy's (1977) classic phrase, "transcultural psychiatry should begin at home."

Culture-Bound Syndromes: Ontological Assumptions

The publicity given the culture-bound syndromes appears to be based on two principal assumptions, both usually implicit and unexamined and both challenged in this chapter:

1. The culture-bound syndromes form a unique and distinctive class of generic phenomena of presumed psychiatric interest (as contrasted with being simply objects of a superficial labeling difference).
2. Such syndromes afflict only, or at least principally, the "others," those peoples established, by some criterion, as outside the "mainstream" population (however defined). Such groups are commonly referred to as ethnic groups or minorities. (From an American Psychiatric Association point of departure, of course, this includes most people in "developing" parts of the world.)

In this chapter I contest both assumptions by suggesting that terminological puzzlement over what the phrase "culture-bound syndrome" means dissolves if the conceptual framework for analysis is placed at a primary level and in a pre-categorical naturalistic scenario of a person relating to a particular and specific sociocultural environment. Specifically, this is to suggest a broadened perspective that derives from the holistically minded cultural anthropologist, a perspective akin to that used by Menninger (1963) when he spoke of "the life process in mental health and illness" (p. x) or that of Meyer (1957), whose "psychobiological" approach ("viewing human behavior as a dynamic process" [1957, p. 46]; see also Foss and Rothenberg 1987) takes common sense at its word and deed, and works with performances as found and chosen for their importance in actual problems, from full-fledged activities and reactions and attitudes of the individual to the most economizing symbolization as thought, image, and feeling" (Meyer 1951, p. 285). This is an approach in which "we must have the courage to turn to the real experiences of real persons, to train ourselves to get the best possible grasp on the facts as they occur in their actuality, as seen by others and by the self" (Meyer 1957, p. 75). Meyer's use of "common sense" was often disparaged by his colleagues. Alexander H. Leighton, one of Meyer's students (and one of my mentors), pointed out to me that "common sense" to Meyer meant the sense (i.e., meaning) of common events (Meyer, personal communication, 1951; also hand-written note in Meyer 1957) (see also Bruner [1990, p. 35]: "folk psychology," or you may prefer 'folk social science' or even, simply, 'common sense'"). Furthermore, and on a grander scale, "The whole of science is nothing more than a refinement of everyday thinking" (Einstein 1950, p. 59), or "Science is self-conscious commonsense" (Quine 1960, p. 3).

Rutter (1986) reinforced Meyer's approach, which "had, as its cornerstone the need to understand how life experiences had effects on the organism and why there were such large individual differences in people's responses to events and circumstances. Particular emphasis was placed on the meaning of happenings for the individual, on their interpretation, on coping mechanisms in terms of both cognitive and affective processes, and on assets and protective factors" (p. 1077). Another commentator suggested that "we are again in need of the Meyerian spirit, a holistic perspective" (Neill 1980, p. 464).

Such a conceptual orientation encases a fundamental biological principle: namely, the profound individuality of the lived experience, which the eminent biologist Ernst Mayr (1982), has phrased as beginning with recognition of "the uniqueness of everything in the organic world" (p. 46). That orientation—a return to the foundational source of conceptualizations of culture-bound syndromes—has implications that pervade all consideration of the life process and its adaptational attempts. First, it requires sensitive attention to primary empirical data before they are evaluated and packaged into diagnoses; it certainly is required in the search for clarity in thinking about this class of observables, that is, the culture-bound syndromes.

In attempting to establish the ontological status of the culture-bound syndromes, therefore, we must go behind the semantic affliction of "label-grip," that is, that paralysis of analytic acumen often created by such a connotatively powerful phrase as "culture-bound syndromes." One must ask, "What is the generic difference (if any) between the culture-bound syndromes and non-culture-bound syndromes? On what basis(es) have the culture-bound syndromes been so peremptorily set apart from the other (conventional) syndromes?"

Data are needed to respond to that question; especially useful would be detailed clinical reports. Unfortunately such data are in scarce supply. However, as a basis for considering whether a standard diagnostic system should explicitly incorporate the phenomena referred to by the phrase "culture-bound syndromes," let us look at a few examples of such syndromes often cited in the literature, which can serve as pro tempore candidates for possible inclusion.

Culture-Bound Syndromes: A Sampler

Hwa-Byung

This is a fairly common disorder conceptualized and labeled in traditional Korean culture ("most Korean health professionals are familiar with the condition" [Lin 1983, p. 106]). With the immigration of several hundred thousand Koreans to the United States since the 1970s, there is an increasing likelihood that patients in this country may present with symptoms that a non-Korean professional might simplistically assign to an inappropriate DSM category. Epigastric pain is a common presenting symptom, along with the fear that such pain will lead to death. Other symptoms often include excessive tiredness and insomnia, acute panic, loss of appetite or other digestive disorders, dyspnea, palpitation, and muscle aches and pains.

Reflection on this syndrome in relation to its cultural setting suggests directions in which the patient's culturally structured world should be explored in the interest of better management. For example, in the Korean language, *byung* refers to sickness, and *hwa* is fire or anger. As in other traditional Asian medical systems (e.g., Chinese), "fire"—one of the basic elements constituting culturally structured "reality"—and "anger" are related. Illness occurs when there is imbalance or inharmonious relationship among such elements. If the element of fire is excessive, anger is the indicator of lack of such harmony. Korean folk etiological beliefs center on anger as the precipitant of numerous illnesses, and case reports frequently discuss a diagnosis of depression engendered by negative life circumstances and expressed by patients as somatic complaints (Lin 1983). (One can speculate as to how an American Psychiatric Association DSM diagnostic formulation might look if its base point of departure were the folk labeling [*hwa* = anger], which has the simplicity of folk sagacity in forthrightly going to anger as the source of the depression. To say the least, it is intriguingly suggestive of a psychoanalytic etiological formulation of depression!)

Ataques de Nervios

Even in metropolitan areas of the contemporary United States, numerous patients of Hispanic cultural background seek help from indigenous practitioners for "folk" syndromes, one of which is *ataques de nervios* (Garrison 1977; Guarnaccia et al. 1989). Characteristically, a sudden-onset dissociative outburst is accompanied by a variety of symptoms: dyspnea, chest tightness, memory loss, trembling, sense of heat or of needles sticking in the limbs, palpitations, and dizziness. The patient's etiological belief—deriving from a particular cultural explanatory matrix—is that he or she is being attacked by evil spirits, and the only form of therapeutic response likely to have any efficacy is an elaborate series of public rituals that incorporate not only clear evidence of social support but also religious and symbolic elements from both Old and New World cultural traditions.

Susto

A common disorder afflicting Hispanic patients is *susto*, typical symptoms of which are found in other parts of the world and known, therefore, by different indigenous terms (Simons and Hughes 1985). A wide range of symptoms are indicators of the presumed primary cause, which is loss of spirit or soul: anxiety, irritability, anorexia, insomnia, phobias, trembling, sweating, tachycardia, diarrhea, depression, vomiting, and others. A traumatic and frightening incident to one's self or someone close, such as a child or other family member, is the triggering "cause," the event believed to result in detachment of the person's spirit or soul from the body. Often the stimulus for emergence of symptoms is a recalled past event, the symptoms being a delayed response to rumination over the event.

This often cited instance of a culture-bound syndrome may not be structurally comparable with some of the others, in the sense that there is not the close relationship to salient cultural values in the numerous contexts in which it is found characteristic of other culture-bound syndromes. It appears to be more a post hoc folk etiological formulation for dealing with stresses, and its symptoms and folk etiological involvement with spiritual forces represent a common adaptive

mechanism in human societies. Therapy typically occurs in a ritualized setting and includes a variety of somatic treatments (e.g., sweating and massage) and behavioral restrictions (e.g., diet), as well as social support techniques.

Taijin Kyofusho

In this syndrome, named from its prevalence in Japan, the patient typically presents with complaints that one's body, its parts or functions, are offensive to other people in appearance, odor, expression (as in facial demeanor), or movements. Particularly manifested in interpersonal situations, the disorder is so prevalent that social support groups have been developed to aid patients. Often the condition is diagnosed in Western nosology as neurasthenia, anxiety neuroses, or obsessive-compulsive reactions (Caudill and Doi 1963). The Japanese term clearly expresses articulation with a specific cultural matrix that provides an emulative "model of madness" or disorder (*taijin* referring to interpersonal context, *kyofu* meaning "fear," and *sho* translating as "syndrome"). Given the deeply entrenched values in Japanese culture concerning proper decorum in all social contexts, evidences of a folk etiological conceptualization are compelling (Kirmayer 1991).

Koro

At the symptomatic level, *koro* is perhaps one of the most bizarre disorders ("bizarre" to the Euro-American observer, primarily because it does not fit neatly into conventional diagnostic categories and may therefore be considered exotic). The term itself is of Malay origin, and its principal reported incidence has been in South Asian and Chinese populations. In recent years, however, there have been reports of its occurrence in Euro-Canadian and African contexts as well (thereby belying a simplistic assertion of its cultural "uniqueness" or specificity; cf. Simons and Hughes 1985).

The symptoms are dramatic. A patient suddenly grasps his penis, fearing that it will shrink into his abdomen and thereby cause death. Family members and friends are frequently called upon to grasp the penis to prevent its retraction into the body. This can continue for several days; and insights from the Asian cultural context are intriguingly suggestive that, by contrast with the Euro-American tradition, the incidence might have a singularly close tie to cultural symbols and values in the patient's culture that relate to the body and its processes. For example, "semen anxiety," a widespread belief in eastern and southeastern Asian cultures that a sufficient supply of semen is vital in maintaining health, offers a possible predisposing explanatory mechanism for both etiology and behavioral form (Bernstein and Gaw 1990).

"Voodoo Death"

Also known as *hex*, *rootwork*, and numerous other terms (in Spanish, for example, *mal puesto*), belief in witchcraft—the putative power of other people to bring about misfortune, disability, and death through "spiritual" (here the outside analyst may read "psychological") mechanisms—has been universal in human history. The belief persists among people in both the developing and "developed" world, and clinicians not familiar with the nexus of perceptual, explanatory, and prognosticatory beliefs of a patient from, for example, a Hispanic or black background even in the contemporary United States may overlook important resources for optimal patient management (Wintrob 1973). One of the most critical of those resources is the patient's confidence in the scope of the healer's knowledge and his or her nonjudgmental acceptance of any kind of reported presenting symptom.

Among many black Americans a distinction is made between "natural" diseases (afflictions that can be expected as a result of "God's plan") and "unnatural" diseases (those representing disharmony, conflict with God's will, or evil) (Snow 1974). Witchcraft affliction—the "hex" that may lead to "voodoo death"—falls in the latter category and often but not exclusively manifests in the form of somatic disturbances. Because "unnatural" diseases are considered to emanate from evil powers (the "devil"), a physician suggesting therapy that does not explicitly take account of the patient's explanatory model can well be frustrated by noncompliance and failure in terms of successful outcome. In developing an effective treatment plan, it may therefore be critical that the clinician accept as "normal" the fearfulness expressed by the patient on finding that a piece of his or her clothing has been snipped off, or the obsessive need to pick up one's fingernail or hair clippings.

By all accounts, the problem is not exotic or rare: Snow (1974) estimates that "one third of the black patients treated at a Southern psychiatric center believe that they are the patients of witchcraft" (p. 85), and Snell (1967) has asserted that the affliction is found among whites as well. In a striking illustration of the power of belief, a case report of a clinical pathological conference from the Department of Pathology at the Johns Hopkins University Medical School speaks of a patient who had been admitted with shortness of breath and episodes of chest pain and syncope of 1 month's duration. She was thoroughly evaluated medically and, aside from relatively minor problems, "the physical findings were normal." Manifestly terrified, the patient had been "hexed" since birth and was doomed to die before her 23rd birthday. The patient did, in fact, die the day before her 23rd birthday (Clinico-Pathologic Conference 1967). Engel (1968, 1970) and Cappannari et al. (1975) have reviewed numerous other mortal events similarly triggered by psychopathological etiology.

Type A Behavior Pattern

An additional candidate being considered as a culture-bound syndrome is based on behavior not unfamiliar to Western physicians, the so-called Type A behavior pattern (Helman 1987), a condition that dramatically shows a disease process in relation to salient background cultural factors. In this instance, of course, the most striking pathology is cardiac in nature, although it is fostered by psychopathological dimensions.

Central definitional elements are the patient's perception of chronically struggling against time and the frustrations experienced in failing to achieve goals; hyperaggressiveness and ambition; "workaholism"; and impatience in interpersonal relations. Personal nonwork social and familial responsibilities usually suffer as a result of a single-minded focus on work, and long-term "follow-up studies have shown that individuals with this behavior pattern are about twice as likely to develop CHD [coronary heart disease] as other adults of similar age group without these traits" (Helman 1990, p. 260). Numerous commentators have pointed out the striking congruence of such a behavior pattern with the background cultural configuration that emphasizes acquisitiveness, "success orientation" (especially of a material nature), competition, and other values characteristic of an industrialist, capitalistic society.

Culture-Bound Syndromes: Semantic Considerations

Is there a common denominator in these examples that could point the way toward seeking a conceptual core that distinguishes the culture-bound syndromes from conventional syndromes? A semantic dissection of possible meanings suggests several hypotheses, any one of which could be the focus for discussion:

1. There is such disparity in empirical referents in discussion of the culture-bound syndromes, as well as in levels of abstraction and analysis used, that productive and comparative analysis is difficult at best, perhaps impossible. So why bother?

2. The syndromes are simply unusual and striking patterns of behavior found in other cultural contexts but are not necessarily pathological (an extreme cultural relativist's position).

3. There is no theoretical justification for establishing this or any other assemblage of syndromes as uniquely and singularly influenced by culture, and hence the American Psychiatric Association categories such as found in the newest version of the diagnostic manual, DSM-IV, are perfectly capable of assimilating them.

4. On the contrary, standard diagnostic categories (DSM type) are inadequate simply because they themselves are so culture-bound that they cannot conceptually accommodate the syndromes (seen, for example, in culturally structured conceptions of what is defined as "disease" or "disorder," or in a Eurocentric psychodynamic interpretation of behavior patterns).

5. However, in recognition of the need for categorization, perhaps appropriate expansion of the existing nosological and assessment framework could accommodate what have been called the culture-bound syndromes (modified from Hughes 1985a), or do we need an entirely new set of categories to prevent further metastasis of classificatory types and subtypes, which appears to be the inexorable trajectory of the current standard diagnostic systems? Compare *taxa*, which has been suggested as a term specifically useful for understanding the dynamics of the culture-bound syndromes (Simons 1985); or, for the entire range of psychiatric disorders, *prototypes* (Cantor et al. 1980), ideal types or *typifications* (Schwartz and Wiggins 1987a, 1987b), *levels of dysfunction* (Menninger 1963), or *ergasiatrics* (Meyer 1951). Although such an idea is appealing, as an anthropologist I am familiar with the ponderous nature of entrenched institutionalized schemata as well as social organizations; at this

point I doubt the feasibility—although not the advisability—of a radical over-haul toward a new (and, perhaps by virtue of that, more rational and less cum-bersome categorical scheme). In the current context, however, the assigned task appears primarily to be that of "tinkering" with an existing diagnostic system, and perhaps the most that can be hoped for is incorporation of lim-ited structural additions that will systematically infuse the general diagnostic schema with the concept of culture.

Possibly Defensible Bases for the Presumed Justification of a Culture-Bound Syndrome Label

How did the culture-bound syndromes get singled out for special categorization in the first place? What criteria would argue for such a special status? Are the defining features based on

- Peculiarities of the diagnostic process used?
- Deviant aspects of the etiology of such disorders?
- Unique meanings of the term *bound* when used with the term *culture* (i.e., culture-bound)?
- Special characteristics of the symptoms displayed?

Diagnosis

Simplistically, the diverse diagnostic labels found in discussions of these syndromes can be traced to two sources: 1) folk diagnosis—definitions and labels embedded in the particular cultural situation—and 2) professional "psychiatric" diagnosis by outsiders. Are the culture-bound syndromes only those deviant and/or "abnor-mal" behavior patterns labeled by folk and folk practitioners as pathological, whereas all other behavior patterns experienced by those with different language and con-ceptual structures are the province of professionals trained in the Western bio-medical tradition?

Is the basis for designation of a special class of purportedly culture-bound syndromes found in the generic peculiarities and cultural location of the diagnos-tic process the pathway by which one label or another gets applied? Perhaps. How-ever, one must remember that a native healer (often called a *diviner* when in this phase of the overall role) goes through a "diagnostic" process that contains many steps in patient assessment similar or analogous to those used by the Western psy-chiatrist (Opler 1936). In a typical example, the healer

1. Gathers data (often by talking with the family as well as the patient).
2. Brings to bear his or her own observations of the patient's life situation— including disturbances in interpersonal relations (witnessed first-hand because of living in the same community as the patient).
3. Names the "cause" of the disturbance, using familiar words and terms that are consonant with the patient's own beliefs about forces in the world—natural as well as supernatural—that bring disturbance and disaster.

4. Prescribes a regimen of treatment appropriate to the presumed cause (i.e., pharmacological, behavioral, interpersonal, and preventive in nature). Frequently some portion of the treatment consists of a ritual process in which the patient, surrounded by family (which provides the well-known power of social support in the therapeutic process), is exorcised of the pathological or malignant forces (Hughes 1990).

Although both "folk" healers and psychiatrists use drugs—and the ameliorative effects of folk psychopharmacology are impressive—what is perhaps the greatest of all "drugs"—the physician whose presence and activities can create a profound "placebo effect" (Balint 1957)—is a major differentiating feature. Some analysts suggest that this is better effectuated in folk medical procedures than in Western medicine (Frank 1973).

Etiology

One major difference, of course, between the diagnostic and evaluation process found in Western psychiatry ("divining"?) and that in many other groups is in the cultural construction of "cause," for example, spirits or a broken taboo on the one hand, and the psychodynamics of repression or stress-related coping responses on the other. The latter is a Western science mode, one in which the premises of the belief differ from those in a typical "folk" conceptual system. Presumably many of the same phenomena are the source for the different formulations, but different "explanatory models" are used by the patient and the clinician (Kleinman et al. 1978). However, is that sufficient reason to establish an entirely new and distinctive class of syndromes? (It reminds one of the difference between a purportedly all-case-relevant "biological" as contrasted to an all-case "psychosocial" explanation of schizophrenia, for example.)

Reflection on the Term *Bound*

Reflection on the term *bound* when used in the phrase *culture-bound* provides another hypothesis as to why these syndromes arguably might be set apart. Is the special discriminatory status of culture-bound syndromes, with their bizarre, "deviant" (from a Eurocentric perspective) ways of being deviant, based on social learning processes that are inherently different from what is found elsewhere? If so, this would mean that the socialization/enculturation process that provides the grounding and behavioral models for pathology in "folk" societies does not exist in industrialized societies. This is an indefensible proposition.

The failure to fully integrate the shaping effects of a person's cultural background into the clinical appraisal and to go behind such stereotypic masking labels as *culture bound* is to miss what may be the most essential element in the presentation of the clinical picture: namely, that many of the symptoms, the forms by which the "disorders" are expressed, are dynamically as well as pathoplastically derived from salient features of the patient's particular cultural setting, a setting that may be strikingly different from that of the therapist.

Therefore, beyond the person as the locus of the problem, there is the inverse question: what are the specific features of the environment, the cultural setting to which the symptoms putatively are bound? No person lives in a generalized, non-specific cultural environment, and the importance of this fact in a person's life is acknowledged in DSM-IV by the introduction of an axis to incorporate data on this feature (Axis IV-Psychosocial and environmental problems).

"Culture" as an analytic category is undifferentiated and devoid of specific content, yet no lived environment for any given person is the same as that for any-one else, which is recognized in DSM-IV. One must therefore be wary of the fallacy of the assumption of a homogeneous cultural environment. Cultural and social dimensions of the total environment are differentiated, as are physical and geographical features. There are flat, sandy plains; mountains and valleys; humid forests, and so forth, each of which places particular demands on the organism and structures the possibilities of response. Analogously, one must look to the specifics, the particulars, of a specific person's social as well as cultural environment, such as population density and varieties of ethnically defined peoples, as well as differentiated values, normatively dictated behavior patterns, role conflicts, prestige sources, and religious and cosmological assumptions, all of which act as a "software pro-gramming system" for so much of social behavior. Indeed, increasingly there seems to be emerging something of a consensus that the most useful meaning of *bound* lies in specifying the dynamic, interactive relations between specific value and situational emphases in a cultural scenario and the person's behavioral performance of themes provided by that cultural script.

Symptoms

In psychiatric disorders, as in any other type of disorder or disease, symptoms are the basis for formulation of a diagnosis, and these indicators of possible disordered functioning are manifested only in the particular person. Therefore, it is important to turn to some examples of such data—symptoms—commonly included under the rubric culture-bound syndromes and ask whether they are so markedly different in nature from symptoms of non–culture-bound syndromes that they can serve as useful shorthand markers for a discriminantly separate class of disorders.

To answer this, one must get as close as possible to data pertaining to the individual person who is experiencing symptoms and conceptualize disorders as disorders of the life process, not as "diseases" having autonomous ontological status apart from that specific life-process (Tempkin 1977; Williams 1956). In short, one must reframe the issue in terms of mutually reinforcing informational feedback loops between person and cultural environment, and not as static, fixed entities on either side of this interacting duality (Foss and Rothenberg 1987; von Foerster 1984).

For clarity in analysis, therefore, it is necessary to go to the level of "micro-detail" urged by Simons (1985); to Feinstein's (1977) "elementary level of first order observation and characterization of data" (p. 202) and "concentrate on raw evidence and on standardization of elements of evidence" (p. 205); or to Meyer's (1957) injunction to "cultivate a method of working with behavior data which is in principle identical with what ordinary common sense offers, only with an even more definite preference for concrete doings" (p. 93). As much as possible, such "first-order" observations must obviously also include a sense of the individual person's world; in the phrase of the biologist Adolf Portmann (1990), they must incorporate that quality of "inwardness, . . . which we can know from our conscious experience most intensely, and which can be measured . . . by those dimensions that are 'mechanisms for the articulation of meaning' . . . that in human beings are represented allegorically by language" (p. 458).

As desirable as such a course of action would be, the literature does not provide an extensive inventory of highly detailed case reports. Too often, discussions of the culture-bound syndromes are framed at a higher and therefore less specific level of analysis. For example, one frequently finds what in effect are dismissals of the analytic problem—that such disorders are "psychosomatic" or "hysterical" reactions. It would be useful, therefore, to review an assemblage of indicators at the level of observable symptoms to assess whether they are significantly different as a class from symptoms found in a conventional population. The question of where to find such an assemblage remains.

One collection useful in this regard is a glossary of such reputed disorders that contains 185 distinctive folk designations of such phenomena (Hughes 1985b). It includes isomorphic patterns found in various societies that other authors have asserted represent equivalences, reactions known by indigenous and therefore different names. It also presents typical symptom patterns for each such entry. In all, the total of 159 entries of designated terms or synonyms contains an aggregate total of 479 reported symptoms. (The total list contains 184 syndrome entries, but it collapses to 159 when alleged comparable syndromes are counted as one entry.) Grouped into rough working "diagnostic" categories, the symptoms listed reveal a familiar epidemiological profile in that they contain a variety of psychophysiological, psychoneurotic, behavioral, and somatic complaints. (See Appendix for the complete tally of reported symptoms phrased in the specific language used by authors of the various reports. Obviously it is a crude and incomplete epidemiology, but its overall contribution to the question is worthwhile as a first approximation.)

In comparing epidemiological findings in community populations elsewhere with the above glossary tally, it becomes clear that it is not the types of symptoms per se that sets these syndromes apart (Dohrenwend and Dohrenwend 1982). In fact, a particularly relevant study from Canada (Ross et al. 1990) noted that "dissociative disorders are common in the general population and decline with age" (p. 1547) and "5.0% of the general population scored above 30 on the Dissociative Experiences Scale, 8.5% above 25, and 12.8 [above 20]." Scores higher than 20 are indicative of a substantial number of dissociative experiences in an individual's life. The question arises, When are dissociative experiences pathological?

> The dissociative disorders, including multiple personality disorder, may be relatively common, with a prevalence that may be in the range of 5%–10% of the general population. If this prediction is borne out, it will be clear that a major form of psychopathology in North America has been almost entirely missed by most mental health professionals. Since dissociative experiences are common in the general population,

we suspect that dissociative symptoms may occur in a wide range of psychiatric disorders, just as anxiety and depression can be components of many different diagnostic entities. (Ross et al. 1990, p. 1547)

Conclusion

If it is not the disjunctive character of the symptoms, or the meaning of the term *bound*, or generic aspects of etiology, or essentials of the diagnostic process, then what is the criterion (or criteria) that could distinguish this putative class of disorders from conventional ones, and why should it be thus differentiated?

On the basis of the arguments developed in this chapter, it seems clear that there is no satisfactory essentialist or exclusionary definition for the label. It is time to discard unanalyzed use of such a classification and attempt a melding of the generics of this notion with familiar concepts.

Colophon

The clinical encounter itself can be the base for the therapist's learning not only about the patient but also about himself or herself. The therapist can use empathy, observation, and insight—insight into oneself as a step toward achieving the same end with the patient (when an analysis of cultural factors indicates its appropriateness, and it must be remembered that development of "insight" is not always acceptable, such as with traditional ethnic Chinese patients). Because a major therapeutic goal often is to enhance the patient's insight, why should not the same be applicable to the therapist? One can conduct a series of reflexive, self-analytic, introspective probes that question one's own assumptions about inferences and "cultural" formulations (Hughes 1991) or undertake what Stein (1982) has called a "clinical ethnography" (see also Ewing 1987).

The concept of "insight" is so taken for granted that there probably is no essential quarrel with Kolb's (1977) statement that it "refers to the patient's ability to observe and understand himself—the extent of his self-knowledge" (p. 213). Going beyond intensive introspective psychodynamic analyses of oneself acquired during the course of psychotherapeutic training, should not the same criterion be appropriate for the therapist with regard to a self-assessment of cultural sensitivity and ability to reframe cultural assumptions? To do so would better position the clinician to "concentrate upon the person and upon the individual clinical case" (Sabshin 1990) without the distortions introduced by interposed and conceptually incomplete diagnostic frameworks, thereby greatly facilitating the clinical goal of fully contextualizing the patient in his or her world as the basis for assessment and therapy.

References

American Psychiatric Association: Diagnostic and Statistical Manual of Mental Disorders, 3rd Edition, Revised. Washington, DC, American Psychiatric Association, 1987

American Psychiatric Association: Diagnostic and Statistical Manual of Mental Disorders, 4th Edition. Washington, DC, American Psychiatric Association, 1994

Balint M: The Doctor, His Patient and the Illness. New York, International Universities Press, 1957

Bernstein R, Gaw AC: Koro: proposed classification for DSM-IV. Am J Psychiatry 147:1670–1674, 1990

Bruner J: Acts of Meaning. Cambridge, MA, Harvard University Press, 1990

Cantor N, Smith ES, French RS, et al: Psychiatric diagnosis as prototype categorization. J Abnorm Psychol 89:181–193, 1980

Cappannari SC, Rau B, Abram HS, et al: Voodoo in the general hospital: a case of hexing and regional enteritis. JAMA 232:938–940, 1975

Caudill W, Doi LT: Interrelations of psychiatry, culture, and emotions in Japan, in Man's Image in Medicine and Anthropology. Edited by Galdston I. New York, International Universities Press, 1963, pp 374–421

Clinico-Pathologic Conference: Case presentation. Johns Hopkins Med J 120:186–199, 1967

Dohrenwend BP, Dohrenwend BS: Perspectives on the past and future of psychiatric epidemiology. Am J Public Health 72:1271–1279, 1982

Einstein A: Out of My Later Years. Westport, CT, Greenwood Press, 1950

Engel GI: A life-setting conducive to illness: the giving-up–given up complex. Ann Intern Med 69:293–300, 1968

Engel GL: Sudden death and the 'medical model' in psychiatry. Can Psychiatr Assoc J 15:527–537, 1970

Ewing KP: Clinical psychoanalysis as an ethnographic tool. Ethos 15(1):16–37, 1987

Feinstein AR: A critical overview of diagnosis in psychiatry, in Psychiatric Diagnosis. Edited by Rakoff VM, Stancer HC, Kedward HB. New York, Brunner/Mazel, 1977, pp 189–206

Foss L, Rothenberg K: The Second Medical Revolution: From Biomedicine to Infomedicine. Boston, MA, New Science Library (SHAMBHALA), 1987

Frank JD: Persuasian and Healing: A Comparative Study of Psychotherapy. Baltimore, MD, Johns Hopkins University Press, 1973

Frank JD, Frank JB: Persuasion and Healing: A Comparative Study of Psychotherapy, 3rd Edition. Baltimore, MD, Johns Hopkins University Press, 1991

Freedman AM, Kaplan HI, Sadock BJ: Comprehensive Textbook of Psychiatry—II. 2nd Edition, Vol 1. Baltimore, MD, Williams & Wilkins, 1975

Freedman AM, Kaplan HI, Sadock BJ: Modern Synopsis of Comprehensive Textbook of Psychiatry—II, 2nd Edition, Vol 2. Baltimore, MD, Williams & Wilkins, 1976

Garrison V: The 'Puerto Rican syndrome' in psychiatry and espiritismo, in Case Studies in Spirit Possession. Edited by Crapanzano V, Garrison V. New York, Wiley, 1977, pp 383–449

Griffith EEH: Psychiatry and culture, in The American Psychiatric Press Textbook of Psychiatry. Edited by Talbott J, Hales RE, Yudofsky SC. Washington, DC, American Psychiatric Press, 1988, pp 1097–1115

Guarnaccia PJ, Rubio-Stipec M, Canino G: Ataques de nervios in the Puerto Rican Diagnostic Interview Schedule: the impact of cultural categories on psychiatric epidemiology. Cult Med Psychiatry 13:275–295, 1989

Haldipur CV: The idea of 'cultural' psychiatry: a comment on the foundations of cultural psychiatry. Compr Psychiatry 21:206–211, 1980

Helman CG: Heart disease and the cultural construction of time: the Type A behaviour pattern as a western culture-bound syndrome. Soc Sci Med 25:969–979, 1987

Helman CG: Culture, Health and Illness: An Introduction for Health Professionals. London, England, Wright, 1990

Hill P, Murray R, Thorley A (eds): Essentials of Postgraduate Psychiatry. London, Grune & Stratton, 1986

Hughes CC: Culture-bound or construct-bound?: the syndromes and DSM-III, in The Culture-Bound Syndromes: Folk Illnesses of Psychiatric and Anthropological Interest. Edited by Simons RC, Charles C. Hughes. Dordrecht, The Netherlands, D Reidel, 1985a

Hughes CC: Glossary of 'culture-bound' or folk psychiatric syndromes, in The Culture-Bound Syndromes: Folk Illnesses of Psychiatric and Anthropological Interest. Edited by Simons RC, Hughes CC. Dordrecht, The Netherlands, D Reidel, 1985b, pp 469–505

Hughes CC: Ethnopsychiatry in medical anthropology: contemporary theory and method. Edited by Johnson TM, Sargent, CF. New York, Praeger, 1990, pp 132–148

Hughes CC: Culture in clinical psychiatry, in Culture, Ethnicity, and Mental Illness. Edited by Gaw AC. Washington, DC, American Psychiatric Press, 1991

Kaplan HI, Sadock BJ: Modern Synopsis of Comprehensive Textbook of Psychiatry—IV, 4th Edition. Baltimore, MD, Williams & Wilkins, 1985

Kaplan HI, Sadock BJ: Synopsis of Psychiatry: Behavioral Sciences and Clinical Psychiatry, 5th Edition. Baltimore, MD, Williams & Wilkins, 1988

Kendell RE, Zealley AK (eds): Companion to Psychiatric Studies, 3rd Edition. Edinburgh, Scotland, Livingstone, 1983

Kirmayer LJ: The place of culture in psychiatric nosology: taijin kyofusho and DSM-III-R. J Nerv Ment Dis 179:19–29, 1991

Kleinman M, Eisenberg L, Good B: Clinical lessons from anthropologic and cross-cultural research. Ann Intern Med 88:251–258, 1978

Kolb LC: Modern Clinical Psychiatry, 8th Edition. Philadelphia, PA, WB Saunders, 1977

Lazare A (ed): Outpatient Psychiatry: Diagnosis and Treatment. Baltimore, MD, Williams & Wilkins, 1989

Lin KM: Hwa-byung: a Korean culture-bound syndrome? Am J Psychiatry 140:105–107, 1983

Littlewood R, Lipsedge M: Culture-bound syndromes, in Recent Advances in Clinical Psychiatry. Edited by Granville K. New York, Livingstone, 1985, pp 105–142

Mayr E: The Growth of Biological Thought: Diversity, Evolution, and Inheritance. Cambridge, MA, Belknap Press of Harvard University Press, 1982

Menninger K: The Vital Balance: The Life Process in Mental Health and Illness. New York, Viking Press, 1963

Meyer A: The Collected Papers of Adolf Meyer, Vol III. Edited by Winters E. Baltimore, MD, Johns Hopkins University Press, 1951

Meyer A: Psychobiology—A Science of Man. Springfield, IL, Charles C Thomas, 1957

Murphy HBM: Transcultural psychiatry should begin at home. Psychol Med 7:369–371, 1977

Neill J: Adolf Meyer and American psychiatry today. Am J Psychiatry 137:460–464, 1980

Nicholi AM (ed): The New Harvard Guide to Psychiatry. Cambridge, MA, Belknap Press of Harvard University Press, 1988

Opler ME: Some points of comparison and contrast between the treatment of functional disorders by Apache shamans and modern psychiatric practice. Am J Psychiatry 92:1371–1387, 1936

Portmann A: On the uniqueness of biological research. J Med Philos 15:457–472, 1990

Prince R, Tcheng-Laroche F: Culture-bound syndromes and international disease classifications. Cult Med Psychiatry 11:3–19, 1987

Quine WVO: Word and Object. Cambridge, MA, MIT Press, 1960

Ross CA, Joshi S, Currie R: Dissociative experiences in the general population. Am J Psychiatry 147:1547–1552, 1990

Rutter M: Meyerian psychobiology, personality development, and the role of life experiences. Am J Psychiatry 143:1077–1087, 1986

Sabshin M: Turning points in twentieth-century American psychiatry. Am J Psychiatry 147:1267–1274, 1990

Schwartz MA, Wiggins OP: Diagnosis and ideal types: a contribution to psychiatric classification. Compr Psychiatry 28:277–291, 1987a

Schwartz MA, Wiggins OP: Typifications—the first step for clinical diagnosis in psychiatry. J Nerv Ment Dis 175(2):65–77, 1987b

Simons RC: Sorting the culture-bound syndromes, in The Culture-Bound Syndromes: Folk Illnesses of Psychiatric and Anthropological Interest. Edited by Simons RC, Hughes CC. Dordrecht, The Netherlands, D Reidel, 1985, pp 25–38

Simons RC, Hughes CC (eds): The Culture-Bound Syndromes: Folk Illnesses of Psychiatric and Anthropological Interest. Dordrecht, The Netherlands, D Reidel, 1985

Snell J: Hypnosis in the treatment of the 'hexed' patient. Am J Psychiatry 124:311–316, 1967

Snow L: Folk medical beliefs and their implications for care of patients: a review based on studies among black Americans. Ann Intern Med 81:82–96, 1974

Stein H: The ethnographic mode of teaching clinical behavioral science, in Clinically Applied Anthropology: Anthropologists in Health Science Settings. Edited by Chrisman N, Maretzki TW. Dordrecht, The Netherlands, D Reidel, 1982, pp 61–82

Swartz L: Anorexia nervosa as a culture-bound syndrome. Soc Sci Med 20:725–730, 1985

Talbott J, Hales RE, Yudofsky SC (eds): The American Psychiatric Press Textbook of Psychiatry. Washington, DC, American Psychiatric Press, 1988

Tempkin O: The scientific approach to disease: specific entity and individual sickness, in The Double Face of Janus and Other Essays in the History of Medicine. Edited by Tempkin O. Baltimore, MD, Johns Hopkins University Press, 1977, pp 441–455

von Foerster H: On constructing a reality, in The Invented Reality: How Do We Know What We Believe We Know? Contributions to Constructivism. Edited by Watzlawick P. New York, WW Norton, 1984, pp 41–61

Williams RJ: Biochemical Individuality: The Basis for the Genetotrophic Concept. New York, Wiley, 1956

Wintrob RM: The influence of others: witchcraft and rootwork as explanations of behavior disturbances. J Nerv Ment Dis 156:318–326, 1973

Appendix

A Symptom Distribution in Glossary of "Culture-Bound" Syndromes

Amnesia: 3

Anxiety (= worries = fearfulness = breathlessness): 17

Apathy (= withdrawal = silence = passivity = social isolation): 15

Autistic talk: 4

Behavior (aimless)= wandering, running away: 4

Behavior (angry, aggressive) = temper tantrum = rage: 18

Behavior (bizarre, unconventional, eccentric, anti-social)= taking off clothing, shouting "dirty" words, inappropriate shouting, dancing, hitting head against wall, screaming, jumping): 26

Behavior (homicidal): 7

Behavior (hyperactive, excited, or agitated)= excessive restlessness, acute nervous tension, tenseness: 12

Behavior (suicidal): 6

Behavior (violent) (= angry = tantrum = kicking): 4

Bewitched (feelings of being): 12

Compulsivity (= obsessiveness): 9

Concentration (= inability to concentrate; wandering thoughts): 3

Confusion (mental): 7

Convulsion (= convulsive): 17

Crawling (sensations somewhere in body): 2

Death (impending fear of): 2

Depression (= despair = brooding = sadness = melancholy): 14

Dissociative (= dissociated, trance, loss of consciousness): 15

Echolalia: 2

Echopraxia (= mimicry, imitation, including hypersuggestibility): 4

Epilepsy: 1

Fatigue (= exhaustion): 11

Fear of cold: 1

Fear of offending or meeting other people: 3

Fear of wind: 1

Fever: 2

Gastrointestinal symptoms (= abdominal complaints = diarrhea = vomiting = constipation): 34

General reference, undifferentiated: 15

Genito-urinary complaints: 7 [also sexual dysfunction (including fear of impotence): 1]

Ghosts (fear of): 2

Glossolalia (= neologisms, including nonsensical talk): 6

Guilt (feelings of): 2

Hallucination (visual, auditory)= fantasy = irrationality: 14

Headache: 4

Hysteria (= hysterical: 4 [general]; hysterical aphonia): 1
Immobility (= mutism, automatism, passivity [excessive]): 2
Irritability, quarrelsomeness: 4
Laughing (inappropriate): 2
Loss of appetite (= lack of appetite = anorexia): 16
Loss of weight (= weight loss): 3
Malaise: 3
Numbness in limbs: 3
Pain (chest): 2
Pain in various parts of body: 8
Palpitations (= tachycardia): 5
Panic: 2
Paralysis: 9
Paranoid or persecutory ideas: 5
Possessed (feelings of being): 7
Posturings and tics: 1
Pouting: 1
Psychophysiological (possibly) complaints [= somatization]
Psychotic symptoms [includes postpartum psychosis, puerperal, senile dementia, schizoid behavior]: 13
Respiratory complaints (= congestion = cough = breathlessness): 7
Sleeplessness (= inability to sleep, insomnia, nightmares, somnambulism): 18
Specific reference: conjunctivitis (1), pleurisy (1), pneumonia (1), tingling (1), feeling of being strangled (1), feeling of having been beaten (1), giddiness or dizziness (5), sensation of heat (1), sensation of burning in parts of body (4), feeling of tightness around head (1), tremors (1), trembling (3), shaking (1), skin rashes (1), eczema (1), itching (1), infection (1), miscarriage (believed caused by) (1), sweating (1), thumping in head (1), sore throat (1) staring: 1
Startle (= fright): 1
Suicidal thoughts: 4
Trauma (psychological); fright: 4
Unconsciousness: 8
Vision (= dimness of sight, "dazzling" of eyes): 7
Weakness (= loss of vitality = muscular weakness): 6
Weeping (= tearfulness = pouting): 7

Source. Developed from Hughes CC: Glossary of 'culture-bound' or folk psychiatric syndromes, in "The Culture-Bound Syndromes: Folk Illnesses of Psychiatric and Anthropological Interest." Edited by Simmons RC, Hughes CC. Dordrecht, The Netherlands, D Reidel 1985, pp 469–505.

Chapter 40

Cultural Comments on Culture-Bound Syndromes: I

Roland Littlewood, M.B., D.Phil.

The proposed association of DSM-IV (American Psychiatric Association 1994) and ICD-10 (World Health Organization 1991) argues for a system that will have some international validity. It is not grandiose to anticipate that our conclusions will be the subject of comment, scrutiny, and criticism in future years; the absence of psychiatrists from the Third World will be raised as a matter of considerable concern.

Are Culture-Bound Syndromes Redundant as a Category?

The issues are most salient in the case of those patterns historically described by psychiatrists and anthropologists as "culture-bound syndromes" (Simons and Hughes 1985): local, usually non-Western, patterns of experience, action, and belief that are regarded as pathological by observers but have not been slotted into the "classic" patterns recognized in the West. Whether we regard them as merely local variants of universal disorders or as discrete patterns that can be understood only through a "complete" knowledge of a particular society or, indeed, as essentially patterns of Western thinking developed in the political interaction between European and non-European elements (Littlewood 1991), how do we present this body of data for psychiatrists in any society? If, for instance (Option A), we rewrite the criteria for all DSM categories to demonstrate that they themselves are socially constructed, and that the observed "behaviors" are reflexively constituted by observer and subject in a particular context, or (Option B) we argue more modestly for a sixth, cultural axis, then grouping the familiar "culture-bound syndromes" in a separate category would probably be redundant, and we could redistribute our phenomena among the existing (albeit revised) DSM categories.

Against the preservation of culture-bound syndromes as a separate category (Option C), I would argue the following:

- All psychiatric patterns are to an extent culturally constituted.
- Certain patterns generally identified in Western societies in particular (such as bulimia nervosa) are already included as DSM-III-R (American Psychiatric Association 1987) and DSM-IV categories (Littlewood and Lipsedge 1987).
- With increasing recognition in general psychiatry that "disorders" are less objects of perception than explanatory and descriptive theories, themselves dependent on the culture of the observer and using local data that involve cultural shaping and recognition (perhaps "generation"), "culture" has become a recognized element within general psychiatric theory, and any "culture-bound" patterns will become less of an "afterthought" (see Chapter 39).
- The distinction between identifiable and discrete culture-bound syndromes is far from clear. Epidemiological and phenomenological data are generally lacking.
- The traditional culture-bound syndromes, which are largely the popular idea of transcultural psychiatry, are themselves likely to disappear in an increasingly homogeneous world culture.

A reason for preserving the category of culture-bound syndromes is that psychiatry is not ready to take on cultural context to the extent of providing a true international system of classification; the form of DSM-IV exported to the Third World will inevitably be Eurocentric, leaving the psychiatrists in the developing world to fit local patterns into this schema as best they can, thus confirming the whole classificatory system as one that emphasizes individual (biological and psychological) differences as the essential determinants of psychopathology. Keeping the list of culture-bound syndromes would be some small guard against this.

Option C: Representation of the Culture-Bound Syndromes as a Separate Category in an Appendix

This is the easiest option at this stage. This new DSM category should be considered provisional, and pending more detailed epidemiological and the multivariate analysis of the defining criteria (social, psychological, and physiological), the culture-bound syndromes could eventually be reallocated to new, existing, or modified categories in the body of the text. The appendix could

- Be titled "Syndromes Usually Specific to Particular Societies That May Come to Medical Attention and That May Require Further Study."
- Have a short introduction detailing the history and epistemological and diagnostic problems of the syndromes.
- Emphasize the paucity of epidemiological data but that further work may well include most of these syndromes in a modified form of the existing DSM

categories; offer examples of how this might be done (e.g., amok in impulse control disorders, tabanka in dysthymia, latah perhaps in some developmental category).

- Note the problem of distinguishing actually observable behavior-experience complexes from local ideas: for example, a single local explanation (say, spirit possession) may encompass a variety of patterns from the observer's point of view (dissociation state, rite of passage, or simply an explanation of misfortune); conversely, the observer's category (dissociation state) may be locally understood in diverse ways (shamanic vision quest, voodoo possession) (Littlewood and Lipsedge 1985).

- Emphasize that local understandings may not necessarily place the pattern in some category of "sickness" analogous to physical illness but that the reason these are potentially of psychiatric interest is because observers have certainly done this.

- Decide which are the most significant syndromes on which to carry out epidemiological and phenomenological studies (for which Hughes has provided some appropriate ground rules in Chapter 39) so as to demonstrate differences from, or approximate identity with, existing DSM categories, and then to press for inclusion there or else modify the DSM category. (We cannot, of course, presume that the addition of Third World data will inevitably lead to a broadening of any DSM category: we should expect that in certain instances we will contribute to narrowing them.) Clearly this will be a major undertaking, and we should argue that a continuing working group is set up under the auspices of the World Health Organization or another competent body to refine these questions, seek funds, and organize appropriate field research. It might be appropriate to start with one well-known culture-bound syndrome and devise an appropriate methodology of comparison.

Conclusion

The three options are not altogether exclusive. We may plausibly make a case for

- A "cultural" statement for DSM-IV, providing clinical, statistical, and research advice for the psychiatrist faced with local data that do not "fit" DSM categories, perhaps even a handbook called *The International Use of DSM-IV.*
- The criteria for a "cultural axis," possibly an optional one, or for "cultural paragraphs" for each existing category.
- Providing evidence now for including certain of our culture-bound syndromes in certain existing DSM categories (or slightly modified forms of them).
- Providing an appendix of culture-bound syndromes (as in Option C).
- Setting up a continuing working group (as in Option C) to press for a more radical "cultural" conception of all disorders but also to provide an appropriate body of information to argue the uniqueness or generality of any syndrome.

Glossary

Culture-bound syndrome: The patterns recognized as such by traditional transcultural psychiatry (*latah*, *amok*, etc).

Local: The socially specific context in which the pattern is developed, recognized, and perhaps resolved (cf. emic).

Observed: The universalizing attempt, essentially Western (cf. etic).

References

American Psychiatric Association: Diagnostic and Statistical Manual of Mental Disorders, 3rd Edition, Revised. Washington, DC, American Psychiatric Association, 1987

American Psychiatric Association: Diagnostic and Statistical Manual of Mental Disorders, 4th Edition. Washington, DC, American Psychiatric Association, 1994

Littlewood R: Against pathology: the "new psychiatry" and its critics. Br J Psychiatry 159:696–702, 1991

Littlewood R, Lipsedge M: Culture-bound syndromes, in Recent Advances in Clinical Psychiatry, 5th Edition. Edited by Granville-Grossman K. Edinburgh, Scotland, Livingstone, 1985

Littlewood R, Lipsedge M: The butterfly and the serpent: culture, psychopathology and biomedicine. Cult Med Psychiatry 11:289–335, 1987

Simons RC, Hughes CC (eds): The Culture-Bound Syndromes: Folk Illnesses of Psychiatric and Anthropological Interest. Dordrecht, The Netherlands, D Reidel, 1985

World Health Organization: International Classification of Diseases, 10th Revision. Geneva, Switzerland, World Health Organization, 1991

Chapter 41

Cultural Comments on Culture-Bound Syndromes: II

Ronald M. Wintrob, M.D.

In Chapter 39, Hughes begins his analysis of psychiatry's and psychiatrists' encounters with the culture-bound syndromes with a lament: the encounters have been very difficult to handle. As a consequence, Hughes suggests, the subject has been largely overlooked, ignored, and set aside in the psychiatric literature. No diagnostic category existed in DSM-III-R and ICD-9—called *culture-bound syndrome* (American Psychiatric Association 1987; World Health Organization 1977). Perhaps the reason is that it would be too daunting an enterprise to categorize all the culture-specific conditions that have been described by physicians, social scientists, and other observers in the course of fieldwork all over the world. The listing of emic categories relevant to psychiatry would be far more exhaustive than the "sampler" Hughes includes in his review. Hughes includes six fairly typical examples of culture-bound syndromes: three from Asian cultural settings, two from Latin America, and one from the Caribbean. He also includes an unexpected emic case from North America and Western Europe: Type A behavior. By including Type A behavior, Hughes brings into focus the implicit ethnocentric bias of the term *culture-bound syndromes*—that is, these syndromes are thought of as strange and unusual phenomena that occur in preindustrial societies and are likely to steadily decrease as those societies evolve as part of the contemporary technological global community. By including Type A behavior as a culture-bound syndrome, Hughes also makes us recognize that within an emic perspective, these conditions are neither strange nor exotic but common and easily understood in the context of our everyday behavior.

Hughes's sampler includes brief descriptions of each condition. However, he does not attempt to categorize each one according to DSM-III-R or DSM-IV criteria. Instead, he addresses what he calls the "conceptual core" of culture-bound syndromes, discussing the cultural significance of diagnosis and etiology and of the clinical appraisal of presenting symptoms.

Hughes considers that the failure to fully integrate the shaping effects of a person's cultural background into the clinical appraisal and go behind such stereotypic masking labels as "culture bound" is to miss what may be the most essential element in the presentation of the clinical picture: namely, that many of the symptoms, the forms by which the "disorders" are expressed, are dynamically as well as pathoplastically derivative from salient features of the patient's particular cultural setting, a setting that may be very different from that of the therapist.

Simons and Hughes (1985) have been working to bring some conceptual and diagnostic order to this subject for a number of years. In *The Culture Bound Syndromes: Folk Illnesses of Psychiatric and Anthropological Interest,* they proposed to categorize these syndromes, according to manifest behavior or core symptomatology, as "taxons." This approach allowed for phenomena that occur in widely different cultural settings to be coherently grouped together, for example, in the startle response taxon (Simons 1985). This kind of grouping has several features that are heuristically appealing. First, it allows for emic phenomena to be grouped together under etic descriptive labels, thereby reducing the number of separate categories of phenomena to manageable proportions. Second, it allows for inclusion of "cultural orphans," that is, cases of typical culture-bound syndrome presentations occurring in a cultural setting strikingly different from the one(s) in which the syndrome is best known; examples would be a startle response syndrome in a Euro-American, a genital retraction syndrome such as koro affecting a Dane, or perhaps the phenomena characteristic of bulimia nervosa affecting a young Samoan woman. Third, it encourages consideration of possible underlying etiological factors that are generalizable and not culture specific, etiological factors that could be as much neurobiological as sociocultural.

Hughes has previously addressed the issue of how to incorporate the richness and complexity of culture-bound syndromes into cross-culturally useful and scientifically valid diagnostic categories (Hughes 1991). He does so again in Chapter 39, cautioning that the diagnostician should not try to squeeze the local meaning out of the primary data in the interests of conforming to an established system that has not exhaustively investigated the entire range of empirical and theoretically important possibilities.

I believe Hughes is justified in pointing out psychiatry's and psychiatrists' wish to avoid comprehensive assessment and classification of the numerous strange-sounding, difficult-to-comprehend conditions known as culture-bound syndromes. Critics point to the great variability and uneven quality of case descriptions, the possible confounding factors of concurrent illnesses (e.g., chronic infectious disease), and the lack of systematic prospective and outcome studies that could help identify the core features of distinct syndromes, as well as how they compare cross-culturally.

One can readily agree with Hughes's suggestion that greater cultural sensitivity among clinicians would benefit their patients and themselves. It seems reasonable and feasible to incorporate in psychiatric resident training programs the kinds of fundamental approaches to enhancing cultural knowledge and sensitivity described by Foulks (1980), Kendrick et al. (1988), and Yager et al. (1989).

However, we are still left with the need—the obligation—to categorize symptoms, to diagnose, so that we can offer relief from distressing conditions. We therefore must account for culture-bound syndromes in terms of Axis I categorization. We must do this in addition to giving greater emphasis, as Hughes proposes, to the specific cultural influences on Axes IV and V.

The very diversity of the culture-bound syndromes requires consideration of the ageless issue of defining normality, or at least drawing its boundaries. I will start with that consideration. I will then draw on some of my own clinical experience as a cultural psychiatrist practicing in contexts in which culture-bound syndromes are very commonly encountered. This will enable me to review some of the characteristics of culture-bound syndromes and use one or two of them as paradigms for purposes of categorization. I follow this review with some suggestions for accommodating these conditions within Axis I categories.

Considerations Concerning Normal and Abnormal

DSM-III-R contains a caveat about the need for cultural sensitivity in applying constructs—including diagnoses—from the cultural context familiar to the clinician to other contexts that are less familiar or unfamiliar. However, we need to be reminded that normal behavior is both intraculturally and cross-culturally variable and changes over time. In our own time and in the "mainstream" cultural context of the United States, such conditions as homosexuality, obesity, anorexia (nervosa), posttraumatic stress disorder, conversion hysteria, gambling, abortion, nicotine use, and voyeurism raise the enduring, emotionally intense, and hotly debated issues about what our culture in this century or generation or psychohistorical moment considers to be normal, eccentric, deviant, dangerous, illegal, and/or pathological. In recognition of the complexity of these issues, DSM-IV (American Psychiatric Association 1994) attempts to avoid moral judgment and stick to observable and replicable data, leading to categories such as alcohol use disorders, with subcategories for intoxication, dependence, abuse, and withdrawal. How are we to judge whether repeated binge drinking episodes or hallucinogenic drug use among members of some Native American tribes, occurring in the context of religious ritual, represents normal, excessive, deviant, or pathological behavior, or whether trance behavior and spirit possession, so widespread in Brazil (i.e., *candomble*) and in the Caribbean (i.e., *voodoo* and *obeah*) are normal, deviant, or pathological?

A Cultural Psychiatrist's Clinical Experience

During the year I was in Laos and the 2 years I practiced in Liberia in West Africa, most of the patients I treated presented with symptoms that they, as well as their families and communities, attributed to spirit possession or to witchcraft. Witchcraft was the term used as a generic referent for what anthropologists would define as malign magic, or more specifically, sorcery: the belief that one has been victimized by an angry and envious relative, friend, or other member of one's group (see Wintrob 1973b for a more detailed description). Patients in Liberia were from many tribes from all over the country. They often presented with florid disturbances of behavior, thinking, and affect and could readily be diagnosed as psychotic. However, regardless of how intense the symptoms were, it was much more difficult to characterize those patients as schizophrenic on the basis of a single episode or even recurrent episodes of acutely disturbed behavior, precisely because of the complicating factor of witchcraft beliefs. The categories of schizoaffective or schizophreniform disorders could more easily accommodate the inherent difficulties of categorization for the short term. Ultimately, treatment outcome and long-term observation of many of these patients—those who were able or felt the need to remain in contact with the treatment center—made it more possible to distinguish between acute psychotic episodes, described by Collomb (1973) as *boufée delirante,* and schizophrenia (chronic, undifferentiated). However, there were other concurrent medical conditions that could and often did complicate—even confound— psychiatric diagnosis. For example, both anemia and malaria were endemic in West Africa. Routine admission laboratory testing for both conditions often confirmed the presence of one or both disorders in patients presenting with psychotic symptoms. However, there was no clear correlation between the severity of these complicating medical conditions and the severity or duration of the psychotic episode (see Wintrob 1973a for details).

Liberian tribes that were in close, prolonged contact with American-Liberian settlements along the coast and were influenced by active missionary movements revealed in their presenting symptomatology syncretic beliefs involving both Christian and animist traditions. Likewise did many of the nominally Christian American-Liberians, who shared many traditional tribal beliefs in hex, malign magic, and witchcraft, reflecting syncretic beliefs of the 19th-century southeastern United States plantation culture, which in turn reflected the influence of Caribbean voodoo and traditional West African beliefs in supernatural influence.

Tribes living in the interior of Liberia were strongly influenced by centuries of contact with the Muslim populations and traditions of the Saharan region and Arab North Africa. Consequently, their clinical presentations revealed the somatic preoccupations, and especially the dramatic neuromuscular movement disorders (e.g., tics, dystonia, pseudoparalysis), that have been well documented by Bennegadi (1990) among migrants from the Maghreb to France. A central feature of the clinical presentation of these Liberian tribal patients was their explanation of their condition as a result of the influence of malevolent spirits called *jinns* or *genii* (Wintrob 1966), terms that reflect Anglicization and Europeanization ("genies") of commonly encountered Muslim, Arabic beliefs in possession by troublesome spirits called *Djinnoun* (Bennegadi 1990). Although the "explanatory models" (Kleinman 1980) of patients from these diverse Liberian tribes were different, the salient point is that the presenting clinical features were very similar. Furthermore, such presentations were, in turn, strikingly similar to those in patients I encountered in Connecticut years later, who attributed their disturbed behavior to the influence of hex or "rootwork" (Ness and Wintrob 1981; Snow 1974).

The impact of cultural change in Liberia also had great importance in clinical practice. Urbanization, detribalization, and movement toward a technological, industrial society resulted in great value being placed on educational achievement. Students were invested with the hopes of their families. Through their accomplishments, status, prestige, and substantial economic advantages were expected to accrue to the family and to the tribe. Little wonder, then, that highly achieving students could become fearful of failure or that some in Nigeria would attribute their chronic fatigue, distractibility, recurrent headache, and other symptoms to "brain fag" (Prince 1964), whereas others in Liberia would attribute those symptoms, and more severe ones, too, to envious fellow students or relatives putting a hex on them to prevent them from succeeding and thereby giving a competitive advantage to the perpetrators or the perpetrators' family members (Wintrob 1967, 1973b)

Spirit possession disorders I have encountered in Liberia often begin with the spirit revealing itself in a dream that precedes the appearance of any disturbed or disturbing behavior—sometimes by a long time. The spirit manifests itself as the special protector of the subject, promising success in the subject's financial, interpersonal, and/or educational aspirations. Only later does the subject report demands made by the spirit that progressively limit the subject's initiative, interests, and activities and lead to manifest disturbances in thinking, affect, and behavior. This cycle can last months or even years. The prototypical spirit cited by Liberian patients was called *mammy water,* representing a syncretism of European beliefs in water spirits (i.e., the Lorelei myth and the mermaid myth) and traditional animistic tribal beliefs about benign, mischievous, and malevolent spirits inhabiting river banks and marshy areas (Wintrob 1970).

Culture-Bound Syndromes: Spirit Possession as a Paradigm

My clinical experience in Liberia convinced me that culture-bound syndromes are common in societies in which traditional tribal organization persists and also in conditions of culture change involving protracted education, urbanization, and loosening of traditional extended family roles and obligations. Adoption of urban social organization or of Christian or Muslim religious participation does not lead to incorporation of a Western, scientific worldview. (Neither has our own society universally or consistently abandoned supernatural or unscientific explanatory beliefs about misfortune, including those concerning illness.) Because spirit possession remains a very common phenomenon worldwide, it can serve as a useful paradigm for analysis as a prototype culture-bound syndrome—that is, if we can adequately take account of the manifestations of spirit possession that clinicians encounter, we can categorize this condition in etic terms compatible with DSM-IV Axis I classification.

In the same way that limited alcohol use may be a normal behavior at an American cocktail party, so, too, can spirit possession beliefs be normal in the particular cultural context that I have described in Liberia. However, spirit possession can lead to unusual, more deviant behavior characterized by preoccupation; distractibility; irritability; social withdrawal; and neglect of personal, familial, and occupational responsibilities. The condition can progress to obviously psychotic manifestations of thinking, affect, and behavior, with the spirit demanding that the subject act in ways that are dangerous for the individual and others with whom the subject interacts. At various points in this progression, the condition could be comprehensively categorized as culturally normative, not pathological, and proceed in the direction of a dissociative disorder. As the severity of the behavioral manifestations of dissociation increases, the condition can be more accurately described as a psychotic disorder.

This categorization seems to make the best clinical sense of the clinical data and allows for Axis I diagnosis. It also compels the clinician to carefully take into account all of the essential components of Axis IV diagnosis (psychosocial stressors). The clinician could also determine the Axis V global assessment of functioning, using the rating periods for current functioning and functioning during the previous year. These determinations would be based on observable data resulting from the subject's, and relatives' or friends', accounts of the extent to which preoccupation with spirit possession has interfered with normal functioning in that specific cultural context.

At this point, we must consider once again the appropriateness of Axis I diagnostic categories.

Toward a Culturally Sensitive Axis I Categorization of Culture-Bound Syndromes

Just as tuberculosis can produce quite different symptom clusters depending on the organ systems predominantly infected by the bacilli, as well as the extent and duration of that infection, so, too, can spirit possession become manifest as different types and severity of presenting symptoms, with different behavioral consequences. Several of the DSM-IV Axis I diagnostic categories seem to fit the need quite readily. Brief psychotic disorder seems very appropriate for the more severe, psychotic manifestations of possession states, such as those I have described in Liberia, as well as for cases of sorcery and witchcraft victimization. At the less severe, less symptomatic end of the scale, the dissociative disorder category of acute stress disorder seems to be a good fit.

However, neither the anxiety disorder categories nor the adjustment disorder diagnosis seems to adequately account for the low-intensity, nonpsychotic manifestations of possession states and similar phenomena that can go on for months or years without leading to personality deterioration or significant impairment in usual psychosocial functioning. It seems, therefore, that one additional diagnostic category is needed in the anxiety disorders section, because neither generalized anxiety disorder nor posttraumatic stress disorder seems to do justice to the clinical data. The additional category could be called *chronic stress disorder*. It seems more consistent with the chronic anxiety-engendering nature of protracted spirit possession or malign magic victimization beliefs and their manifest symptomatology to include chronic stress disorder as an anxiety disorder rather than a dissociative disorder.

In the meantime, I believe that adherence to the principles outlined in Chapter 39, and in this commentary engendered by it, will bring clinicians closer to fulfilling their aspirations to become culturally sensitive therapists for their ethnically and culturally diverse patients.

References

American Psychiatric Association: Diagnostic and Statistical Manual of Mental Disorders, 3rd Edition, Revised. Washington, DC, American Psychiatric Association, 1987

American Psychiatric Association: Diagnostic and Statistical Manual of Mental Disorders, 4th Edition. Washington, DC, American Psychiatric Association, 1994

Bennegadi R: "Khala" among Tunisian migrants to France. Paper presented at the annual meeting of The Society for the Study of Psychiatry and Culture, Timberline, OR, October 1990

Collomb H: L'avenir de la psychiatrie en Afrique. Psychopathologie Africaine 9:343–370, 1973

Foulks EF: The concept of culture in psychiatric residency education. Am J Psychiatry 137:811–816, 1980

Hughes CC: Culture in clinical psychiatry, in Culture, Ethnicity, and Mental Illness. Edited by Gaw AC. Washington, DC, American Psychiatric Press, 1991

Kendrick EA, Reid K, Lomax JW: Cultural psychiatry education during psychiatric residency. Journal of Psychiatric Education 12(2):90–101, 1988

Kleinman A: Patients and Healers in the Context of Culture: An Exploration of the Borderland Between Anthropology, Medicine and Psychiatry. Berkeley, University of California Press, 1980

Ness R, Wintrob RM: Folk healing: a description and synthesis. Am J Psychiatry 138:1477–1481, 1981

Prince R: Indigenous Yoruba psychiatry, in Magic, Faith, and Healing. Edited by Kiev A. New York, Free Press of Glencoe, 1964

Simons RC: Sorting the culture-bound syndromes, in The Culture-Bound Syndromes: Folk Illnesses of Psychiatric and Anthropological Interest. Edited by Simons RC, Hughes CC. Dordrecht, The Netherlands, D Reidel, 1985

Simons RC, Hughes CC (eds): The Culture-Bound Syndromes: Folk Illnesses of Psychiatric and Anthropological Interest. Dordrecht, The Netherlands, D Reidel, 1985

Snow L: Folk medical beliefs and their implications for care of patients: a review based on studies among black Americans. Ann Intern Med 81:82–96, 1974

Wintrob RM: Psychosis in association with possession by genii in Liberia. Psychopathologie Africaine 2:249–258, 1966

Wintrob RM: A study of disillusionment: depressive reactions of Liberian students returning from advanced training abroad. Am J Psychiatry 123:1593–1598, 1967

Wintrob RM: Mammy water: folk beliefs and psychotic elaborations in Liberia. Can Psychiatr Assoc J 15:143–157, 1970

Wintrob RM: Malaria and the acute psychotic episode. J Nerv Ment Dis 156:306–317, 1973a

Wintrob RM: The cultural dynamics of student anxiety: report from Liberia. Psychopathologie Africaine 9:267–283, 1973b

World Health Organization: International Classification of Diseases, 9th Revision, Geneva, Switzerland, World Health Organization, 1977

Yager J, Chang C, Karno M, et al: Teaching transcultural psychiatry. Academic Psychiatry 13(3):164–171, 1989

Chapter 42

Nosological Comments on Culture-Bound Syndromes

Harold A. Pincus, M.D.

ughes presents in Chapter 39 an extraordinary, useful analysis of the issues for including so-called culture-bound syndromes in DSM-IV (American Psychiatric Association 1994) from both a conceptual and a substantive perspective. In considering the inclusion of these syndromes in DSM-IV, we approached this issue in two ways that incorporate assumptions both contested and suggested by Hughes:

- We considered these syndromes as new diagnostic categories, not unlike any other proposals for such categories that have emanated from researchers and clinicians inside and outside of the DSM process.
- We also sought to elaborate issues of cultural presentation and the need for the assessment of ethnic and cultural issues in psychiatric diagnosis throughout the manual.

As discussed by my colleagues and I (Pincus et al. 1992), there are potential benefits and risks in all proposals for new diagnostic categories. We asked each of the DSM-IV Work Groups to explicitly consider these benefits and risks and to evaluate the available empirical data that might be relevant to these issues.

Furthermore, we asked that the Work Groups establish a relatively high threshold for recommending the entry of new diagnoses into DSM-IV. So-called culture-bound syndromes have been explicitly included among the more than 100 new categories that have been suggested for inclusion in DSM-IV and are assessed by the same process applied to non–culture-bound syndromes.

In the early stages of the development of DSM-IV, we held a methods conference aimed in part at specifying the criteria to be applied in making decisions about adding or subtracting categories. Participants agreed that it was important to have information on how a proposed diagnostic category would facilitate communication and clinical utility, reliability, and descriptive validity of the category. Especially important is the examination of external validators that include antecedent validators (e.g., demographic characteristics, premorbid personality, family history, and precipitating factors), concurrent validators (e.g., biological, physiological, and psychological variables), and predictive validators (e.g., diagnostic consistency; social, occupational, and other follow-up variables; and treatment response). Proposals for possible incorporation of new diagnostic categories (non–culture-bound as well as culture-bound) will require systematic, objective, and comprehensive reviews of the literature on all of these factors (Widiger et al. 1990). Many of the criteria explicitly discussed by Hughes are incorporated among the factors listed above.

At the same time, we also tried to integrate consideration of ethnic and cultural issues throughout the manual by

- Expanding the discussion of the role of culture and ethnicity in the evaluation of psychiatric patients in the Introduction to the manual.
- Including within the text for each of the disorders in the DSM-IV manual a section discussing cultural presentations (as well as variable age and gender presentations) of the disorders.
- Having persons familiar with cultural issues review the criteria suggested for each disorder with regard to potential misinterpretation and misapplication of the criteria.
- Including reviews of cross-cultural issues in the *DSM-IV Sourcebook* (Widiger et al., in press).

Cultural Approaches in DSM-IV

Hughes also makes four very useful, specific suggestions for disorders that have been labeled culture-bound syndromes:

1. Emphasizing use of "atypical" or "not otherwise specified" categories. Clinicians have informed us that many patients do not fully meet criteria for specific disorders, and they often feel pressured to put "round pegs in square holes." Not otherwise specified categories have always been available for use by clinicians in these circumstances. The "Use of the Manual" chapter in DSM-IV is more encouraging of the use of these categories. We have also included, where appropriate, so-called culture-bound syndromes as examples in the unspecified categories.
2. Including culture in the index, along with some direction about how the concept should be used in the clinical process. In addition, we have included, as an appendix, a glossary of culture-bound syndromes that includes a brief definition of each term.
3. Including a "cultural axis." Although there was an initial discussion regarding a cultural axis, there has not been a formal and plausible proposal for such a cultural axis. Instead a Cultural Formulation Outline has been included.
4. Expanding training of clinicians on basic concepts of cultural awareness. It is important to distinguish between DSM-IV as a tool for the communication of

the results of a clinician's assessment of a given patient from the whole process of psychiatric evaluation. The National Institute of Mental Health Conference on Culture and Diagnosis in Pittsburgh, this book, and the many reviews related to culture and ethnicity in the DSM-IV Sourcebook (Mezzich et al., in press), all constitute major elements of a strategy to improve the education of clinicians and their awareness of cultural factors. They are not, however, a substitute for training of psychiatrists and other health and mental health professionals. We can never hope to include in a DSM manual everything that one must know in order to do a competent psychiatric evaluation. Yet, the "cultural" innovations for DSM-IV are very much in keeping with the spirit of what Hughes suggests.

References

American Psychiatric Association: Diagnostic and Statistical Manual of Mental Disorders, 4th Edition. Washington, DC, American Psychiatric Association, 1994

Mezzich JE, Kleinman A, Fabrega H, et al (eds): Cultural Issues Section, in DSM-IV Source Book, Vol 2. Edited by Widiger T, Frances A, Pincus HA, et al. Washington, DC, American Psychiatric Press (in press)

Pincus HA, Frances AJ, Davis WW, et al: DSM-IV and new diagnostic categories: holding the line on proliferation. Am J Psychiatry 149:112–117, 1992

Widiger TA, Frances AJ, Pincus HA, et al: DSM-IV literature reviews: rationale process and limitations. Journal of Psychopathology and Behavior Assessment 12:189–202, 1990

Widiger TA, Frances AJ, Pincus HA, et al (eds): DSM-IV Source Book, Vol 2. Washington, DC, American Psychiatric Press (in press)

Section XI

Multiaxial Issues

Chapter 43

Culture and Multiaxial Diagnosis

Juan E. Mezzich, M.D., Ph.D.

Multiaxial diagnosis represents a challenging reconceptualization of the diagnostic formulation. As contrasted with the traditional disease entity approach, it involves a schematic and comprehensive statement designed to portray more thoroughly and effectively the patient's condition, to facilitate comprehensive treatment planning, and to maximize prognosis of multiple outcomes. Codification of such a statement is required to respond to the ever-growing need for efficient processing of key clinical information. The informational richness and the scaling flexibility afforded by the multiaxial approach provide an opportunity for describing more penetratingly the clinical realities of the patients to be served.

With regard to the need to enhance the cultural sensitivity and meaningfulness of a diagnostic system, the multiaxial approach constitutes both a challenge and an opportunity. As a more complex statement than the single-label categorical diagnosis, it presents greater demands for appraising the cultural suitability of its various components for the populations of interest. For the case of DSM-IV, one does not need to leave the borders of the United States to realize the intricacy of the requirements presented by multicultural diversity, highlighted by the substantial presence of Native American, Asian American, African American, and Latin American populations (Mezzich et al. 1992). In this increasingly interconnected world, the flow of migrants and refugees and the realities of international travel and communication add to the challenge.

In this chapter I present a synopsis of the literature on cultural and the multiaxial approach. The chapter is broadly organized by comments on the international roots and overall architecture of the multiaxial model and on key individual axes, particularly those contained in DSM-IV (American Psychiatric Association 1994).

International Grounds

To appreciate the potentialities of the multiaxial approach, one must consider its historical roots and trajectory.

The first clearly multiaspectual formulations of standard psychiatric diagnosis involving the separation of syndrome and causation were those separately proposed by Essen-Möller and Wohlfahrt (1947) in Sweden and Lecomte et al. (1947) in France. Shortly after that, Bilikiewicz (1951) in Poland and Leme Lopes (1954) in Brazil independently designed triaxial diagnostic schemata encompassing axes on general psychiatric syndromes, personality conditions, and etiopathological constellations.

In more recent decades, at least 17 general psychiatric multiaxial schemata have been published. In all, 11 different countries spanning three continents have been the sources of multiaxial proposals; this does not include those diagnostic schemata focusing on just one psychiatric disorder or situation. Particularly noteworthy have been the classifications of child psychiatric disorders developed by Rutter and colleagues (1969, 1975a, 1975b) in Great Britain (which used the term *multiaxial* for the first time), and the pentaxial systems structuring DSM-III, DSM-III-R (American Psychiatric Association 1980, 1987), and DSM-IV. These diagnostic systems explicated by Williams (1985) have extended worldwide the visibility of the multiaxial model (Mezzich 1987).

The World Health Organization, in collaboration with members of the World Psychiatric Association Section on Classification, Diagnostic Assessment and Nomenclature, started to design some years ago a multiaxial schema for ICD-10 (Mezzich 1988). The final architecture includes three axes: I, Clinical Diagnoses; II, Disabilities; and III, Contextual Factors (Mezzich 1992; Janca et al., in press).

Cultural Considerations for the Design of Multiaxial Systems

The design of multiaxial systems involves decisions on the number, types, and content of their constitutive axes as well as on the scaling principles (categorical or dimensional) and specific measurement tools to be used.

Regarding the conceptualization of the content of a multiaxial schema, it is important to consider axes prevalently included in published multiaxial systems. This may accord a certain degree of convergent or face validity to the selected axes. Further enriching such conceptualization would be broader considerations such as normality or health as contrasted with pathology or illness (Kastrup and Wig 1986; Perales et al. 1989; Sabshin 1989). In fact, some of the most powerful influences that have emerged as crucial for extending the depth and reach of the multiaxial diagnostic model correspond to comprehensive concepts of health status. These views identify physical health, mental condition, functioning levels, and quality of life as key elements of health status assessment. Each of these elements, in increasing order, is influenced by cultural factors (Patrick et al. 1985). Consequently, assessment of individuals from ethnically identified groups requires familiarity with their culture on the part of the evaluator (Dana 1984).

From a methodological perspective, resourcefulness and creativity in the design process and rigorousness in the empirical evaluation of the reliability and validity of multiaxial schemata are clearly needed. Illustrative of welcome resourcefulness is the schema designed by Bech et al. (1987) combining DSM-III and ICD-8 (World Health Organization 1967) components along with severity considerations.

Cultural Considerations and Proposals, Axis by Axis

Axes I and II: Mental Disorders

The mental disorder aspects of the multiaxial diagnostic formulation contain the central characterizations of the psychiatric condition. Cultural factors may affect the list of categories (as in the case of the so-called culture-bound syndromes), the diagnostic definitions, and the qualifiers presented in the text.

Limited experience exists at present regarding the measurement of severity and course of specific syndromes to serve as the bases of specific cultural recommendations on these issues. However, given the salience of cultural concerns on these topics, it would be appropriate for a standard diagnostic system to recommend attentiveness to cultural factors when assessing severity and course of illness. For example, the comparatively high expressiveness described in Latin American and African American groups and the prominent number and level of complaints often presented by members of these groups as cultural idioms may lead some clinicians to make unwarranted ratings on severity of illness.

Axis III: General Medical Disorders

There is growing awareness of connections between ethnicity and specific physical disorders. These connections can reflect epidemiological observations on the variation of specific conditions across populations. They can involve genetic factors (as in the case of sickle cell anemias and African ethnicity) as well as social factors (as in the case of tuberculosis being facilitated by poor sanitary conditions, which are disproportionately more prevalent in some plurally deprived, ethnically identified minorities). Furthermore, cultural factors can powerfully influence the emergence, meaning, and ramifications of well-known disorders as well as of ill-defined and difficult-to-diagnose health problems often seen in primary care.

Axis IV: Psychosocial and Environmental Factors

The importance of psychosocial and environmental factors for a comprehensive diagnostic formulation has been widely recognized since the proposals of Rutter et al. (1975b), despite the modest satisfaction reported with the specific procedures developed for the assessment of this axis. The importance of this domain appears to be significant not only for psychiatric conditions but for general health as well (House et al. 1988). It should be noted that scaling of stressors and supports assumes an implicit cultural norm and that lists of stressors and supports may be culturally specific.

In any case, the need to consider general environmental factors, specific precipitating factors, and levels of support and cultural factors influencing all of these is widely recognized. For example, Tseng (1985) has emphasized the need to understand the anthropology of the family to effectively assess pertinent stressors and coping patterns. Pierloot and Ngoma (1988) have documented that psychosocial stressors tend to originate in large group interactions in the case of African American patients, as compared with more restricted family interactions in patients with a European background. Vargas-Willis and Cervantes (1987) have discussed the loss of family relations and cultural change faced by Latino and Latina immigrants to the United States.

Diagnostic proposals on psychosocial factors should be empirically validated in the major ethnically identified populations. Also, recommendations should be prepared for the clinical evaluator to keep in mind the cultural and ethnic status of the patient when assessing this particular axis.

Axis V: Global Functioning

The structure and content of the important global functioning axis are the subjects of numerous competing perspectives. One of these refers to focusing this aspect on adaptive functioning only, without considering symptomatology. This perspective is based on the arguments that symptomatology is most relevant to the clinical syndromic axes and that the inclusion of symptoms in the functioning axis tends to attract the clinician's attention to them, to the detriment of attention to social functioning. Furthermore, it can be argued that the severity of symptoms may be best handled by severity guidelines furnished for psychopathological (Axes I and II) diagnoses.

Another proposal involves the separate assessment of key functioning areas such as occupational and interpersonal performances. It has been extensively explicated that cultural factors can crucially affect the design and application of measurement instruments in this area, as pointed out by Alarcon (1983), particularly in the case of personality disorders. To illustrate further, Kunce and Vales (1984) have discussed the need for sensitivity in the assessment of the functioning of Mexican Americans, taking into consideration differences in behavioral expectations, values, and styles.

As in the case of Axis IV, it seems clear that the cultural relevance of measurement instruments must be empirically examined and that sensitivity to cultural diversity is required in their administration.

Cultural considerations were minimally incorporated in the DSM-IV multiaxial scheme, which remained basically as a standardized, monothetic statement.

Proposals for Additional Axes

Proposals for additional axes include, first, the octoaxial schema designed by Efren Ramirez and implemented in Puerto Rico for several years (E. Ramirez, personal communication, April 2, 1989). This schema gives emphatic and differentiated consideration to psychosocial and religious or spiritual factors found to be highly significant for Puerto Rican and perhaps other Latin American populations.

Another important proposal is that for a cultural axis, advanced by Good and Good (1986). Such an axis would represent an evaluation of the patient's condition from the patient's own perspective and that of the patient's primary social group. This is in line with the importance of personal experience cogently argued by Fabrega (1987), Hopper (1991), and Kleinman (1988). It is based on evidence suggesting that the cultural meaning of a disorder has important influences on the reality of the illness, its accompanying social disability, and its course. The authors recommend that the evaluator record in this axis the culture-specific illness category, explanatory model, illness idiom, predominant care-seeking patterns, and the perceived level of disability. This proposal seems to represent a formulation of important information, similar in level of discourse to those dealing with familial genetic and psychodynamic factors. To the extent that this proposal is effectively structured and codified, it approaches the prevalent concept of a diagnostic axis beyond what may be a useful narrative statement.

Proposals for additional axes need to be considered carefully, given the unmanageable burden they may impose on the regular clinical use of the diagnostic system. Alternatively, they could be placed in an investigative or experimental appendix of the diagnostic manual.

The DSM-IV Cultural Formulation Outline

The NIMH Culture and Diagnosis Group developed, as part of a broader contribution to DSM-IV, a Cultural Formulation Outline (Mezzich et al. 1993). Its purpose is to facilitate clinicians' attention to the cultural framework of the patient's identity, illness experience and context, as well as of the clinician-patient relationship. Instead of using a standardized or nomothetic scaling approach (characteristic of multiaxial diagnostic schemata) it is organized and presented as an idiographic or personalized statement, utilizing the descriptive richness of natural language.

The components of the DSM-IV Cultural Formulation Guideline follow:

A. Cultural identity of the individual
B. Cultural explanations of the individual's illness
C. Cultural factors related to psychosocial environment and levels of functioning
D. Cultural elements of the relationship between the individual and the clinician
E. Overall cultural assessment for diagnosis and care

The Cultural Formulation Outline was published in the ninth appendix of DSM-IV. Such placement drastically limits the visibility and accessibility of this development. Furthermore, its publication in a skeletal form and without illustrative examples has reduced its immediate usability. To remedy this situation, the NIMH Culture and Diagnosis Group is preparing both an Introductory Booklet to the DSM-IV Cultural Formulation and a Cultural Casebook (containing a sample of real cases from a cross-section of the general population of the United States, evaluated in terms of DSM-IV multiaxial diagnosis and Cultural formulation).

Summary

The multiaxial diagnostic system, as a more comprehensive diagnostic model, represents a challenge to the determination of cultural suitability, as well as an opportunity to enrich the description of the patient's condition. Consequently, cultural factors should be pointedly considered in the development and instrumentation of the various axes, and field trials should address the reliability and validity of the multiaxial system across pertinent ethnic groups and subcultures. Not as a standardized or monothetic axis but rather as an idiographic or formalized statement, DSM has included for the first time in an official diagnostic system a Cultural Formulation Outline.

References

Alarcon RD: Latin American perspective on DSM-III. Am J Psychiatry 140:102–105, 1983

American Psychiatric Association: Diagnostic and Statistical Manual of Mental Disorders, 3rd Edition. Washington, DC, American Psychiatric Association, 1980

American Psychiatric Association: Diagnostic and Statistical Manual of Mental Disorders, 3rd Edition, Revised. Washington, DC, American Psychiatric Association, 1987

American Psychiatric Association: Diagnostic and Statistical Manual of Mental Disorders, 4th Edition. Washington, DC, American Psychiatric Association, 1994

Bech P, Hjortso S, Lund K, et al: An integration of the DSM-III and ICD-8 by global severity assessments for measuring multidimensional outcomes in general hospital psychiatry. Acta Psychiatr Scand 75:297–306, 1987

Bilikiewicz T: Próba ukladu nozograficznego etioepigenetycznego w psychiatrii. Neurol Neurochir Pol 1:68–78, 1951

Dana RH: Personality assessment: practice and teaching for the next decade. J Pers Assess 48(1):46–57, 1984

Essen-Möller E, Wohlfahrt S: Suggestions for the amendment of the official Swedish classification of mental disorders. Acta Psychiatr Scand Suppl 47:551–555, 1947

Fabrega H: Psychiatric diagnosis: a cultural perspective. J Nerv Ment Dis 175:383–394, 1987

Good BJ, Good M-JD: The cultural context of diagnosis and therapy: a view from medical anthropology, in Mental Health Research and Practice in Minority Communities (U.S. Department of Health and Human Services Publ No (ADM) 86-1466). Edited by Miranda MR, Kitano HHL. Washington, DC, U.S. Government Printing Office, 1986

Hopper K: Some old questions for the new cross-cultural psychiatry. Medical Anthropology Quarterly 5:299–330, 1991

House JS, Landis KR, Umberson D: Social relationships and health. Science 241:540–545, 1988

Janca A, Kastrup MC, Katschnig H, et al: The ICD-10 mulitaxial system for use in adult psychiatry: structure and applications. J Nerv Ment Dis (in press)

Kastrup M, Wig NN: The transcultural perspectives of the multiaxial classification. Indian Journal of Social Psychiatry 2:289–300, 1986

Kleinman A: Rethinking Psychiatry: From Cultural Category to Personal Experience. New York, Free Press, 1988

Kunce JT, Vales LF: The Mexican American: implications for cross-cultural rehabilitation counseling. Rehabilitation Counseling Bulletin 28(2):97–108, 1984

Lecomte M, Damey A, Delage E, et al: Essai d'une statistique synoptique de médicine psychiatrique. Techniques Hospitaliers 18:5–8, 1947

Leme Lopes J: As Dimensões do Diagnóstico Psiquiátrico. Rio de Janeiro, Brazil, Agir, 1954

Mezzich JE: International use and impact of DSM-III, in An Annotated Bibliography of DSM-III. Edited by Skodol AE, Spitzer RL. Washington, DC, American Psychiatric Press, 1987

Mezzich JE: On developing a psychiatric multiaxial schema for ICD-10. Br J Psychiatry 152(suppl 1):38–43, 1988

Mezzich JE: Multiaxiale Diagnostik und internationale Klassifikation in der Psychiatrie. Fundamenta Psychiatrica 6:150–153, 1992

Mezzich JE, Fabrega H, Kleinman A: Cultural validity and DSM-IV. J Nerv Ment Dis 180:4, 1992

Mezzich JE, Good BJ, Lewis-Fernández R, et al: Cultural Formulation Guidelines, in Revised Cultural Proposals for DSM-IV. Edited by Mezzich JE, Kleinman A, Fabrega H, et al. Technical Report, NIMH Group on Culture and Diagnosis, Pittsburgh, PA, September 1993

Patrick DL, Sittampalam Y, Somerville SM, et al: A cross-cultural comparison of health status values. Am J Public Health 75:1402–1407, 1985

Perales A, Leon R, Mezzich JE: Proposición de un modelo de normalidad en salud mental y clasificación multiaxial. Anales de Salud Mental 5:11–28, 1989

Pierloot TA, Ngoma M: Hysterical manifestations in Africa and Europe: a comparative study. Br J Psychiatry 152:112–115, 1988

Rutter M, Lebovici S, Eisenberg L, et al: A triaxial classification of mental disorders in childhood. J Child Psychol Psychiatry 10:41–61, 1969

Rutter M, Shaffer D, Sturge C: A Guide to a Multiaxial Classification Scheme for Psychiatric Disorders in Childhood and Adolescence. London, England, Institute of Psychiatry, 1975a

Rutter M, Shaffer D, Shepherd M: A Multiaxial Classification of Child Psychiatric Disorders. Geneva, Switzerland, World Health Organization, 1975b

Sabshin M: Normality and the boundaries of psychopathology. Journal of Personality Disorders 3:259–273, 1989

Tseng W-S: Cultural aspects of family assessment. International Journal of Family Psychiatry 6:19–31, 1985

Vargas-Willis G, Cervantes RC: Consideration of psychosocial stress in the treatment of the Latina immigrant. Special issue: Mexican immigrant women. Hispanic Journal of Behavioral Sciences 9:315–329, 1987

Williams JBW: The multiaxial system of DSM-III: where did it come from and where should it go? Its origins and critiques. Arch Gen Psychiatry 42:175–180, 1985

World Health Organization: Manual of the Eighth Revision of the International Classification of Diseases. Geneva, Switzerland, World Health Organization, 1967

Chapter 44

Cultural Comments on Multiaxial Issues

Peter J. Guarnaccia, Ph.D.

The multiaxial system provides considerable opportunities for incorporating social and cultural information into patient evaluation. However, the limited utilization of Axes IV and V as they are defined in recent versions of the DSM makes one pause before being either too enthusiastic or too comprehensive in selecting new axes for. As Mezzich (Chapter 43) makes clear, well-developed systems can have several axes, which are used to enhance the utility and cultural sensitivity of diagnostic systems. Such an expanded system could be used to codify a more complete assessment of patients and provide an improved framework for clinicians and researchers.

Some of the lack of use of the current Axes IV and V may come from their attempt to summarize multiple and complex issues in too brief a form. "Unpacking" these axes and providing additional ones might make them more useful. One possibility, suggested by Mezzich (Chapter 43) and by Frances and colleagues (1991), would be to develop multiple axes to accompany the three diagnostic axes and to allow more flexible use of these axes depending on the needs of the clinician or researcher.

From a cultural point of view, a major problem in the conceptualization of Axis IV the instructions were suggesting that rating the severity of the stressor should be based on the assessment of "an 'average' person in similar circumstances and with similar sociocultural values . . ." (American Psychiatric Association 1987). This instruction required the clinician to make a generalization about the "average" person from a sociocultural value system that may be quite different from that of the clinician. At the same time, it led the clinician to ignore the assessment of the patient. Such a generalization is quite difficult unless the patient's culture is well-known by the clinician and runs the risk of being stereotypic. The force of psychosocial stressors results from the meaning of those events to the person who experiences them. Thus, identifying the specific stressors (as now indicated in DSM-IV) and their meaning for the person seems more appropriate, both clinically and for research purposes. In the area of specific stressors, particular attention needs to be paid to the migration experience for individuals recently arrived from other countries or moving from rural to urban areas within countries. The reasons for migration, the migration process itself, and the situation in the new country are all potent sources of social stressors. Particularly stressful migration experiences may play either exacerbating or etiological roles in different psychiatric disorders.

Rather than confounding stressors and social supports as the present system does, construction of a separate axis on social supports would be very useful. The level of social support has been shown to both be a vulnerability factor in the onset of disorder (Brown and Harris 1978) and a key issue in treatment planning. Cultural factors influence both the structure of social supports and the evaluation of the effectiveness of support. Clinically, the nature of social ties is critical both to therapy and to treatment planning. Assessing the degree of social support is also a key area in social research on mental health (Barrera 1980).

Axis V also combines two issues that are not easily subsumed into one score: symptomatology and social functioning. I concur with Mezzich that the severity of symptomatology is best handled with the severity criteria already provided for Axis I diagnoses. Thus, Axis V could focus on social functioning. Alarcon's (1983) commentary on DSM-III highlights the problems of assessing social functioning cross-culturally, specifically in the case of antisocial personality disorder. For example, in sectors of American society where unemployment is widespread, an assessment of occupational functioning may be quite difficult. In this axis, two assessments—one based on the broader norms of society and the other based on the evaluation of significant others close to the patient—might be quite useful.

The proposal for a cultural axis (Good and Good 1986) has considerable merit. Research in medical anthropology and cross-cultural psychiatry (much of it summarized in Kleinman 1988) has strongly demonstrated the role of culture in shaping psychiatric disorder and the importance of examining popular illness categories in comparison with psychiatric diagnoses. I recommend using the cultural axis both for popular illness categories and for recording the patient's understanding of his or her disorder. The presence of a separate axis is preferable to adding cultural syndromes to Axis I. This allows for simultaneous exploration of cultural categories in relation to psychiatric diagnoses and for developing appropriate clinical interventions for culturally defined syndromes.

At least three additional areas for a cultural axis seem central to the issue of diagnosis, particularly given the multicultural dynamism of United States society. One important area is the assessment of language use and multilingualism. Considerable evidence has been presented on the influence of the language of assessment on the outcome of the diagnosis; particularly notable is the work of Marcos et al. (1973). An area or subaxis is needed that can assess the language abilities and preferences of multilingual individuals. A detailed assessment of language abilities and preferences is central to accurate diagnosis, to treatment, and to research on the cultural and cognitive processes in psychiatric disorder.

The area of acculturation, or preferably biculturalism, is another important sphere for axis development. Early work on acculturation focused on developing a unidimensional scale assessing an individual's affiliation on a continuum from totally involved in their culture of origin to totally assimilated to the host culture (Cuellar et al. 1980). More recent conceptualizations (Szapocznik et al. 1980) have focused on biculturalism and the parallel assessment of involvement in both the culture of origin and the host culture (see Rogler et al. 1991 for an excellent review of the acculturation literature). To assess the impact of culture on expressions of distress and recovery from psychiatric disorder, clinicians and researchers need an accurate assessment of the cultural background of the patient. Labels that focus only on national origin miss the complexities of cultural affiliation. There also is a sizeable literature on the contribution of acculturative stresses to the emergence of mental disorder. There is a growing literature on the adaptive value of biculturalism. Evaluation of these propositions, both from clinical and research perspectives, requires a more rigorous and more uniform assessment of biculturalism than currently exists. Also, the bulk of the literature has focused on Latin Americans, and more work must be done to develop similar assessments for other ethnic groups in the United States.

The third axis I propose addresses issues of religious belief and practice. Religious beliefs provide one framework for structuring an individual's relationship to the world. When an individual's world becomes disordered, religious belief and practice can provide a sense of coherence that in itself may be therapeutic (Antonovsky 1979). At the same time, religious ideas may also provide the content for hallucinations and delusions. Sorting out those ideas that are culturally consonant and those that are indicative of disorder requires an assessment by the clinician and significant others of the role of religion in the person's life and the degree to which a person's ideas are culturally appropriate. Mezzich (1989) noted that Ramirez in Puerto Rico has already developed a schema for such an axis that could serve as the basis for broader developments in this area.

Given the current focus on and reality of the multicultural nature of U.S. society, it is incumbent on us to develop diagnostic systems that are responsive to the realities already faced by clinicians and mental health researchers working in the United States and cross-culturally. DSM-IV, like its predecessors, will be used internationally and should be responsive to multicultural issues in assessment and diagnosis. A major way to expand the cultural scope of DSM-IV is through the creative enhancement of the multiaxial system.

References

Alarcon R: A Latin American perspective on DSM-III. Am J Psychiatry 140:102–105, 1983

American Psychiatric Association: Diagnostic and Statistical Manual of Mental Disorders, 3rd Edition, Revised. Washington, DC, American Psychiatric Association, 1987

American Psychiatric Association: Diagnostic and Statistical Manual of Mental Disorders, 4th Edition, Washington, DC, American Psychiatric Association, 1994

Antonovsky A: Health, Stress and Coping. San Francisco, CA, Jossey-Bass, 1979

Barrera M: A method to assess social support networks in community research. Connections 3:8–13, 1980

Brown GW, Harris T: Social Origins of Depression. New York, Free Press, 1978

Cuellar I, Harris LC, Jasso R: An acculturation scale for Mexican American normal and clinical populations. Hispanic Journal of Behavioral Sciences 2:199–217, 1980

Frances A, Pincus HA, Widiger TA, et al: DSM-IV: work in progress. Am J Psychiatry 147:1439–1448, 1991

Good B, Good MJD: The cultural context of diagnosis and therapy, in Mental Health Research and Practice in Minority Communities (U.S. Department of Health and Human Services Publ No (ADM) 86-1466). Edited by Miranda M, Kitano HHL. Washington, DC, U.S. Government Printing Office, 1986

Kleinman A: Rethinking Psychiatry. New York, Free Press, 1988

Marcos LR, Urcuyo L, Kesselman M, et al: The language barrier in evaluating Spanish-American patients. Arch Gen Psychiatry 29:655–659, 1973

Mezzich J: International diagnostic systems and Latin-American contributions and issues. Br J Psychiatry 154:84–90, 1989

Rogler L, Cortes DE, Malgady RG: Acculturation and mental health status among Hispanics. Am Psychol 46:585–597, 1991

Szapocznik J, Kurtines WM, Fernandez T: Bicultural involvement in Hispanic American youths. International Journal of Intercultural Relations 4:353–365, 1980

Chapter 45

International Comments on Multiaxial Issues

Marianne C. Kastrup, M.D., Ph.D.

C lassificatory systems should be evaluated in the context of culture, and an increased respect for the psychiatric viewpoint from less industrialized countries has revealed unresolved issues in the prevailing systems (Sartorius 1990). However, no country can seclude itself from the mainstream of the constantly advancing psychiatric knowledge. To strike the proper balance, multiaxial classification may be a useful instrument (Wig 1983).

Multiaxial Classification

Plurinational from its conception and inception, the multiaxial approach has revealed common patterns despite national diversity (Mezzich 1988). From an international perspective, the idea of a cultural axis deserves special attention. A classificatory system may cover cultural factors independently of social stressors (Schulsinger 1988), but consideration should be paid to the root cause of mental health problems.

Empirical Studies

Several international surveys have concentrated on the perceived clinical use of the various multiaxial schemata as a professional instrument (Mezzich et al. 1985; Williams 1987). With this end in view, a survey was carried out (Mezzich et al. 1985) with the participation of 175 diagnosticians from 52 countries. The study focused on recognized clinicians, and may not reflect the usage by regular practitioners, but revealed that most respondents were familiar with the multiaxial system and considered it highly useful.

Critical Comments

By and large, reports on the multiaxial schemata have been favorable. The critical comments have focused on the DSM-III and its successors, the most widely known multiaxial system. The axis on psychosocial stressors (Williams 1987) has been subject to close scrutiny. This reflects the severity of the "average" person's reaction in similar circumstances and with similar sociocultural values to a given stressor and not the eventual idiosyncratic reaction of the person in question; in addition the etiological requirement may be problematic and difficult to assess. A certain circularity between axes may also be inherent in a multiaxial system as specific impairment on one axis simultaneously may be the criterion for a diagnosis on another (Schrader et al. 1986). Furthermore, the combination of all stressors into one rating of severity implies that the different stressors work through the same mechanism (Kendell 1983).

Multiaxial Aspects of ICD-10

The multiaxial schema of the ICD-10 (World Health Organization 1991) is designed with consideration of the experiences gathered from multiaxial systems regarding the number and types of axes, the measuring instruments for these, and the conceptual interrelationships between them (Mezzich 1988). Three axes are included: the first groups together the psychiatric core syndrome, the personality, and the concomitant physical conditions. The second is concerned with a global assessment of the degree of disability in functioning areas such as 1) personal care and survival, 2) occupational function (i.e., performance of expected role as worker/homeworker), 3) functioning with family (i.e., interaction with spouse and relatives), and 4) functioning in other roles and activities (e.g., the community at large). The third identifies environmental and circumstantial factors of relevance for the psychiatric condition with selected Z codes for ratings.

Utilization of Services

The relationship among the utilization of the mental health services, the clinical severity, and the ratings on the different axes has been the focus of limited interest. Chronically mentally ill persons in contact with psychiatric hospitals undergo the most severe stress and have the lowest premature level of functioning (Gordon and Gordon 1987), and a clear correlation between the level of functioning and the decision of whether or not to hospitalize has been reported (Mezzich et al. 1984). Such findings indicate the important utility of the multiaxial system in estimating the need for services, in identifying the "heavy user" patient population, and thus in providing an instrument for a better allocation of the available mental health services. In the World Health Organization program Health for All Year 2000, it is emphasized that resources should be distributed according to need and that services ensure physical, economic, and cultural acceptability to the population. Organizing the available mental health care resources according to need is a major problem in many countries that have populations with different cultural backgrounds. Many factors must be taken into consideration to ensure rational utilization of existing resources. For these objectives, a widely acceptable multiaxial system may be an important tool in recognizing the psychiatrically ill patients who need care most.

Implications

The multiaxial systems of psychiatric classification are still in a process of evolution, but undoubtedly they are here to stay. Prior to this time, empirical studies were primarily carried out in industrialized countries and concerned the usefulness and applicability of the systems developed. We still need transcultural experiences to elucidate the specific problems encountered in different cultural settings.

To be truly international, a multiaxial classification should help in overcoming some of the shortcomings experienced by the current classifications. These shortcomings are based primarily on cultural differences, health services, and clinical grounds (Wig 1990). International classifications have special responsibilities. The classifications should be sufficiently simple and understandable to allow easy use by those dealing with commonly encountered disorders (Sartorius 1990). Furthermore, they should act as a servant rather than a master of classifications already in existence—that is, they should not replace regional classifications but should instead be a tool of information exchange to generate translations of national classifications into the reference classification. The development of an internationally acceptable and applicable classification system is a never-ending process. The introduction of the multiaxial approach, considering the complex interaction of psychopathology, biology, environmental stressors, sociocultural factors, and adaptive functioning (Kastrup and Wig 1988), has not made the process any easier but hopefully more rewarding.

References

Gordon RE, Gordon KK: Relating Axes IV and V of DSM-III to clinical severity of psychiatric disorders. Can J Psychiatr 32:423–424, 1987

Janca A, Kastrup MC, Katschnig H, et al: The ICD-10 multiaxial system for use in adult psychiatry: structure and applications. J Nerv Ment Dis (in press)

Kastrup M, Wig NN: Multiaxial classification with particular reference to the transcultural aspects. Paper presented at the World Psychiatric Association Regional Symposium, Sydney, New South Wales, Australia, May 1988

Kendell RE: A major advance in psychiatric nosology, in International Perspectives on DSM-III. Edited by Skodol AE, Spitzer RL. Washington, DC, American Psychiatric Press, 1983

Mezzich JE: On developing a psychiatric multiaxial schema for ICD-10. Br J Psychiatry 152(suppl 1):38–43, 1988

Mezzich JE, Evanczuk KJ, Mathias RJ, et al: Admission decisions and multiaxial diagnosis. Arch Gen Psychiatry 41:1001–1004, 1984

Mezzich JE, Fabrega H, Mezzich AC: An international consultation on multiaxial diagnosis, in Psychiatry—the State of the Art. Edited by Pichot P, Berner P, Wolfe R, et al. London, England, Plenum, 1985

Sartorius N: Introduction, in Sources and Traditions of Classifications in Psychiatry. Edited by Sartorius N et al. Toronto, Ontario, Canada, Hogrefe & Huber, 1990

Schrader G, Gordon M, Harcourt R: The usefulness of DSM-III Axis IV and Axis V assessments. Am J Psychiatry 143:904–907, 1986

Shulsinger F: Classification from a sub-Saharan perspective, in International Classification in Psychiatry. Edited by Mezzich JE, von Cranach M. Cambridge, England, Cambridge University Press, 1988

Wig NN: DSM-III: its strengths and weaknesses: a perspective from the third world, in International Perspectives on DSM-III. Edited by Skodol AE, Spitzer RL. Washington, DC, American Psychiatric Press, 1983

Wig NN: The third world perspective on psychiatric diagnosis and classification, in Sources and Traditions of Classification in Psychiatry. Edited by Sartorius N, et al. Toronto, Ontario, Canada, Hogrefe & Huber, 1990

Williams JBW: Multiaxial diagnosis, in An Annotated Bibliography of DSM-III. Edited by Skodol AE, Spitzer RL. Washington, DC, American Psychiatric Press, 1987

World Health Organization: International Classification of Diseases, 10th Revision. Geneva, Switzerland, World Health Organization, 1991

Chapter 46

Nosological Comments on Multiaxial Diagnosis

Janet B. W. Williams, D.S.W.

There seems to be general endorsement of the notion that the DSM multiaxial system affords an important opportunity to enrich the description of a patient or client in a systematic way. However, we are also faced with the fact that the multiaxial system is not as widely used as we had hoped it would be. Why is it not? The reasons may be multidetermined or as simple as the fact that no prototypic recording form was made available with the publication of DSM-III (American Psychiatric Association 1980), and many facilities do not have readily available the expertise to redo their own forms to accommodate multiaxial ratings. A multiaxial report is now offered in DSM-IV (American Psychiatric Association 1994, p. 34). Another serious but very real possibility is that clinicians simply do not find the multiaxial system useful.

There are many things a clinician needs to know to formulate an adequate treatment plan: family history; previous treatment response; history of life traumas; the patient's perception of his or her own illness; and the patient's cultural background, religion, and native language, to name a few. We should ask about all of these things. However, the specific areas of information that are formally included in the multiaxial system must be limited, lest the system be made so complicated that it is not used at all. Therefore, the DSM-IV Multiaxial Issues Work Group asked: What few areas fulfill the purposes of the multiaxial system (i.e., usefulness for treatment planning and predicting outcome), and are universally relevant to all patients and all clinicians? The decision of what these few areas are must reflect the need to balance usefulness with simplicity.

Axis IV

Axis IV of DSM-III-R (American Psychiatric Association 1987) provides a scale for rating the severity of psychosocial stressors that the clinician believes are related to the initiation or exacerbation of the current mental disorders listed in Axes I and II. Many have criticized the fact that the severity rating is based on how stressful the clinician decides the relevant stressors would be to the "average" person, given similar circumstances and sociocultural background to those of the person being evaluated. The reason for this convention is that a rating of how stressful the patient found the stressors to be would be redundant with the Axis I and II diagnoses and severity ratings and would not add much new information. What is then of interest is any discrepancy between the severity of stressors recently experienced and the person's reaction to them (i.e., the Axis I and II ratings). Therefore, it would be of potential importance to note that a person developed a psychotic episode after a stressor that the "average" person would find very mild, even though the person being evaluated (i.e., who became psychotic) found it very stressful. This discrepancy gives an indication of the person's personal vulnerability to stress, which is a prognostic indicator.

As already mentioned, Axis IV is not as widely used as had been hoped. It is possible that clinicians do not find the axis useful because, unlike the diagnostic criteria of Axes I and II that challenge the clinician to organize his or her clinical findings into a summary statement (i.e., a diagnosis), merely locating a severity level on a scale once the stressors are known may not help the clinician come to any greater understanding of the patient's condition or develop an awareness of any new factors.

More promising seems to be to consider the fact that all people are inherently social animals; social relationships are common to all cultures. In all cultures there is a need for social ties, and the importance of social relationships is recognized. These relationships may take different forms, such as families, large groups, and individuals, but all people need them for normal functioning.

There is abundant evidence that social supports are strongly related to morbidity and mortality (Cohen et al., in press). Studies finding a relationship between social support and mental health have done so in clinical and normal populations, in case-control studies, and in studies of adjustment to life crises. Intervention studies, in which a group receiving a particular type of support is compared with another group not receiving the support, have strongly suggested that social support has a protective effect against psychological distress. Social supports have been found to serve as a major coping resource for elderly individuals, helping to delay the decline of mental health (Haug et al. 1989). Adaptation to illness is another area in which social support appears to be of considerable benefit.

Because of the strong relationship between social support and mental health, a scale for the measurement of social support deserves serious consideration for inclusion in future multiaxial systems. A proposal was made during the development of DSM-IV to use Axis IV for a simple rating of the adequacy of social supports. It was hoped that such a rating would help the clinician summarize the overall adequacy of the person's social supports, including family and peers. Such a scale would focus attention on an area of functioning that is clearly related to treatment adherence and outcome. For the patient, this measure would ensure that this very significant aspect of his or her life is not overlooked; for the clinician, focus on social supports might reveal additional resources that could aid in the treatment plan or deficiencies that need to be addressed in the treatment plan. It is possible that development of adequate supports could be a specific goal of treatment.

An alternative proposal was made, and eventually incorporated in DSM-IV, for including a psychosocial problem checklist that would list problem categories, such as occupational problems, environmental problems, inadequate social supports/interpersonal losses, etc. The clinician would check off all problem areas that might adversely affect the individual and might be associated (either causally or in a contributory fashion) with mental disorders and write in the specific problems in his or her own words.

As pointed out in Chapter 43, both of these new proposals need to incorporate cultural factors. Axis IV should be amended to be more culturally sensitive, for example, by including stressors such as immigration.

Axis V

In Chapter 43 Mezzich describes the proposals to disaggregate the current Axis V Global Assessment of Functioning Scale into separate scales for social/occupational functioning and psychological functioning. Clearly, whether this scale is disaggregated or not, in the future, it will need to be reviewed by a group of cultural experts.

Other Proposals

Several experts have suggested adding specific cultural axes. In general, the proposals presented are too complex for a general, already complicated manual and run the very real danger of overloading the system.

Therefore, what can be done to enhance the cultural sensitivity of a standard diagnostic system? Many productive suggestions have been formed, including expanding the section on cross-cultural issues in the introduction to DSM-IV and modifying the text description of some of the disorders. I offer some additional specific suggestions. First, it would be useful to develop an outline for a "cultural case formulation" that would specify what areas of cultural functioning should be assessed and how best to assess them. The Cultural Formulation Outline published in DSM-IV is a pertinent contribution. If this information were published in a widely read journal, it would go a long way toward enhancing the cultural sensitivity of many clinicians and researchers. Second, it would be useful to form a committee that is willing to review future proposed axes to enhance their cultural sensitivity.

References

American Psychiatric Association: Diagnostic and Statistical Manual of Mental Disorders, 3rd Edition. Washington, DC, American Psychiatric Association, 1980

American Psychiatric Association: Diagnostic and Statistical Manual of Mental Disorders, 3rd Edition, Revised. Washington, DC, American Psychiatric Association, 1987

American Psychiatric Association: Diagnostic and Statistical Manual of Mental Disorders, 4th Edition. Washington, DC, American Psychiatric Association, 1994

Cohen C, Williams JBW, Rabkin JG: A proposed axis for social supports: rationale and review of the literature, in DSM-IV Source Book. Edited by Widiger T, Frances A, Pincus HA, et al. Washington, DC, American Psychiatric Press (in press)

Haug MR, Breslau N, Folmar SJ: Coping resources and selective survival in mental health of the elderly. Res Aging 11:468–491, 1989

Chapter 47

Epilogue:

Knowledge, Power, and Diagnosis

Byron J. Good, Ph.D.

A s this book goes to press, the American Psychiatric Association (1994) has already published DSM-IV. This volume therefore serves as a record—after the fact—of more than 3 years of efforts to influence the final text of DSM-IV. The chapters in this volume were first written for a national conference on culture and psychiatric diagnosis held in Pittsburgh, Pennsylvania, in April 1991. That conference was intended to provide an assessment of specific categories within the DSM-III-R (American Psychiatric Association 1987) from the perspective of culture and ethnicity and to chart a course for engaging the DSM-IV committees, with the goal of making the new manual a less culturally parochial instrument. The most powerful realization to emerge from the gathering in Pittsburgh, Pennsylvania, was the extent of our current knowledge about cultural data relevant to psychiatric diagnosis, particularly our knowledge about the phenomenology of mental illnesses across cultures and across groups within our society who live in radically diverse social environments. At this conference were assembled a group of researchers and clinicians—psychiatrists, epidemiologists, psychologists, and anthropologists—with personal experience in attempting to apply the criteria of the DSM-III-R among patient populations for whom some aspects of the manual were wholly inadequate. In preparing for the conference, it became apparent that the evidence necessary for evaluating the DSM formulations was quite limited for some diagnostic categories. For many of the most critical categories of the manual, however, a large body of empirical data from many culturally diverse populations could be marshalled to assess the validity of the normative judgments present in the manual. Furthermore, the consensus of the group was that these findings were important for contemporary psychiatric practice and could be integrated into the body of the new manual. A decision was thus made to join in the process that would lead to the writing of DSM-IV, to attempt to influence the particular committees revising sections of the manual as well as the leadership of the overall process.

At this date, the steering committee of the National Institute of Mental Health (NIMH) Culture and Diagnosis Group is in the process of producing a systematic assessment of the outcome of our efforts to influence DSM-IV. Several things, however, are apparent. On the one hand, culture has not been added as an afterthought to this manual, represented in one or two paragraphs in the Introduction lifted from a letter from Arthur Kleinman, as was the case with DSM-III (American Psychiatric Association 1980) (see Kleinman's remarks in Chapter 2). Cultural concerns are represented in the Introduction, in the introduction to the multiaxial structure, in the text associated with particular categories (as "cultural considerations"), in a glossary of cultural terms (culture-bound syndromes and idioms of distress), and in an outline of an approach to culturally sensitive assessment appearing in one of the Appendices of DSM-IV. All this is an advance. On the other hand, many of the substantive recommendations made by the task force—the wording of particular symptom criteria, variations in duration criteria, widespread evidence for new or revised categories (a mixed anxiety-depression category, culturally distinctive forms of dissociative disorders, neurasthenia as seen and diagnosed in many Asian cultures)—were not incorporated into the body of the diagnostic manual, in spite of strong empirical data from the cross-cultural research literature. The primary thrust and philosophical commitments of the DSM-IV remain largely impervious to the empirical and ultimately political claims of those at the cultural margins of American society.

There are obvious reasons for the difficulties faced by members of this task force in gaining a hearing by many of the committees who devised the DSM-IV. There are generic difficulties in attempting to make a diagnostic manual truly reflect the diversity of a multicultural society. As Kleinman, Fabrega, and many others in this volume demonstrate, the DSM-IV is organized around particular cultural commitments—normative views of the person and societal judgments about what constitute the most critical forms of "antisocial" behavior—basic categories, and distinctions (e.g., thought vs. affect, somatic vs. affective) that are implicit in the entire structure of the diagnostic process. This is hardly surprising. Any diagnostic system is culturally situated; there can be no "God's eye point of view" free of culture from which to assess a person suffering a mental illness. Furthermore, any efforts to represent psychiatric disorders as unique to particular "cultures" leads rapidly to cultural essentialism, stereotyping, and increased possibilities of stigmatization. The glossary of cultural terms developed by this task force for inclusion as an appendix of DSM-IV is almost certain to be interpreted in this way by some. There are no easy means to incorporate what we know about cultural diversity within a document such as the DSM.

There are more fundamental issues at stake, however, in the resistance to incorporating the messages of this volume into the text of DSM-IV. Members of the Culture and Diagnosis Work Group are deeply committed to a view of psychopathology as social and cultural. This in no way implies a discounting of the role of human biology, but it does represent a basic critique of a particular vision of psychopathology and psychiatric practice. It represents a critique of a too-sharp distinction between "disease" and "illness," between psychiatric diseases viewed as universal biological entities and the forms of experience and cultural interpretations of that experience that occur in individuals and social groups. It represents a critique of the hegemony of particular forms of science, of the failure to match our commitment to furthering knowledge of the neurobiology of mental illnesses with an equal commitment to recognizing and understanding the social origins of psychopathology and to developing effective social interventions. It also represents a critique of all too easy assumptions about universality, assumptions that what one learns from an upper middle class white American population in a tertiary care anxiety disorder clinic is generalizable to all humans, because one is learning about basic human (i.e., biological) processes. To claims that the view represented by the chapters in this volume leads inevitably toward relativism or cultural essentialism, we can only echo the anthropologist Edwin Ardener (1982): "when issues are big enough there is no recourse but to firmly universalistic principles. Yet cross-cultural (or subcultural) misunderstanding on supposedly trivial issues (whatever the possibility on greater ones) is a very real problem at the level of close interactions between individuals, so much so that it is itself a human universal, and whether we like it or not language looms very large in these situations" (p. 3).

Psychiatric diagnosis is one of those forms of close interaction where cross-cultural and subcultural misunderstandings are indeed a very real problem. It is because so much is at stake in this form of misunderstanding that the many members of the Culture and Diagnosis Work Group have devoted such energy to a process that from the outset was certain to have limited effects. At stake is not only the integrity of psychiatry's claims to knowledge as a science of the human mind but also, more importantly, the care of many of the most disadvantaged members of American society—psychiatric patients who are recent immigrants, members of minority populations, or persons who are poor and living on the margins of our society. Research provides strong evidence for quite high rates of psychiatric misdiagnosis among such persons (Neighbors et al. 1989; see also Good 1993 for a summary review of the literature). Although the full implications of these data are not known, some evidence suggests that the inappropriate prescription of some medications (such as neuroleptics) and the failure to prescribe potentially effective medications (such as antidepressants) may be all too common. Misdiagnosis is almost certainly associated with inordinately high rates of involuntary confinement of African American men and with less than optimal patterns of treatment in outpatient care, inpatient units, and substance abuse treatment centers (Lindsey and Paul 1989; Nordhoff and Bates 1989). If the evidence we have supporting these claims is indeed valid, cultural misunderstanding at the level of "close interactions" between clinician and patient and apparently trivial issues of wording in the DSM may turn out to be very crucial issues for the integrity of psychiatric practice.

It is because we accept the claim of those central to the development of the DSM-IV that diagnosis matters, that it matters for the care of patients whether a diagnostic assessment is formulated well (or correctly) or badly, that members of the DSM-IV Culture and Diagnosis Group took the task seriously and in due course produced a set of recommendations as substantive as any from the DSM-IV Work Groups. It is frankly troubling that concern about the development of reliable research instruments by much of the leadership of the psychiatry profession should not be matched by concern about the reliable use of diagnostic instruments in community practice. Engaging these issues, however, takes psychiatric research to the social margins, to clinicians who are struggling under adverse conditions to care for homeless men and women who are mentally ill, to providers caring for persons experiencing both mental illness and the effects of the use of alcohol and other drugs, to Native American patients in emergency departments of rural hospitals, to poor Latin American or African American men and women in crowded urban clinics, to recent arrivals to our country suffering the traumatic effects of state violence and living in continuing terror that they will be deported. It takes psychiatric research to everyday uses of language, to the pragmatic effects of a diagnostic judgment, to the effects of using the label *antisocial personality disorder* for minority youths (while refusing to label racism as a personality disorder; see Chapter 3).

The chapters in this volume are written by scholars whose primary concern is not finding a biological marker for a specific subtype of anxiety but who link their concerns for scientific accuracy with a commitment to human rights. It is for this reason that we recognize that our struggle to be heard, the disqualification of certain forms of scientific evidence, and the reluctance to incorporate knowledge generated at the social margins are issues of power. It is also the reason that those who contributed to this volume are optimistic, for this is an era of multiculturalism. Change is occurring. The door has been opened and it will not close until much more substantive materials on culture and ethnicity are made part of the diagnostic manual. Disappointment with DSM-IV, we expect, will lead to greater efforts so that future revisions will create a diagnostic system appropriate to our multicultural society and our globally interconnected world.

Only time will tell whether we have chosen wisely in selecting psychiatric diagnosis and the DSM-IV as a site for engaging what we believe are crucial issues of our day. Clearly it is a small part of what must be done if psychiatric care is to be improved for many of the least powerful members of our society. The DSM-IV now is a part, however—a part to which the scholars who have contributed to this book have devoted years of research and academic writing. This volume provides a record of those efforts, large efforts that rebuke disappointment; they are a sign along the way of what is to come.

References

American Psychiatric Association: Diagnostic and Statistical Manual of Mental Disorders, 3rd Edition. Washington, DC, American Psychiatric Association, 1980

American Psychiatric Association: Diagnostic and Statistical Manual of Mental Disorders, 3rd Edition, Revised. Washington, DC, American Psychiatric Association, 1987

American Psychiatric Association: Diagnostic and Statistical Manual of Mental Disorders, 4th Edition. Washington, DC, American Psychiatric Association, 1994

Ardener E: Social anthropology, language and reality, in Semantic Anthropology. Edited by Parkin D. London, England, Academic Press, 1982, pp 1–14

Good B: Culture, diagnosis and comorbidity. Cult Med Psychiatry 16:1–20, 1993

Lindsey KP, Paul GL: Involuntary commitments to public mental institutions: issues involving the overrepresentations of blacks and assessment of relevant functioning. Psychol Bull 106:171–183, 1989

Neighbors HW, Jackson JS, Campbell L, et al: The influence of racial factors on psychiatric diagnosis: a review and suggestions for research. Community Ment Health J 25:301–311, 1989

Nordhoff G, Bates E (eds): Inside looking out. Southern Exposure 17, 1989

Index

*Page numbers in **boldface** type refer to figures and tables.*